C000284921

MENTAL CAPACITY: THE NEW LAW

MENTAL CAPACITY: THE NEW LAW

General Editor and contributor

District Judge Gordon R Ashton
Deputy Master of the Court of Protection
Visiting Professor in Law at Northumbria University

Contributors

Penny Letts
Policy Consultant

Laurence Oates
Official Solicitor and Public Trustee

Martin Terrell
Solicitor, partner with Rix & Kay

JORDANS

Published by
Jordan Publishing Limited
21 St Thomas Street
Bristol BS1 6JS

Whilst the publishers and the author have taken every care in preparing the material included in this work, any statements made as to the legal or other implications of particular transactions are made in good faith purely for general guidance and cannot be regarded as a substitute for professional advice. Consequently, no liability can be accepted for loss or expense incurred as a result of relying in particular circumstances on statements made in this work.

Crown Copyright material is reproduced with kind permission of the Controller of Her Majesty's Stationery Office.

British Library Cataloguing-in-Publication Data

A catalogue record for this book is available from the British Library.

ISBN 0 85308 976 0
ISBN 978 0 85308 976 6

Typeset by Etica Press Limited

Printed in Great Britain by Antony Rowe Limited

To the memory of

PAUL JOSEPH SCHOLES ASHTON

who died at the age of 28 years on 26 January 2004
before he could benefit from this much needed legislation.

Preface

It is 17 years since the Law Society's *Mental Health Sub-Committee* (as it then was) first drew public attention to the legal vacuum in which people who lacked mental capacity were obliged to exist. This provoked the Law Commission to take this topic on board and, after several years of consultation, recommendations were made for a statutory mental incapacity jurisdiction. Different governments then pursued further consultation whilst lacking the will to introduce legislation, but pressures to do so became overwhelming with the introduction of community care policies, disability discrimination laws and ultimately human rights legislation. The Mental Capacity Act 2005 is the result, but a consequence of the changed climate is that it must meet higher standards than were expected when the need was first identified.

This Act builds upon enduring powers of attorney and the existing jurisdiction of the Court of Protection, and follows most of the Law Commission's recommendations in creating a broad and viable framework. The devil will be in the detail that has yet to emerge through forms, Codes of Practice, regulations and Court rules. There is an inevitable tension between protection and empowerment, and inadequate support may lead to a denial of both. Those who complain that the jurisdiction is too controlling may be the first to express outrage when abuse is not prevented. But we do not live in a 'nanny state' and there are issues as to who should fund the new jurisdiction. The existing Court of Protection can seek to be self-funding because it only opens its doors to those who have money. The new jurisdiction may find itself addressing the needs of some of the most financially disempowered people in the community. Is it in reality an extension of our health and social services notwithstanding that it functions through a Court? The legal rights of individuals who lack the capacity to pursue them must be addressed, but this can only be done in the context of support and care provision which become the ultimate responsibility of the state.

No one should allow themselves to be fooled by the familiar terms 'Public Guardian' and 'Court of Protection'. The former is a new incarnation with a statutory role rather than a mere administrative body, and only time will tell how far this role will develop. The latter is a new regional court working within the mainstream courts and enjoying a wider jurisdiction exercised under different principles. Those already working within the existing system do not know how the new regime will develop, so for practitioners and others there must be an element of speculation.

This book is an attempt by four concerned authors who have throughout been committed to the reforms to explain what is going on and provide some insight into the issues that must be faced. Although the detailed law must be set out, however tedious this may be, we have endeavoured to breathe life into the provisions and procedures. We have also tried to face up to some of the potential pitfalls and difficulties that will inevitably arise in implementing new legislation in this complex area.

I wish to thank my co-authors for their dedicated contributions, each being highly experienced in the topics that they have covered. As to the rest I must accept responsibility. We do not claim to be experts – who is in this field? – but for my part I have drawn on 28 years of general legal practice, 13 years as a generic judge and 5 years involvement within the existing Court of Protection. Above all, I have been influenced by my family experience of a child with severe learning disabilities and the insight this gave me into a different philosophy which should influence the legal system more in the future than it has in the past. I have campaigned for this jurisdiction from the inception and wish to see it improve the quality of life of those who lack capacity, their families and carers. Whether it does so will depend upon all those who play a part in the process, but by picking up this book you have indicated that you are one of those people. Thank you for your support.

Gordon R Ashton
Grange-over-Sands
January 2006

Contents

Table of Cases

References are to paragraph numbers.

Table of Statutes

References are to paragraph numbers.

Table of Statutory Instruments

References are to paragraph numbers.

Table of European and International Materials

List of Abbreviations

Legislation

2005Act/the Act	Mental Capacity Act 2005
2004 Act	Civil Partnership Act 2004
2001 Rules	Court of Protection Rules 2001
1998 Act	Human Rights Act 1998
1995 Act	Disability Discrimination Act 1995
1983 Act	Mental Health Act 1983
1979 Act	The Sale of Goods Act 1979
1959 Act	Mental Health Act 1959
AWI Act	Adults with Incapacity (Scotland) Act 2000
CPR	Civil Procedure Rules 1998
FPR 1991	Family Proceedings Rules 1991

Other

ADR	Alternative Dispute Resolution
ANH	Artificial nutrition and hydration
CAB	Citizens Advice Bureau
CPA	Continuing power of attorney
DCA	Department for Constitutional affairs
DWP	Department of Work and Pensions
EPA	Enduring power of attorney
GMC	General Medical Council
GSI	Government Secure Intranet
IMCAs	Independent mental capacity advocates
JAC	Judicial Appointments Commission
JCHR	Joint Committee on Human Rights
JSB	Judicial Studies Board
LPA	Lasting power of attorney
OPG	Office of the Public Guardian
PGO	Public Guardianship Office
PREMA	Preston E-mail Applications
PTO	Public Trust Office
PVS	Persistent vegetative state

Chapter 1

Background

PRELIMINARY

Overview

Issues

1.1   We all assume that fellow citizens are able to make their own decisions.[1] Those who cannot do so depend upon the support of others and are vulnerable to abuse or neglect. A civilised society must make provision for such people in its laws, but this assumes that they can be properly identified.

Capacity

1.2   The assessment of capacity is not an easy matter for society. To deprive people who are capable of making their own decisions of the right to do so would be an abuse, yet failure to recognise lack of capacity results in continuing vulnerability. It is possible to stigmatise a person as lacking capacity for a variety of reasons and our history provides many examples of this.[2] Is the objective to protect the individual or society? Is it to afford power to one section of society over another by categorising some people as being unable to make decisions? We accept that children may be denied capacity especially during their formative years, but the age at which capacity becomes recognised by the law has progressively reduced during recent years. It is only within the past century that all people in our society have been recognised as equals, and this means that some objective justification must exist before personal capacity is denied to an adult. That justification is generally to be found in the diagnosis of some form of mental impairment.

---

[1]   The *Concise Oxford Dictionary* defines a decision as 'a conclusion or resolution reached after consideration'.

[2]   Women, felons and lunatics have all at some time been treated as incompetent. The Mental Deficiency Act 1913 extended to 'moral imbeciles' and thus unmarried mothers could be deprived of their liberty.

1.3   Legal incompetence is thus to be found when there is lack of capacity
        due to a mental disability. It may arise for a variety of reasons and may
        be merely temporary or a permanent condition. The lack of capacity
        may be partial or total. In so far as an individual does have capacity any
        decisions that are made should be recognised and an 'all or nothing'
        approach should not be adopted. Some decisions require little thought
        and may be identified from a mere assent or even body language.
        Others require knowledge and understanding and need to be
        communicated in a reasoned manner.

Decision-making

1.4   When lack of capacity is temporary it may be possible to defer
        decisions until capacity is restored. But if it is of lasting duration or
        permanent, or if an urgent decision otherwise needs to be made, there
        must be some legally recognised procedure whereby necessary
        decisions can be made by some other person or body. The decision-
        maker must be identified so that any decision that is made will be
        recognised by others.

1.5   There are different types of decision that we all make. We have to
        manage our financial affairs, and those who enter into transactions with
        us must be satisfied that these are enforceable and not likely to be set
        aside due to lack of competence on our part or lack of authority on the
        part of the person who transacts them for us. Decisions about medical
        treatment may also need to be made and should not simply be left to
        doctors, especially if they could have a serious effect upon the rest of
        our lives. Many personal welfare decisions are trivial, but some may
        have implications for other persons and lead to disputes within
        families.[3] Each of these three types of decision-making needs to come
        within any jurisdiction afforded by the law.

1.6   If personal choices are to be made for us then there must be a
        recognised basis on which this should be done. Is the decision-maker
        free to make whatever decisions he or she thinks best, which might be
        subjective and influenced by personal interests, or is an objective basis
        to be adopted? What might that basis be? There seems to be general
        acceptance that the paternalistic approach adopted in respect of children
        is not appropriate for an adult.

        It is not acceptable for one person to assume dominion over another
        without the facility for this to be questioned and it is a function of the
        law to provide this facility. Although various procedures may be
        devised to resolve disputes, as a last resort it is the courts that are

---

[3]   Compare decisions about what to wear and what to eat with decisions about where to live or
        with whom.

usually relied upon to undertake this task. They need to be legally empowered to do so, but it is not only disputes that may need to be referred to the courts: where there is uncertainty as to what may be done or what would be lawful, the courts are usually expected to determine this.

Communication

1.7   There is no magic about decision-making: it merely means making a choice, but this does require the ability to identify the range of possible choices and the implications of each. It also requires the ability to communicate the choice once this has been made. Communication is a two-way process: it is as important to ensure that the person understands what is being said to them as that their attempts to respond are understood. Impairment of communication does not necessarily indicate lack of mental capacity and where there is doubt a medical report may establish the capacity of the individual.

If we are to empower people we must not rely solely upon normal methods of communication but must explore and adopt any method that will achieve effective communication.[4] This may involve using available aids or an interpreter where this will assist. If verbal dialogue is not possible, written notes or sign language may facilitate communication. A simple response to questions, such as movement of a finger, may be found reliable but in that event questions must be phrased so as to facilitate a range of responses.

Conclusion

1.8   These are the fundamental issues that should be addressed by any legal system, but until recently only the provinces in Canada, states of Australia, and New Zealand have through their legislation over the years developed an adult guardianship law. The Mental Capacity Act 2005 is the first attempt to remedy this shortcoming in England and Wales and it contains some innovative features.[5] A slightly different approach has already been adopted in Scotland.[6]

Legal competence

1.9   The law assumes that an adult has the capacity to make and the ability to communicate personal decisions so there is a vacuum if someone is not able to do this. Concerns may also arise as to whether an individual

---

[4]   The phrase 'locked in syndrome' is used to describe a person who can reason and make decisions but is unable to communicate.

[5]   The implementation date is presently April 2007 and it will probably be adopted in Northern Ireland thereafter by regulations.

[6]   Adults with Incapacity (Scotland) Act 2000.

is competent to make a particular decision or acquiesce in the decisions of others even though he or she purports to do so. In a legal context we are assessing whether the choice would be recognised by the law.

When talking about competence we are considering the ability to understand, make a choice and then make this clear to others, even though assistance may be needed to carry the choice into effect. It follows that neither age nor physical or sensory impairment should by itself affect competence. Lack of legal competence may arise through mental incapacity, an inability to communicate or a combination of the two but every effort should be made to overcome communication difficulties.

Tests of mental capacity

1.10   Although the term 'mental incapacity' conveys a fairly consistent impression to most people it does not have a precise meaning. It would be convenient if there were a universal definition, so that we could readily identify those members of society who are eligible for special treatment, but this could never be the case because very few people are incapable in all things. Legal tests of capacity must vary according to the circumstances.

The classic definition of a 'patient' which is found in the Mental Health Act 1983 and elsewhere has only recently been interpreted by the appeal courts.[7] In some situations specific tests have been developed by case-law, so textbooks are able to identify testamentary capacity and the capacity required to sign an enduring power of attorney, conduct civil proceedings in the courts, enter into a marriage, or make a gift. Otherwise general principles must be relied upon and these are now based upon function rather than status or the outcome of decisions. Furthermore, it is the individual's understanding rather than judgment that is relevant – we are all entitled to make unwise decisions.

Assessment of mental capacity

1.11   Doubts about capacity may arise for several reasons but these should not be confused with tests of capacity. Thus the status of the individual (such as being elderly and living in a nursing home), the outcome of a decision (viewed by others as illogical), or the appearance or behaviour of the individual may cause capacity to be questioned. Yet it is not unusual for outward appearances to create a false impression of incapacity and conversely, the absence of any of these indications does not mean that the individual is capable. In all these situations a proper assessment should be made according to appropriate criteria.

---

[7]   *Masterman-Lister v Brutton & Co and Jewell & Home Counties Dairies* [2002] EWCA Civ 1889, [2002] All ER (D) 297 (Dec).

1.12 One of the difficulties is that the various professionals who may be involved approach the question of capacity from different standpoints so often reach different conclusions. In case of dispute, capacity is a question of fact for the court to decide on the balance of probabilities with a presumption of capacity. The opinions of professionals will be admitted as 'expert' evidence but considered alongside factual evidence from those who know the individual and will only be persuasive if they have been given all relevant information and applied the appropriate legal test.

The medical profession tends to be concerned with diagnosis and prognosis rather than the severity and implications of mental disability. The doctor may well be able to identify the cause of the disability and indicate its likely future consequences, but what is in issue to the lawyer is the effect on the individual at this moment in time.[8] Care workers classify people according to their degree of independence, which involves consideration of levels of competence in performing skills such as eating, dressing, communication and social skills. These skills may be affected by mental or physical causes. An assessment based upon a medical diagnosis is of little use to the care worker other than to explain the reason for the present impairment and indicate whether improvement or deterioration is to be expected. The carer may become concerned as to the vulnerability of the person cared for and the entitlement of others to take decisions on that person's behalf.

1.13 The lawyer wishes to establish whether the individual is capable of making a reasoned and informed decision, although there may be the need to assess the degree of dependence, for example when considering what financial provision should be made. There can be no universally applied test because the capacity required will depend upon the nature of the decision to be made, but the medical diagnosis will be largely irrelevant except in so far as it points to the degree of capacity that may be anticipated and the carer's view may be helpful but will not be based on any particular legal test. Thus the lawyer may need to consult the doctor and carer (or social worker) but their views merely form part of the evidence when considering the question of legal capacity. Having gathered this evidence the lawyer is in the best position to form a considered view as to legal capacity or to refer the issue to the court for determination.

---

[8] The Law Society and the British Medical Association have produced guidance in a book entitled *Assessment of Mental Capacity: Guidance for doctors and lawyers* (London: BMJ Books, 1995 – 2nd edn, 2004).

Incapacitated adults

1.14   Children are adequately catered for under the law of England and Wales.[9] Those adults who may lack capacity fall into four main groups. The largest group comprises elderly people who are deprived of their capacity by senile dementia but have previously been able to manage their own affairs. At the other extreme are those with learning disabilities which may be so severe that they have never been able to enjoy personal autonomy. In between are those who encounter a period of mental illness or suffer brain damage rendering them incapable of making decisions that others should recognise. The situation is made more complicated by the fact that, for some, capacity may fluctuate and in every instance there is the potential for partial capacity.

Decision-making

1.15   Decisions fall into three broad categories: financial, personal welfare and healthcare. When an adult is incapable of making decisions special procedures should be available for these to be taken on his or her behalf if that is appropriate. This raises the questions of when decision-making powers should be delegated, who should then be empowered to take the decisions and the basis on which they should be taken.

Delegated decision-making

1.16   Although under general legal principles a specific decision may be held to be invalid due to lack of competence this may be merely a 'one-off' situation[10] and something more is needed if decision-making powers are to be delegated. This is presently the existence of a 'mental disorder' which causes the lack of capacity. It is then clear that an ongoing problem needs to be addressed.

'Mental disorder' is defined in the Mental Health Act 1983 as: 'mental illness, arrested or incomplete development of mind, psychopathic disorder and any other disorder or disability of mind', but does not include the effect of alcohol or drugs.[11] This definition is extremely wide but provides a useful screening process because merely being eccentric should not be a basis for being deprived of one's rights.

---

[9]   The Children Act 1989 contains the necessary powers for intervention by the courts and the High Court wardship jurisdiction remains.

[10]   The individual may be under the influence of alcohol or drugs at the time.

[11]   Mental Health Act 1983, s 1(2) and (3).

Decision-makers

1.17 There is at present a list of persons who may represent the interests of a mentally disabled individual to a greater or lesser extent. This includes:[12]

> *appointee* for state benefits;
>
> *receiver* by Court of Protection for financial affairs;
>
> *attorney* under an enduring power for financial affairs;
>
> *trustees* for financial affairs;
>
> *litigation friend* for civil proceedings;[13]
>
> *next friend* or *guardian ad litem* for family proceedings;[14]
>
> *personal advocate* – used in practice but not recognised in law.

Despite the length of this list, the authority of such representatives extends to very few ordinary decisions for the individual and there are large gaps where no one has any power to make such decisions.

1.18 In a climate where many marriages end in separation or divorce and 'living together relationships' have become almost the norm, it would no longer be acceptable for a spouse or designated blood relative to be given special status by the law as decision-maker. Preserving personal autonomy requires that the incapacitated individual has the opportunity to make the choice of decision-maker in advance (if then capable) and to influence that choice even after losing mental capacity to the extent that wishes can be ascertained. Introducing such flexibility creates its own problems but there must be a procedure whereby the appointment of a nominee can be challenged on established principles.

Best interests

1.19 There has been much debate about the basis on which delegated decisions are to be made. Should this be what the decision-maker thinks best or what the incapacitated individual would have decided had he or she been capable? The former is too paternalistic for contemporary society whereas the latter is not feasible for those who have never been able to express their own wishes. The concept of best interests has emerged, which is an attempt to combine respect for the wishes of the individual with the views of others in a climate of minimum intervention. But what exactly does this mean in practice?

---

[12] This list applies to England and Wales. A different list could be produced for Scotland.

[13] Civil Procedure Rules 1989, Part 21.

[14] Family Proceedings Rules 1991, Part IX.

A special jurisdiction

1.20   There are more adults who lack mental capacity and have property or
        financial affairs that need to be dealt with. This is partly because the
        population is living longer with greater home ownership, and partly
        because more brain-damaged children survive – some with substantial
        damages awards. Existing procedures allow these affairs to be dealt
        with but there is a vacuum in our law for other forms of decision-
        making.

        It is a nonsense that financial management should control personal
        welfare: none of us run our own lives in that way. We decide what we
        wish to do and how we wish to live our lives and then temper this
        according to what we can afford. It is also unacceptable that uncertainty
        prevails on issues such as where the individual should live, with whom
        he or she should have contact and what medical treatment should be
        given. It was inevitable that sooner or later legislation would have to be
        introduced to tackle this issue. The Mental Capacity Act 2005
        superimposes a procedure for decision-making on our existing law.

1.21   It has to be acknowledged that any jurisdiction whose role is to address
        the needs of 'adults with incapacity'[15] has little relevance to the work of
        most lawyers and, apart from an occasional high-profile case, is of little
        interest to the public at large. But to anyone who encounters a decline in
        the mental capacity of a loved one, and to the professionals involved,
        the manner in which issues that arise are addressed is seen as a test of
        the integrity of the legal system. No one can afford to ignore reform in
        this area, because this is not a 'them and us' situation. Any of us may
        encounter a period when we lack capacity whether temporary,
        progressive or permanent, especially as we grow older. We and our
        loved ones will then depend on the new jurisdiction established by the
        Mental Capacity Act 2005.

1.22   The new jurisdiction must also set standards for others to follow in the
        field of disability. Disabled people must be assured of equal access to
        justice and that the discrimination they still encounter in society will not
        be reproduced within the system of justice. This applies to the legal
        principles that are applied, the procedures that are followed, the
        facilities available and the attitudes of those involved. There will be
        many lessons to be learnt by the Public Guardian and the new Court of
        Protection, but hopefully these will be well learned and thereafter
        permeate throughout the legal system.[16]

---

15   This is the terminology now creeping into use, based on the title to the Scottish legislation,
     but it is questionable. It may be thought that referring to those who 'lack capacity' is
     demeaning and to be discouraged, but it is illogical to refer to someone as being with
     something that they are without.

16   Guidance to judges is available from the Judicial Studies Board in the *Equal Treatment*

Confidentiality

1.23　Doctors, lawyers and professional persons generally[17] owe a duty of confidentiality to their patients or clients, which means that personal information should only be revealed to others with the consent of the patient or client.[18] This duty is not absolute and may be overridden where there is a stronger public interest in disclosure.[19] Where the individual lacks the mental capacity to consent to (or refuse) disclosure, it may be desirable to permit disclosure in certain circumstances. This has been expressed as follows:[20]

> 'C's interest in protecting the confidentiality of personal information about himself must not be underestimated. It is all too easy for professionals and parents to regard ... incapacitated adults as having no independent interests of their own: as objects rather than subjects. But we are not concerned here with the publication of information to the whole wide world. There is a clear distinction between disclosure to the media with a view to publication to all and sundry and disclosure in confidence to those with a proper interests in having the information in question.'

During an assessment as to mental capacity it is essential that information is shared by the professionals involved. The patient's consent should be obtained to this wherever possible, but in the absence of this relevant disclosure may be permitted. However, this does not extend to confidential information about the patient unrelated to the assessment. Disclosure will be based upon a need to know and the overall test will be the best interests of the patient.

Undue influence

Assisted decision-making

1.24　One of the problems when dealing with individuals who are frail or of borderline mental capacity is undue influence. Some adults prefer to have many of their decisions made by others and tests of capacity encourage the acceptance of support from others even though this may amount to influence.[21] But there may be cause for concern if an individual is too easily influenced or becomes too much under the

---

Bench Book which can be accessed at www.jsboard.co.uk/etac/etbb/index.htm. A summary in PDF format can be downloaded at www.jsboard.co.uk/downloads/fairness_guide_final.pdf.

[17]　Including social workers.

[18]　This may be imposed by codes of professional conduct or by the law, eg Data Protection Act 1998 or European Convention on Human Rights, Art 8.

[19]　*W v Egdell* [1990] Ch 359 at p 419.

[20]　*R (on the application of Ann Stevens) v Plymouth City Council and C* [2002] EWCA Civ 388, per Hale LJ.

[21]　Once we have the new decision-making jurisdiction (see **1.24**) the real problem is likely to become undue influence of those whose capacity is impaired but not lacking.

influence of another person. Also, understanding of relevant factors may be corrupted by the manner and selectivity in which information is provided. A person who is constantly given incomplete or even incorrect information is likely to make choices that they would not otherwise have made. The ability to make a choice may also be affected by threats, perceived or actual. Thus a decision which appears to have been competently made could be the outcome of at best a limited perception of the choices available or at worst fear of the consequences of making a different decision.

This problem is magnified by the fact that those seeking to challenge a decision may themselves be seeking to exert an influence over the individual. All too often these situations of conflict develop from a power struggle between otherwise concerned relatives with the vulnerable person becoming a pawn in the game. A tendency by this person to agree with the party who presently has their audience either because of a short-term desire for peace or the strength of that party's personality merely provides evidence which fuels the problem. Experience in the Court of Protection demonstrates that many of the disputes arise from the abuse of power or desire of another individual for control over the patient.

1.25   Perhaps of more concern is the situation where undue influence is not recognised and financial or emotional abuse is taking place. An individual who needs assistance from others before making significant personal decisions is vulnerable. There is a tendency to delegate decisions to others who demonstrate a willingness to take them over, and when those others are influenced by personal gain or improper motives there is likely to be abuse. The courts are prepared to set aside transactions adverse to an individual when these are the result of undue influence, but these matters can be expensive to litigate and the interaction between improper influence and mental capacity has yet to be fully developed.

The legal position

1.26   People may not be saved from their own foolishness but will be protected from being victimised by other people. The common law developed a principle of duress but equity supplemented this by enabling gifts and other transactions to be set aside if procured by undue influence or if they are otherwise unconscionable. The manner in which the intention to enter into the transaction was secured may be investigated and if produced by an unacceptable means, the law will not permit the transaction to stand. There are thus three situations where transactions may be set aside:

1. where duress or undue influence has been expressly used for the purpose of achieving a gift or benefit – the burden of proof is on the party alleging this;
2. where undue influence is presumed – the burden is then on the other party to justify the transaction;
3. where a contract of an improvident nature has been made by a poor and ignorant person acting without independent advice, and the other party cannot show that it was fair and reasonable – this is a fall-back remedy for unconscionable conduct.

1.27 The law has appeared to approach the issue of undue influence according to the specific relationship between the parties, but the question is whether one party has placed sufficient trust and confidence in the other, rather than whether the relationship between the parties is of a particular type.[22] However, a presumption may arise in two ways:

1. *The type of relationship*: where there is a recognised relationship in which one party acquires influence over another who is vulnerable (for example, client and solicitor, patient and doctor, beneficiary and trustee). There is then an irrebuttable presumption of influence and it is not necessary to establish that the relationship was based upon trust and confidence. If it appears that this influence has been inappropriately exercised then the party with influence must prove that this was not the case.
2. *The evidential presumption*: where there is evidence that the relationship was based on trust and confidence in relation to the management of the complainant's financial affairs, coupled with a transaction giving rise to suspicions which must be addressed. There may then be a rebuttable presumption of undue influence and it is for the other party to produce evidence to counter the inference which otherwise should be drawn.

There are thus two prerequisites to the burden of proof shifting to the other party. First, that trust and confidence was placed in the other party, or that party was in a position of dominance or control. Second, that the transaction is not readily explicable by the relationship of the parties. The mere existence of influence is not enough, but it is not essential that the transaction should be disadvantageous to the pressurised or influenced person, either in financial terms or in any other way.[23] However, questions of undue influence will not usually arise where the transaction is innocuous.[24]

---

[22] Treitel *The Law of Contract* (10th edn, 1999) pp 380–381.

[23] The label 'manifest disadvantage' adopted by Lord Scarman in *Morgan's Case* [1985] 1 All ER 821 can give rise to misunderstanding and should no longer be adopted – see the judgment of Lord Nicholls in *Bank of Scotland plc v Etridge (No 2)* referred to above.

[24] *CIBC Mortgages plc v Pitt* [1993] 4 All ER 433, [1994] 1 AC 200, HL.

Current law

Historical

Parens patriae

1.28   Until 1959 the High Court and its predecessors had jurisdiction over the lives of incompetent adults pursuant to the rights of the Crown, known as the Royal Prerogative or *parens patriae* jurisdiction which was given statutory recognition in 1339.[25] In practice this meant state involvement in the financial affairs of the mentally incapacitated citizen and there was no equivalent of the modern welfare state or social services.[26] The Mental Health Act 1959 abolished the delegation of the Royal Prerogative in respect of adults[27] and established a completely statutory jurisdiction but, although this was not realised at the time, it deprived the courts of jurisdiction over personal welfare and healthcare decisions other than in the context of treatment for a mental disorder.[28] This became apparent after it was held that the statutory jurisdiction of the Court of Protection only extended to financial affairs.[29]

1.29   Even if there was no need for decisions to be made on behalf of those who lacked capacity, it was necessary for the courts to decide whether decisions could be made by the individual or whether those purported to have been made were effective. There was confusion in the legal terms found in statutes and law reports well into the twentieth century which pointed to a general condition but did not assist in determining the specific implications. Undefined and stigmatising phrases such as 'of unsound mind',[30] 'mentally defective' and 'mentally disordered' were sometimes used with little attempt to define or assess the implications in any particular case. These terms reflected the period when used rather than the interpretation that should now be placed on the words chosen.

---

[25]   Statute de Prerogativa Regis, 17 Edw II (1339) St I cc 9, 10. The earliest reference is to be found in a semi-official tract known as the *De Praerogativa Regis* ('On the King's Prerogative') dating from the reign of Edward I (1272–1307).

[26]   The background to the financial jurisdiction of the Court of Protection is outlined in **CHAPTER 6**.

[27]   It is suggested that the Royal Prerogative still exists and only delegation to the High Court was abolished. That court's powers continue in the Wardship jurisdiction in respect of children (infants). The Republic of Ireland still relies on a *parens patriae* jurisdiction (although not on the basis of the Royal Prerogative!).

[28]   The High Court has recently developed a declaratory jurisdiction, initially for serious healthcare decisions – see **CHAPTER 5**.

[29]   *Re W* [1971] Ch 123; [1970] 2 All ER 502.

[30]   This phrase is actually defined in the Trustee Act 1925 as 'incapable from infirmity of mind of managing his own affairs'. Typical of the 1925 property legislation, this has stood the test of time.

1.30 Lawyers too failed to distinguish mental illness, mental handicap (now known as learning disability) and brain injury or to realise that although any of these conditions may result in lack of mental capacity they did not inevitably do so. Their approach tended to concentrate upon the nature of the condition rather than its effect on the individual. Unless a status test applied they relied on doctors to assess capacity and little guidance was given as to the specific test to be applied. An 'all or nothing' approach tended to be adopted rather than asking whether the individual was capable of making the particular decision in question. Thus there were people who were without doubt capable and those who clearly lacked capacity, but between these extremes was a grey area for the most part avoided by lawyers.

Mental health legislation

1.31 The Lunacy Act 1890 gave various powers to the Office of the Master in Lunacy (which was not renamed the Court of Protection until 1947) and these are the basis of the provisions now contained in Part VII of the Mental Health Act 1983.[31] The present Court of Protection has powers over the property and affairs of an individual who is 'incapable, by reason of mental disorder, of managing and administering his property and affairs'. Usually someone will be appointed as a *receiver* to handle those affairs under the supervision of the court, but a *short order* is available for small or straightforward cases.

Recent developments

Enduring Powers of Attorney Act 1985

1.32 Demand for a less expensive and simpler procedure of choice[32] coupled with the inability of the Court of Protection to cope with the financial affairs of all mentally incapacitated persons, resulted in recommendations by the Law Commission in 1983[33] and the passing of the Enduring Powers of Attorney Act 1985. This overcame the problem with ordinary powers of attorney that they were revoked by the subsequent mental incapacity of the donor[34] under normal agency principles. Some formality has been introduced into the documentation and an application must be made to the Public Guardianship Office for the power to be registered with the Court of Protection upon the donor becoming mentally incapable but there is no supervision although the Court has power to intervene.

---

[31] These largely re-enact Part VIII of the Mental Health Act 1959.
[32] Ie the choice of the person whose affairs are to be dealt with.
[33] *The Incapacitated Principal*, Law Com No 122 (Cmnd 8977).
[34] Ie the person who granted the power.

Enduring powers have proved to be a great success but they have their limitations (only financial decisions can be dealt with in this way) and leave scope for financial abuse. In terms of numbers they have far surpassed receivership orders. The development of enduring powers into lasting powers dealing with a wider range of decision-making is considered in **CHAPTER 3**.

High Court declarations

1.33   The High Court has found it necessary to facilitate decisions in extreme cases and has done so by making *declarations* as to best interests. This was initially in respect of serious healthcare decisions.[35] More recently this remedy has been extended to personal welfare decisions. In 1995, Mrs Justice Hale not only applied the procedure to a personal welfare decision[36] but also backed it up with an injunction and was upheld by the Court of Appeal.[37] In that same year, the High Court held that the court had jurisdiction to grant a declaration that a child with cerebral palsy and learning difficulties was upon attaining majority entitled to choose where to live and with whom to associate, and to restrain the parents by injunction from interfering.[38] However, it should be noted that the making of a declaration or an injunction is a discretionary remedy and this procedure is inordinately expensive and scarcely available for everyday situations even though these do arise.

THE NEW CLIMATE

The social climate

General

1.34   There is now a new social and legal climate that emphasises personal autonomy, favours community care and disapproves of discrimination in any form. It should not be overlooked that those who lack mental capacity frequently have other physical or mental impairments as well, so the combined implications of mental and physical disabilities have to be considered.

---

[35]   This power was first recognised by the House of Lords in *F v West Berkshire Health Authority* [1989] 2 All ER 545 and confirmed in *Airedale NHS Trust v Bland* [1993] 2 WLR 316. See, generally, **CHAPTER 5**.

[36]   *Re S (Adult Patient: Jurisdiction)* [1995] 1 FLR 302. An injunction was granted to stop the wife of an elderly, infirm man taking him abroad out of the care of his mistress.

[37]   *Re S (Hospital Patient: Court's Jurisdiction)* [1996] Fam 1, [1995] 1 FLR 1075.

[38]   *Re V (Declaration against Parents)* [1995] 2 FLR 1003, Johnson J.

Community care

1.35 New community care policies were introduced in 1993. There are many facets to community care, but of particular relevance to disabled people are the requirement for their needs to be assessed, the duty placed upon the social services departments of local authorities (subject to available funding) to ensure that these needs are met rather than expecting the individual to cope with whatever services are available, and the move away from institutional care to care in the community. The consequence is that people with disabilities are more visible in society and both they and their family/carers have greater expectations as to how they will be treated. Their rights are increasingly being recognised and enforced, by others if not by themselves.

Discrimination

1.36 Discrimination is not always intentional. It may be due to pure ignorance or mere thoughtlessness (ie treating people in an insensitive way), but stereotyping and prejudice also give rise to discrimination. Unwitting or unconscious prejudice – demonstrating prejudice without realising it – is difficult to tackle. Ignorance of the cultures, beliefs and disadvantages of others encourages prejudices and these are best dispelled by greater awareness. For people with disabilities it is not just a question of avoiding these forms of discrimination because any special needs also have to be addressed. Providing equal treatment may involve different treatment so as to ensure equal opportunity.

1.37 Discrimination takes many forms: it may be actual or perceived and it may be direct or indirect. *Direct* discrimination occurs where a person is treated less favourably, on grounds of race, colour, religion, gender, ethnic or national origin, or disability, than others would be in similar circumstance. *Indirect* discrimination occurs where a requirement is applied equally to all groups, but has a disproportionate effect on the members of one group because a considerably smaller number of members of that group can comply with it.

Discrimination may also be found in an entire organisation through its processes, attitudes and behaviour.[39] A culture of prejudice may have grown up within an organisation which is seen as acceptable by those involved and results in unquestioning behaviour that disadvantages a section of the community.[40] If this arises in the legal system or in any environment it should be addressed in an appropriate way.

---

[39] This was one of the conclusions of *The Stephen Lawrence inquiry – Report by Sir William Macpherson* (HMSO, Cmnd 4264-1). 'Institutional racism' was identified in the police force.

[40] Eg failure to provide assistance to wheelchair users or to communicate in a friendly manner with people from ethnic minorities.

1.38   Discrimination in any form is now disapproved of as it means being
        treated unfairly or denied opportunities. It should be avoided even if not
        intended. Indirect discrimination should not be tolerated unless it can be
        objectively justified by a legitimate aim and the means of achieving that
        aim are appropriate and necessary. Even if there is no discrimination
        every effort should be made to avoid the perception that there has been.

Attitudes to disability

1.39   Attitudes to disability in general have also changed in three significant
        respects:

1. We have moved away from the medical model of disability, which
    concentrates on the limitations of the individual, to a social model
    which identifies the barriers created in society. Thus lack of access
    to a building is not seen as being due to the fact that the individual
    is a wheelchair user but rather that the building has been
    constructed with steps but no ramp. In other words, don't blame the
    individual but blame the way society is structured. It is the barriers
    that should be removed (or not put there in the first place) rather
    than the individual that should be given special treatment.

2. Stereotyping has been recognised as the most significant form of
    discrimination that affects people with disabilities. This is exhibited
    in the unjustified assumption that people who meet particular
    criteria will behave in a particular way. In other words, we must be
    careful not to apply labels to people, often unconsciously, and then
    make assumptions based thereon. People who have a specific
    condition should not all be assumed to have the same limitations or
    approach to life – they should be treated as 'people first' rather than
    identified by their perceived disability.

3. There is a greater awareness of mental health problems and
    arguably less social stigma involved, although it is still prevalent in
    certain sections of the community.[41] There are many myths about
    people with mental health problems, in particular that they are
    dangerous and violent, can't work and are incapable of making their
    own decisions. Contrary to popular belief, mental health problems
    are not rare and unusual. However, there remains a tension,
    reflected in the debate about a new Mental Health Act, between the
    need to protect society and the best interests of the individual.
    Society and politicians still tend to be obsessed with those few cases
    where the individual has become a public danger when in the vast
    majority of cases any risk is purely to the individual.

---

[41]   Stigma arises from negative stereotypes associated with the symptoms or diagnosis of
       mental health problems.

Terminology

1.40 How we refer to people is important. Use of inappropriate terms can cause great offence to the individual and also demonstrates prejudicial attitudes towards disabled people. Also, if we attach labels to people there is a danger that we then use these, however inadvertently, to take away their rights by making assumptions that are not in fact justified. Comparisons should never be made with 'normal'[42] and we should not refer to 'the disabled' or 'the handicapped' as if these are a class of person.[43] Terminology that suggests a value judgment should also be avoided.[44] One of the difficulties is that defined medical or legal terms have over the years tended to become used in a derogatory manner[45] and then new neutral terms have to be found. Thus 'mental handicap' has been replaced by 'learning disability' and efforts are being made to find a new term for 'mentally ill'.[46]

Use of appropriate terminology is not just political correctness but is also an attitude of mind: we should recognise the person rather than any disability. Organisations such as *People First* prefer that we state 'people with disabilities' for this reason. More recently the *Disability Rights Commission* has opted for 'disabled people' because this emphasises that the individual is disabled by society (the social model of disability).

Attitudes of minority ethnic communities

1.41 It has become apparent that some minority ethnic communities have a distrust of mental health authorities, try to deal with problems within the family and view the Public Guardianship Office as 'interfering'. It is essential that any new mental incapacity jurisdiction reaches out to such communities and recognises cultural norms. The problems that are faced may be illustrated by reference to two communities.

1.42 Asian communities in the UK have tended to be young with the men mainly working and in consequence controlling the finances. This is changing as they move into the second and third generation, and as members become older more are presenting with senile dementia. There

---

[42] Instead refer to non-disabled or able bodied.

[43] These terms are grammatically incorrect! Similarly 'the blind' or 'the deaf' – instead use 'people with impaired sight' or 'people with impaired hearing'.

[44] Eg referring to someone as 'a victim of ...', 'suffering from ...', 'afflicted by ...' or 'wheelchair bound'.

[45] Eg the terms *idiot, imbecile, lunatic, cretin, moron,* all of which have appeared in earlier legislation or medical textbooks. The Mental Deficiency Act 1913 used the defined terms 'idiot' and 'imbecile'.

[46] MIND, the national organisation, tends to use 'people who experience mental distress' or 'people with mental health problems' but at one time the expression 'mentally challenged' was advocated.

is a stigma associated with mental health problems which tend to be concealed with a consequent delay in accessing services. Many unwritten transactions take place within the community so incapacity issues are not being faced up to. There is a need to raise awareness of the legal position because families react with disbelief when told that they have no authority over the finances of an incapacitated member.

1.43   The Jewish community ranges across a religious spectrum from liberal to ultra-orthodox and increased numbers come from a range of racial groups, mainly Asian and African. They generally live in urban areas situated around local and regional centres close to religious, education and cultural venues. Some are assimilated into the general community but others lead segregated lives. Parents tend to request the continuation of a Jewish life and value base for their children of whom they have high expectations. Jews have a different experience, both historically and culturally, from the mainstream population. They would define themselves as an ethnic minority and carry a shared past and present experience of persecution and discrimination.

National statistics tend to show a higher than average incidence of mental health problems especially in students and young people. This is coupled with a lack of knowledge and awareness of mental health issues and a feeling of stigma within families who have difficulty in accepting problems. In consequence these are often concealed and not regularly acknowledged as a Jewish issue. There are a large number of Jewish social care agencies and care tends to be segregated in the Jewish community with culturally specific services – kosher food, prayer facilities and religious activities.

Role of the law

1.44   People with disabilities are vulnerable to neglect, abuse and exploitation and may need support, protection and empowerment.

Support

1.45   There are three sources of support, all regulated by the law:

1.   DWP – the Department of Work and Pensions,[47] which through the *Benefits Agency* provided state benefits, generally on a weekly basis. These may be contributory, non-contributory[48] or a means-tested top-up to ensure that everybody has a minimum income to meet their requirements.[49] The Benefits Agency has since been

---

[47]   Formerly known as the Department of Social Security (DSS), and previously the Department of Health and Social Security (DHSS).

[48]   Eg disability benefits. Contributory benefits are generally for earnings replacement, eg retirement pension and incapacity benefit.

[49]   Often referred to as 'welfare benefits'.

replaced by *Job Centre Plus* (for adults of working age), the *Disability and Carers Service* (for disability related benefits) and the *Pensions Service* (for people over pension age);

2. SSD – the social services departments of local authorities[50] which are responsible for providing or arranging community care services and services for disabled persons. These must generally be paid for, subject to a means test;

3. NHS – the National Health Service which, largely now through NHS Trusts, provides free hospital and nursing care and general medical services.[51]

The respective roles of these providers are changing and overlapping, with social services applying means tests which may take away state benefit yet now providing cash to pay for services, whilst state benefits are withdrawn from those in 'hospital'.[52] In some areas, Care Trusts provide both health and social care services, particularly mental health and learning disability services and care for older people.

Protection

1.46 The law must also ensure protection and may do so by providing a representative in the form of an *appropriate adult* for police interviews and a *statutory guardian* or *nearest relative* for Mental Health Act functions. The authorities should investigate and intervene where there is a suspicion of abuse but their powers are limited at present when compared with those under the Children Act 1989 and there is no duty to act – which means that often they do not do so despite conflict or perceived abuse.[53]

Empowerment

1.47 Empowerment means enabling individuals to take decisions for which they are competent. There must be a proper assessment of capacity and any communication difficulties should be overcome. A suitable person should be empowered to take decisions for individuals who are not competent. At present we have a number of potential representatives but coverage is not comprehensive.[54]

---

[50] Not all local authorities have such departments and reference is often now made to 'local authorities with social services responsibilities'.

[51] Older readers will remember the DHSS (Department of Health and Social Security) when health and social security came within the same government department.

[52] The definition of 'hospital' for benefits purposes is wider than the generally recognised meaning.

[53] Some local authorities have set up Adult Protection procedures under the *No Secrets* guidance.

[54] See **1.17** above.

Problems

1.48   There have been four significant problems in our present law and
        procedures:

(a) a lack of adequate public funding to cover the needs of disabled
    people and a lack of ring-fencing of the funds that could be
    available;

(b) buck-passing between the Department of Work and Pensions, local
    authorities and health authorities with the disabled individual
    becoming a pawn in the funding game, and money that could have
    been expended on unquestionable needs being wasted on the
    argument over which funder must provide. In recent years many
    appeal decisions have sought to define responsibilities but to some
    extent the problem has been alleviated by the introduction of joint
    commissioning of services by health and social services;

(c) the delicate balance between protection and empowerment, because
    protection involves taking away the personal autonomy it is desired
    to preserve. This dilemma is frequently encountered in our courts
    when dealing with vulnerable persons;

(d) no adequate legally authorised representatives in many situations
    because of the piecemeal nature of our present system, in particular
    the lack of procedures for personal and medical decision-making.

The new jurisdiction introduced by the Mental Capacity Act 2005 will
address the third and fourth of these problems and assist family and
carers to address the second, but will not assist where there is
inadequate funding for care needs.

Role of lawyers

1.49   Lawyers have developed considerable skills in negotiating on behalf of,
        and promoting the rights of, individuals who for one reason or another
        are at a disadvantage in looking after their own interests. The lawyer
        can also act as a whistle-blower to draw attention to situations where the
        rights of a vulnerable person are being overlooked or abuse is taking
        place.

Who is the client?

1.50   It is essential for any adviser in these situations to start by identifying
        the client. The identity of the client does not change just because of
        communication difficulties or even lack of capacity. Undue reliance
        should not be placed on relatives or carers in identifying the wishes of
        the client especially where these persons may be affected by the
        outcome of any decision. Any potential conflicts of interest should be
        identified at an early stage and, if appropriate independent legal advice
        recommended either for the would-be client or for the relatives or
        carers.

1.51 A solicitor receiving instructions from a third party on behalf of an individual who is or may become mentally incapacitated should at all times remember that this individual is the client, not the third party. This is so even if the third party has legal authority to represent the individual, either as receiver appointed by the Court of Protection or attorney acting under a registered enduring power of attorney. The third party is merely an agent with a duty to act in the best interests of the incapacitated principal, and any solicitor who accepts instructions shares this duty even if it brings him or her into conflict with the agent through whom he or she receives instructions. In such situations the incapacitated person may need to be independently represented by a solicitor and any new procedures should address this.

The legal climate

General

1.52 Driven by these social forces the legal climate has also changed over the past decade. Lawyers and the courts are having to cope with the needs of infirm elderly and disabled people. Some practitioners concentrate upon this aspect of the law and have developed considerable expertise. There have also been significant legislative initiatives which provide the basis for the growth of legal activity and a wide range of new outcomes from the courts.

Legal publishing

1.53 A new approach to legal publishing and the practice of the law was also developing. In July 1992 *Mental Handicap and the Law* was published, having been 5 years in gestation.[55] The aim was to address the needs of people with learning disabilities and their families and carers. This was followed by further books by the same author relating to elderly people[56] which represented a radical new approach to the law based on the needs of client groups rather than the coverage of legal topics as hitherto favoured by practitioners, authors and academics.

Elderly client practices

1.54 With the encouragement of the Law Society, solicitors have developed 'elderly client practices' providing a full range of services targeting the needs of older clients that go beyond the traditional wills and enduring

---

[55] Sweet & Maxwell, 1992. The author, Gordon Ashton, is the General Editor of the present work and has contributed this Chapter.

[56] *The Elderly Client Handbook*, (The Law Society, 1994, 3rd edn, 2004); *Elderly People and the Law*, (Butterworths, 1995); *Butterworths Older Client Law Service* (looseleaf) (Butterworths, 1997). Further books have followed by other authors.

powers of attorney.[57] These developments have resulted in a wider range of legal services being available to the public thereby increasing expectations and creating a greater awareness of the weaknesses of our existing legal system in regard to incapacitated people.

National Health Service and Community Care Act 1990

Background

1.55   Care in the community is not a new concept. For many it had been the reality for years, but meant living alone or being cared for by family with little support from the state in an indifferent society. The need became apparent to reduce institutional care and provide alternative services in a community setting, and increasing pressure from concerned people and organisations to recognise the rights and freedoms of people who need care or support found expression in policies which have become known as *community care*.

It was also recognised that this meant more than just the provision of a home in the community for former hospital patients; a whole range of support and services had to be provided for all persons needing care, including those already living in their own family homes. The emphasis should be upon enabling them to remain in their own homes or otherwise in the community when they, their family and friends could no longer cope without support. In the absence of a suitable range of services the only alternative had been long-term care in a residential home or hospital.

Reports

1.56   In 1986 the Audit Commission carried out a review of community-based care services and identified many problems which needed to be tackled. Resources, staffing and training were all directed towards the more institutional forms of care, organisation was fragmented, and there was a lack of effective joint working and planning between the different agencies involved in the provision of services. The Commission regarded community care as providing clients with a full range of services, and a wide range of options; bringing services to people, rather than people to services; the adjustment of services to meet the needs of people, rather than the adjustment of people to meet the needs of services.[58]

---

[57]   First advocated by this author at the Annual Conference of the Law Society in 1992. A new professional body *Solicitors for the Elderly Limited* (SFE) now has several hundred members, runs conferences and has a website at: www.solicitorsfortheelderly.com.

[58]   *Making a Reality of Community Care* (Report of 1986).

1.57 A further review, *Community Care: Agenda for Action*, was published in 1988.[59] It acknowledged the need to promote 'the provision of services to individuals, developed from a multi-disciplinary assessment of their needs and made with proper participation of the individuals concerned, their families and other carers'. This was followed in 1989 by the publication of a White Paper *Caring for People: Community Care in the Next Decade and Beyond* in which it was stated:

> 'Community care means providing the services and support which people who are affected by problems of ageing, mental illness, mental handicap or physical or sensory disability need to be able to live as independently as possible in their own homes, or in homely settings in the community.'

Legislation

1.58 Although the legislation seen as introducing community care policies and procedures is the National Health Service and Community Care Act 1990 ('the 1990 Act'), this devotes only nine sections[60] to the topic in England. The 1990 Act does not create new rights to new services, and although it imposes a new duty upon local authorities to assess anyone who appears to them to need a community care service which they may provide, it relied heavily on the following earlier legislation some of which had existed for many years:

> National Assistance Act 1948 (Part III);
>
> Health Services and Public Health Act 1968;
>
> Chronically Sick and Disabled Persons Act 1970;
>
> Housing Act 1985;
>
> National Health Service Act 1977;
>
> Disabled Persons Act 1981;
>
> Mental Health Act 1983;
>
> Health and Social Services and Social Security Adjudications Act 1983;[61]
>
> Disabled Persons (Services Consultation and Representation) Act 1986.

Further legislation has followed and this has proved a prolific area for litigation with many appeal cases contributing to the implementation of the policy.

1.59 The 1990 Act extended the role of local authorities in the provision of residential accommodation and welfare services, enabling them to make agency arrangements with other organisations and persons whilst

---

[59] Report to the Secretary of State for Social Services by Sir Roy Griffiths (*the Griffiths Report*).

[60] See Part III of the 1990 Act.

[61] Known as the HASSASSA Act.

restricting their powers to provide accommodation. It amended the provisions as to charges for residential accommodation and other community care services and dealt with recovery of such charges. Local authorities were required, following consultation with health and housing authorities, to prepare and publish a community care plan. They had to assess the care needs of any person who might appear to them to require community care services and decide what services needed to be provided. Disabled individuals were given a right to an assessment. Further provisions dealt with the inspection of certain premises used for community care services, access to information and the transfer of staff from health authorities to local authorities. Finally, local authorities had to provide a complaints procedure and comply with directions from the Secretary of State in carrying out their social services functions failing which default powers became available.

Circulars and directions

1.60   The legislation is supplemented by government guidance and circulars, and by directions issued by the Secretary of State. A local authority may only be obliged to take account of advice contained in circulars and having done so may not be under a duty to comply,[62] though where an appeal to the Secretary of State is provided for it may be expected that he or she will follow his or her own advice. The policy documents of a local authority (including its community care plan) should reflect any directions and guidance in circulars and these are likely to be quoted in court proceedings and could form the basis for a legal challenge of an authority's action or inaction. The Secretary of State is empowered to issue directions to local authorities in regard to the exercise of their social services functions, and these must be observed with the sanction being the use of default powers.

Race Relations Act 1976

1.61   This legislation, which established the *Commission for Racial Equality*, makes it unlawful to discriminate on grounds of colour, race, nationality, ethnic or national origin. The Race Relations (Amendment) Act 2000 promotes race equality by imposing specific duties on public authorities and these will apply to the new Office of the Public Guardian. Positive steps will have to be taken to promote equality and to reach communities which may hitherto have had little knowledge of the Court of Protection or sought to avoid involvement.

---

[62]   Local Authority Social Services Act 1970, s 7. In this respect there may be a difference between general guidance and a direction, but the other view is that guidance is instruction that must be followed – see *R v North Yorkshire CC, ex p Hargreaves* (1994) *The Times*, November 9.

Disability Discrimination Act 1995

Overview

1.62   According to the Disability Rights Commission, there are approximately 9.8 million disabled adults in Britain, over 17 per cent of the population. Increased awareness of the effects of discrimination has resulted in disability discrimination legislation in parallel to that in relation to race and gender. The Disability Discrimination Act 1995 ('the 1995 Act') (as amended) is supplemented by Regulations and *Codes of Practice* which provide detailed information and must be taken into account when interpreting the statutory material.[63]

1.63   'Disability' in this context is defined in the following manner:[64]

> '... a person has a disability for the purposes of this Act if he has a physical or mental impairment which has a substantial and long-term adverse effect on his ability to carry out normal day-to-day activities.'

This definition is amplified in Sch 1 to the 1995 Act and various regulations[65] and is more complex than it first appears. It does not cover all types of disability (eg people with HIV and other progressive conditions who have not developed any symptoms) but it is not dependent upon being 'registered disabled' with the local authority or receipt of disability benefits under the social security system.

1.64   The 1995 Act makes it unlawful to discriminate against people with disabilities and provides new rights in the areas of employment, the provision of goods, services and facilities, and the buying or renting of land or property. It also places a duty on service providers and employers to take reasonable steps to change any practice, policy or procedure which makes it impossible or unreasonably difficult for disabled persons to make use of a service which they provide to other members of the public. This extends to providing auxiliary aids and services and, from 1 October 2004, to removing physical barriers to service.

Provision of services

1.65   Under Part III of the 1995 Act it is unlawful for a provider of services to discriminate against a disabled person:[66]

---

[63]   Disability Discrimination Act 1995, s 53.

[64]   Disability Discrimination Act 1995, s 1.

[65]   See in particular Disability Discrimination (Meaning of Disability) Regulations 1996, SI 1996/1455.

[66]   Disability Discrimination Act 1995, s 19.

(a) in refusing to provide, or deliberately not providing, to the disabled person any service which he provides, or is prepared to provide, to members of the public;

(b) in failing to comply with any duty imposed on him [to make adjustments] in circumstances in which the effect of that failure is to make it impossible or unreasonably difficult for the disabled person to make use of any such service;

(c) in the standard of service which he provides to the disabled person or the manner in which he provides it to him; or

(d) in the terms on which he provides a service to the disabled person.

Where an auxiliary aid or service would assist, it is the duty of the service provider to take reasonable steps to provide this. 'Services' includes 'goods or facilities' and it is irrelevant whether a service is provided on payment or without payment.

1.66   A provider of services discriminates against a disabled person:

(a) if, for a reason which relates to the disabled person's disability, he treats him less favourably than he treats or would treat others to whom that reason does not or would not apply, and he cannot show that the treatment in question is justified; or

(b) if he fails to comply with the duty to make adjustments and he cannot show that his failure to comply with that duty is justified.

Specified examples include access to and use of information services, facilities by way of banking or insurance or for grants, loans, credit or finance and the services of any profession or trade, or any local or other public authority all of which are relevant to a mental capacity jurisdiction.

1.67   The duty of a provider of services to make adjustments is set out as follows:[67]

'Where a provider of services has a practice, policy or procedure which makes it impossible or unreasonably difficult for disabled persons to make use of a service which he provides, or is prepared to provide, to other members of the public, it is his duty to take such steps as it is reasonable, in all the circumstances of the case, for him to have to take in order to change that practice, policy or procedure so that it no longer has that effect.'

1.68   In dealing with this tort the court has all usual remedies and damages may include compensation for injury to feelings.[68] An employer of a provider is liable for the actions of an employee or agent, acting within the course of his or her duties, unless the employer took reasonable steps to prevent the discrimination.

---

[67]   Disability Discrimination Act 1995, s 21.
[68]   Disability Discrimination Act 1995, s 25.

Comment

1.69 Most claims to date have been in respect of employment and these are dealt with by the Employment Tribunals, but claims relating to the supply of goods and services come before the county courts. These are generally dealt with in the small claims track and there have been relatively few so far because disabled people were expected to bring their own claims but the Disability Rights Commission now runs test cases.[69]

1.70 The courts are not exempted from these provisions; they provide legal services and could find themselves in breach of this legislation if they do not take into account the needs of disabled people.[70] It is not clear whether this applies only to court buildings and the facilities provided within them or also to the role of the court staff, and further whether there is immunity for judicial acts as distinct from administrative arrangements. Nevertheless, the Office of the Public Guardian and the Court of Protection must be fully conversant with these provisions both as regards the manner in which they deal with disabled people and the expectations that they have for incapacitated persons when dealing with their financial, social welfare and healthcare decisions.

Human Rights Act 1998

The Convention

1.71 The *European Convention on Human Rights*[71] is a treaty of the Council of Europe.[72] It was signed in 1950 and ratified by the UK in 1951 which means that under international law the UK became obliged to abide by its terms, although the right of individual petition was only afforded in 1966. But this did not mean that Convention rights could be relied upon in proceedings in our courts. The treaty has subsequently been amended by *Protocols* which are either mandatory or optional, the latter only binding states that choose to ratify them.

The legislation

1.72 The long title to the Human Rights Act 1998 ('the 1998 Act') states that it is 'to give further effect to' the Convention rights and it was said to be 'bringing rights home' on the basis that individuals within the UK

---

[69] There is an interesting summary of cases on their website: www.drc-gb.org/.

[70] The Court Service has already found itself having to admit liability in a claim involving access to the courts for a hearing impaired person.

[71] The full title is the *Convention for the Protection of Human Rights and Fundamental Freedoms*.

[72] This is a separate organisation from the *European Union* and now comprises more than 40 member states. For further information see www.coe.int.

would be enabled to rely on their rights in their home courts,[73] although the right to bring a case in Strasbourg is not prevented. The 1998 Act is a compromise, representing an attempt to incorporate the Convention into our law whilst still recognising the traditions of the common law and the sovereignty of Parliament. Every new Bill must, when introduced, be supported by a *statement of compatibility* by the Minister responsible.[74]

1.73   Only certain of the rights contained in the Convention have been designated as 'Convention rights' for the purpose of the 1998 Act,[75] but those omitted must no doubt be 'taken into account'. Those of particular relevance in the present context are:

Article 2 – the right to life, which has implications for the health services and especially decisions as to whether to treat those who would otherwise die;

Article 3 – the prohibition of inhuman or degrading treatment, which is of particular relevance to the abuse and neglect of vulnerable people;

Article 5 – the protection of liberty, which may affect detention in a home or hospital;

Article 6 – the right to a fair trial, which concerns participation and ensuring an independent and impartial tribunal;

Article 8 – respect for private and family life, home and correspondence, which extends to bodily integrity, access to information, confidentiality and sexual relations;

1st Protocol, Article 2 – protection of property.

Some of these are 'absolute' in the sense that they do not include any qualification or allow for any derogation[76] by a ratifying country and others are qualified by some limitation or restriction.[77] Non-discrimination operates within all other rights pursuant to Art 14.[78]

Interpretation

1.74   The courts must interpret our primary and secondary legislation 'so far as it is possible to do so' in a way which is not incompatible with the Convention whilst not having power to overrule any such legislation.[79]

---

[73]   See the White Paper *Bringing Rights Home*, Cm 3782 (1997).

[74]   Human Rights Act 1998, s 19.

[75]   Human Rights Act 1998, s 1. The text of these Articles is set out in Sch 1 to the 1998 Act.

[76]   An exceptional limitation imposed by the ratifying country on a particular right in specified circumstances. It must be in accordance with the law, directed to a 'particular purpose' and 'necessary in a democratic society'.

[77]   This relates to some existing law of the country concerned, which is not to be affected.

[78]   A breach of another Convention right does not need to be established, but the circumstances must fall within the ambit of a Convention provision.

[79]   Human Rights Act 1998, s 3.

Where this cannot be done a *declaration of incompatibility* may be made[80] and it then becomes a matter for Parliament (which has a fast-track procedure for remedying the incompatibility[81]), although in the meanwhile the legislation must still be applied.[82] So legislation must henceforth be interpreted so as to give effect if possible to Convention rights.

It has been stated that an Act must receive a 'generous and purposive' interpretation to ensure that Convention rights are effective rather than illusory. Techniques may include 'reading down' (choosing between two possible interpretations and opting for the narrower) and 'reading in' (inserting words to make the statute compatible). Strasbourg jurisprudence must be 'taken into account' by our courts and tribunals,[83] which means that decisions of the European Court now become part of our case-law.

1.75   The European Court has recognised that the obligations of states under the Convention are not limited to refraining from interfering with individual human rights. There is a positive obligation to ensure that one person's rights are protected from violation by another person and this has led to five duties being imposed on states in relation to Convention rights:

1.   to have a legal framework providing effective protection;
2.   to prevent breaches;
3.   to provide information and advice;
4.   to respond to breaches;
5.   to provide resources to individuals to prevent breaches.

Remedies

1.76   When a Convention right is found to have been breached (or is about to be breached) the court may grant such relief or remedy, or make such order, within its powers as it considers 'just and appropriate'.[84] The 1998 Act does not give additional powers and the normal routes of an appeal or judicial review apply. There can be no claim for damages in respect of a judicial act done in good faith except in the case of a breach of liberty.

---

[80]   Human Rights Act 1998, s 4. This power is restricted to the High Court, Court of Appeal and House of Lords and the Crown is entitled to make representations.

[81]   Human Rights Act 1998, s 10. This procedure will also be appropriate when a finding of the European Court in proceedings against the UK renders a provision incompatible.

[82]   If subordinate legislation (eg a statutory instrument) is incompatible with Convention rights, and the incompatibility is not required by primary legislation, either the courts will find ways of interpreting it so as to be compatible or will set it aside.

[83]   Human Rights Act 1998, s 2(1).

[84]   Human Rights Act 1998, s 8(1).

New concepts

1.77   It follows that each branch of government (legislature, executive and
        judicial) is responsible for giving effect to Convention rights when
        exercising public powers. However, various concepts apply in the
        interpretation and application of Convention rights which will not be
        familiar to lawyers brought up on the common law and statute law:

1. Not only can proceedings be brought against a public authority in
    relation to Convention rights (the 'vertical' effect), but as the courts
    are public authorities they must apply Convention rights when
    adjudicating on proceedings between private individuals (the
    'horizontal' effect). So litigants can argue their human rights in the
    courts and these must be respected.

2. To some extent the European Court adopts a hands-off approach to
    the way that individual countries apply Convention rights, although
    this 'margin of appreciation' has no application to national courts.
    This reflects the fact that those courts are in a better position to
    assess the needs and standards of their own society and the national
    authorities should be deferred to (especially in moral matters and
    social policy) as long as the whole process is fair and the outcome is
    true to the Convention.

3. Where a state interferes with a Convention right, the means ('the
    limitation') must be balanced against the end ('the permitted
    purpose') and shown to be necessary. There must be a reasonable
    relationship between the goal pursued and the means employed.
    This follows from the fact that any limitation on a Convention right
    must be in accordance with law and 'necessary in a democratic
    society',[85] and has become the principle of 'proportionality'.

4. A 'principle of legality' is derived from the use by the Convention
    of the phrases 'in accordance with the law' and 'prescribed by law'
    and the use of the word 'lawful'. It has been stated to mean:[86]

    (a) that the legal basis for any restriction on Convention rights must
        be identified and established by the domestic law;

    (b) that law must be accessible and not interpreted according to
        unpublished criteria; and

    (c) that the law must be clear to those affected by it so that they can
        understand it, although it may allow some discretion as long as
        the limits are clear.

---

[85]   A 'democratic society' means a society which is pluralistic and tolerant. The interests of
       minorities and individuals must be carefully considered.
[86]   Keir Starmer *European Human Rights Law* (Legal Action Group, 1999) at para 4.29.

Application to the Court of Protection and Public Guardian

1.78 Not only must the courts apply Convention rights but rather than giving individuals personal rights the 1998 Act also imposes a new statutory duty on 'public authorities' not to act in contravention thereof. This term is not defined but a function-based test is to be applied. Courts and tribunals are expressly included, as is 'any person certain of whose functions are functions of a public nature' which would include the Public Guardian. It is 'unlawful for a public authority to act in a way which is incompatible with a Convention right'[87] and even a failure to act would be construed as non-compliance. An individual who claims that a public authority has acted in an incompatible way may bring proceedings against that authority either directly or within the context of other proceedings.[88]

Where the public body determining the civil rights or obligations is not a court or tribunal[89] a two-limbed test is applied: either that body must comply with the right to a fair hearing under Art 6 or there must be a right of appeal or review from that body to a court or tribunal which fully complies. The previous right to apply for judicial review is not sufficient because the Administrative Court cannot make findings of fact.[90]

Comment

1.79 People who lack capacity do not lose their human rights, but the rights of others must also be respected. In delivering its services the new jurisdiction must not overlook the human rights of anyone, but there will be many situations when there is a conflict between the rights of those involved, whether the incapacitated individual, family members or others. An appropriate balance must then be achieved. It has hitherto been the view of government, when considering the involvement of the Court of Protection, that only the decision that an individual lacks capacity affects human rights, and that once delegated decision-making powers arise there are no further human rights implications. That may be the position for the incapacitated person, but family and personal relationships also give rise to human rights in others.

1.80 The Convention is a living instrument so, unlike the common law where previous decisions of higher courts create precedents, it must be interpreted in accordance with present-day conditions. This means that what was decided yesterday may be decided differently tomorrow,

---

[87] Human Rights Act 1998, s 6.
[88] Human Rights Act 1998, s 7.
[89] Eg a local housing authority, a health authority, social services and probably the Public Guardian.
[90] *W v UK* (1987) 10 EHRR 29 at para 82.

although this may be a whole generation later. The difficulty lies in determining what the contemporary standards are which merit protection. However, the Convention is intended to guarantee rights that are practical and effective rather than theoretical and illusory.[91]

Civil Partnership Act 2004

Background

1.81   This recent legislation reflects more liberal social attitudes. It has become widely accepted that it is both logically and morally indefensible to prevent homosexual couples from access to formal recognition of their relationships and to the 'next of kin' rights and the tax, pension and other advantages that flow from marriage. Encouraging stability in relationships, whether heterosexual or homosexual, should involve the same sorts of protections as come with marriage, and the Civil Partnership Act 2004 ('the 2004 Act') addresses these issues in considerable detail.

The legislation

1.82   The 2004 Act[92] will introduce greater recognition for same sex relationships in England and Wales, Scotland and Northern Ireland by an option of registration as 'civil partners'. A 'civil partnership' is defined as:[93]

> '... a relationship between two people of the same sex ... which is formed when they register as civil partners of each other ...'.

It ends only on death, dissolution or annulment. Heterosexual couples are specifically excluded because they have the option of marriage. The general approach is to make detailed provision for the formation and ending of civil partnerships, and for the consequences that flow from them. It deals with these matters by treating civil partners in very much the same way as married couples. There is provision for recognition of overseas relationships.

1.83   To create a civil partnership a specific document is required, signed in the presence of each other and of a civil partnership registrar and two witnesses. No religious service is to be used during the registration formalities, and it cannot take place in religious premises. A couple cannot register if one is already married or a civil partner of someone else, nor if either is under 16 or within prohibited degrees of relationship.

---

91   *Artico v Italy* A/37 (1980) 3 EHRR 1.
92   It has 196 sections arranged in 8 Parts and there are 22 Schedules.
93   Civil Partnership Act 2004, s 1.

The provisions for court proceedings to end partnerships,[94] and as to children and finances in most cases, mirror existing provisions for married couples. In the case of disputes about property either civil partner may apply to the county court, and the court may make such order with respect to the property as it thinks fit, including an order for sale. Contributions to property improvement if substantial and in money or money's worth are recognised.

1.84 Other amendments align civil partners with married persons, for example in certain parts of the law relating to housing and tenancies, in domestic violence proceedings[95] and under the Fatal Accidents Act 1976. Interpretation of statutory references to step relationships (eg stepson, stepmother, etc), and the terms '...in-law' (eg brother-in-law and daughter-in-law) are amended to apply in Civil Partnerships. There are amendments to the Sex Discrimination Act 1975, social security, child support and tax credits legislation. Civil Partners will have an insurable interest in each other.

Implementation will involve significant changes in many areas, for example in court rules, the registration service, training and guidance for employers. The 2004 Act does not address the problems in the legal treatment of those cohabiting without registration by marriage or by civil partnership.

Incapacity issues

1.85 Civil partnership is not merely a matter of contract but affects status and creates a completely new legal relationship. Clearly this will have implications for any mental capacity jurisdiction. The civil partner must be recognised to the same extent as a spouse when decisions are to be made, whether relating to financial matters, personal welfare or healthcare. Comparable duties and responsibilities may also arise on the part of the civil partner.

1.86 The civil partner must also be afforded the same status as a spouse as regards participation in any of the procedures. This is not as radical as it may seem, because the new social attitudes have already resulted in domestic partners being involved in many situations, and this has included same sex partners even in the absence of a civil partnership. To this extent there has been a move away from relationships of blood and marriage to *de facto* relationships. The Adults with Incapacity (Scotland) Act 2000 provided 'next of kin' rights to same sex partners by including them within the definition of nearest relative whose views must be taken into account,[96] and the equivalent provision under the

---

[94] Including nullity, presumption of death and separation orders.
[95] Under Family Law Act 1996, Part IV.
[96] Adults with Incapacity (Scotland) Act 2000, ss 1(4)(b) and 87(2).

Mental Capacity Act 2005 includes 'anyone engaged in caring for the person or interested in his welfare' as well as 'anyone named by the person as someone to be consulted on the matter in question or matters of that kind'.[97]

LAW REFORM

Origins

Law Society of England and Wales

A discussion paper

1.87   During recent years it has become apparent that the law and procedures in England and Wales fail to address in a comprehensive manner the problems raised by those who are incompetent in the sense that they cannot make their own decisions. The courts do not have adequate powers to fill the vacuum and such legislation as there has been is piecemeal and not based upon an underlying philosophy. Comprehensive reform in this area is essential. This was first highlighted in a paper produced by the Law Society in 1989 which posed the following questions:[98]

> 'What happens where an adult does not have the mental capacity to make reasoned decisions? Who should make decisions on behalf of a dependent adult – the carer or nearest relative, an appointed representative, the court? The law is hopelessly confused and clearly inadequate, making provision only for limited financial management. Where legislation exists, it provides a multiplicity of procedures with varying criteria, and its effects are often inappropriate. In practice it is widely ignored, leaving dependent adults unprotected and open to exploitation and abuse.'

1.88   After considering the identification of incapacity and reasoning that a test based on 'functional ability as a decision-maker' is to be preferred to tests based upon the outcome of decisions or status, the paper suggested that there was a need for change:

> '... the existing legal mechanisms providing for decision-making in relation to mental incapacity are complicated, inflexible and piecemeal. Limited provision exists for the management of financial affairs, and in some circumstances, for consent to medical treatment. But there is no provision for other, and more day-to-day, life decisions, or for particular groups of clients.'

---

[97]   Mental Capacity Act 2005, s 4(7).
[98]   *Decision-making and Mental Incapacity: A Discussion Document*, Memorandum by the Law Society's Mental Health Sub-Committee, January 1989.

The paper then compared the 'substituted judgment' and 'best interests' approaches to decision-making and concluded by identifying what has become the underlying problem in devising a statutory procedure for decision-making:

> 'There is however a conflict of opinion between those who believe a change in the law will provide much-needed protection for dependent adults with those who consider that such a change would further restrict the rights of dependent adults, removing from them the power to make any decisions, including those they are capable of making. It appears that changes in the law are necessary, which can be tested against stringent safeguards and which must also be accompanied by better provision or advocacy, assistance and representation.'

A conference

1.89 A conference was then arranged[99] and the speakers included Professor Brenda Hoggett who had recently been appointed as a Law Commissioner. She provided an overview of the legal problems and possible approaches to finding solutions to them, and was followed by Dr Raanan Gillon[100] who pointed out the differences between incompetence and vulnerability when intervening in people's lives and between those who had never achieved and those who had lost their autonomy. Other speakers were from MENCAP, Age Concern, MIND and the Scottish Law Commission who were also considering proposals for change.

The Law Commission

Consultation

1.90 The Law Commission of England & Wales was set up by Parliament to recommend ways in which the law may be improved, kept up to date and made more simple. Prompted by the Law Society initiative it embarked upon a consideration of the whole question of decision-making and mental incapacity.[101] Professor Brenda Hoggett was the Law Commissioner responsible.[102] Serious deficiencies were identified during a protracted consultation and it became clear that reform was badly needed.

---

[99] *Decision-making and Mental Incapacity* (The Law Society, 5 May 1989).

[100] Professor of Medical Ethics at Imperial College, London and Editor of the Journal of Medical Ethics.

[101] A similar review was undertaken by the Law Commission of Scotland.

[102] She later became Mrs Justice Hale and rapidly progressed through the Court of Appeal to become the first lady to sit in the House of Lords. In these capacities she has had the opportunity to shape the law in accordance with her previous thinking.

An overview

1.91   The first consultation paper published in March 1991[103] provided an invaluable overview of the present state of the law and its procedures. It recognised that the existing law was inadequate to cope with the range of decisions that needed to be made on behalf of mentally incapable people but that the issue was large and complex. Further consultation followed.

A new jurisdiction

1.92   The second consultation paper published in December 1992[104] dealt with private law aspects and proposed procedures whereby decisions relating to the personal care and financial affairs of incapacitated people could be made.

Medical treatment

1.93   A third consultation paper published in March 1993[105] explored legal procedures whereby substitute decisions about medical treatment could be authorised at an appropriate level.

Public law protection

1.94   The fourth consultation paper followed soon after in April 1993.[106] It considered the powers of public authorities and was expanded to cover vulnerable as well as mentally incapacitated people.

Report

1.95   The Law Commission published its final Report in March 1995[107] with the almost unanimous support of charities and others concerned with the welfare of mentally incapacitated people. This set out comprehensive recommendations and included a draft Mental Incapacity Bill.

The basic approach

1.96   The Law Commission recommended that there should be a single comprehensive piece of legislation[108] to make new provision for people

---

[103]   'Mentally Incapacitated Adults and Decision-Making: An Overview' – No 119.

[104]   'Mentally Incapacitated Adults and Decision-Making: A New Jurisdiction' – No 128.

[105]   'Mentally Incapacitated Adults and Decision-Making: Medical Treatment and Research' – No 129.

[106]   'Mentally Incapacitated and Other Vulnerable Adults: Public Law Protection' – No 130.

[107]   'Mental Incapacity' – No 231.

[108]   This would move these problems away from the Mental Health Act and facilitate a different approach to the needs of incapacitated persons from that of mental health professionals.

who lack mental capacity.[109] This should provide a coherent statutory scheme to which recourse can be had when any decision (whether personal, medical or financial) needs to be made for a person aged 16 or over who lacks capacity. Two concepts were identified as being fundamental to any new decision-making jurisdiction, namely capacity and best interests.[110]

Capacity

1.97   It was proposed that:

> 'a person should be regarded as unable to make a decision if at the material time he or she is:
>
> (a) unable by reason of mental disability to make a decision on the matter in question; or
>
> (b) unable to communicate a decision on that matter because he or she is unconscious or for any other reason.'

An 'inability to make a decision' means an inability to:

> 'understand or retain the information relevant to the decision, including information about the reasonably foreseeable consequences of deciding one way or another or of failing to make the decision; or
>
> make a decision based on that information.'

1.98   The new term 'mental disability'[111] would mean 'a disability or disorder of the mind or brain, whether permanent or temporary, which results in an impairment or disturbance of mental functioning'.

Best interests

1.99   A new general rule was proposed that anything done for a person who is without capacity should be done in that person's 'best interests', and although this term was not defined in the draft Bill four factors were listed which should be taken into consideration:

1. the ascertainable past and present wishes and feelings of the person concerned and the factors which he or she would consider if able to do so;

2. the need to permit and encourage that person to participate, or to improve his or her ability to participate, in anything done for and any decision affecting him or her;

---

[109]   The annexed draft Mental Incapacity Bill would comprise such legislation.

[110]   These concepts have been further developed in the Mental Capacity Act 2005.

[111]   The use of this new term was intended to avoid associations with the medical term 'mental disorder'. A different approach has been adopted in the Mental Capacity Act 2005 but the references to 'an impairment or disturbance' and 'the mind or brain' have been retained.

3. (if it is practicable and appropriate to consult them) the views as to that person's wishes and feelings and as to what would be in the best interests of that person of:

    (i)   any person named by him or her as someone to be consulted;
    (ii) any person[112] engaged in caring for or interested in the person's welfare;
    (iii) the donee of a continuing power of attorney granted by him or her; and
    (iv) any manager appointed by the court;

4. whether the purpose for which any action or decision is required can be as effectively achieved in a manner less restrictive of the person's freedom of action.

General authority to act reasonably

1.100 One of the uncertainties of the present law was what action might lawfully be taken by someone caring for a person without capacity or what medical treatment a doctor could give to such a person. It was proposed that it should be lawful to do anything for the personal welfare or healthcare of a person who was, or was reasonably believed to be, without relevant capacity if it was in all the circumstances reasonable for it to be done by the person who did it and it was in the best interests of the incapacitated person.[113] In view of the risks of abuse it would be a criminal offence for anyone to ill-treat or wilfully neglect a person in relation to whom he had these powers. There remained, however, decisions which can only ever be taken by the individual personally.[114]

This general authority would not authorise:
1. the threat or use of force to overcome an objection by the individual;
2. the detention or confinement of the individual;
3. doing anything contrary to the directions of, or inconsistent with a decision made by, an attorney or manager acting within the scope of his or her authority;
4. medical treatment contrary to an advance refusal;
5. any medical treatment which requires the approval of a second doctor or the court.

1.101 It would be lawful for the person acting to pledge the other's credit so as to recover any expenditure incurred, and a new statutory scheme was proposed whereby certain financial institutions might[115] make payments,

---

[112] Eg a spouse, relative or friend or other person.
[113] This concept has been carried forward into the Mental Capacity Act 2005 but was not adopted in Scotland.
[114] Eg consenting to marriage or sexual relations, and voting at an election.
[115] Subject to financial and time limits.

which would otherwise be made to the person without capacity, to someone acting on his or her behalf.

Healthcare

1.102 The principle that people be encouraged and enabled to take their own decisions was extended to future healthcare. In summary it was recommended that living wills[116] be authorised and given statutory authority subject to safeguards. Independent supervision of certain medical and research procedures was also proposed, and this might involve approval by a second doctor or the court or the consent of a 'manager or attorney'. The withdrawal of artificial feeding from patients in a persistent vegetative state was given special consideration.

Continuing power of attorney

1.103 The policy aim[117] extended to anticipatory decision-making by people who, knowing or fearing that their decision-making faculties may fail, wished to make plans for what was to happen to them should they lose capacity. The Enduring Power of Attorney ('EPA') only dealt with decisions about property and affairs so would be replaced by a Continuing Power of Attorney ('CPA') which could extend to matters relating to a donor's:

1. personal welfare (for example whom the donor should see);
2. healthcare (whether to accept or refuse medical treatment); and
3. property and affairs, including the conduct of legal proceedings.

The CPA might confer general authority or be subject to such restrictions or conditions as the donor wished to impose.[118] The donee (ie attorney) would have authority to make and implement decisions on behalf of the donor which the donor lacked capacity to make, but should act in the best interests of the donor according to the above criteria.

1.104 A new registration procedure was proposed and the donee would have no power to act unless the power was registered. A donor who had capacity could object to registration which would be an administrative act with any disputes being resolved by the court[119] which would have defined powers.

---

[116] Including advance refusals of medical treatment and the appointment of someone to take treatment decisions.

[117] Ie of enabling and encouraging people to take for themselves those decisions which they are able to take.

[118] The 'Lasting Power of Attorney' ('LPA') to be found in the Mental Capacity Act 2005 adopts a similar approach.

[119] Ie the court exercising the new jurisdiction – see below.

Decision-making by the court

1.105 An integrated statutory jurisdiction was proposed for the making of all types of decision on behalf of persons without capacity. Where specific problems or disputes arose concerning such a person a single court would be available to resolve the issue.[120] This court would be able to make declarations and one-off orders or, where appropriate, appoint a manager with substitute decision-making powers. The making of an order was to be preferred to the appointment of a manager. In its decisions the court would be required to act in the best interests of the person without capacity and have power to make declarations in relation to the capacity of a person and the validity or applicability of an advance refusal of treatment. The court would have power to make an order making a decision on behalf of a person who lacks capacity to make that decision or appointing a manager to be responsible for making decisions on behalf of such person.

These powers could extend to matters relating to personal welfare, healthcare and property and affairs. Managers appointed by the court would only have such powers as were expressly granted and no appointment could last for more than 5 years. Any manager appointed by the court should act in the best interests of the person without capacity and the Public Trustee would exercise a supervisory role and may also be appointed as a manager. The court might require managers to give to the Public Trustee such security as the court thought fit, and to submit such reports at such intervals as the court determines.

A new Court of Protection

1.106 In order to exercise this statutory jurisdiction a new Court of Protection would be established with a central registry in London and regional hearing centres. It would be made up of nominated district and circuit judges and nominated judges of the Chancery and Family Divisions of the High Court. Cases would be heard by judges at the appropriate level with the necessary experience and expertise.[121]

Codes of Practice

1.107 It was recommended that the Secretary of State should, after consultation, prepare and from time to time revise Codes of Practice to accompany the proposed legislation, providing guidance for persons:[122]

1. assessing whether a person is or is not without capacity to make a particular decision;

---

[120] This court would also have the role of approving certain serious medical treatments. The Mental Capacity Act 2005 adopts this proposal.
[121] The Mental Capacity Act 2005 fully adopts this approach.
[122] There will be Codes of Practice under the Mental Capacity Act 2005.

2. acting under the general authority; and
3. acting as managers appointed by the court.

Public law protection

1.108 The Law Commission, having concluded that the existing law was outdated and ineffective, extended its consultation to cover vulnerable people who might be at risk. A 'vulnerable person' was identified as being any person aged 16 or over who:

1. is or may be in need of community care services by reason of mental or other disability, age or illness; and
2. is or may be unable to take care of himself or herself, or unable to protect himself or herself against significant harm or serious exploitation.

It was recommended that local social services departments should be under a duty to investigate where they have reason to believe that a vulnerable person is suffering or likely to suffer significant harm or serious exploitation. Where the department was being prevented from carrying out an investigation it should have the power to enter premises and interview the person concerned and to apply to the court for an entry warrant, 'assessment order' or 'temporary protection order'. Magistrates' courts and single justices of the peace[123] would be able to grant warrants or make these orders for the protection of vulnerable people. It would be an offence to obstruct an 'authorised officer' in the exercise of his or her powers or to obstruct any person acting under one of these orders. These powers would not be exercisable where it was known or believed that the person concerned objected, unless that person was believed to suffer from mental disability.[124]

The Government's response

More consultation

1.109 Unfortunately publication of the Law Commission Report *Mental Incapacity* coincided with an emotional but less well considered attack on the Law Commission by the *Daily Mail* in support of 'family values'.[125] Living wills were singled out for condemnation and little was said of the many other recommendations in this Report. The Government immediately announced that it did not intend to proceed

---

[123] As well as the new Court of Protection, but that jurisdiction would be rarely exercised.

[124] These proposals, which went beyond the initial Law Commission brief, have not been adopted.

[125] The main casualty was the new Domestic Violence and Matrimonial Homes Bill which was withdrawn but since reappeared with few amendments in Part IV of the Family Law Act 1996.

with legislation 'in its present form' but would undertake further consultation on the Report. That consultation did not materialise.

1.110 On 23 October 1997, the new Lord Chancellor, Lord Irvine of Lairg, announced that he intended to issue a consultation paper seeking views on the Report. He added:

> '[It] is a thorough and detailed examination of the current law. It provides a coherent framework for reform. The Government recognises, however, that the report addresses sensitive issues on which strong personal views may be held. The Government does not consider that it would be appropriate to legislate without fresh public consultation. It therefore hopes to issue a consultation paper by the end of the year seeking views on the full range of the Law Commission's recommendations.'

To those who were concerned about euthanasia he added this:

> 'the ... Report does not make any recommendations concerning euthanasia. The Government is of the certain view, in line with the House of Lords Select Committee on Medical Ethics, that euthanasia cannot be sanctioned in any circumstances. The consultation paper will therefore not seek views on this subject.'

'Who Decides?'

General

1.111 In December 1997, the Lord Chancellor's consultation document *Who Decides? Making Decisions on Behalf of Mentally Incapacitated Adults*[126] was published with a relatively short period for consultation. This was in addition to an ambitious programme of law reform which included a Human Rights Bill to give effect to the European Convention on Human Rights in the UK and the continuance of civil justice reforms following Lord Woolf's Report *Access to Justice*.

Contents

1.112 Although the Green Paper is freestanding it was structured to follow the Law Commission's Report *Mental Incapacity*. The Government accepted that there was a clear need for law reform in this area and contemplated that there would be Codes of Practice dealing with specific areas. Whilst emphasising that there would be no move towards euthanasia (which is illegal) the Government supported many of the Law Commission's recommendations and expressed the wish to consult further on how they might best be implemented and those that might be controversial.

---

[126] Cm 3803 issued by the Lord Chancellor's Department.

Recommendations accepted

1.113 The principles underlying the following recommendations were accepted:

1. definition of incapacity;
2. framework for carers;
3. more extensive powers for the Court of Protection so that decisions can be made regarding a person's healthcare, personal welfare and finance within the same jurisdiction;
4. powers of attorney for the care of the person.

Further consultation was to be directed towards practical issues and safeguards.

Matters for consultation

1.114 The following areas were identified as raising issues of particular moral and ethical sensitivity where further consultation was needed:

1. advance statements about healthcare;
2. non-therapeutic research.

Although advance refusals of treatment were accepted to be currently binding it was necessary to consider whether these should be put on a statutory footing.

Resources

1.115 At this stage the issue of resources arose for the first time.[127] Three questions were posed in the consultation:

1. What resource implications would arise from implementation of the proposals?
2. Would the likely benefits render the costs incurred worthwhile?
3. How would these costs be met?

The judicial forum

1.116 The Law Commission realised that if decision-making issues were to be referred to the courts, this must be to locally available judges trained to understand the special demands made of them. The new Court of Protection should not be seen as a separate and distinct court, but needed to function in part through trained judges working on a regional basis within the existing court system. There were three reasons for this:

1. the need for personal access to the judicial process;
2. the prohibitive cost of coping with hearings in London;
3. the need in some instances for a judge to sit in a dual jurisdiction.

---

[127] There has been no analysis of the cost to society of coping with mentally incapacitated persons in the present climate of uncertainty.

The Government initially rejected this approach and stated that the existing Court of Protection could cope despite the extension of the jurisdiction from financial matters to personal and healthcare decisions. This no doubt reflected funding implications for the administration of the courts, but overlooked the additional cost for everyone else involved.

'Making Decisions'

1.117 In October 1999, the Lord Chancellor published the Government's proposals in the Report *Making Decisions*. Much, but not all, of the Law Commission's recommendations survived.[128] This Report stated that there would be:

1. a new test of capacity based on a functional approach with a presumption against lack of capacity and an emphasis on assisting people to communicate their decisions;
2. a best interests approach to decision-making with statutory guidance as to how this should be determined;
3. a general authority for carers to act reasonably subject to restrictions but with authority for expenditure to be incurred including a 'necessaries' rule;
4. continuing powers of attorney subject to safeguards;
5. decision-making by the court either through one-off orders or the appointment of a manager with specified powers and subject to supervision;
6. a new Court of Protection with a regional presence to exercise the new jurisdiction;
7. further consultation on a 'release of payments scheme'.

The Lord Chancellor announced in November 1999 that there would be legislation 'when Parliamentary time allows' but much of the detail had still to be worked out. In the meanwhile some of the recommendations of the Law Commission were already finding their way into our law through decisions of the courts, and Scotland had legislation based on the Scottish Law Commission proposals.

Legislation

Adults with Incapacity (Scotland) Act 2000

1.118 Scotland achieved legislation first.[129] The Adults with Incapacity (Scotland) Act 2000 ('the AWI Act'), which followed recommendations

---

[128]   In particular the proposals for public law protection have not been followed up.
[129]   The fifth Act passed by the new Scottish Parliament but the first lengthy piece of legislation to be considered.

of the Scottish Law Commission[130] and was widely welcomed as a significant and much-needed reform of the law, received Royal Assent on 16 May 2000 and came into force in stages.[131] It protects the rights and interests of adults in Scotland who are incapable of managing their own affairs, acknowledged to be one of the most vulnerable groups in society.[132] There are regulations under the AWI Act and Codes of Practice which provide guidance on the legislation itself and offer further practical information for those people and organisations that have functions given to them by the AWI Act.

A number of different agencies are involved in supervising those who take decisions on behalf of the adult:

1. the Public Guardian has a supervisory role and keeps registers of attorneys, people who can access an adult's funds, guardians and intervention orders;
2. local authorities look after the welfare of adults who lack capacity;
3. the Mental Welfare Commission protects the interests of adults who lack capacity as a result of mental disorder.

1.119 The AWI Act changes the system for safeguarding the welfare, and managing the finances and property, of adults (aged 16 or over) who lack the capacity to take some or all decisions for themselves because of mental disorder or inability to communicate by any means. It allows other people to make decisions on behalf of these adults, subject to safeguards. All decisions made on behalf of an adult with impaired capacity must:

- benefit the adult;
- take account of the adult's wishes and the wishes of the nearest relative or primary carer, and any guardian or attorney;
- restrict the adult's freedom as little as possible while still achieving the desired benefit;
- encourage the adult to use existing skills or develop new skills.

The main ways that other people can make decisions for an adult with impaired capacity are summarised below.

Power of attorney

1.120 Individuals can arrange for their welfare to be safeguarded and their affairs to be properly managed in future should their capacity

---

[130] *Report on Incapable Adults*, No 151 dated July 1995.

[131] Available at www.opsi.gov.uk/legislation/scotland/s-acts.htm. Information about implementation, which is updated at intervals, is to be found on the Scottish Executive website: www.scotland.gov.uk.

[132] Up to 100,000 adults in Scotland and their relatives and carers are affected by incapacity at any time.

deteriorate by giving another person[133] power of attorney. This may be to look after some or all of their property and financial affairs and/or to make specified decisions about their personal welfare, including medical treatment. All continuing and welfare powers of attorney granted from 2 April 2001 need to be registered with the Public Guardian to be effective.

Access to the adult's funds

1.121 Individuals (normally relatives or carers) can apply to the Public Guardian to gain access to the funds of an adult incapable of managing those funds. This applies to funds held in, for example, a bank or building society account in the sole name of the adult.[134] Authorised care establishments can manage a limited amount of the funds and property of residents who are unable to do this themselves.

Medical treatment and research

1.122 The AWI Act allows treatment to be given to safeguard or promote the physical or mental health of an adult who is unable to consent.[135] Where there is disagreement a second medical opinion can be sought and cases can be referred to the Court of Session in certain circumstances. The AWI Act also permits research involving an adult incapable of giving consent but only under strict guidelines.

Intervention and guardianship orders

1.123 Individuals (and also local authorities or any person claiming an interest in the adult's affairs) can apply to their local Sheriff Court for:

1. an *intervention order* where a one-off decision or short-term help is required;[136]
2. a *guardianship order*, which may be more appropriate where the continuous management of affairs or the safeguarding of welfare is required.

Mental Incapacity Bill

1.124 On 27 June 2003, the Government published a draft Mental Incapacity Bill. Lord Filkin CBE, Parliamentary Under-Secretary at the new Department for Constitutional Affairs[137] stated:

---

[133] This could be a relative, carer, professional person or trusted friend.
[134] The AWI Act also includes provisions to allow access to a joint account to continue where one account holder has become incapable of managing the funds.
[135] Special provisions apply where others such as attorneys have been appointed under the AWI Act with powers relating to medical treatment.
[136] Eg selling property or signing a document.
[137] This has replaced the Lord Chancellor's Department.

'The current law on decision making ... has grown up in a piecemeal way. Different rules apply in different circumstances. It is difficult to plan ahead for a time when you might lose capacity. Carers, family members and professionals may find that there is insufficient information available to guide them in decision making.

The current law is not as helpful to carers and professionals as it could be. About one adult in seven in the UK cares for another adult – nearly 6 million carers in all. Many of these people care for adults who lack capacity and they need to make decisions for them. On a daily basis professionals come into contact with adults who lack capacity and they need to know how to go about the decision making process.

We want to improve the lives of all these people and introduce a comprehensive decision making framework for all people who may lack capacity. The Mental Incapacity Bill aims to provide a clear, simple, informal system that will ensure people can maintain a maximum level of autonomy. People would be able to choose someone who can make decisions for them when they cannot do so themselves. And there would be clear rules on how decisions should be taken, making sure that vulnerable people were not left open to abuse.'

Summary

1.125 The draft Bill, which was to be scrutinised by a joint committee of both Houses of Parliament,[138] would:

- define the concepts of 'persons who lack capacity' and 'best interests';
- provide a 'general authority to act' (with restrictions) and an obligation to pay for 'necessary' goods and services;
- establish 'lasting powers of attorney'[139] which may, subject to greater safeguards, deal with personal welfare (including medical treatment) as well as property and financial affairs;[140]
- give the new Court of Protection power to make declarations as to capacity and to make (and enforce) decisions or appoint deputies[141] to do so under supervision;[142]
- put the common law relating to 'advance refusals of (medical) treatment' on a statutory footing;
- make provision for Codes of Practice;
- create a new offence of 'ill-treatment and neglect' on the part of carers, donees and deputies;

---

[138] The Committee received over 1,200 written submissions and heard oral evidence from 61 witnesses.

[139] Note the change of terminology from 'continuing powers of attorney'.

[140] Enduring powers of attorney are abolished, subject to transitional provisions.

[141] This replaces the previously proposed term 'managers'.

[142] The jurisdiction under the Mental Health Act 1983, Part VII would be abolished.

- establish a new Court of Protection which would function on a regional basis through nominated judges with power to call for reports from several sources;
- create a statutory role for the Public Guardian.

Joint Committee Report

1.126 The Joint Committee published its response in November 2003[143] and the Government commented on some of those recommendations.[144] The title was to be changed to the *Mental Capacity Bill* and it was considered that draft *Codes of Practice* should be available before the Bill was passed.[145] Key points were:

- Statement of principles – the Bill should be re-drafted so as to commence with a statement of principles which would include the assumption of capacity, full participation in making decisions, the right to make unwise decisions, decisions made in the best interests of the person incapacitated and to be the least restrictive.
- The general authority required consideration so that it looked less interventionist but was more restricted in its scope. A second opinion should be required for some medical decisions or in case of dispute, and other serious medical decisions might be excluded and dealt with by the courts.
- Advocacy (of more relevance for persons with learning disabilities) was unlikely to be formalised but the present provision of advocacy services be investigated so as to identify current policy and practice and any shortfalls in provision.
- Standards of conduct be set out in Codes of Practice and professionals be under a duty to comply with these. Attorneys and deputies would be expected to have regard to Codes of Practice but it might not be reasonable to expect others to do so when acting under the general authority.
- Lasting powers of attorney ('LPA') – more measures be introduced to tackle abuse and consideration given to the implications of appointing separate attorneys for financial and welfare matters.
- Advance directions – consideration be given to the practicability of requiring advance decisions to refuse medical treatment to be recorded in writing and witnessed by two independent people with no financial interest in the person's estate.

---

[143] Report of the Joint Committee on the Draft Mental Incapacity Bill, Vols I & II (HL Papers 189-1 & 189-II, HC 1083-1 & 1083-II) (London: TSO, 2003).

[144] The Government's Response to the Scrutiny Committee's Report on the draft Mental Incapacity Bill, Cm 6121 (London: TSO, 2004).

[145] There was still a lack of reliable estimates as to the likely cost of the Bill in terms of resources.

- Court of Protection – various proposals for greater accessibility to the new Court (including legal aid in some circumstances) and more guidance as to when the Court should be involved were not commented on by the Government.

- Medical research – the Joint Committee made very strong recommendations for the inclusion of provisions in the legislation to enable medical research involving people lacking capacity to consent, governed by strict controls and safeguards. The Government's response was more cautious at first, promising further consultation, before it finally agreed to include such provisions.

- Protection from abuse and exploitation – the Government did not comment on the recommendation that statutory authorities should be given additional powers of investigation and intervention in cases of alleged physical, sexual or financial abuse of vulnerable adults.

- Access to information – the Government was to take advice as to the extent that financial LPAs would be able to access health and welfare information and vice versa (this remains a troubled area).

1.127 The Joint Committee considered that priority should be given to the Bill so that account could be taken of its provisions when framing new mental health legislation. The Law Society remained a strong supporter of the Bill and accepted most of the recommendations of the Joint Committee.

Mental Capacity Act 2005

1.128 A Bill, by then called the Mental Capacity Bill, incorporating the changes to the draft Bill which had been recommended by the Joint Committee and which were accepted by the Government, was introduced in Parliament in June 2004. This Bill (as amended) was finally passed in April 2005 as the Mental Capacity Act 2005 ('the Act') and extends to England and Wales only. It will come into force in accordance with provisions made by the Lord Chancellor.[146] The Act does not provide all the answers but lays down the principles, creates a statutory framework and authorises Rules, Practice Directions and Codes of Practice to be made. Much now depends upon the manner in which these are implemented. The new social and legal climate will dictate the content but this will change over the years.

---

[146] Mental Capacity Act 2005, s 68. The target date is April 2007 but different days may be appointed for different provisions.

Human rights compatibility

1.129 Explanatory notes[147] prepared by the Department for Constitutional
        Affairs and the Department of Health state that the Mental Capacity Act
        2005 meets the state's positive obligation under Art 8 of the European
        Convention on Human Rights to ensure respect for private life. The
        following issues are acknowledged to arise:

> '*Article 8 – private life*
>
> This Article is engaged in connection with sections 5, 6, 9 and 11 and
> could also be engaged as a result of section 20 and a court order made
> under section 16(2). Any interference pursues the legitimate aim of
> protecting the health and wellbeing of the person lacking capacity and
> ensures that those who care for and treat persons who lack capacity are
> protected from certain liabilities where appropriate. The principles in
> section 1, the criteria for lack of capacity (section 2), the checklist as to
> best interests (section 4) and the safeguards within the sections
> themselves create a framework within which any interference will be
> proportionate to this legitimate aim.
>
> Section 49(7) to (9), allows the court to direct a medical examination or
> interview of the person concerned and the examination of his health
> and social services records although the court is bound by the
> principles in section 1 and the best interests checklist. Sections 35(6),
> 58(5) and (6) and 61(5) and (6) also make provision whereby particular
> persons may interview the person concerned and examine relevant
> records. Again, any interference is justified as being for the protection
> of that person's own health and welfare and proportionate to that aim.
> The powers are given to the relevant officials for the purpose of
> enabling them to carry out their functions, which are directed to the
> protection of the interests of the person who lacks capacity.
>
> *Article 1 of the First Protocol – protection of property*
>
> These rights may be engaged in connection with sections 7 to 9 and 12
> which provide for the control of a person's property and affairs and
> payment on his behalf for necessary goods and services. The statutory
> rules are intended to be clear and precise and are designed to strike a
> fair balance between the property interests of the person lacking
> capacity, his own wider welfare interests and the interests of others
> (persons supplying necessary goods and services to the person lacking
> capacity, anyone bearing the cost and, in the case of section 12, persons
> related to or connected with him).
>
> Sections 10(2) and 13(8) and (9) prevent a bankrupt from acting as a
> donee of a lasting power of attorney (an "LPA") where the power
> covers property and affairs and suspend that power where there is an
> interim bankruptcy restrictions order. Article 8 and Article 14 rights

---

[147] These do not form part of the Act and have not been endorsed by Parliament.

may be engaged but any difference of treatment has the legitimate aim of protecting an incapacitated donor from the possibility of financial abuse and is proportionate to that end.

Articles 2 and 3 – right to life and prohibition from torture

A donee of a lasting power of attorney (an "LPA") can be given power to refuse to give consent to life-sustaining treatment on behalf of the donor (see section 11(7) and (8)). A person can also make an advance decision to refuse treatment, including life-sustaining treatment. Section 25(5) provides that an advance decision will not apply to any treatment necessary to sustain life unless the advance decision is in writing and is signed and the signature is witnessed. Further, there must be a statement that the decision stands even if life is at risk (and this statement must also be in writing and be signed and the signature must be witnessed). Sections 6(7) and 26(5) provide that action can be taken to preserve life or prevent serious deterioration while the court resolves any dispute or difficulty. These provisions are designed to protect a person's Article 2 and 3 rights, while also discharging the obligation to respect the Article 8 rights of those who choose to give powers to a donee under an LPA or to make an advance decision.

Article 14 – prohibition of discrimination

Sections 35 to 39 may engage these rights in connection with Article 8 by providing for an independent mental capacity advocate to represent and support people who lack capacity where they are being treated and cared for by the NHS or a local authority and there is no one who could be consulted about that treatment or care. Any relevant difference in treatment which there might be would have the legitimate aim of protecting the Article 8 rights of incapacitated persons.

Article 6 – right to a fair trial

The comprehensive jurisdiction of the new Court of Protection (sections 15 to 21 and 45 to 56) ensures protection for any rights engaged in connection with the provisions of the Act. The Government is satisfied that sections 50 (certain applicants to obtain permission to apply), 51(2)(d) (exercise of jurisdiction by officers or staff) and 54 (court fees) do not breach Article 6 rights.'

1.130 This analysis concentrates upon the rights of the incapacitated person. Procedures for decisions to be made on behalf of such persons may also have an impact upon the human rights of other persons, and especially members of the family. Experience of the present Court of Protection shows that there may be strong sibling rivalry for control over the financial affairs of a parent and that the person in control of the finances, although not legally empowered to make personal welfare decisions, has a strong influence over where the individual lives. This may impact upon the human rights of other members of the family to respect for family life. The new jurisdiction will be better able to tackle these issues but must do so in a way that is human rights compliant for all concerned.

Conclusion

1.131   At last we are to have in England and Wales a statutory jurisdiction for decision-making in respect of mentally incapacitated adults. The need for this has been clearly demonstrated and the legislation is overdue, but will it fill the vacuum in our legal system? The general principles contained in s 1 are relatively innovative so far as UK legislation is concerned and have been much praised.

Of key importance are the statutory formulae for assessing a lack of capacity and determining best interests. We now have a benchmark against which people with a mental impairment are to be assessed and interventions must be justified. This should apply beyond the specialist jurisdiction of the Court of Protection and be adopted by all courts and tribunals when they encounter people with impaired capacity. There is now the potential for the specialist judges to sit in a dual jurisdiction but the benchmark should become second nature to all professionals working in this field. There is also a developing awareness of the need to identify incapacity as a discrete area of law divorced from provisions that deal with the treatment of those who are mentally ill.

1.132   The new procedures to implement decision-making over a wider range of content are intended to empower those members of our families and society who lack capacity but must also ensure that they are protected from abuse. This is a delicate balance and where that balance should be struck depends upon one's viewpoint and how one interprets the statistics. It should not be assumed that everyone is satisfied with the present balance.[148] There is a range of diversity within mental incapacity and a 'one size fits all' approach cannot be adopted. There is a world of difference between the needs of a wealthy senior citizen who develops Alzheimer's, an autistic young person dependent on means-tested benefits and a brain-injured individual who has recovered compensation of several million pounds. There is also a difference between the incapacitated adult with dedicated family carers and the similarly incapacitated adult who has been abandoned by family.

---

[148]   The Law Society paper of 1989 was concerned about protection and the Law Commission proposals were perhaps the high point of empowerment. The continuing consultation appeared to swing back towards protection but the emphasis in the Mental Capacity Act 2005 appears to be empowerment.

Those working in this field become very concerned about vulnerability, but of course this does not feature in the test of mental capacity. In a recent decision of the Court of Appeal it was stated:[149]

> '... the courts have ample powers to protect those who are vulnerable to exploitation from being exploited; it is unnecessary to deny them the opportunity to take their own decisions if they are not being exploited. It is not the task of the courts to prevent those who have the mental capacity to make rational decisions from making decisions which others may regard as rash or irresponsible.'

Many practitioners working in this field would question the suggestion that the courts have ample powers to protect those who are vulnerable. However, where vulnerability is perceived it becomes appropriate to inquire why this should be so and a thorough investigation may reveal that the underlying cause is a mental impairment. Although there may be sufficient understanding, resulting personal qualities such impulsiveness, recklessness and being easily manipulated may mean that there is an inability to make and implement decisions based on that understanding.

1.133 The procedures need to be publicly known and accessible. There is a role for the new Office of the Public Guardian in this respect but that role should extend to resolving uncertainties where these exist and assisting in facilitating the resolution of disputes as to best interests. We also have a specialist Court charged with the responsibility of interpreting the statutory criteria and exercising the new jurisdiction. But although empowering a new court to make all types of decisions or to authorise other persons to do so is a *sine qua non*, delivering that which is needed depends upon those called upon to implement the new jurisdiction at all levels. Where will these people come from and how will they be trained? The success or failure of this much needed initiative depends on the guidance available and the availability of professionals who are familiar with the new law and procedures.

Any new court or administrative body that is established to implement the new mental capacity jurisdiction will be judged by people whose needs have for too long been overlooked but who have now become vocal in support of their increased expectations of the legal system. It must not only be compatible with the new social and legal climate but also set a good example to other courts and bodies.

---

[149] Chadwick LJ in *Masterman-Lister v Brutton & Co and Jewell & Home Counties Dairies* [2002] EWCA Civ 1889, [2002] All ER (D) 297 (Dec).

1.134 The following pages address the manner in which these issues have
       been addressed. It is too much to expect that all of the objectives will be
       met initially, but within the framework established by the Mental
       Capacity Act 2005 there is the prospect of a ground-breaking
       improvement in the lives of those who have the misfortune to be unable
       to structure these for themselves.

Chapter 2

The New Jurisdiction

Introduction

2.1   The Mental Capacity Act 2005 ('the Act') establishes a comprehensive statutory framework setting out how decisions should be made by and on behalf of adults whose capacity to make their own decisions is in doubt. It also clarifies what actions can be taken by others involved in the care and medical treatment of people lacking capacity. The framework provides a hierarchy of processes, extending from informal day-to-day care, to decision-making requiring formal powers and ultimately to court decisions and judgments. The full range of processes is intended to govern the circumstances in which necessary acts of caring can be carried out, and necessary decisions taken, on behalf of those lacking capacity to consent to such acts or make their own decisions.

2.2   This Chapter is in three parts:
   (a) Part 1 gives a brief overview of the new jurisdiction created by the Act and discusses the role and status of the Code (or Codes) of Practice which will guide its operation.
   (b) Part 2 looks in detail at the guiding principles that underline the Act's key messages and govern how the Act is to be interpreted and implemented. The two fundamental concepts – capacity and best interests, which form the basis of the new statutory framework – are discussed and their definitions explained.
   (c) Part 3 looks at the provisions in the Act which permit actions to be taken in relation to the care and treatment of people lacking capacity to consent to those actions. Some types of decisions are excluded from the Act's provisions and these are explored. Finally, an explanation is given of the new criminal offence created under the Act to deal with cases of ill-treatment or wilful neglect of people lacking capacity to protect themselves from such abuse.

PART 1: OVERVIEW

Key elements

General

2.3   The Act sets out a new integrated jurisdiction for the making of personal welfare decisions, healthcare decisions and financial decisions on behalf of people without the capacity to make such decisions for themselves. The Act's starting point is to enshrine in statute the existing presumption at common law that an adult has full legal capacity unless it is established that he or she does not. It also includes provisions to ensure that people are given all appropriate help and support to enable them to make their own decisions or to maximise their participation in the decision-making process.

2.4   The Act also enshrines in statute current best practice and former common law principles concerning people who lack capacity and those who take decisions on their behalf. The statutory framework is based on two fundamental concepts:[1] lack of capacity and best interests. For those who lack capacity to make particular decisions, the Act provides a range of processes, extending from informal arrangements to court-based powers, to govern the circumstances in which necessary decisions can be taken on their behalf and in their best interests.

Essential provisions

2.5   The essential provisions of the Act are intended to:

- set out five guiding principles to underpin the Act's fundamental concepts and to govern its implementation;
- define people who lack decision-making capacity;
- set out a single clear test for assessing whether a person lacks capacity to take a particular decision at a particular time;
- establish a single criterion (best interests) for the taking of decisions on behalf of people who lack capacity to take those decisions;
- clarify the law when acts in connection with the care or treatment of people lacking capacity to consent are carried out in their best interests, without formal procedures or judicial intervention, but with clear restrictions on the use of restraint and, in particular, acts resulting in deprivation of liberty;

---

[1]   A full discussion of the meaning of these concepts is set out in Law Commission Report, *Mental Incapacity*, Law Com No 231 (London: HMSO, 1995), Part III. See also Part 2 below.

- extend the provisions for making powers of attorney which outlast capacity (lasting powers of attorney ('LPAs')) covering health and welfare decisions as well as financial affairs, with improved safeguards against abuse and exploitation;
- provide for a decision to be made, or a decision-maker (deputy) to be appointed, by a new specialist Court of Protection;
- make statutory rules, with clear safeguards, for the making of advance decisions to refuse medical treatment;
- set out specific parameters for research involving, or in relation to, people lacking capacity to consent to their involvement;
- provide for the appointment of Independent Mental Capacity Advocates to support people without capacity who have no one to speak for them;
- provide statutory guidance, in the form of Codes of Practice, setting good practice standards for the guidance of people using the Act's provisions.

The new public bodies

2.6   The Act also creates two new public bodies to support and implement the statutory framework:

1. a superior court of record, the Court of Protection, with jurisdiction relating to the whole Act and its own procedures and nominated judges;
2. a Public Guardian, whose office will be the registering authority for LPAs and deputies, and will supervise deputies and respond to any concerns raised about donees or deputies.

The Code(s) of Practice

The draft Code

2.7   It has long been recognised that complex legislation of this sort will require an accompanying Code (or Codes) of Practice for the guidance of practitioners using the Act and those affected by its provisions, and also to assist with interpretation and implementation of the Act.[2] Provision for such statutory guidance is made in the Act.[3] Following parliamentary pre-legislative scrutiny of the Draft Mental Incapacity Bill in 2003, the Joint Scrutiny Committee specifically recommended that the Bill should not be introduced into Parliament unless it could be considered alongside a draft Code of Practice.[4]

---

[2]   Law Com No 231, para 2.53.
[3]   Mental Capacity Act 2005, s 42.
[4]   Report of the Joint Committee on the Draft Mental Incapacity Bill, Vol 1 (HL Paper 189-1, HC 1083-1) (London: TSO, 2003) para 229.

A draft Code was placed in the libraries of both Houses of Parliament on 8 September 2004 and was made available on the Department for Constitutional Affairs ('DCA') website.[5] Members of both the House of Commons and the House of Lords were able to refer extensively to the Code during debates on the passage of the Bill.

2.8   At the same time as the Mental Capacity Act received Royal Assent, the Government issued a summary of the revisions expected to be made to the Code to reflect amendments made during the passage of the Bill through both Houses.[6] The updated Code is also anticipated to include changes suggested by members in both the Commons and the Lords and points arising from dialogue with stakeholders.

Prior to implementation of the Act (which is intended to be in April 2007) a revised version of the draft Code will be issued for formal consultation.[7] It is anticipated that the final version of the Code (or Codes) will contain extensive cross-references and signposting to other relevant guidance and sources of information.

2.9   At the time of writing, it is not yet known what the format of the final Code or Codes will be, the extent to which its contents will differ from the draft Code, or the expected date of publication. In the meantime, reference to the 2004 Draft Code of Practice is made throughout this book.

Application

2.10   The Lord Chancellor is required to prepare and issue one or more Codes of Practice and the Act specifies the particular issues, as well as particular categories of people, that guidance in the Code(s) must address.[8] These are:

1. persons involved in assessing capacity;
2. persons acting in connection with the care or treatment of a person lacking capacity;
3. donees of lasting powers of attorney;
4. deputies appointed by the Court of Protection;
5. persons carrying out research involving people lacking capacity;
6. Independent Mental Capacity Advocates ('IMCAs');
7. the provisions in the Act covering advance decisions to refuse treatment;
8. any other matters concerned with the Act as the Lord Chancellor thinks fit.

---

[5]   Available at www.dca.gov.uk/menincap/mcbdraftcode.pdf.
[6]   *Hansard,* HC Deb, col 103WS (4 April 2005); *Hansard,* HL Deb, col WS62 (4 April 2005).
[7]   Mental Capacity Act 2005, s 43(1).
[8]   Mental Capacity Act 2005, s 42(1).

The Codes are intended to give practical guidance and examples to illustrate the provisions of the Act, rather than imposing any new legal or formal requirements. It is intended that the Codes will be revised as and when required[9] and the Lord Chancellor may delegate the preparation or revision of the whole or any part of a Code as he considers expedient.[10]

Legal effect

2.11   The Codes of Practice are statutory guidance in that the Act imposes a duty on certain people to 'have regard to any relevant Code' when acting in relation to a person lacking capacity.[11] The specified people are those acting in one or more of the following ways:

1. as a donee of a lasting power of attorney;
2. as a deputy appointed by the Court;
3. as a person carrying out research under the Act;
4. as an Independent Mental Capacity Advocate;
5. in a professional capacity;
6. for remuneration.

2.12   The statutory duty to have regard to the Codes will therefore apply to those exercising formal powers or duties under the Act, and to professionals (including lawyers, health and social care professionals) and others acting for remuneration (such as paid carers). The position of informal carers, such as family members, was considered by the Joint Committee on the Draft Bill:[12]

> 'The position is different with regard to guidance issued to assist non-professional or informal decision-makers, such as family members and unpaid carers acting under the general authority. It is essential that family members and carers carrying out such responsibilities are provided with appropriate guidance and assistance, both to promote good practice and also to impress upon them the seriousness of their actions and the need to be accountable for them. However, we accept that it would be inappropriate to impose on them a strict requirement to act in accordance with the codes of practice.'

Sanctions for non-compliance

2.13   The Act provides that a provision of a Code, or a failure to comply with the guidance set out in a Code, can be taken into account by a court or tribunal where it appears relevant to a question arising in any criminal or civil proceedings.[13] There is no liability for breach of the Code itself,

---

[9]   Mental Capacity Act 2005, s 42(2).
[10]   Mental Capacity Act 2005, s 42(3).
[11]   Mental Capacity Act 2005, s 42(4).
[12]   Joint Committee Report, Vol I, para 232.
[13]   Mental Capacity Act 2005, s 42(5).

but compliance or non-compliance may be an element in deciding the issue of liability for breach of some other statutory or common law duty. For example, the need to have regard to the Code is highly likely to be relevant to a question of whether someone has acted or behaved in a way which is contrary to the best interests of a person lacking capacity. Breach of a Code might also be relevant to an action in negligence or to a criminal prosecution.

2.14   This will apply, not only to those categories of people who have a duty to have regard to the Code of Practice, but also to those who are not under a duty. This is because informal carers still have an obligation to act in accordance with the principles of the Act and in the best interests of a person lacking capacity.[14] The provision will therefore remain applicable where any such person is facing civil or criminal proceedings and the court or tribunal considers the Code to be relevant.

Creation

Consultation

2.15   The Act sets out the procedures required for the preparation or revision of the Code(s) and for parliamentary approval.[15] In particular, there must be formal consultation with anyone whom the Lord Chancellor considers appropriate before a Code is prepared or revised.[16] Since health and social care responsibilities are devolved in relation to Wales, the National Assembly for Wales must specifically be consulted and involved in the preparation of the Codes. During the parliamentary debates, the Government committed itself to wide consultation:[17]

> 'By the time the code is published it will have undergone a long process of formal and informal consultation. That is important; the more collaborative and informed the process, the better the code ... I also want to make sure the code speaks to all the different groups of people that it needs to address, and that they clearly understand it, and we can only do that if we get input from those people. This process will take many months and the draft that is finally laid before Parliament will have been informed and improved by both laymen and experts.'

Procedure for approval

2.16   A draft of the Code(s) must be laid before Parliament.[18] The Code will take effect after 40 days unless, within that time, either House has

---

[14]   See Part 2 below.

[15]   Mental Capacity Act 2005, s 43.

[16]   Mental Capacity Act 2005, s 43(1).

[17]   *Hansard*, HC Standing Committee A, col 375 (4 November 2004).

[18]   Mental Capacity Act 2005, s 43(2).

resolved not to approve it (known as the 'negative resolution' procedure).[19] Neither the Law Commission nor the Joint Committee on the Draft Mental Incapacity Bill suggested that any procedure, other than laying the Code before Parliament, was in fact necessary. However, the Government decided that some form of parliamentary scrutiny was desirable in view of the importance and scope of the statutory guidance provided in the Code(s). Parliament's *Delegated Powers and Regulatory Reform Committee* accepted that the negative resolution procedure would be appropriate.[20]

2.17   Several amendments were proposed to the Bill, suggesting that closer parliamentary scrutiny was required, for example through the affirmative resolution procedure requiring Parliament to debate and approve the Codes and any changes made to them. This was rejected by the Government as too cumbersome and unnecessary, not least because it would be very difficult to find the necessary parliamentary time. The Under Secretary of State for Constitutional Affairs, Baroness Ashton said:[21]

> 'So my issue with the amendment is not that I object to coming to your Lordship's House and debating the matter. The negative procedure enables the House to debate the matter if someone feels strongly that we have got it wrong. But I do not accept the idea that the code will have validity only when it goes through the affirmative process.'

Publication

2.18   The Lord Chancellor is allowed considerable flexibility in arranging for the Codes to be produced in the most appropriate format and for bringing the guidance to the attention of everyone who needs to know about it.[22] This may mean that separate Codes are produced for different types of decisions or aimed at different decision-makers.

The Government has made a commitment to publish accessible versions of the Codes in various formats, and in particular to make the Codes available to people who may lack capacity.[23] The Department for Constitutional Affairs, in conjunction with the Department of Health and the Public Guardianship Office, has established a *Mental Capacity Implementation Programme* to undertake a wide-ranging awareness raising campaign to ensure that everyone who could be affected is aware of the implications of the Act, and in particular to seek views on the content and format of the Code.[24]

---

[19]   The 40-day period is defined in s 43(4)–(5).

[20]   *Hansard*, HL Deb, col 220 (1 February 2005).

[21]   *Hansard*, HL Deb, col 1533 (17 March 2005).

[22]   Mental Capacity Act 2005, s 43(3).

[23]   *Hansard*, HL Deb, cols 217–218 (1 February 2005).

[24]   DCA, DH and PGO, *Mental Capacity Implementation Programme Newsletter*, July 2005.

PART 2: PRINCIPLES AND CONCEPTS

The principles

Background

2.19   Much of the evidence submitted to the Joint Committee undertaking
        pre-legislative scrutiny of the Draft Mental Incapacity Bill was
        concerned with the principles said to underlie the provisions of the Bill.
        In particular, commentators stressed the need for a clear statement of
        those principles to be set out on the face of the legislation.[25]
        Comparisons were made with s 1 of the Adults with Incapacity
        (Scotland) Act 2000 ('the AWI Act') which sets out five general
        principles to govern all 'interventions' in the affairs of an adult taken
        under or in pursuance of the AWI Act.[26]

2.20   It is important to note that while some of the specific provisions of the
        AWI Act and the draft Bill (and subsequently the Act) are similar, there
        are significant differences in the underlying intentions and operation of
        both pieces of legislation as well as in the respective jurisdictions. Both
        are based on the recommendations of the respective Law Commissions,
        each of which adopted a different approach as a result of their separate
        consultation exercises. There are also differences in drafting styles.

        The Joint Committee examined these differences in approach, and were
        persuaded that the statement of principles in the AWI Act provided not
        only necessary protection for people with impaired capacity and a
        framework for ensuring that appropriate action is taken in individual
        cases, but also that the specified principles were extremely helpful in
        pointing the way to solutions in difficult or uncertain situations.[27] In
        conclusion, the Joint Committee commented:[28]

> '... we were struck by the absence of a specific statement of principles on
> the face of the Bill as an initial point of reference, as had been done in the
> Scottish Act. Although the principles of the draft Bill may be discernible to
> lawyers from the opening clauses of the draft Bill, they may not be so
> obvious to the majority of non-legal persons who will have to deal with the
> Bill in practice.'

---

[25]   See in particular the evidence submitted by the *Making Decisions Alliance*, Joint
        Committee Report, Vol II (HL Paper 198-II, HC 1083-II) (London: TSO, 2003) Ev 85.

[26]   Adults with Incapacity (Scotland) Act 2000, s 1.

[27]   *Evidence for the Law Society of Scotland*, Joint Committee Report, Vol II, Ev 2.

[28]   Joint Committee Report, Vol I, para 39.

The statement of principles

2.21 The Joint Committee's strong recommendations[29] that a statement of principles be incorporated on the face of the Act were accepted by the Government. As a result, s 1 of the Act now sets out five guiding principles designed to emphasise the underlying ethos of the Act, which is not only to protect people who lack capacity, but also to maximise their ability to participate in decision-making. This section provides as follows:

'(1) The following principles apply for the purposes of this Act.

(2) A person must be assumed to have capacity unless it is established that he lacks capacity.

(3) A person is not to be treated as unable to make a decision unless all practicable steps to help him to do so have been taken without success.

(4) A person is not to be treated as unable to make a decision merely because he makes an unwise decision.

(5) An act done, or decision made, under this Act for or on behalf of a person who lacks capacity must be done, or made, in his best interests.

(6) Before the act is done, or the decision is made, regard must be had to whether the purpose for which it is needed can be as effectively achieved in a way that is less restrictive of the person's rights and freedom of action.'

2.22 In his Ministerial statement announcing the publication of the Mental Capacity Bill and its introduction into Parliament, David Lammy, Parliamentary Under Secretary of State for Constitutional Affairs said:[30]

'The overriding aim of the Bill is to improve the lives of vulnerable adults, their carers, families and professionals. It provides a statutory framework for decision making for people who lack capacity, making clear who can take decisions, in which situations and how they should go about this.

The Bill is based on clearly defined principles. Its starting point is that everyone has the right to make his or her own decisions, and must be assumed to have capacity to do so unless it is proved otherwise. No-one should be labelled as incapable – each decision should be considered individually and everyone should be helped to make or contribute to making decisions about their lives. The Bill sets out clear guidelines for, and limits on, other people's role in decision making.'

2.23 The statement of principles was warmly welcomed, not only by voluntary and professional organisations involved with people who lack capacity,[31] but also by MPs and Peers commenting on the principles

---

[29] Joint Committee Report, Vol I, Recommendations 4 and 5.

[30] *Hansard*, HC Deb, col 67WS (18 June 2004).

[31] See, eg, Making Decisions Alliance, *Briefing for 2nd Reading debate in House of Commons*, 11 October 2004, pp 7–9.

during the parliamentary debates. In particular, during the Bill's second reading in the House of Lords, the Lord Bishop of Worcester, said:[32]

> 'The result is not just a Bill with important protections for vulnerable people; Clause 1 contains a statement about a vision of humanity and how humanity is to be regarded. I hope children in generations to come will study that as one of the clearest and most eloquent expressions of what we think a human being is and how a human being is to be treated ...
>
> I believe that [the Bill] states what is fundamentally right. In the course of Committee we shall no doubt improve and tighten some of the wording, but we shall never take away the powerful and eloquent statement in Clause 1. That should underlie our treatment of one another in all circumstances and for all purposes.'

2.24   The following paragraphs consider the origins of each of the key principles and their operation in practice.

Presumption of capacity

2.25   Practitioners will already be familiar with the presumption, at common law, that an adult has full legal capacity unless it is established that he or she does not. If a question of capacity comes before a court, the burden of proof is generally on the person who is seeking to establish a lack of capacity and the matter is decided according to the usual civil standard, the balance of probabilities.

Law Commission proposals

2.26   Taking account of responses to consultation and in keeping with its proposal to establish a single comprehensive jurisdiction, the Law Commission recommended that the new statutory provisions should expressly include and re-state both the common law principle of presumption of capacity and the relevant standard of proof.[33]

The legislation

2.27   The Joint Committee also supported the principle of presumption of capacity and recommended that this principle should be given primacy of place in the legislation:[34]

> 'This is because it better reflects the positive nature of the Bill's purpose and will increase confidence in the operation of this legislation.'

The presumption of capacity therefore appears in s 1(2) as the first principle relating to the Act.

---

[32]   *Hansard*, HL Deb, cols 53–54, 55 (10 January 2005).

[33]   Law Com No 231, para 3.2. In Scotland, the presumption of capacity is established under common law and is not re-stated in the AWI Act.

[34]   Joint Committee Report, Vol 1, paras 66–67.

The Draft Code of Practice

2.28   The Draft Code of Practice stresses that the starting point for assessing someone's capacity to make a particular decision is always the assumption that the individual does have capacity:[35]

> 'Some people may need help or support to be able to make a decision or communicate a decision ... but the need for help and support does not automatically mean that they cannot make that decision.'

Capacity must then be judged in relation to the particular decision at the time that decision needs to be made, and the presumption of capacity may only be rebutted if there is acceptable evidence that the person is incapable of making the decision in question. In relation to day-to-day decisions in connection with the person's care and treatment, a 'reasonable belief' that the person lacks capacity is sufficient, so long as reasonable steps have been taken to establish this.[36]

Practicable steps to help decision-making

2.29   The second of the Act's key principles[37] clarifies that a person should not be treated as unable to make a decision until everything practicable has been done to help the person make his or her own decision. All practicable steps to enable decision-making must first be shown to be unsuccessful before the person can be assessed as lacking capacity.

Law Commission proposals

2.30   The Law Commission had originally proposed that it would only be necessary for 'reasonable attempts' to be made to understand a person who has difficulty in communicating a decision.[38] However, many respondents to the consultation paper made the point that the reference to 'reasonable attempts' was too weak and, for people who are not simply unconscious, 'strenuous steps must be taken to assist and facilitate communication before any finding of incapacity is made'.[39] Other respondents stressed the need for help and support to maximise a person's potential to make their own decisions, not just those with communication difficulties.

---

[35]   Mental Capacity Bill: Draft Code of Practice, para 3.3.

[36]   Mental Capacity Act 2005, s 5(1). See **2.67–2.68**.

[37]   Mental Capacity Act 2005, s 1(3).

[38]   Law Commission, *Mentally Incapacitated Adults and Decision-Making: A New Jurisdiction,* Consultation Paper No 128 (London: HMSO, 1993) para 3.41.

[39]   Law Com No 231, para 3.21.

The legislation

2.31   This requirement has now been translated into the Act's guiding
        principles in s 1(3). There are a number of ways in which people can be
        given help and support to enable them to make their own decisions, and
        these will vary depending on the decision to be made, the timescale for
        making the decision and the individual circumstances of the person
        wishing to make it. The practicable steps to be taken might include
        using specific communication strategies, providing information in an
        accessible form, or treating an underlying medical condition to enable
        the person to regain capacity.

The Draft Code of Practice

2.32   The Draft Code of Practice gives a number of pointers to prompt
        consideration of a range of practicable steps which may assist decision-
        making, although the relevance of the various factors will vary
        depending on each particular situation.[40] As a minimum, the following
        steps should be considered:

    1. Try to minimise anxiety or stress by making the person feel at ease.
        Choose the best location where the client feels most comfortable
        and the time of day when the client is most alert.
    2. If the person's capacity is likely to improve, wait until it has
        improved (unless the decision is urgent). If the cause of the
        incapacity can be treated, it may be possible to delay the decision
        until treatment has taken place.
    3. If there are communication or language problems, consider using a
        speech therapist or interpreter, or consult family members on the
        best methods of communication.
    4. Be aware of any cultural, ethnic or religious factors which may have
        a bearing on the person's way of thinking, behaviour or
        communication.
    5. Consider whether or not a friend or family member should be
        present to help reduce anxiety. But in some cases the presence of
        others may be intrusive.

Unwise decisions

The legislation

2.33   The third principle underlying the Act, set out in s 1(4), confirms the
        right of a person to make unwise decisions. The intention here is to
        reflect the nature of human decision-making. Different people will
        make different decisions because they give greater weight to some
        factors than to others, taking account of their own values and

---

[40]   Mental Capacity Bill: Draft Code of Practice, paras 3.15–3.22.

preferences. Some people are keen to express their own individuality or may be more willing to take risks than others. The diagnostic threshold requiring evidence of some mental impairment or disturbance[41] will to some extent ensure that the capacity of those who are merely eccentric is not challenged unnecessarily. However, people who have mental disabilities which could affect their decision-making capacity should not be expected to make 'better' or 'wiser' decisions than anyone else.

Law Commission proposals

2.34   Originally, the Law Commission had suggested that it was unnecessary to make such provision in the Act. The right to make unwise decisions has been part of the common law since at least 1850.[42] In a consultation paper the Law Commission argued:[43]

> 'If it is feared that a function test along these lines is not strong enough, interference in the lives of the merely deviant or eccentric could be expressly excluded. New Zealand law (Protection of Personal and Property Rights Act 1988, s 1(3)) provides that the fact that the client "has made or is intending to make any decision that a person exercising ordinary prudence would not have made or would not make is not in itself sufficient ground for the exercise of its jurisdiction by the court." A similar safeguard is proposed by the Scottish Law Commission, with a stipulation that "the fact that the person has acted or intends to act in a way an ordinary prudent person would not should not by itself be evidence of lack of capacity" (Discussion Paper No 94, para 4.40). We, however, doubt the need for any such stipulation, in the light of the definition we have proposed, which clearly directs an assessor to the decision-making process, rather than its outcome. We invite views on this.'

The views received by the Law Commission were strongly in favour of explicit provision being made in the legislation:[44]

> 'Those we consulted, however, overwhelmingly urged upon us the importance of making such an express stipulation. This would recognise that the "outcome" approach to capacity has been rejected, while recognising that it is almost certainly in daily use. We recommend that a person should not be regarded as unable to make a decision by reason of mental disability merely because he or she makes a decision which would not be made by a person of ordinary prudence.'

Evidence before the Joint Committee

2.35   During pre-legislative scrutiny of the draft Bill, the Joint Committee received evidence from some witnesses expressing concern that a

---

[41]   See **2.48–2.49**.

[42]   *Bird v Luckie* (1850) 8 Hare 301.

[43]   Law Commission, *Mentally Incapacitated Adults and Decision-Making: A New Jurisdiction*, Consultation Paper No 128 (1993) para 3.25.

[44]   Law Com No 231, para 3.19.

person with apparent capacity may be able to make repeatedly unwise decisions that put him or her at risk or result in preventable suffering or disadvantage.[45] Particular concerns were raised by Denzil Lush, Master of the Court of Protection, who drew attention to the distinction between decision-specific capacity and more general ongoing incapacity. He gave examples of cases where people had made unwise decisions, each of which they appeared capable of making, but where they in fact lacked an overall awareness or understanding of the implications of those decisions.[46] Master Lush has explained his concerns as follows:[47]

> 'Even though they may be suffering from a condition that restricts their ability to govern their life and make independent choices, so long as they have the basic ability to consider the options and make choices, we must not intervene against their will. By intervening against their will, even for their own good, we show less respect for them than if we had allowed them to go ahead and make a mistake. This lack of inter-personal respect is potentially a more serious infringement of their rights and freedoms than allowing them to make an unwise decision.'

Some caution may therefore need to be applied in operating this principle in practice. Although as a general rule, capacity should be assessed in relation to each particular decision or specific issue, there may be circumstances where a person has an ongoing condition which affects his or her capacity to make a range of interrelated or sequential decisions. One decision on its own may make sense but the combination of decisions may raise doubts as to the person's capacity or at least prompt the need for a proper assessment. But equally, an unwise decision should not, by itself, be sufficient to indicate lack of capacity.

Best interests

The Law Commission proposals

2.36   In seeking to establish a clear legal framework for making decisions with, or on behalf of people who lack capacity, the Law Commission proposed a single criterion to govern all decision-making:[48]

> 'Although decisions are to be taken by a variety of people with varying degrees of formality, a single criterion to govern any substitute decision can be established. Whatever the answer to the question "who decides?", there should only be one answer to the subsequent question "on what basis?".
>
> We explained in our overview paper that two criteria for making substitute decisions for another adult have been developed in the literature in this

---

45   Joint Committee Report, Vol I, paras 72, 78.
46   Joint Committee Report, Vol II, Ev 184, Q495–Q496.
47   Denzil Lush 'The Mental Capacity Act and the new Court of Protection', *Journal of Mental Health Law* 12, 34.
48   Law Com No 321, paras 3.24–3.25.

field: "best interests" on the one hand and "substituted judgment" on the other. In Consultation Paper No 128 we argued that the two were not in fact mutually exclusive and we provisionally favoured a "best interests" criterion which would contain a strong element of "substituted judgment". It had been widely accepted by respondents to the overview paper that, where a person has never had capacity, there is no viable alternative to the "best interests" criterion. We were pleased to find that our arguments in favour of a "best interests" criterion found favour with almost all our respondents, with the Law Society emphasising that the criterion as defined in the consultation papers was in fact "an excellent compromise" between the best interests and substituted judgment approaches. We recommend that anything done for, and any decision made on behalf of a person without capacity should be done or made in the best interests of that person.'

2.37   It is notable that the Scottish Law Commission took a different approach in formulating proposals which led to the AWI Act:[49]

'We consider that "best interests" by itself is too vague and would require to be supplemented by further factors which have to be taken into account. We also consider that "best interests" does not give due weight to the views of the adult, particularly to wishes and feeling which he or she had expressed while capable of doing so. The concept of best interests was developed in the context of child law where a child's level of understanding may not be high and will usually have been lowered in the past. Incapable adults such as those who are mentally ill, head injured or suffering from dementia at the time when a decision has to be made in connection with them, will have possessed full mental powers before their present incapacity. We think it is wrong to equate such adults with children and for that reason would avoid extending child law concepts to them. Accordingly, the general principles [of the AWI Act] are framed without express reference to best interests.'

The Joint Committee's view

2.38   The Joint Committee on the draft Bill compared the two approaches and came down in favour of including the concept of best interests within the Act's key principles:[50]

'We heard evidence that the concept of best interests has been usefully developed by the courts and that its inclusion in statute would assist in promoting awareness and good practice, thereby ensuring some consistency in approach.'

The legislation

2.39   Section 1(5) establishes in statute the common law principle that any act done, or any decision made, under the Act for or on behalf of a person who lacks capacity must be done, or made, in that person's best

---

[49]   Scottish Law Commission, *Report on Incapable Adults*, Scot Law Com No 151 (Scottish Executive, 1995) para 2.50.
[50]   Joint Committee Report, Vol I, para 82.

interests. Further details on the meaning and determination of best interests are set out in the Act.[51]

Least restrictive alternative

The Law Commission proposals

2.40   The Law Commission originally proposed that the 'least restrictive alternative' principle should be included in the new legislation as one of the factors to be taken into account in determining the best interests of a person who lacks capacity.[52] The Commission considered that the principle had been developed over many years by experts in the field so as to become widely recognised and accepted.[53] The Draft Mental Incapacity Bill therefore included this principle in the proposed statutory checklist for best interests.[54]

The legislation

2.41   However, in response to the Joint Committee's recommendation[55] the Government agreed to incorporate the least restrictive option in s 1(6) as the fifth key principle to guide the use of the Act generally, rather than just one factor in the best interests checklist.

Before any action is taken, or any decision is made under the Act in relation to a person lacking capacity, the person taking the action or making the decision must consider whether it is possible to act or decide in a way that interferes less with the person's rights and freedom of action. Where there is more than one course of action or a choice of decisions to be made, all possible options or alternatives should be explored (including whether there is a need for any action or decision at all) in order to consider which option would be the least restrictive. However, other options need only be considered so long as the desired purpose of the action or decision can still be achieved.

The Scottish approach

2.42   This formulation differs from the principles set out in the AWI Act, which starts with a specific 'no intervention' provision[56] – that there shall be no intervention in the affairs of an adult unless the intervention

---

[51]   Mental Capacity Act 2005, s 4, and see **2.92–2.110**.
[52]   Law Com No 231, paras 3.28, 3.37.
[53]   For a discussion of the origins and development of the principle of least restrictive alternative, see Denzil Lush 'The Mental Capacity Act and the new Court of Protection' in *Journal of Mental Health Law* 12, 37–38.
[54]   Draft Mental Incapacity Bill, Cm 5859-I (TSO, 2003) cl 4(2)(e).
[55]   Joint Committee Report, Vol I, para 44.
[56]   Adults with Incapacity (Scotland) Act 2000, s 1(2).

will benefit the adult and that such benefit cannot reasonably be achieved in any other way. This is then followed by the 'least restrictive option' principle.[57] The Joint Committee considered this approach, but took the view that the least restrictive alternative principle would involve decision-makers in having to consider whether any intervention at all was in fact necessary.[58]

Application to the Court of Protection

2.43   Although the Court of Protection is subject to the principles set out in s 1,[59] including best interests and the least restrictive alternative, specific provision is made to limit the scope of any intervention where court proceedings are contemplated. The Act requires the Court, in deciding whether to grant permission for an application to it, to consider the reasons for the application, the benefit to the person lacking capacity and whether the benefit can be achieved in any other way.[60] In addition, the Act imposes an obligation on the Court to make a single order in preference to appointing a deputy, and where the appointment of a deputy is considered necessary, that the powers conferred on the deputy should be as limited in scope and duration as possible.[61]

Defining lack of capacity

The functional approach

2.44   The lack of a clear statutory definition of capacity (or lack of capacity) has caused confusion and difficulty for all concerned, not least for professionals called on to assess someone's decision-making capacity. There are also significant differences in approach between legal and medical or psychological concepts of capacity.[62] Case-law has offered a number of tests of capacity depending on the type of decision in issue.[63] The Law Commission recommended that, in order to provide certainty and clarity in using the new jurisdiction, a single statutory definition of capacity should be adopted.[64] Therefore, having set out the key principles governing its operation, the Act goes on to define the people affected by its provisions.

---

[57]   Adults with Incapacity (Scotland) Act 2000, s 1(3).

[58]   Joint Committee Report, Vol I, para 96.

[59]   Mental Capacity Act 2005, s 16(3).

[60]   Mental Capacity Act 2005, s 50(3).

[61]   Mental Capacity Act 2005, s 16(4). See **CHAPTER 4**.

[62]   The Law Society and British Medical Association attempted to address this problem by providing much needed guidance in *Assessment of Mental Capacity: Guidance for Doctors and Lawyers* (London: BMA, 1995; BMJ Books, 2nd edn, 2004).

[63]   See **2.65–2.66**.

[64]   Law Com No 231, para 3.7.

2.45   Section 2 of the Act sets out the definition of a person who lacks
       capacity. Section 3 sets out the test for assessing whether a person is
       unable to make a decision and therefore lacks capacity. By applying
       these together, the Act adopts a functional approach to defining
       capacity, requiring capacity to be assessed in relation to each particular
       decision at the time the decision needs to be made, and not the person's
       ability to make decisions generally. This means that individuals should
       not be labelled 'incapable' simply on the basis that they have been
       diagnosed with a particular condition, or because of any preconceived
       ideas or assumptions about their abilities due, for example, to their age,
       appearance or behaviour. Rather it must be shown that they lack
       capacity for each specific decision, or type of decision, at the time the
       particular decision needs to be made. The following paragraphs
       consider in turn each element of the Act's definition and test of
       capacity.

People who lack capacity

2.46   Section 2(1) sets out the definition of a person who lacks capacity as
       follows:

> 'For the purposes of this Act, a person lacks capacity in relation to a matter
> if at the material time he is unable to make a decision for himself in relation
> to the matter because of an impairment of, or a disturbance in the
> functioning of, the mind or brain.'

Capacity is therefore decision-specific and the inability to make the
particular decision in question must be *because of* 'an impairment of, or
a disturbance in the functioning of, the mind or brain' (ie a mental
disability or disorder). It does not matter whether the impairment or
disturbance is permanent or temporary.[65] A person can lack decision-
making capacity even if the loss of capacity is partial or temporary or if
his or her capacity fluctuates. In particular, a person may lack capacity
in relation to one matter but not in relation to others.

The two-stage test of capacity

2.47   In order to decide whether an individual has capacity to make a
       particular decision, a two-stage procedure must be applied:

1.   it must be established that there is an impairment of, or disturbance
     in the functioning of, the person's mind or brain; and
2.   it must be established that the impairment or disturbance is
     sufficient to render the person incapable of making that particular
     decision.

---

[65]   Mental Capacity Act 2005, s 2(2).

If there is no indication of impairment or disturbance, the individual should be presumed to have capacity and his or her ability to make decisions should not be questioned.

A diagnostic threshold

2.48   During its consultation processes, the Law Commission considered the finely balanced arguments for and against having a diagnostic threshold, requiring a 'mental disability' to be established before someone is deemed to lack capacity.[66] The Commission concluded that a diagnostic 'hurdle' would serve a useful gate-keeping function, to ensure that decision-making rights are not taken over prematurely or unnecessarily and to make the test of capacity stringent enough *not* to catch large numbers of people who make unusual or unwise decisions. It was felt that the protection offered by a diagnostic threshold outweighs any risk of prejudice or stigma affecting those who need help with decision-making.[67]

2.49   Instead of using the term 'mental disability', the Act refers to 'an impairment of, or a disturbance in the functioning of, the mind or brain'. This covers a wide range of conditions. For example, people taken to casualty requiring treatment for a physical disorder who are incapacitated in the short-term through alcohol or drug misuse, delirium, or following head injury, may need urgent attention which cannot wait until their capacity has been restored. People in such situations are entitled to the protections and safeguards offered by the Act in the same way as those found to lack the capacity to make specific financial, health or welfare decisions as a result, for example, of mental illness, dementia, learning disabilities, or the long-term effects of brain damage.

Principle of equal consideration

2.50   During the Bill's Report stage in the House of Lords, an amendment was passed to make it clear that lack of capacity cannot be established merely by reference to a person's age or appearance, or any condition or aspect of his/her behaviour which might lead others to make unjustified assumptions about the person's capacity.[68] This amendment was originally proposed by the *Making Decisions Alliance*[69] as a 'principle of non-discrimination and equal consideration' which the Alliance sought to have included in the Act's statement of principles, in order to

---

[66]   The arguments are set out in Law Commission Consultation Paper No 128, paras 3.10–3.14.

[67]   Law Com No 231, para 3.8.

[68]   Mental Capacity Act 2005, s 2(3).

[69]   A coalition of around 40 charities that campaigned for the Mental Capacity Act.

ensure that people with impaired capacity are treated no less favourably
than people with capacity:[70]

> 'Our concerns stem from evidence, anecdotal and otherwise, that prejudices
> and attitudes about the quality of life of a person with serious learning
> disabilities, mental health problem or a head injury or other condition that
> leads to loss of capacity can get in the way of supporting that person and
> how they are, what they want and what they need.'

2.51   While the Government was sympathetic to these concerns, the drafting
        of a broad 'equal consideration' principle proved unworkable. Instead
        the Government put forward two amendments, one relating to the
        definition of capacity and the second concerning best interests
        determinations[71] in order to:[72]

> '… reinforce the belief, shared across the House, that no-one should be
> assumed to lack capacity, excluded from decision-making, discriminated
> against or given substandard care and treatment simply, for example, as a
> result of disability.'

The amendment therefore ensures that individuals should not be
labelled 'incapable' because of their age or appearance, or because of
any preconceived ideas or prejudicial assumptions about their abilities
due to their particular condition or behaviour. The reference to
'condition' covers a range of factors, including both mental or physical
disabilities and temporary conditions such as drunkenness.
'Appearance' is also deliberately broad, covering visible medical
problems, disabilities, skin colour, religious dress and so on.

Qualifying age

2.52   It has always been the intention that the new jurisdiction should apply
        only to *adults* who lack capacity, leaving disputes about the care and
        welfare of children and young people to be resolved under the Children
        Act 1989. However, the Law Commission commented that a number of
        the statutory provisions in the Children Act 1989 do not apply to 16–18
        year olds or only in 'exceptional' circumstances. The Law Commission
        concluded that:[73]

> 'If continuing substitute decision-making arrangements are needed for
> someone aged 16 or 17, this is likely to be because the young person lacks
> mental capacity and not because he or she is under the age of legal
> majority.'

---

[70]   Making Decisions Alliance, *House of Lords Briefing*, Second Reading, 10 January 2005,
        p 3.
[71]   See **2.94**.
[72]   *Hansard*, HL Deb, col 1318 (15 March 2005).
[73]   Law Com No 231, para 2.52.

2.53　It followed that the provisions of the new jurisdiction, rather than the Children Act 1989, should apply in those circumstances for young people aged 16 or 17, and not just where there is no one available to exercise parental responsibility. For example, there may be circumstances where it is in the young person's best interests for someone other than a person with parental responsibility to be appointed as deputy to make financial or personal welfare decisions. Or it may be appropriate for the Court of Protection to make welfare decisions, for example where the young person should live, or medical treatment decisions concerning a young person lacking capacity where it is considered that those with parental responsibility are not acting in the young person's best interests. It was suggested that the resultant overlap would pose no great problems in practice.

2.54　Section 2(5) therefore makes it clear that the Act's provisions apply in general only to people lacking capacity who are aged 16 years or over. However, as is the case under the current law, the Act's powers to deal with property and financial affairs might be exercised in relation to a child whose disabilities will cause a lack of capacity to manage those affairs to continue into adulthood.[74]

2.55　In cases where legal proceedings are required to resolve disputes or make legally effective arrangements for someone aged 16 or 17, the Law Commission pointed out that it would not make sense to require two sets of legal proceedings to be conducted within a short period of time where the problems arising from the young person's incapacity are likely to continue after the age of 18. The Act, therefore, makes provision for transfer from the Court of Protection to the children's courts, and vice versa.[75] The choice of court will depend on what is appropriate in the particular circumstances of the case. Practice Directions are likely to be issued giving guidance on the types of cases appropriate to each jurisdiction.

Inability to make decisions

2.56　The second stage of the test of capacity[76] requires it to be shown that an impairment of, or disturbance in the functioning of, the mind or brain is sufficient to make the person unable to make the decision in question. Section 3 sets out the test for assessing whether a person is unable to make a decision for him or herself. This is a 'functional' test, focusing on the personal ability of the individual concerned to make a particular decision and the processes followed by the person in arriving at the

---

74　Mental Capacity Act 2005, ss 2(6) and 18(3).
75　Mental Capacity Act 2005, s 21.
76　See **2.47**.

decision, not on the outcome. A person is unable to make a decision if
he or she is unable:[77]

> '(a) to understand the information relevant to the decision,
>
> (b) to retain that information,
>
> (c) to use or weigh that information as part of the process of making the
>   decision, or
>
> (d) to communicate his decision (whether by talking, using sign language
>   or any other means).'

If someone cannot undertake one of the first three aspects of the
decision-making process, then he or she is unable to make the decision.
The fourth criterion in subsection (d) relates only to a residual category
of people who are totally unable to communicate.[78]

Understand the information relevant to the decision

2.57   Information relevant to the decision will include the particular nature of
the decision in question, the purpose for which the decision is needed
and the likely effects of making the decision. It must also include the
likely consequences of deciding one way or another or of making no
decision at all.[79]

2.58   Following lobbying by the Making Decisions Alliance, amendments
were made to the Bill in both Houses of Parliament to require
communication support, as is *appropriate* to meet individual needs, to
be provided to help people with impaired capacity to express their
views and, wherever possible, to make their own decisions.[80] As a
result, the Act[81] requires every effort to be made to provide an
explanation of all information relevant to the decision in question in a
way that is appropriate to the circumstances of the person concerned
and using the most effective means of communication (such as simple
language, visual aids or any other means) to assist their understanding.
Cursory or inadequate explanations will not be acceptable.

The threshold of understanding is quite low, requiring an ability to
understand an explanation of what is proposed and any possible
consequences given in broad terms and simple language – it is not
always necessary to understand all the details. This approach is
consistent with the desire to enable people to take as many decisions as
possible for themselves, while also ensuring that the more serious the

---

[77]   Mental Capacity Act 2005, s 3(1).

[78]   See **2.63–2.64**.

[79]   Mental Capacity Act 2005, s 3(4).

[80]   See, eg, *Re AK (Medical Treatment: Consent)* [2001] 1 FLR 129 where strenuous efforts
were made to communicate with someone able only to move one eyelid.

[81]   Mental Capacity Act 2005, s 3(2).

consequences of any decision, the greater the degree of understanding required.

Retain the information

2.59   The ability to retain information for a short period only should not automatically disqualify the person from making the decision.[82] The person must be able to retain the information for long enough to make a choice or take an effective decision and the length of time will therefore depend on what is necessary for the decision in question. The Draft Code of Practice suggests that mechanical aids, such as videos and voice recorders, could be used to assist retention and recording of information.[83]

2.60   It has been suggested that the Act's failure to define for how long the information must be retained may cause confusion for those seeking to assess a person's capacity. It is possible that applications may be made to the Court of Protection to provide clarification on this point.

Use or weigh the information

2.61   A number of cases have come before the courts where the person concerned had the ability to understand information but where the effects of a mental disability prevented him or her from using that information in the decision-making process.[84] The Law Commission gave examples of certain compulsive conditions (such as anorexia) which cause people, who are quite able to absorb information, to make decisions which are inevitable (eg not to eat) regardless of the information and their understanding of it. To reflect these concerns, the Law Commission originally proposed that in order to have capacity, a person must be able to make a 'true choice'.[85] However, in its final report, the Commission recognised that:[86]

> 'Common to all these cases is the fact that the person's eventual decision is divorced from his or her ability to understand the relevant information. Emphasising that the person must be able to use the information which he or she has successfully understood in the decision-making process deflects the complications of asking whether a person needs to "appreciate" information as well as understand it. A decision based on a compulsion, the overpowering will of a third party or any other inability to act on relevant information as a result of mental disability is not a decision made by a person with decision-making capacity.'

---

[82]   Mental Capacity Act 2005, s 3(3).
[83]   Draft Code of Practice, para 3.11.
[84]   See, eg, *Re MB* [1997] 2 FLR 426; *R v Collins and Ashworth Hospital Authority ex parte Brady* [2001] 58 BMLR 173.
[85]   Law Commission Consultation Paper No 128, paras 3.31–3.35.
[86]   Law Com No 231, para 3.17.

2.62   The courts have further defined the process as the ability to weigh all relevant information in the balance as part of the process of making a decision and then use the information in order to arrive at a decision. Section 3(1)(c) translates this common law provision into statute.

Unable to communicate

2.63   The final criterion which would indicate an inability to make a decision is the fact that the person is *unable to communicate the decision* by any possible means.[87] There are obvious situations, such as unconsciousness, which would result in a person being unable to communicate a decision. Other types of cases may include people in a permanent vegetative state or with the condition known as 'locked-in syndrome'. The Law Commission intended this to be very much a residual category affecting a minority of people:[88]

> 'This test will have no relevance if the person is known to be incapable of deciding (even if also unable to communicate) but will be available if the assessor does not know, one way or the other, whether the person is capable of deciding or not.'

2.64   Strenuous efforts must first be made to assist and facilitate communication before any finding of incapacity is made. The Draft Code of Practice recommends that in cases of this sort, professionals with specialist skills in verbal and non-verbal communication will be required to assist in the assessment.[89]

Existing common law tests of capacity

2.65   The definition and two-stage test of capacity set out in the Act are expressed to apply 'for the purposes of this Act'[90] and Sch 6 makes consequential amendments to existing statutes, inserting the new statutory definition. There are also several *common law* tests of capacity set out in case-law.[91] Examples are as follows:

> capacity to make a will;[92]
> capacity to marry;[93]
> capacity to make a gift;[94]

---

[87]   Mental Capacity Act 2005, s 3(1)(d).
[88]   Law Com No 231, para 3.20.
[89]   Draft Code of Practice, para 3.14.
[90]   Mental Capacity Act 2005, s 2(1).
[91]   Details of the existing common law tests of capacity can be found in BMA/Law Society, *Assessment of Mental Capacity: Guidance for doctors and lawyers* (London: BMJ Books, 2004).
[92]   *Banks v Goodfellow* (1870) LR 5 QB 549.
[93]   *Sheffield City Council v E & S* [2005] 1 FLR 965.
[94]   *Re Beaney (deceased)* [1978] 2 All ER 595.

contractual capacity;[95]
capacity to litigate.[96]

2.66   The Act's new definition of capacity is intended to expand on, rather than contradict, the terms of existing common law tests.[97] As cases come before the court, it is likely that judges will consider the new statutory definition and adopt it if they see fit and use it to develop common law rules in particular cases.

Reasonable belief of lack of capacity

2.67   In most day-to-day decisions or actions involved in caring for someone, it will not be appropriate or necessary to carry out a formal assessment of the person's capacity. Indeed many informal carers or others exercising powers under the Act will not be equipped to carry out a detailed assessment. Rather, it is sufficient for them to 'reasonably believe' that the person lacks capacity to make the decision or consent to the action in question,[98] but they must be able to point to objective reasons to justify why they hold that belief.

2.68   This is based on the Law Commission's explanation that:[99]

> 'It would be out of step with our aims of policy, and with the views of the vast majority of the respondents to our overview paper, to have any general system of certifying people as "incapacitated" and then identifying a substitute decision-maker for them, regardless of whether there is any real need for one. In the absence of certifications or authorisations, persons acting informally can only be expected to have reasonable grounds to believe that (1) the other person lacks capacity in relation to the matter in hand and (2) they are acting in the best interests of that person.'

The assessment of capacity

Background

2.69   By making a judgment on an individual's decision-making capacity, anyone with authority over that person can deprive him or her of civil rights and liberties enjoyed by most adults and now safeguarded by the Human Rights Act 1998. Alternatively, such a judgment could permit a person lacking capacity to do something, or carry on doing something, whereby serious prejudice could result, either putting that person at risk

---

[95]   *Boughton v Knight* (1873) LR 3 PD 64.

[96]   *Masterman-Lister v Brutton & Co and Jewell & Home Counties Dairies* [2003] 3 All ER 162, CA.

[97]   Law Com No 231, para 3.23.

[98]   Mental Capacity Act 2005, ss 4(8) and 5(1).

[99]   Law Com No 231, para 4.5.

or causing harm or inconvenience to others. It is therefore essential that anyone called upon to assess another person's capacity must understand what they are being asked to judge and be prepared to justify their findings.

2.70   The Joint Committee on the Draft Mental Incapacity Bill received evidence from a number of organisations expressing concern that the Bill made no specific provisions for the assessment of capacity, despite the far-reaching implications of the outcome of assessment.[100] These concerns were discussed during the Bill's Committee stage in the House of Lords, when Lord Carter put forward a probing amendment, seeking to impose a statutory duty on public bodies to carry out a formal assessment of a person's capacity where it may be relevant in the context of any assessment of needs or the provision of services to meet those needs. The Minister responded:[101]

> 'This is important – I recognise that – but I am not sure that is something I want to see covered in primary legislation. The purpose of the Bill is to set out the broad principles and absolutes ... to be followed, but we cannot lay out on the face of the Bill the practical detail of how professionals should operate ... The details of the assessment procedure must be a matter for professional judgement in relation to the case, with support from the code of practice in training and guidance.'

2.71   The following sections draw on the guidance given in the Draft Code of Practice and on the professional guidance for doctors and lawyers on assessment of mental capacity issued jointly by the BMA and the Law Society.[102]

When should capacity be assessed?

2.72   According to the principles of the Act, the starting point should be the presumption of capacity. Doubts as to a person's capacity may arise for a number of reasons, either because of the person's behaviour or circumstances, or through concerns raised by someone else, but any concerns must be considered specifically in relation to the particular decision which needs to be made. Where doubts are raised about a person's decision-making abilities, the following questions should first be considered:

1.   Does the person have all the relevant information needed to make the decision in question? If there is a choice, has information been given on any alternatives?

---

[100]   Joint Committee Report, Vol I, para 242.
[101]   *Hansard*, HL Deb, col 1230 (25 January 2005).
[102]   BMA/Law Society *Assessment of Mental Capacity: Guidance for doctors and lawyers* (BMJ Books, 2nd edn, 2004).

2. Could the information be explained or presented in a way that is easier for the person to understand?
3. Are there particular times of day when the person's understanding is better, or particular locations where they may feel more at ease? Can the decision be put off until the circumstances are right for the person concerned?
4. Can anyone else help or support the person to make choices or express a view, such as an advocate or someone to assist communication?

If all these steps have been taken without success in helping the person make a decision, an assessment of their capacity to make the decision in question should be made.

Who should assess capacity?

2.73 In keeping with the functional approach, the question of who assesses an individual's capacity will depend on the particular decision to be made. For most day-to-day decisions, the carer most directly involved with the person at the time the decision has to be made assesses his or her capacity to make the decision in question. Carers acting informally are not expected to be experts in assessing capacity, but they must be able to show they have reasonable grounds for believing that the person lacks capacity to make the decision or do the act in question, at that particular time.[103] Formal processes are rarely required unless the assessment is challenged, for example by the person whose capacity is being assessed or by another family member. In such circumstances, the assessor must be able to point to objective reasons as to why they believe the person lacks capacity.

2.74 Where consent to medical treatment or examination is required, the doctor proposing the treatment must decide whether the patient has capacity to consent and should record the assessment process and findings in the person's medical notes. Where a legal transaction is involved, such as making a will or a power of attorney, the solicitor handling the transaction will need to assess whether the client has capacity to give instructions – this requires the solicitor to assess whether the client has the required capacity to satisfy the relevant legal test, perhaps assisted by an opinion from a doctor.

2.75 The more serious the decision, the more formal the assessment of capacity may need to be, but whoever assesses capacity must be prepared to justify their findings. Ultimately, if a person's capacity to do something is disputed, it is a question for the court to decide. Cases referred to the new Court of Protection will require formal evidence of the assessment of capacity, either to enable the Court to make a

---

[103] Mental Capacity Act 2005, ss 4(8) and 5(1). See **2.67–2.68**.

declaration as to whether the person has or lacks capacity or to confirm that the Court has jurisdiction to deal with the matter in question.[104]

The need for formal assessment

2.76   For certain more complex or serious decisions, a formal assessment of capacity may be required, sometimes involving different professionals. Doctors are generally regarded as experts in the assessment of capacity, and in many cases all that may be needed is an opinion from the person's GP or family doctor. Where the person has been diagnosed with a particular condition or disorder, it may be more appropriate to seek an opinion from a specialist, such as a consultant psychiatrist or psychologist who has extensive clinical experience of the disorder and is familiar with caring for patients with that condition. In other cases, a multi-disciplinary approach is best, using the skills and expertise of different professionals.

2.77   Doctors or other experts should never express an opinion without first conducting a proper assessment of the person's capacity to make the decision in question and applying the appropriate test of capacity. Solicitors requesting a professional assessment should send full letters of instruction, setting out details of the requisite test of capacity and how this should be applied in relation to the client's particular circumstances.[105] However, a doctor's opinion may not necessarily be given greater weight than other relevant evidence, such as the views of a solicitor where capacity to undertake a legal transaction is involved.[106]

Legal requirements

2.78   In some cases it is a requirement of the law that a formal assessment of capacity be carried out. These include the following situations:

1.   where a doctor or other expert witness certifies a legal document (such as a will) signed by someone whose capacity could be challenged (the so-called 'golden rule' established in *Kenward v Adams*[107]);

---

[104]   See **Chapters 4** and **6**.

[105]   Sample letters have been provided in BMA/Law Society *Assessment of Mental Capacity* (BMJ Books, 2004) and Denzil Lush *Elderly Clients: A Precedent Manual* (Jordans, 2nd edn, 2005).

[106]   *Richmond v Richmond* (1914) 111 LT 273; *Birkin v Wing* (1890) 63 LT 80.

[107]   (1975) *The Times*, November 29. The need to observe this 'golden rule' was repeated in *Re Simpson (Deceased), Schaniel v Simpson* (1977) 121 SJ 224, *Buckenham v Dickinson* [1997] CLY 661 and more forcefully in *Great Ormond Street Hospital v Pauline Rushie* (unreported) 19 April 2000, in which the solicitor was strongly criticised for failing to follow the 'golden rule'.

2. to provide a certificate of capacity to make a lasting power of attorney;[108]

3. to establish that a particular person requires the assistance of the Official Solicitor;[109]

4. to establish that a particular person comes within the jurisdiction of the Court of Protection;[110]

5. where the court is required to determine a person's capacity to make a particular decision.[111]

Other expert assessments

2.79 In other cases, a judgment will need to be made as to whether the particular circumstances make it appropriate or necessary to seek a formal assessment of capacity by obtaining an opinion from a doctor or other expert. The Draft Code of Practice suggests that any of the following factors might indicate the need for a formal assessment:[112]

1. the gravity of the decision or its consequences;

2. where the person concerned disputes a finding of incapacity;

3. where there is disagreement between family members, carers and/or professionals as to the person's capacity;

4. where the person concerned is expressing different views to different people, perhaps through trying to please each one or tell them what he or she thinks they want to hear;

5. where the person's capacity to make a particular decision may be subject to challenge, either at the time the decision is made or in the future – for example a person's testamentary capacity may be challenged after his or her death by someone seeking to contest the will;

6. where there may be legal consequences of a finding of capacity – for example in a settlement of damages following a claim for personal injury;

7. where legal proceedings are contemplated (eg divorce proceedings) and the person's capacity to litigate may be in doubt;

8. where the person concerned is repeatedly making decisions that put him or herself at risk or could result in preventable suffering or damage.

---

[108] Mental Capacity Act 2005, Sch 1, para 2(1)(e).

[109] Civil Procedure Rules 1998, r 21.1; Practice Note (*Official Solicitor: Declaratory Proceedings: Medical and welfare decisions for adults who lack capacity*) [2001] 2 FLR 158, para 7.1. (Note: Both will require amendment to take account of the Act.)

[110] Mental Capacity Act 2005, ss 15(1), 16(1).

[111] *Masterman-Lister v Brutton & Co and Jewell & Home Counties Dairies* [2002] EWCA Civ 1889, CA at 54.

[112] Draft Code of Practice, para 3.37.

How capacity is assessed

2.80   Where there are doubts about capacity, it is important that people are
       assessed when they are at their highest level of functioning because this
       is the only realistic way of determining what they may or may not be
       capable of doing. Many of the practicable steps which can be taken to
       enable a person to make his or her own decisions[113] may also be helpful
       in creating the best environment for capacity to be assessed. Once this
       has been done, the two-stage test of capacity[114] must then be applied, ie:

       1.   Is there an impairment of or disturbance in the functioning of the
            person's mind or brain? If so,
       2.   Is the impairment or disturbance sufficient to render the person
            incapable of making that particular decision?

       In the majority of cases, it is likely to be obvious whether there is any
       impairment or disturbance which could affect the person's decision-
       making capacity. For example, there may have been a previous
       diagnosis of an ongoing mental illness or learning disability, or
       recognisable symptoms to indicate the recurrence of illness or the
       disabling effects of a head injury. However, in other cases, such as
       dementia, the onset of debilitating illness is gradual and the point at
       which capacity is affected is hard to define. During the period when
       capacity is borderline, a medical opinion may be required.

2.81   People should not be considered 'incapable' simply on the basis that
       they have a particular diagnosis or condition, but this must be shown to
       affect their ability to make a decision at the time the decision needs to
       be made. The following questions must be considered:

       1.   Does the person have a general understanding of what the decision
            is and why he or she is being asked to make it?
       2.   Does the person have a general understanding of the consequences
            of making, or not making, this decision?
       3.   Is the person able to understand and weigh up the information
            relevant to the decision as part of the process of arriving at it?

       In borderline cases, or where there is any element of doubt, the person
       doing the assessment must be able to show that it is more likely than not
       that the answer to the above questions is 'No'.

Confidentiality

2.82   Carrying out an assessment of capacity requires the sharing of
       information about the personal circumstances of the person being
       assessed. Yet doctors, lawyers and other professionals are bound by a
       duty of confidentiality towards their clients, imposed through their

---

[113] See **2.29–2.32**.
[114] See **2.47**.

professional ethical codes and reinforced by law. As a general principle, personal information may only be disclosed with the client's consent, even to close relatives. However, there are circumstances when disclosure is necessary in the absence of consent.[115]

In relation to people who lack capacity to consent (or refuse) disclosure, a balance must be struck between the public and private interests in maintaining confidentiality and the public and private interest in permitting, and occasionally requiring, disclosure for certain purposes. Some guidance has been offered in the case of *S v Plymouth City Council and C* which established:[116]

> '... a clear distinction between disclosure to the media with a view to publication to all and sundry and disclosure in confidence to those with a proper interest in having the information in question.'

2.83 A similar balancing act must be carried out by professionals seeking or undertaking assessments of capacity. It is essential that information concerning the person being assessed which is directly relevant to the decision in question is made available to ensure that an accurate and focused assessment can take place. Every effort must first be made to obtain the person's consent to disclosure by providing a full explanation as to why this is necessary and the risks and consequences involved. If the person is unable to consent, relevant disclosure – that is the minimum necessary to achieve the objective of assessing capacity – may be permitted where this is in the person's best interests.[117] However, this does not mean that everyone has to know everything.

Refusal to be assessed

2.84 There may be circumstances in which a person whose capacity is in doubt refuses to undergo an assessment of capacity or refuses to be examined by a doctor. It will usually be possible to persuade someone to agree to an assessment if the consequences of refusal are carefully explained. For example, it should be explained to people wishing to make a will that the will could be challenged and held to be invalid after their death, while evidence of their capacity to make a will would prevent this from happening.

2.85 If the person lacks capacity to consent to or refuse assessment, it will normally be possible for an assessment to proceed so long as the person is compliant and this is considered to be in the person's best interests. In some cases, a 'reasonable belief' of lack of capacity will be sufficient.[118] However, where a formal assessment is needed, no one can be forced to

---

[115] *W v Egdell and others* [1990] 1 All ER 835 at 848.
[116] [2002] EWCA Civ 388 at 49.
[117] Further guidance is given in the Draft Code of Practice, chapter 13.
[118] See **2.67–2.68**.

undergo an assessment of capacity in the face of an outright refusal unless required to do so by a court in legal proceedings. Even then, entry to a person's home cannot be forced and a refusal to open the door to the doctor may be the end of the matter. Where there are serious concerns about the person's mental health, an assessment under mental health legislation may be warranted so long as the statutory grounds are fulfilled.[119]

Recording assessments of capacity

2.86   The majority of decisions made on behalf of people lacking capacity will be informal day-to-day decisions and as such, those caring for them on a daily basis will be able to assess their capacity and carry out acts in connection with their care and treatment in accordance with s 5 of the Act.[120] No formal assessment procedures or recorded documentation will be required. However, if the carer's assessment is challenged, they must be able to point to the grounds which justified a reasonable belief of lack of capacity.[121]

Professional records

2.87   Where professionals are involved, it is a matter of good practice that a proper assessment of capacity is made and the findings recorded in the relevant professional records. This includes, for example:

1.   an assessment of a patient's capacity to consent to medical treatment made by the doctor proposing the treatment and recorded in the patient's clinical notes;
2.   an assessment of a client's capacity to instruct a solicitor to carry out a legal transaction (where necessary supported by a medical opinion) made by the solicitor and recorded on the client's file.

Formal reports or certificates of capacity

2.88   In some cases, a more detailed report or certificate will be required, for example:

1.   for use in court proceedings;
2.   as may be required by Regulations made under the Act (eg in relation to lasting powers of attorney);
3.   as may be required by the new Court of Protection Rules.

---

[119]   Mental Health Act 1983, ss 2, 3. A refusal to be assessed is in no way sufficient grounds for assessment under the Mental Health Act 1983.
[120]   See **2.119–2.130**.
[121]   See **2.67–2.68**.

Determining best interests

Background

2.89   The principle of acting in the best interests of a person who lacks capacity has become well established in the common law and the concept has been developed by the courts in cases relating to incapacitated adults, mainly those concerned with the provision of medical treatment.[122] Section 1(5) of the Act enshrines this principle in statute as the overriding principle that must guide all actions done for, or all decisions made on behalf of, someone lacking capacity.[123] Section 4 goes on to describe, for the purposes of this Act, the steps that must be taken in determining what is in a person's best interests.

2.90   Given the wide range of decisions and acts covered by this legislation and the varied circumstances of the people affected by its provisions, the concept of best interests is not defined in the Act. In considering the need for a definition, the Law Commission acknowledged that:[124]

> '... no statutory guidance could offer an exhaustive account of what is in a person's best interests, the intention being that the individual person and his or her individual circumstances should always determine the result.'

Instead, the Law Commission recommended that statute should set out a checklist of common factors which should always be taken into account. It also set out some important considerations as to how a statutory checklist should be framed:[125]

> 'First, a checklist must not unduly burden any decision-maker or encourage unnecessary intervention; secondly it must not be applied too rigidly and should leave room for all considerations relevant to the particular case; thirdly, it should be confined to major points, so that it can adapt to changing views and attitudes.'

2.91   The Joint Committee on the Draft Mental Incapacity Bill agreed with this approach:[126]

> 'We agree that no list of "best interest" factors can ever be comprehensive or applicable in all situations. We therefore endorse the approach recommended by the Law Commission that a checklist of common factors to be considered in all cases should be set out in statute. However, it should be made clearer in the Bill that in addition to these common factors, all other matters relevant to the incapacitated individual and the decision in question must also be considered.'

---

[122]   See, eg, *Re A (Male Sterilisation)* [2000] 1 FLR 549; *Re S (Sterilisation: Patient's Best Interests)* [2000] 2 FLR 389; *Re F (Adult Patient: Sterilisation)* [2001] Fam 15.
[123]   See **2.36–2.39**.
[124]   Law Com No 231, para 3.26.
[125]   Law Com No 231, para 3.28.
[126]   Joint Committee Report, Vol I, para 85.

Both as a result of recommendations made by the Joint Committee and amendments made during the parliamentary process, the best interests checklist contained in s 4 has been extended and made more prescriptive in relation to certain types of decisions, in particular those involving end-of-life decisions. The specific requirements for determining best interests are considered in detail in the following paragraphs.

The best interests checklist

2.92 Under the Act, a person's capacity to make the decision or take the action in question must first be assessed. Section 4 only comes into play once it has been established (or there are reasonable grounds for believing) that the person lacks capacity to make the decision in question and needs someone else to decide or act on his or her behalf. It then sets out a checklist of factors which must be considered in deciding what is in a person's best interests aimed at identifying those issues most relevant to the individual who lacks capacity (as opposed to the decision-maker or any other persons). Not all the factors in the checklist will be relevant to all types of decisions or actions, but they must still be considered if only to be disregarded as irrelevant to that particular situation.

2.93 The serious nature of this task was recognised by the Joint Committee:[127]

'We acknowledge that consideration of best interests requires flexibility, by allowing and encouraging the person [lacking capacity] to be involved to the fullest possible extent but also enabling the decision-maker to take account of a variety of circumstances, views and attitudes which may have a bearing on the decision in question. This flexibility is particularly important in cases of partial or fluctuating capacity. Determining best interests is a judgement, requiring consideration of what will often be conflicting or competing concerns, while seeking to achieve a consensus approach to decision-making.'

Principle of equal consideration

2.94 Similar to the 'equal consideration' requirement imposed as an amendment to the definition of people who lack capacity,[128] s 4(1) begins with a clear statement that a determination of someone's best interests must not be based merely on the person's age or appearance, or any condition or aspect of his or her behaviour which might lead others to make unjustified assumptions about the person's best interests. As in s 2(3), the reference here to 'condition' covers a range of factors, including both mental or physical disabilities as well as temporary

---

[127] Joint Committee Report, Vol I, para 89.
[128] See **2.50–2.51**.

conditions. 'Appearance' is also deliberately broad, covering visible medical problems, disabilities, skin colour, religious dress and so on.

This is intended to ensure that people with impaired capacity are treated no less favourably than people with capacity. Thus, decisions about best interests must not be based on any preconceived ideas or negative assumptions, for example about the value or quality of life experienced by older people or people with mental or physical disabilities who now lack capacity to make decisions for themselves.

All relevant circumstances

2.95 A determination of a person's best interests involves identifying those issues most relevant to the individual who lacks capacity in the context of the decision in question. The statutory checklist sets out the minimum necessary considerations but all other matters relevant in the particular situation must also be taken into account. Section 4(2) therefore requires the person making the determination to consider 'all the relevant circumstances' as well as following the steps set out in the checklist.

It is recognised that the person making the determination may not be in a position to make exhaustive inquiries to investigate every issue which may have some relevance on the incapacitated person or the decision in question. Therefore relevant circumstances are defined as those:[129]

(a) of which the person making the determination is aware, and
(b) which it would be reasonable to regard as relevant.

Regaining capacity

2.96 Following further consultation on the checklist suggested by the Law Commission for the determination of best interests, the Government proposed an additional factor – whether the person is likely to regain capacity.[130] One of the Act's key principles is that before a person is found to be incapable of making a decision, all practicable steps must be taken to help the person make that decision.[131]

In keeping with this approach, when looking at best interests, it is important to consider whether the individual concerned is likely to have capacity to make that particular decision in the future and if so, when that is likely to be.[132] It may be possible to put off the decision until the person can make it him or herself. This delay may allow further time for additional steps to be taken to restore the person's capacity or to provide

---

[129] Mental Capacity Act 2005, s 4(11).
[130] Lord Chancellor's Department, *Making Decisions*, Cm 4465 (TSO, 1999) para 1.12.
[131] Mental Capacity Act 2005, s 1(3). See **2.29–2.32**.
[132] Mental Capacity Act 2005, s 4(3).

support and assistance which would enable the person to make the decision.

2.97   The Draft Code of Practice on the Mental Capacity Bill suggests some factors which may indicate that a person may regain capacity:[133]

  1.   'The cause of the incapacity can be treated, either by medication or some other form of treatment or therapy.

  2.   The incapacity may decrease in time (for example where caused by the effects of medication or alcohol, or following a sudden shock).

  3.   People may learn new skills or be subject to new experiences which increase their capacity to make certain decisions, for example a young adult with learning disabilities who leaves his parental home to live in supported accommodation and gains new skills as a result.

  4.   The person may have a condition which causes capacity to fluctuate (such as some forms of mental illness) so it may be possible to arrange for the decision to be made during a lucid interval.

  5.   A person previously unable to communicate may learn a new form of communication.'

Permitting and encouraging participation

2.98   Section 4(4) requires that, even where a person does not have capacity to make an effective decision, he or she should be both permitted and encouraged to participate, or to improve his or her ability to participate as fully as possible in the decision-making process or in relation to any act done for him or her. It will always be important to consult the person on the particular act or decision to be made and to try to seek their views, not only to encourage the development of decision-making skills, but also as an important contribution in determining best interests. The practicable steps to enable decision-making will also be relevant here.[134]

Life-sustaining treatment

2.99   A specific best interests factor relates to decisions concerning the provision of life-sustaining treatment, which is defined as treatment which a person providing healthcare regards as necessary to sustain life, usually the life of a person lacking capacity to consent to that treatment.[135] Section 4(5) clarifies that in determining whether the treatment is in the best interests of someone who lacks capacity, the

---

[133]   Draft Code of Practice, para 4.16.

[134]   See **2.29–2.32**.

[135]   Mental Capacity Act 2005, s 4(10). In parliamentary debate, it was also clarified that 'in the case of a pregnant woman we want to ensure that the life of the baby, not only the life of the mother, must be considered' *Hansard*, HL, Vol 668, col 1184 (25 January 2005). However, an unborn child does not have an independent set of interests to be weighed against the mother's best interests (*St George's Healthcare NHS Trust v S* [1998] 3 All ER).

person making the determination must not be motivated by a desire to bring about the individual's death.

2.100 A great deal of the debate in both Houses of Parliament concerned life and death decisions affecting people who lack capacity. In order to provide clarity and reassurance on these very difficult issues, the Government agreed to a number of amendments introducing specific statements in the legislation. In particular, s 62 confirms that the Act does not have the effect of authorising or permitting euthanasia or assisted suicide. Secondly, in relation to decisions about whether the provision or continuance of life-sustaining treatment would be in a person's best interests, s 4(5) clarifies that the decision-maker must not be motivated by a desire to bring about the person's death.

2.101 This particular factor was introduced as an amendment in the House of Lords after an undertaking was given in correspondence between the Lord Chancellor and the Roman Catholic Archbishop of Cardiff, Peter Smith, that the Act would make this point absolutely clear. Commenting on a situation where no advance decision has been made about whether treatment should be continued or refused, the Lord Chancellor said:[136]

> 'The decision about whether to continue to give life-sustaining treatment will then fall to be taken by the doctor, acting with an attorney who has relevant powers ... In some cases a decision ... will still be taken by the court. The Bill preserves the jurisdiction exercised in the Tony Bland case and restates the principles applied in that case. These are very difficult decisions, even for a court. In making them the decision-maker must act in the best interests of the patient. Above all, he must make an objective assessment. The decision cannot simply be the personal value judgement of the decision-maker – the decision-maker cannot say "If I were in the patient's position, I would want to die" – nor can it be motivated by the desire to bring about the death of the patient.'

2.102 Any decision about life-sustaining treatment for a person lacking capacity will take as its starting point the assumption that it is in the person's best interests for life to continue. However, there will be some cases, for example in the final stages of terminal illness or for some patients in a permanent vegetative state where there is no prospect of recovery, where it may be in the best interests of the patient to withdraw treatment or to give palliative care that might incidentally shorten life.[137] All the factors in the best interests checklist must be considered, but the person determining best interests must not be motivated in any way by the desire to bring about the person's death.

---

[136] *Hansard*, HL Deb, cols 14–15 (10 January 2005).
[137] See **CHAPTER 5**.

The person's wishes and feelings, beliefs and values

2.103 A particularly important element of the best interests checklist is the consideration, so far as these can be ascertained, of:[138]

> '(a) the person's past and present wishes and feelings (and in particular, any relevant written statements made by him when he had capacity),
>
> (b) the beliefs and values that would be likely to influence his decision if he had capacity, and
>
> (c) the other factors that he would be likely to consider if he were able to do so.'

This places the focus firmly on the person lacking capacity, taking into account the issues most important to him or her and what he or she would have wanted to achieve. It also reflects the need to make every effort to find out whether the person has expressed any relevant views in the past, whether verbally, in writing or through behaviour or habits, as well as trying to seek his or her current views.

2.104 The Draft Code of Practice acknowledges that, while this factor establishes the importance of individual views, those views will not automatically determine the outcome.[139] Indeed, in some cases, there may be a conflict between the person's past and present wishes, so that these must be weighed against each other and considered alongside other factors in the checklist.

2.105 The reference to written statements was included as a Government amendment in the House of Lords in response to lobbying by the Making Decisions Alliance and other stakeholder organisations. Those organisations had requested that advance statements, particularly those expressing wishes about medical treatment, should be given some form of statutory recognition and should specifically be taken into account in determining a person's best interests. The Minister for Constitutional Affairs, Baroness Ashton confirmed:[140]

> '... the purpose of this amendment is to clarify that if someone with capacity has written down their wishes and feelings in respect of a matter, including positive preferences, those must be explicitly taken into account in a best interests determination.
>
> Patients do not have a right to demand and receive treatment, so advance requests cannot have the same legal effect as advance decisions to refuse treatment. However, the amendment makes clear that preferences about any aspect of a person's life, including treatment, should be respected and taken into account ... The more specific and well thought out the statement, the more likely it will be persuasive in determining best interests.'

---

[138] Mental Capacity Act 2005, s 4(6).
[139] Draft Code of Practice, paras 4.19–4.22.
[140] *Hansard*, HL Deb, cols 1441–1442 (17 March 2005).

2.106 The Draft Mental Incapacity Bill published in 2003 made no mention of the person's 'beliefs and values' but this was added to the Bill in response to a recommendation of the Joint Committee:[141]

> 'The Medical Ethics Alliance suggested to us that the factor involving the need to consider the incapacitated person's "past and present wishes and feelings" should also contain reference to that person's values. Others suggested that specific reference should be made to social, psychological, cultural, spiritual and religious issues. It is anticipated that the need to consider a wide range of issues, in particular religious and cultural concerns, will be spelt out in the Code of Practice. We seek reassurance that the form of words used in the Bill will require a person's values to be given due weight.'

2.107 The reference to factors the person 'would be likely to consider' if able to do so reflects current case-law in relation to the powers exercised by the Court of Protection to make a statutory will, where:[142]

> '... subject to all due allowances ... the court must seek to make the will which the actual patient, acting reasonably, would have made if notionally restored to full mental capacity, memory and foresight.'

Section 4(6)(c) extends this notion as a factor to consider for all decisions or actions, whether or not the person concerned ever had capacity in relation to the matter in question. The Draft Code of Practice suggests that this might also include 'altruistic motives and concern for others as well as duties and obligations towards dependants or future beneficiaries'.[143]

The views of other people

2.108 For the first time, the Act establishes the right for carers, family members and other relevant people to be consulted on decisions affecting the person. People with a right to be consulted include anyone named by the person lacking capacity as someone to be consulted, carers and anyone interested in the person's welfare, donees and deputies.[144] Any person who is determining the best interests of someone lacking capacity is required to take into account the views of these key people, but only if it is 'practicable and appropriate' to consult them.

The Draft Code of Practice suggests:[145]

> 'This is not intended to give absolute discretion to the decision-maker about whom to consult, rather decision-makers will need to show they have thought carefully about whom to consult and be prepared to explain why a

---

[141] Joint Committee Report, Vol I, para 90.
[142] *Re D(J)* [1982] 2 All ER 37 at 43.
[143] Draft Code of Practice, para 4.22.
[144] Mental Capacity Act 2005, s 4(7).
[145] Draft Code of Practice, para 4.23.

consultation which they declined to carry out was either impracticable or inappropriate.'

2.109 The consultation is limited to two matters – first, what those people consider to be in the person's best interests on the matter in question, and secondly whether they can provide any information on the wishes, feelings, values or beliefs of the person lacking capacity. If prior to losing capacity, the person concerned has nominated someone whom he or she would like to be consulted, the named person is more likely to have that information. People who are close to the person lacking capacity, such as relatives, partners and other carers, may also be able to assist with communication or interpret signs which give an indication of the person's present wishes and feelings.

2.110 The requirement for consultation must be balanced against the right to confidentiality of the person lacking capacity. That right should be protected so that consultation only takes place where relevant and with people whom it is appropriate to consult. For example, it is unlikely to be appropriate to consult anyone whom the person had previously indicated should not be involved. However, there may be occasions where it is in the person's best interests for specific information to be disclosed, or where the public interest in disclosure may override the person's private interest in maintaining confidentiality.[146] If professionals are involved in the determination of best interests, they will also need to comply with their own duties of confidentiality in accordance with their professional codes of conduct.

Duty to apply the best interests principle

2.111 The principle set out in s 1(5) confirms that any act done, or any decision made, on behalf of a person lacking capacity must be done in his or her best interests. Section 4(8) confirms that the best interests principle, and the duties to be carried out in determining best interests, also apply in certain circumstances where the person concerned may not in fact lack capacity in relation to the act or decision in question. The specified situations are:

1. where a donee is acting under a lasting power of attorney in relation to financial matters while the donor still has capacity;
2. where someone exercising powers under the Act 'reasonably believes' that the person lacks capacity.

Reasonable belief

2.112 The second situation reflects the position that in most day-to-day decisions or actions involved in caring for someone, it will not be

---

[146] *S v Plymouth City Council and C* [2002] EWCA (Civ 388) at para 49. See **2.82–2.83.**

appropriate or necessary to carry out a formal assessment of the person's capacity. Rather, it is sufficient for them to 'reasonably believe' that the person lacks capacity to make the decision or consent to the action in question.[147]

Similarly, s 4(9) confirms that, in cases where the court is not involved, carers (both professionals and family members) and others who are acting informally can only be expected to have reasonable grounds for believing that what they are doing or deciding is in the best interests of the person concerned, but they must still, so far as possible, apply the best interests checklist and therefore be able to point to objective reasons to justify why they hold that belief.

Section 4(9) also applies to donees and deputies appointed to make welfare or financial decisions as well as to those carrying out acts in connection with the care and treatment of a person lacking capacity. In deciding what is 'reasonable' in any particular case, higher expectations are likely to be placed on those appointed to act under formal powers and those acting in a professional capacity than on family members and friends who are caring for a person lacking capacity without any formal authority.

PART 3: GENERAL POWERS AND DUTIES

Acts in connection with care or treatment – background

The problem

2.113 Hitherto legislation has been silent about what actions could lawfully be taken by carers in looking after the day-to-day personal or healthcare needs of people who lack capacity to consent to those actions. These actions may include helping individuals to wash, dress and attend to their personal hygiene, feeding them, taking them out for walks and leisure activities or taking them to the doctor or dentist.

In consequence, doctors, dentists and other healthcare professionals have been hesitant about carrying out examinations, treatment or nursing care on patients unable to consent to those medical procedures. In the absence of any clear statutory provision, it was left to the courts to establish the common law 'principle of necessity', setting out the circumstances in which actions and decisions could lawfully be taken on behalf of adults who lack capacity.[148]

---

[147] See **2.67–2.68.**
[148] *Re F (Mental Patient: Sterilisation)* [1990] 2 AC 1 at 75.

2.114 The courts have confirmed that where the principle of necessity applied
(ie that it was necessary to act in relation to the well-being of a person
lacking capacity to consent), and the action taken was reasonable and in
the person's best interests, that action which would otherwise amount to
a civil wrong, or even a crime (eg of battery or assault) would in fact be
lawful. The principle of necessity is *not* equivalent to having consent
but may constitute a defence if an action is subsequently challenged.

Such actions might involve touching or interfering with the person's
bodily integrity, or using or interfering with the person's property or
possessions. In such cases, the lack of capacity of the people concerned
means that they cannot give their informed consent and therefore the
proposed actions, if they were to take place, could potentially be
unlawful unless the principle of necessity applied.

The Law Commission proposal

2.115 The Law Commission acknowledged that within the new jurisdiction it
proposed, there should remain scope for caring actions to take place,
and for some informal decision-making 'without certifications,
documentation or judicial determinations'.[149] However, the Commission
recognised that the common law 'principle of necessity' was not widely
understood and there was therefore a need to clarify the confused state
of the law governing such actions:[150]

> 'We suggested in our consultation papers that there was a strong case for
> clarifying in statute the circumstances in which decisions can be taken for
> people who lack capacity, but without anyone having to apply for formal
> authorisation. We did not envisage this as conferring any new power on
> anyone, but rather as a clarification of the uncertain "necessity" principle.
> Respondents gave an enthusiastic welcome to our provisional proposals.
> There was very broad agreement that a statutory provision would be
> invaluable in dispelling doubt and confusion and setting firm and
> appropriate limits to informal action.'

The general authority

2.116 The Law Commission proposed a new statutory authority, which it
called the 'general authority to act reasonably', to codify in statute what
has become practice under common law and to clarify the 'principle of
necessity'. It was intended that the general authority would provide
legal authorisation for acts connected with the personal welfare or
healthcare of a person lacking capacity if it is reasonable in the
particular circumstances for the act to be done by the person who does
it. The legal authorisation would apply to different people acting at
different times, so long as it was appropriate for them to do the act in

---

[149] Law Com No 231, para 4.1.
[150] Law Com No 231, para 4.2.

question and they were acting reasonably and in the best interests of the person lacking capacity.

The views of the Joint Committee

2.117 However, the clauses in the Draft Mental Incapacity Bill making provision for the 'general authority'[151] caused significant concerns and confusion to a number of witnesses giving evidence to the Joint Committee on the Bill:[152]

> 'A number of the concerns which have been brought to our attention seem to be premised on a misunderstanding of the general authority as it is set out in the draft Bill. The extent of the misunderstandings apparent in the evidence we have received suggests that the drafting of this provision is not sufficiently clear. Many interested parties appear to be under the erroneous impression that the general authority would be assumed by a single individual who would then take all decisions on behalf of an incapacitated individual. In fact the general authority is for the relevant person, in the context of a specific decision or action, at a particular point in time, so long as it is reasonable for that person to act. Others have suggested that the general authority may be used by carers to justify taking decisions for which they would otherwise need formal authorisation. In fact the general authority is not intended to convey any new powers on anyone but rather to clarify the uncertain principle of "necessity".

> We have come to the conclusion that the term "general authority" itself has contributed to the misinterpretations apparent within the evidence we have received. The word "authority" implies an imposition of decision making upon an incapacitated individual rather than an enabling process designed to enact decisions taken in their best interests. This may have contributed to perceptions of the general authority as likely to promote "over-paternalistic attitudes" towards incapacitated individuals. We are convinced that semantic issues are important in affecting public perceptions of the draft Bill as well as in determining legal interpretations of the provisions it contains.'

2.118 The Joint Committee recommended radical redrafting to clarify the legislative intent of the 'general authority' and the use of alternative terminology to avoid its misleading connotations. The Government's response was to recast the provisions to allow for a limitation of liability for people who need to act in connection with the care or treatment of a person lacking capacity. Offering protection from liability is intended to enable caring actions to take place in the absence of consent, but also to make clear that anyone acting unreasonably or not in the person's best interests would forfeit that protection.

---

[151] Draft Mental Incapacity Bill, cls 6–7.
[152] Joint Committee Report, Vol I, paras 109–110.

Acts in connection with care or treatment – the legislation

Protection from liability

2.119 Section 5 of the Act makes provision to allow carers (both informal carers, such as family members, and paid carers) and health and social care professionals to carry out certain acts in connection with the personal care, healthcare or treatment of a person lacking capacity. These provisions are intended to give legal backing, in the form of protection from liability, for actions which are essential for the personal welfare or health of people lacking capacity to consent to having things done to or for them. Such actions can be performed as if the person concerned had capacity and had given consent.[153] There is no need to obtain any formal powers or authority to act.

2.120 In introducing the Bill into the House of Commons, the Under Secretary of State for Constitutional Affairs, David Lammy explained:[154]

> 'Clause 5, entitled "Acts in connection with care and treatment", is an important clarification of the law surrounding what someone can do to or for a person lacking mental capacity who is unable to give consent. The current law is based on the poorly understood and obscure "doctrine of necessity". Hon. Members will know of constituents who are worried and uncertain about what they are allowed to do, because they do not understand the law. For example, a nurse may want to restrain someone who is having an epileptic fit. Someone caring for an elderly patient at home may need to help them to use the toilet. Someone whose daughter suffers from bipolar disease may want to go to her house to cook for her and to help her to eat because she is in too much distress.
>
> It is not right that people in such situations should have to rely on what seems to them to be an outdated and obscure legal concept. Clause 5 explains what they can do. It provides that one is protected from liability when the person cannot consent, provided that one takes reasonable steps to establish whether that person lacks mental capacity in relation to the matter in question, that one reasonably believes that the person lacks capacity in relation to the matter, and that what one does is in the person's best interests.'

Section 5 acts

2.121 The types of action which may be carried out with protection from liability under s 5 (referred to as 'section 5 acts') are those carried out *in connection with the care or treatment* of a person who is believed to lack capacity in relation to the matter in question, at the time the act

---

153 Mental Capacity Act 2005, s 5(2).
154 *Hansard*, HC Deb, col 29 (11 October 2004).

needs to be carried out. The Draft Code of Practice provides examples (but not an exhaustive list) as follows:[155]

> 'a) *Acts in connection with personal care –*
>
>> (i) acts of physical assistance such as washing, dressing, attending to personal hygiene, feeding, physically putting someone in a car (e.g. in order to take them to see their doctor)
>>
>> (ii) other assistance, such as doing the shopping, buying essential goods, arranging services required for the person's care
>>
>> (iii) clearing someone's house when they have moved into residential care, washing someone's clothes, taking their car to a garage to be repaired.
>
> b) *Acts in connection with health care and treatment –*
>
>> (i) diagnostic examinations and tests
>>
>> (ii) medical and dental treatment
>>
>> (iii) other healthcare procedures (such as the taking of a blood or other bodily samples, chiropody, physiotherapy)
>>
>> (iv) nursing care.'

Serious acts relating to medical treatment or welfare

2.122 In a briefing on the Mental Capacity Bill, the Making Decisions Alliance expressed concern that the scope of s 5 'remains unclear and is too wide'. It argued that the legislation should:[156]

> '… establish a clear hierarchy of safeguards which reflect the seriousness of the action taken and the consequences for that individual. The MDA recommends that some actions taken under section 5 require additional safeguards to counter against its inappropriate use. For example, we think it is important that a person has the support of an independent advocate when moving home which would involve a change of carer. Similarly, we think that there should be an independent second medical opinion, in relation to serious medical treatment.'

2.123 The Draft Code of Practice confirms that the current case-law requirement to seek a declaration from the court in cases where it is proposed to withdraw or withhold life-sustaining treatment from patients in a permanent vegetative state ('PVS') is unaffected by the Act, and is likely to be confirmed in a Practice Direction by the new President of the Court of Protection. Similarly the proposed non-therapeutic sterilisation of a person lacking capacity may well involve doubts as to the person's best interests and such cases should therefore continue to be referred to the court.[157]

---

[155] Draft Code of Practice, para 5.5.
[156] Making Decisions Alliance *Mental Capacity Bill: Briefing for 2nd Reading* (11 October 2004).
[157] Draft Code of Practice, para 5.23.

2.124 An additional safeguard is provided where serious medical treatment or a change of residence is proposed for a person lacking capacity, but *only* where the person concerned has no family or friends to speak up on his or her behalf. In such cases, the Act makes provision for an independent mental capacity advocate ('IMCA') to be appointed to support and represent the person.[158] In these and any other cases where there is a doubt or dispute about whether a particular section 5 act is in the person's best interests, and the matter cannot be resolved through negotiation or other means of dispute resolution, the Court of Protection has ultimate jurisdiction to resolve the matter.

Who can act in connection with care or treatment?

2.125 It is not intended that s 5 will apply to a single identifiable person involved in the care or treatment of a person lacking capacity, nor does it convey any powers on anyone to make substitute decisions or to give consent on behalf of the person lacking capacity. The intention is to allow carers and healthcare professionals to do whatever is necessary to safeguard and promote the welfare and health of individuals who lack capacity, so long as it is appropriate for the particular carer or professional to take the action in question and the act is in the best interests of the incapacitated person.

2.126 Before doing anything, the person wishing to take action in connection with the care or treatment of another person must take 'reasonable steps' to establish whether the person concerned has capacity in relation to the matter in question.[159] This does not necessarily require a formal assessment of capacity, although professional practice may require this, for example in respect of medical treatment. In any event, steps must be taken to look for objective reasons which would justify a belief of lack of capacity.[160] If it is found that the person has capacity, his or her consent to the action will be required to provide protection from liability.

2.127 Anyone proposing to carry out an act under s 5 must also take account of the Act's key principles set out in s 1.[161] This includes starting with the presumption of capacity and taking all practicable steps to enable the person to express a view about the proposed action. If it is believed the person lacks capacity, the 'least restrictive alternative' principle requires consideration of whether the act is needed at all and if so, whether the purpose for which the act is needed can be achieved in a

---

[158] Mental Capacity Act 2005, ss 35–41. See **CHAPTER 5**.
[159] Mental Capacity Act 2005, s 5(1)(a).
[160] See **2.67–2.68**.
[161] See **2.19–2.43**.

way less restrictive of the person's future choices or would allow him or her the most freedom.

2.128   In addition, the person wishing to act must 'reasonably believe' that what they are doing is in the best interests of the person lacking capacity.[162] Again, they must be able to point to objective reasons to justify that belief. They must be able to show that they have taken account of all relevant circumstances, including those set out in the best interests checklist.[163] If their judgment of best interests is challenged, they will be protected if they can show that it was reasonable in all the circumstances of that particular case for them to have arrived at that judgment. Where professionals are involved, their professional skills and levels of competence will be taken into account in determining what would be considered 'reasonable'.

No protection in cases of negligence

2.129   Professionals and other carers may have duties of care which, if breached, give rise to liability in the tort of negligence. Consent is not a defence to a claim of negligence. Similarly in relation to people who lack capacity to consent, s 5(3) clarifies that protection from liability does not extend to situations where the person taking the action has acted negligently, whether in carrying out the act or by failing to act in breach of duty. Therefore, there is no protection excluding a person's civil liability for any loss or damage, or his or her criminal liability, resulting from his or her negligence in carrying out or failing to do an act.

Effect on advance decisions to refuse treatment

2.130   In cases where an advance decision to refuse treatment is known to exist, is clear and unambiguous and is valid and applicable in the circumstances which have arisen, any health professionals who knowingly provide treatment contrary to the terms of the decision may be liable to legal action for battery or assault, or for breach of the patient's human rights.[164] The provisions of s 5 do not provide protection from liability in these circumstances, since s 5(4) specifically excludes the operation of advance decisions to refuse treatment.

---

[162]   Mental Capacity Act 2005, s 5(1)(b)(ii).
[163]   See **2.92–2.110**.
[164]   Mental Capacity Act 2005, ss 24–26. See also **CHAPTER 5**.

Limitations on permitted acts

2.131 Section 6 imposes two important limitations on the acts which can be carried out with protection from liability under s 5. The first relates to acts intended to restrain a person who lacks capacity and the second to situations where the act might conflict with a decision made by a donee of a lasting power of attorney or a deputy appointed by the court.

Restraint

2.132 As a general rule, any act that is intended to restrain a person lacking capacity will not attract protection from liability[165] and any carer or professional using restraint could be liable to legal action and will be personally accountable for their actions. In particular, no protection from liability is offered to people who use or threaten violence in order to carry out any action in connection with the care or treatment of a person lacking capacity or to force that person to comply with the carers' actions. However, the practicalities of caring for and providing protection for people who are unable to protect themselves are also recognised. The Act therefore permits the use of some form of restraint or physical intervention in limited circumstances in order to protect the person from harm.[166]

2.133 An individual restrains a person lacking capacity if he or she (a) uses, or threatens to use, force to secure the doing of an act which the person resists, or (b) restricts that person's liberty of movement, whether or not there is resistance.[167] Restraint may take many forms. It may be verbal or physical and may vary from shouting at someone, to holding them down, to locking them in a room. It may also include the prescribing of a sedative or other chemical restraint which restricts liberty of movement.

2.134 The Act permits restraint to be used where two conditions are satisfied:[168]

1. the person using it must reasonably believe that it is necessary to do the act in order to prevent harm to the person lacking capacity; and
2. the restraint used must be a proportionate response both to the likelihood of the person suffering harm and the seriousness of that harm.

The Act does not define 'harm', since this will vary according to individual circumstances. Similarly, what is likely to be a 'proportionate response' to harm, both in scale and nature, will depend on the

---

[165] Mental Capacity Act 2005, s 6(1).
[166] Mental Capacity Act 2005, s 6(2).
[167] Mental Capacity Act 2005, s 6(4).
[168] Mental Capacity Act 2005, s 6(2) and (3).

seriousness of the particular circumstances and the desired outcome. However, where there are objective reasons for believing that restraint is necessary to prevent the person from coming to any harm, only the minimum necessary force or intervention may be used and for the shortest possible duration.

2.135 These provisions attracted some criticism from the Joint Committee on Human Rights ('JCHR') in two of its reports on the human rights implications of the Mental Capacity Bill.[169] The Committee was concerned that use of these provisions could lead to deprivations of liberty which are not compatible with Art 5(1) of the European Convention, and in particular could lead to involuntary placement in hospital of a person lacking capacity and thereby deprive them of the procedural safeguards available if they had been detained under Mental Health Act powers:[170]

> 'Although clauses 5 and 6 contain important safeguards against the inappropriate use of restraint ... the combined effect of the two clauses appears to be to authorise (in the sense of protect against liability for) the use of force or the threat of force to overcome an incapacitated person's resistance in certain circumstances, or restrict their liberty of movement, in order to avert a risk of harm. For example, the power in clause 5 could be used to secure the admission into hospital of a person lacking capacity who is resisting such admission, where the person using or threatening force reasonably believes that the person lacks capacity in relation to his treatment, that it is in his best interests for him to be admitted to hospital for treatment and that it is necessary to admit the person in order to prevent harm to himself.
>
> We have written to the minister asking why the Government has not adopted the recommendation of the Joint Committee [on the Draft Mental Incapacity Bill] that the use or threat of force or other restriction of liberty of movement be expressly confined to emergency situations. Without such an express limitation on the face of the Bill, it appears to us that these provisions are likely to lead to deprivations of liberty which are not compatible with Article 5(1) ECHR, because they do not satisfy the Winterwerp requirements that deprivations of liberty be based on objective medical expertise and are necessary in the sense of being the least restrictive alternative. The Bill as drafted therefore does not appear to contain sufficient safeguards against arbitrary deprivation of liberty.'

2.136 The response from the Under Secretary of State, Baroness Ashton, confirmed that 'It has never been the Government's policy that acts in connection with care and treatment in clause 5 might amount to a deprivation of liberty'.[171] The Government therefore moved a series of

---

[169] JCHR, Twenty-third Report of Session 2003–04 *Scrutiny of Bills: Final Progress Report* (HL Paper 210, HC 1282) Part 2; JCHR, Fourth Report of Session 2004–05 *Scrutiny: First Progress Report* (HL Paper 26, HC 224) Part 4.

[170] JCHR, Twenty-third Report of Session 2003–04, paras 2.22–2.23. See also **CHAPTER 5**.

[171] JCHR, Fourth Report of Session 2004–05, Appendix 4, para 11.

amendments in the House of Lords to address the Committee's concerns:[172]

> 'The committee wanted the Bill to confirm expressly that that actions amounting to deprivation of liberty do not fall within the definition of "restraint" used in the Bill. The amendments achieve this ... This means that no-one acting in connection with care or treatment under Clause 5, nor an attorney or deputy, may deprive a person who lacks capacity of his liberty. "Restraint" includes only restrictions of liberty.'

Section 6(5) expressly confirms that someone carrying out an act under s 5 will do more than 'merely restrain' a person lacking capacity if he or she deprives that person of liberty within the meaning of Art 5(1). This section applies not only to public authorities covered by the Human Rights Act 1998 but to anyone carrying out acts in connection with care or treatment under s 5.

2.137 There is clearly a fine line to be drawn between *restriction* of liberty, permitted under the definition of restraint, and *deprivation* of liberty under Art 5(1). This was considered by the European Court of Human Rights in *HL v UK* (the so-called *Bournewood* case) which said:[173]

> '... in order to determine whether there has been a deprivation of liberty, the starting point must be the specific situation of the individual concerned and account must be taken of a whole range of factors arising in the particular case such as the type, duration, effects and manner of implementation of the measure in question. The distinction between a deprivation of, and restriction upon, liberty is merely one of degree or intensity and not one of nature or substance ...
>
> ... the Court considers the key factor in the present case to be that the health care professionals treating and managing the applicant exercised complete and effective control over his care and movements ...'

The interface between the Act and mental health legislation, and the safeguards to be introduced in response to the European Court judgment, is considered in more detail in **CHAPTER 5**.

Decisions of donees or deputies

2.138 The provisions of s 5 provide protection from liability to carers and professionals in circumstances where no formal decision-making powers are required. However, where formal powers already exist, for example under a lasting power of attorney or through an order made by the Court of Protection, these formal decision-making powers will take precedence. Thus, s 6(6) confirms that the provisions of s 5 do not authorise a person to do an act which conflicts with a decision made by a donee of a lasting power of attorney previously granted by the person

---

[172] *Hansard*, HL Deb, col 1468 (17 March 2005).

[173] *HL v The United Kingdom* (Application No 45508/99). Judgment 5 October 2004, paras 89 and 91.

lacking capacity, or by a deputy appointed by the Court, so long as the donee or deputy is acting within the scope of their authority. Anyone acting contrary to a decision of a donee or deputy will not have protection from liability.

2.139 In cases of dispute, for example when carers or health professionals feel that a donee or deputy is acting outside the scope of his or her authority, or contrary to the incapacitated person's best interests, an application may be made for permission to apply to the Court of Protection to resolve the matter. Where the dispute involves serious healthcare decisions, s 6(7) clarifies that life-sustaining treatment, or treatment necessary to prevent a serious deterioration in the person's condition, can be given pending a ruling from the court.[174]

Paying for goods, services and other expenditure

Current law

2.140 The current law already makes provision for the enforceability of contracts, including contracts to purchase goods, which are made 'with' a person who lacks capacity or whose mental capacity is in doubt. In such cases, the courts have had to counterbalance two important policy considerations. One is a duty to protect those who are incapable of looking after themselves, and the other is to ensure that other people are not prejudiced by the actions of persons who appear to have full capacity. So, people without capacity are bound by the terms of a contract they have entered into, even if it was unfair, unless it can be shown that the other party to the contract was aware of their mental incapacity or should have been aware of this.[175] If the other party knows, or must be taken to have known of the lack of capacity, the contract is voidable.

The Sale of Goods Act 1979 ('the 1979 Act') modified this rule when applied to contracts for 'necessaries'. A person without mental capacity who agrees to pay for goods which are necessaries is legally obliged to pay a reasonable price for them. Although the 1979 Act applies to goods, similar common law rules are believed to apply to essential services.

The new jurisdiction

2.141 These rules are now brought together and given statutory force under s 7 of the Act. This clarifies that the obligation to pay a reasonable price applies to both the supply of necessary goods and the provision of

---

[174] Issues around life-sustaining treatment are dealt with in **CHAPTER 5**.
[175] *Imperial Loan Company v Stone* [1892] 1 QB 599.

necessary services to a person without capacity to contract for them, and it is the person who lacks capacity who must pay.

2.142 The definition of 'necessary' set out in s 7(2) is based on that in the 1979 Act,[176] meaning goods and services which are suitable to the person's condition in life (ie his or her place in society, rather than any mental or physical condition) and his or her actual requirements at the time of sale and delivery (eg ordinary drink, food and clothing or the provision of domiciliary or residential care services).

2.143 During parliamentary debate of these provisions, Lord Goodhart put forward some probing amendments to try to protect people with impaired capacity from entering into contracts which may be disadvantageous to them, for example through abusive doorstep selling:[177]

> 'These amendments have been proposed by the CAB [Citizens Advice Bureau] which is concerned with the number of cases in which businesses have entered into contracts with people who lack capacity, and those contracts were unduly disadvantageous to those people. At present under English law, though not under the law of Scotland, a contract entered into by a person lacking capacity can be set aside only if the other party to that contract was aware of the incapacity. The CAB amendment alters this, and it wants to apply to England the rule in Scotland which is that a contract can be set aside on grounds of incapacity even if the other party was not aware of the incapacity.'

The amendments were resisted by the Government on the ground that they may have unintended consequences, either by disempowering people with impaired capacity with whom traders may be reluctant to contract, or by allowing the possibility of abuse by people claiming incapacity in order to avoid being bound by a contract. However, the Minister committed the Government to further work during implementation of the Act to ensure that 'policy development ... on consumer strategy, credit and indebtedness is sensitive to the needs of consumers who lack capacity'.[178]

Responsibility to pay for necessary goods and services

2.144 The Act therefore confirms that the legal responsibility for paying for necessary goods and services lies with the person for whom they are supplied even though that person lacks the capacity to contract for them. The obligation is to pay 'a reasonable price' for them[179] so this

---

[176] Sale of Goods Act 1979, s 3(3).
[177] *Hansard*, HL Deb, col 1396 (27 January 2005). See also HL Deb, cols 1469–1472 (17 March 2005).
[178] *Hansard*, HL Deb, col 1472 (17 March 2005).
[179] Mental Capacity Act 2005, s 7(1).

provision cannot be used to enforce a contract which involves gross over-charging for goods or services.

2.145 Where the person also lacks the capacity to arrange for payment to be made, the carer who has arranged for the goods and services may also have to arrange settlement of the bill. The Law Commission described the problem as follows:[180]

> 'We are not here concerned with ways in which a person may gain access to another person's income or assets. Where assets are held by a bank or other institution, specific authority will certainly be required before they can be transferred to anyone other than the legal owner. We are concerned, rather, with the situation where a carer arranges for something which will cost money to be done for a person without capacity. Family members often arrange for milk to be delivered, or for a hairdresser, gardener or chiropodist to call. More costly arrangements might be roof repairs, or for an excursion or holiday. In many cases it may be reasonable for a family member to arrange such matters, if it is done in the best interests of the person without capacity. Such actions could therefore fall within the confines of the general authority to provide for the person's welfare and care recommended above. Who, however, is to pay the provider of the goods or services supplied?'

2.146 Where it is appropriate for carers to arrange such matters, and so long as the arrangements made are in the best interests of the person lacking capacity, the carers' actions are therefore likely to be considered 'acts in connection with care or treatment' under s 5, providing them with some protection from liability if their actions were to be challenged. However, some further arrangements may need to be made to meet the costs involved or to pay the provider of the goods or services supplied.

Expenditure

2.147 In such cases where necessary goods or services must be paid for, provision is made under s 8 to meet the expenditure involved. This may be done in any one of three ways, described in the Draft Code of Practice as follows (with footnotes added):

> '● If neither the person lacking capacity nor the carer who has arranged for the goods or services can produce the necessary funds, then the carer may promise that the person who may lack capacity will pay (i.e. the carer may pledge the credit of the person who lacks capacity).[181] Of course, it may be that a supplier will not be happy with such a promise, in which case formal steps will be required.

---

[180] Law Com No 231, para 4.7.
[181] Mental Capacity Act 2005, s 8(1)(a).

- If the person lacking capacity has cash in his/her possession, then the carer may use that money to pay for goods or services[182] (e.g. to pay the milkman or the hairdresser).

- The carer may choose to pay for the goods or services with his/her own money and is then entitled to be reimbursed or otherwise indemnified from the money of the person lacking capacity.[183] Again this may involve using cash in the person's possession or running up an IOU. Formal steps would be required before a carer could gain access to any money held by a third party such as a bank or building society.'[184]

2.148 The intention of these provisions is to make it possible for ordinary but necessary goods and services to be provided for people who lack the capacity to organise and pay for them, but without requiring carers to invoke expensive and time-consuming court proceedings to obtain authority to do so. However, s 8 does not give any authorisation to a carer to gain access to the incapacitated person's income or assets or to sell the person's property. A distinction is drawn between the use of available cash already in the possession of the person lacking capacity, on the one hand, and the removal of money from a bank account or selling valuable items of property, on the other. Where a carer has promised that the person lacking capacity will pay for the goods or services supplied (ie has pledged the person's credit), formal authority may then need to be obtained before that promise can be put into effect. Similarly, formal arrangements may need to be made before a carer can be reimbursed if a large amount of expenditure is involved.

2.149 Some carers may already have such formal authority, for example under a lasting power of attorney, as a deputy appointed by the Court of Protection or as a social security 'appointee'. Section 8(3) makes clear that these arrangements are not affected or changed by the above provisions allowing carers to arrange and pay for necessary goods and services on behalf a person lacking capacity to make their own arrangements. However, as confirmed by s 6(6), an informal carer cannot make arrangements for goods or services to be provided for someone lacking capacity if this conflicts with a decision made by a donee or deputy.

---

[182] Mental Capacity Act 2005, s 8(1)(b).
[183] Mental Capacity Act 2005, s 8(2).
[184] Draft Code of Practice, para 5.37.

Excluded decisions

Background

2.150 The Law Commission recognised the need to place some restrictions on carers and others acting under its proposed 'general authority' (now section 5 acts) without the need to apply for formal powers:[185]

> 'One benefit of setting out a clear general authority in statute is that the statute can then specify which matters fall outside the scope of that general authority. The general law already provides that certain acts can only be effected by a person acting for himself or herself. Examples would be entering into marriage or casting a vote in a public election. For the avoidance of doubt, our draft Bill lists certain matters which must be done by a person acting for him or herself ... In many areas, however, it is at present quite unclear whether action may be lawfully taken on behalf of a person without capacity. If no-one is sure what can lawfully be done, then no-one can be sure what must and must not be done.'

The legislation

2.151 The Act therefore seeks to make clear what can and cannot be done by someone else in relation to a person lacking capacity. There are certain acts which cannot be done and certain decisions which can never be made on behalf of a person who lacks capacity to consent to those actions or to make those decisions for him or herself, either because they are so personal to the individual concerned or because they are governed by other legislation. In ss 27–29, the Act lists those specific decisions which are excluded and cannot be made under the Act, whether by a carer or professional acting under s 5, a donee under a lasting power of attorney, a deputy or by the Court of Protection itself.

Family relationships, etc

2.152 Section 27 excludes the following decisions on family relationships from being taken on behalf of a person lacking capacity to make the decision:

> '(a) consenting to marriage or civil partnership,
>
> (b) consenting to have sexual relationships,
>
> (c) consenting to a decree of divorce being granted on the basis of two years' separation,
>
> (d) consenting to a dissolution order being made in relation to a civil partnership on the basis of two years' separation,
>
> (e) consenting to a child's being placed for adoption by an adoption agency,
>
> (f) consenting to the making of an adoption order,

---

[185] Law Com No 231, para 4.29.

    (g) discharging parental responsibilities in matters not relating to a child's property,

    (h) giving a consent under the Human Fertilisation and Embryology Act 1990.'

2.153 Where a person lacking capacity becomes involved in divorce or dissolution proceedings on any basis other than two years' separation, or where someone loses capacity during the course of such proceedings, a next friend or guardian ad litem will be appointed under the Family Proceedings Rules 1991 to give instructions and otherwise act on their behalf in relation to the proceedings.[186] In relation to adoption, if the birth parent lacks capacity to consent to an adoption order, the rules relating to dispensing with consent in adoption legislation will apply.[187] Matters concerned with the discharging of parental responsibilities not related to a child's property will be dealt with under the Children Act 1989.

Mental Health Act matters

2.154 Section 28 states that the Act's decision-making powers cannot be used to give or to consent to treatment for mental disorder if the treatment is regulated by Part IV of the Mental Health Act 1983 ('the 1983 Act'). The purpose of Part IV is to clarify the extent to which treatment for mental disorder can be imposed on detained patients in hospital and to provide specific statutory safeguards concerning the provision of treatment without consent.[188] Section 28 ensures that where a person lacking capacity to consent to treatment has been detained in hospital under the 1983 Act, the powers available under Part IV would 'trump' the decision-making powers under the Mental Capacity Act 2005 in relation to treatment for mental disorder.

This means that the safeguards and procedures of the 1983 Act (or future mental health legislation) relating to treatment for the person's mental disorder cannot be avoided by reference to s 5 or to the consent of a donee or deputy. However, for all other decisions affecting that person, the principles and provisions of the Mental Capacity Act 2005 would apply.

2.155 During the two pre-legislative scrutiny exercises carried out – on the draft Mental Incapacity Bill in 2003 and on the draft Mental Health Bill in 2004–05, both Joint Committees expressed concern about the interrelation between the two pieces of legislation and the potential for overlap and confusion between them.[189] These concerns were also raised

---

[186] Family Proceedings Rules 1991, Part IX.
[187] Adoption and Children Act 2002, s 52.
[188] Mental Health Act 1983, ss 57–58.
[189] Joint Committee on the Draft Mental Incapacity Bill, Vol I (HL Paper 189-I, HC 1083-I)

frequently during the parliamentary debates on the Mental Capacity Bill. Of particular concern were the need to:

1. provide appropriate safeguards in relation to the treatment of adults lacking capacity who are compliant with their care and treatment as required by the European Court judgment in *HL v UK*;

2. ensure that health professionals are clear about which law should be used to provide treatment for serious mental disorder for those lacking capacity to consent.

These matters are considered further in **CHAPTER 5**.

Voting rights

2.156 The final category of excluded decisions concerns voting rights. Section 29 confirms that no one can make a decision on voting or cast a vote at an election or a referendum on behalf of a person lacking capacity to vote.

Ill-treatment or neglect

Background

2.157 The Act creates a number of ways in which someone can acquire powers over another person who lacks some decision-making capacity. For this reason the Law Commission concluded that:[190]

> 'It is right that a person with such powers should be subject to criminal sanction for ill-treating or wilfully neglecting the other person concerned.'

The Government was not at first 'persuaded that the creation of a new offence would be the best way of tackling abuse'.[191] However, a number of high-profile cases concerning abuse and ill-treatment of vulnerable people resulted in such an offence being included in the Draft Mental Incapacity Bill. This proposed the creation of an offence of ill-treatment or neglect with a maximum penalty of 2 years' imprisonment.[192]

2.158 The original impetus for the creation of a specific offence was the *Longcare* case, in which more than 50 adults with learning difficulties were abused at two care homes in South Buckinghamshire between 1983 and 1993. Despite the severity of abuse (which included rape, assault, over-sedation, starvation and neglect over a period of 10 years) existing law meant those responsible only received light sentences. The *Independent Longcare Inquiry*, the report of which was published in

---

Chapter 12; Joint Committee on the Draft Mental Health Bill, Vol I (HL Paper 79-I, HC 95-I) Chapter 4.

[190] Law Com No 231, para 4.38.

[191] Lord Chancellor's Department *Making Decisions* (Cm 4465) (TSO, 1999) para 1.37.

[192] Draft Mental Incapacity Bill, cl 31.

1998,[193] recommended that the Government introduce a new, arrestable offence of harming or exploiting a vulnerable adult, with a maximum penalty of 10 years in prison. Lack of action in implementing any changes led to a campaign called 'Justice for Survivors' launched in 2003 by the journal *Disability Now*[194] and supported by leading disability organisations and charities.

The new offence

2.159 Section 44 of the Act addresses some of these concerns by creating a new offence. The penalty will vary according to the seriousness of the offence, ranging from a fine to a term of imprisonment, but the maximum penalty has been increased to 5 years' imprisonment.[195] This has the effect of making it an 'arrestable offence' under s 2 of the Police and Criminal Evidence Act 1984. It also reflects the potential severity of the crime, with sentences in parallel with those for serious assaults on individuals, including the offences of inflicting grievous bodily harm and assault occasioning actual bodily harm under the Offences Against the Person Act 1861, which both carry maximum sentences of 5 years.

Scope of the offence

2.160 The new offence will have a wide application to 'anyone who has the care of' a person lacking, or reasonably believed to lack, capacity.[196] This will include not only family carers, but also health and social care staff in hospital or care homes or providing domiciliary care. It will also apply to donees of a lasting power of attorney or attorneys of an enduring power of attorney made by the person lacking capacity[197] and to any deputy appointed by the Court of Protection for that person.[198] No lower age limit is specified, so the offence will also apply to the ill-treatment or wilful neglect of children under 16 whose lack of capacity is caused by an impairment of, or disturbance in the functioning of, the mind or brain, not solely by the immaturity of youth.

2.161 During the parliamentary stages, amendments were put aimed at extending the application of the new offence to appointees, appointed by the Department of Work and Pensions ('DWP') to collect and manage social security benefits on behalf of claimants unable to do so for themselves. The Minister clarified that:[199]

---

[193] Tom Burgner *Independent Longcare Inquiry* (Buckingham County Council, 1998).
[194] See www.disabilitynow.org.uk/campaigns/justice/justice_invest_200312.htm.
[195] Mental Capacity Act 2005, s 44(3)(b).
[196] Mental Capacity Act 2005, s 44(1)(a).
[197] Mental Capacity Act 2005, s 44(1)(b).
[198] Mental Capacity Act 2005, s 44(1)(c).
[199] *Hansard*, HL Deb, col 746 (8 February 2005).

'... it is clear that noble Lords are still concerned that because DWP appointees are handling only financial matters they might not be considered as having "care of the person" and, as such, would fall outside the scope of the offence. Again, we made clear during the Report stage in the other place that, in the majority of cases, the appointee will have care of the person and will therefore be covered by the offence.'

The Minister also confirmed that DWP officials were considering ways of introducing more effective monitoring of appointees.

Ill-treatment

2.162   A single act is sufficient to show ill-treatment.[200] For a conviction of ill-treatment, it is necessary to show deliberate conduct by the accused which could properly be described as ill-treatment, whether or not it had caused or was likely to cause harm. The accused must either realise that he or she is inexcusably ill-treating the other person, or be reckless as to whether he or she is doing so.[201]

Wilful neglect

2.163   Ill-treatment and neglect are separate offences.[202] In the context of the offence of wilfully neglecting a child in a manner likely to cause unnecessary suffering or injury to health under s 1 of the Children and Young Persons Act 1933, it has been held that neglect cannot be described as *wilful* unless the person either had directed his or her mind to whether there was some risk (although it might fall far short of a probability) that the child's health might suffer from the neglect and had made a conscious decision to refrain from acting, or had so refrained because he or she did not care whether the child might be at risk or not.[203] Similar considerations are likely to apply in cases of wilful neglect of an adult lacking capacity.

---

[200]   *R v Holmes* [1979] Crim LR 52.

[201]   *R v Newington* (1990) 91 Cr App R 247, CA.

[202]   *R v Newington* (1990) 91 Cr App R 247, CA.

[203]   *R v Sheppard* [1981] AC 394, [1980] 3 All ER 899, HL.

Chapter 3

Lasting Powers of Attorney

BACKGROUND

Powers of attorney

3.1   A power of attorney is simply a formal arrangement, undertaken by deed, whereby one person ('the donor') gives to another person ('the attorney' or 'the donee') authority to act in his or her name and on his or her behalf. A power of attorney is a form of agency which has been recognised at common law and used for centuries to enable the affairs of the donor to be conducted on his or her behalf by an attorney while the donor is away on business, overseas or physically unwell.

Common law principles of agency apply to powers of attorney, although the law relating to powers of attorney has been developed by statute, beginning with the Powers of Attorney Act 1971.[1] This short statute confirmed that powers of attorney must be by deed[2] and provided for the protection of the donee and a third person where they act in good faith without knowledge of revocation of the power.[3]

3.2   Notwithstanding the introduction of statutory rules governing their operation, common law principles concerning the creation, operation and revocation continued to apply, and in particular the principle that a power of attorney is revoked by the supervening incapacity of the donor. The rationale behind this principle is quite straightforward. An act carried out by an attorney is treated as an act carried out by the donor. The attorney can only do what the donor can give authority for him to do and if the donor lacks capacity then he or she cannot give that authority. The attorney and any third party dealing with the attorney can therefore assume, in the absence of any evidence to the contrary, that the donor is able to know and approve of what is being done on his or her behalf.

---

[1]   This implemented the recommendations of the Law Commission's report *Powers of Attorney (1970)* Law Com No 30.

[2]   Law of Property (Miscellaneous Provisions) Act 1989, s 1.

[3]   Powers of Attorney Act 1971, ss 1 and 5.

Limitations

3.3   Any power of attorney has to be understood in the context of the
        common law principles of agency and their limitations. A power of
        attorney confers rights on the attorney as well as responsibilities. And
        while an attorney may, if authorised, do anything that can lawfully be
        done by the donor, this is not an open-ended right to deal with the
        donor's property as he or she wishes. In particular:

- an attorney owes a fiduciary duty to the donor and cannot act so as
  to benefit him or herself or any other person to the detriment of the
  donor or his or her estate. The attorney must act in good faith, keep
  accounts and disclose any conflict;
- an attorney contracts in the name of the donor and while not
  personally liable under the contract, any property acquired or
  money held as attorney should be kept in the donor's name and
  must be kept separate from the attorney's own estate;[4]
- an attorney owes a duty of skill and care commensurate with the
  degree of expertise offered by him or her and whether he or she is
  acting gratuitously or for reward;[5]
- an attorney owes a duty of confidentiality to the donor and cannot
  disclose information unless authorised or to the extent required by
  the agency. This duty survives the operation of the power;
- an attorney cannot generally delegate his or her authority to another
  person;[6]
- an attorney is chosen to exercise personal skill and cannot appoint a
  successor in the same way as a trustee can appoint a new or
  replacement trustee;
- a power of attorney may be revoked by the donor by a deed or other
  act inconsistent with the continued operation of the power, which
  must include the giving of notice to the attorney;[7]
- the authority of the attorney is revoked by the death, incapacity or
  bankruptcy of the attorney;
- the attorney may disclaim the power at any time;
- the attorney may only do such things as may lawfully be done by an
  attorney. Thus an attorney cannot perform an act which can only be
  performed personally, such as swearing an affidavit[8] or executing a

---

[4]   If the attorney holds property of the donor then he holds it as trustee. See *Henry v
      Hammond* [1913] 2 KB 515.

[5]   See, eg, *Chaudhry v Prabhakar* [1988] 3 All ER 718.

[6]   Delegation may be permitted if authorised by the instrument or by statute, if it is purely
      administrative, it is usual practice in the business of the donor or the attorney or if it is due
      to necessity. For example directors of a company may delegate powers to an attorney or
      agent who may in turn delegate all or any of his powers (Art 71 of Table A).

[7]   Thus the creation of a new power does not operate to revoke an earlier one, in contrast to a
      Will under Wills Act 1837, s 20.

[8]   *Clauss v Pir* [1988] 1 Ch 267.

Will.[9] Neither can an attorney perform an act arising by virtue of the donor's office[10] or which is of a personal nature;[11]

- statute further limits an attorney's authority to conduct legal proceedings in the name of the donor;[12]
- a power of attorney is revoked by the incapacity of the donor.[13]

The incapable donor

3.4 It is the last limitation that has been regarded as having the largest impact for most people. The existing law was adequate for businessmen or families going abroad leaving a relative or solicitor to manage their property. It would also help where a donor was physically unable to manage his or her affairs. But it was of no assistance in the increasingly frequent cases where a person was incapable and had property and affairs that required administration. There were two approaches to that situation. Either the person's affairs were neglected or dealt with under a potentially invalid power of attorney or the Court of Protection would appoint a receiver to manage that person's property and affairs.[14]

3.5 The traditional power of the Court to appoint a receiver was reviewed by the Law Commission in its report *The Incapacitated Principal* (1983).[15] This drew attention to the fact that the slow and bureaucratic jurisdiction of the Court of Protection and the Public Trust Office might not be necessary or appropriate in every situation where an incapable person's property and affairs needed to be administered. Surely if a person could plan ahead and choose who would administer their property and affairs in the event of their incapacity, that person should be allowed to do just that without having to undergo a formal judicial process. In such cases a loving spouse or mature and sensible children could look after the affairs of the incapable person without having to go to the expense and indignity of accounting for their conduct. It was also assumed that the existing judicial and administrative framework would not be able to cope with the increasing demands placed upon it by an ageing population.

---

[9] Wills Act 1837, s 9.

[10] The attorney of a judge cannot pass a sentence or the attorney of a bishop ordain a priest.

[11] Thus an attorney cannot, for instance, sit an exam, drive a car, marry or vote on behalf of the donor. These last two circumstances are specifically excluded from the scope of an attorney's authority under a Lasting Power of Attorney by ss 27 and 29 of the Mental Capacity Act 2005.

[12] See *Gregory v Turner* [2003] EWCA Civ 83.

[13] See *Drew v Nunn* (1879) 4 QBD 661, CA; *Yonge v Toynbee* [1910] 1 KB 215, CA.

[14] First under the Mental Health Act 1959 and then under the Mental Health Act 1983.

[15] Law Com No 122.

Statutory powers of attorney

Enduring Powers of Attorney

3.6   In response to the Law Commission report *The Incapacitated Principal*,
        Parliament enacted the Enduring Powers of Attorney Act 1985 ('the
        1985 Act') which came into force on 10 March 1986.[16] This created a
        new type of power of attorney, Enduring Powers of Attorney ('EPAs'),
        which would function in the same way as a conventional power of
        attorney but which, subject to a basic registration process, would
        continue or 'endure' beyond the onset of incapacity.[17]

        The 1985 Act also provided some practical extension to the attorney's
        authority under a conventional power of attorney. Thus an attorney
        would be able to make gifts or provide for the needs of someone the
        donor might be expected to provide for.[18] Thus a husband looking after
        an incapable wife would be able to make gifts at Christmas to
        grandchildren on behalf of his wife and an attorney could use the
        donor's estate to maintain a disabled child or pay a grandchild's school
        fees.[19]

3.7   The 1985 Act further provided a number of safeguards for the
        protection of donors of EPAs and placed the EPA jurisdiction under the
        authority of the Court of Protection. However, such safeguards were the
        result of a compromise between two competing objectives: on the one
        hand, individuals should be able to entrust their affairs to someone with
        as little interference from the state as possible while, on the other, the
        vulnerable would need protection from the unscrupulous as well as the
        inefficient. Any system of protection would also have to be simple to
        operate, cost effective and largely self-financing.

        The result of this tension was a simple system of protection which
        would operate on two levels. On the first level, there would be the
        administrative process of registration which would involve the donor
        and his or her next of kin being notified of an intention to register the
        EPA and having an opportunity to object. The onus would be on the
        donor and his or her family to alert the Court of Protection in the event
        of misuse. On the second level, the civil law would apply to acts carried
        out by an attorney who was acting beyond the scope of his or her
        authority, particularly if the donor were incapable and the power was
        not registered. Acts carried out by an attorney would be invalid and
        provide the donor or his or her estate with a form of redress.[20]

---

[16]   Enduring Powers of Attorney Act 1985 (Commencement Order) 1986, SI 1986/125.
[17]   Enduring Powers of Attorney Act 1985, s 1(1)(a).
[18]   Enduring Powers of Attorney Act 1985, s 3(4), (5).
[19]   *Re Cameron* [1999] Ch 386, [1999] 2 All ER 924, [1999] 3 WLR 394, [1999] 16.
[20]   Although a Scottish case and not directly involving EPAs, this principle was applied in

3.8   The level of protection offered by an EPA, reflecting two opposing ideals, remains an imperfect compromise.[21] The 1985 Act provides the following safeguards:

- The power of attorney must be in a prescribed form[22] and must be executed by the donor and attorney and attorneys.
- The prescribed form contains a brief explanation of the nature and effect of the power.
- The attorney or attorneys must register the EPA with the Court of Protection when they believe that the donor is or is becoming mentally incapable of managing their property and affairs.[23]
- Before applying for registration the attorney or attorneys must notify the donor of their intention and also at least three relatives in a prescribed order of classes of relatives.[24] All the members of a class must be notified, even if there are more than three persons, so that if a donor has one child, one sibling and six grandchildren all eight relatives must be notified.
- The donor must be given notice personally of the intention to register.[25]
- All notices must be served within 14 days of each other and an application to register must be made within 10 days after the service of the last notice.[26]
- Any notices must be in a prescribed form and provide the recipient with details of the applicant and the grounds on which an objection can be made.
- Any person notified of an application to register an EPA, and any other person at any other time (with the leave of the Court) may apply to the Court to refuse registration or to revoke the EPA.
- The Court shall refuse to register a power or cancel the registration of a power if satisfied that the donor has revoked the power, the donor remains capable, the donor has died or become bankrupt, that fraud or undue influence was used to create the power or 'having regard to all the circumstances and in particular the attorney's relationship or connection with the donor, the attorney is unsuitable to be the donor's attorney'.[27]
- The Court of Protection has powers to intervene generally on behalf of the incapable or potentially incapable donor of the EPA. Thus the

---

McDowall v Inland Revenue [2003] UKSC SPC00382 (26 June 2003). Ironically the beneficiary of this case was not the donor's estate but the Inland Revenue.

[21]   Problems with the EPA jurisdiction are considered in more detail at **3.11**.

[22]   Enduring Powers of Attorney Act 1985, s 2(1)(a).

[23]   Enduring Powers of Attorney Act 1985, s 4(1).

[24]   Enduring Powers of Attorney Act 1985, Sch 1, para 2(1).

[25]   Enduring Powers of Attorney Act 1985, Sch 1, para 4(1) and Court of Protection (Enduring Power of Attorney) Rules 2001, SI 2001/825, r 15(1).

[26]   Court of Protection (Enduring Power of Attorney) Rules 2001, SI 2001/825, rr 6(1) and 7.

[27]   Enduring Powers of Attorney Act 1985, ss 6(5) and 8(4).

Court may exercise its powers to determine whether the EPA is effective,[28] give directions as to the management of the donor's affairs and the rendering of accounts or the making of gifts.[29] In addition the Court retains its powers under Mental Health Act 1983 ('the 1983 Act') to intervene in the affairs of an incapable person so that there is an overlap between the two jurisdictions and rules of procedure enacted pursuant to the 1983 Act apply to proceedings under the 1985 Act.[30]

Success of enduring powers

3.9   That the EPA has filled a legal and social need is evident from the substantial number of EPAs in place. Because EPAs are often made for use prior to the onset of incapacity or as an insurance against incapacity, there is no reliable method of knowing how many EPAs have been created. Those that can be measured are those which are registered with the Court of Protection and the number of registrations has increased steadily each year since the first such powers were registered in 1986. In 2004, 16,314 EPAs were registered.[31]

3.10   While the number of registered EPAs has increased, the number of incapable persons whose affairs are subject to the traditional jurisdiction of the Court of Protection has remained stable, at around 30,000. Thus without the introduction of EPAs, it would not have been possible for the existing judicial and administrative system to manage without a significant increase in resources.

There is no doubt that EPAs have, by the measure of their popularity alone, proved useful. They are seen as simple documents and therefore inexpensive to create.[32] The registration process is also easy to operate, with registration forms available from the Public Guardianship Office and a one-off fee of £120 payable on registration.[33]

Problems with enduring powers

3.11   Despite the widespread acceptance and use of EPAs, the jurisdiction has several drawbacks, principally:

- An EPA relates only to the property and affairs of the donor and the attorney has no authority over the personal welfare of the incapable

---

[28]   Enduring Powers of Attorney Act 1985, ss 5 and 8.

[29]   Enduring Powers of Attorney Act 1985, s 8(2).

[30]   Enduring Powers of Attorney Act 1985, s 10.

[31]   National Audit Office *Protecting and promoting the financial affairs of people who lose capacity* (HC 27 Session 2005–2006).

[32]   The prescribed form is readily available and may be downloaded from the Public Guardianship Office website.

[33]   Court of Protection (Enduring Power of Attorney) (Amendment) Rules 2005, SI 2005/668.

donor, covering matters such as where the donor should live, what care he or she should receive or whether a particular treatment can be given or withheld. This is despite the fact that an attorney acting in the best interests of the incapable donor needs to take account of the welfare of the donor. The donor's estate cannot, in practice, be dealt with in isolation from the actual needs of the donor.

- The EPA jurisdiction rests on the principle that the donor's autonomy and right to choose the person to manage his or her affairs needs to be respected, so that the attorney can operate with as little official intervention as possible. This avoids the point of such official intervention, which is to protect the incapable person who is by the nature of his or her situation, vulnerable and at risk from abuse. The Master of the Court of Protection has estimated that financial abuse takes place in about 10–15 per cent of cases.[34] This substantial proportion includes not just cases of actual fraud but also cases of misuse where, for instance, an attorney is acting beyond the scope of his or her authority, and may be overly optimistic in view of the extent to which unregistered EPAs are used beyond the onset of incapacity. An attorney might therefore dispose of an asset belonging to an incapable donor using an unregistered EPA or make gifts which are beyond the scope of his or her authority as an attorney.

- That fraud or misuse takes place so extensively is due to the very limited degree of official supervision provided. There is no means of knowing that a particular EPA is being used, let alone that it is being used correctly. The Court of Protection relies on misuse being notified to it, but this in turn presupposes that an attorney who registers an EPA correctly notifies relatives and they in turn file an objection with the Court of Protection. In one recent instance the manager of a nursing home was attorney for several residents and systematically defrauded them of their savings over several months. The residents had no relatives and, in any event, the EPAs were not registered. Although subsequently the Court of Protection revoked the EPA, the civil and criminal laws offered little recompense. Recovery of the stolen assets was impossible as these had been dissipated and a criminal prosecution was made difficult by the fact that the witnesses could not give evidence for themselves.[35] The

---

[34] This bold assertion was first made by Denzil Lush in 'Taking Liberties: Enduring Powers of Attorney and financial abuse' *Solicitors Journal* (11 September 1998) 808 but has been restated by Denzil Lush in *Cretney & Lush on Enduring Powers of Attorney* (Jordans, 5th edn, 2001) at p 133 and see also oral evidence given by Master Lush to the Joint Committee on the Draft Mental Incapacity Bill (HL Paper 189-11, HC 1083-11 at 188).

[35] In this tragic example, although the Crown prosecuted the former manager, it accepted an admission of liability in respect of only certain counts where the victims were capable of giving evidence. Where the victims were incapable or had subsequently died, there was no conviction in their individual cases, making civil recovery very difficult to pursue.

failure of the system to protect vulnerable adults was recognised officially in the Quinquennial Review of the then Public Trust Office:[36]

> 'An EPA bestows virtually unfettered control of someone's finances once it is brought into force. While its objective (to put someone's financial affairs into the hands of an individual they have pre-selected, rather than surrendering to the Court of Protection) fits entirely with the objective of keeping the state out of family affairs unless there is no alternative, if an EPA goes wrong the results can be catastrophic for the person concerned. Although comparatively rare, there are plenty of instances where the system has been deliberately or accidentally abused and getting the position rectified through the Court is a long and difficult process ...'

- In view of these difficulties, the choice of attorney is crucial to the success or failure of a person's EPA. Unfortunately, many EPAs are made long before they are needed and the donor is unable to foresee changes in his or her circumstances that might otherwise have led him or her to choose a different attorney. The knowledge of the donor and the advice he or she receives at the time the EPA is made is therefore of utmost importance. However, the prescribed form of EPA is easy to obtain and complete and offers little effective protection. The form only requires a signature by the donor and one witness whereupon it is presumed to have been validly executed.[37] There is furthermore no requirement that the donor has any form of legal or independent advice or that there be any assessment of the donor's capacity to create the power. Thus the ability to misuse the EPA is instituted quite easily at the time the form is created.

- An attorney is required to register an EPA once he or she 'has reason to believe that the donor is or is becoming mentally incapable'.[38] Therefore once the EPA has been registered, it appears to anyone dealing with the attorney that the donor is mentally incapable and thereby incapable, by reason of mental disorder, of managing and administering his or her property and affairs.[39] The presumption arises therefore that once the EPA is registered, the donor is unable to manage or administer the full extent of his or her property and affairs. This sits uneasily with the principle that capacity is function specific and that a person may have capacity or lack capacity in respect of different functions.[40] Thus a donor could

---

[36] Ann Chant CB *The Public Trust Office of the Lord Chancellor's Department: A Quinquennial Review* (November 1999) at para 47.

[37] *Re W* (enduring power of attorney) [2001] Ch 609, [2001] 4 All ER 88, [2001] 2 WLR 957.

[38] Enduring Powers of Attorney Act 1985, s 4(1).

[39] Enduring Powers of Attorney Act 1985, s 13.

[40] *Re Beaney* [1978] 2 All ER 595, [1978] 1 WLR 770 and see generally, **Chapter 2**.

be prevented from making decisions in respect of which he or she had capacity. For instance a donor might be able to manage small amounts or collect his or her pension, but their bank or pension administrator would assume, from the fact that the EPA had been registered, that they could not allow him or her any rights whatsoever over their own estate.

Abolition of enduring powers

3.12   The Law Commission considered these inherent failings in the EPA jurisdiction in the context of a review of the law relating to mental incapacity in its report *Mental Incapacity* (1995).[41] This review of the law, considered in more detail in **CHAPTER 1**, led to the passing of the Mental Capacity Act 2005 ('the 2005 Act') in April 2005 and which is expected to come into force in 2007.

3.13   Although no new EPAs may be made after the 2005 Act comes into force, all existing EPAs will continue to remain effective. Rather than convert existing EPAs into new Lasting Powers of Attorney, the 2005 Act provides for existing EPAs to continue to operate under the same legislative basis as they were created.[42]

Lasting Powers of Attorney

3.14   The 2005 Act provides expressly for the revocation of the 1985 Act,[43] and for the creation of a new type of power of attorney, a Lasting Power of Attorney ('LPA').[44]

3.15   LPAs and the 2005 Act jurisdiction cannot be comprehended without reference to EPAs:

- EPAs made before the 2005 Act comes into force will continue to operate under their own jurisdiction, although within the framework of the 2005 Act.[45] Thus different procedures as well as laws will operate side-by-side for many years to come.
- The Public Guardian and the Court of Protection will be responsible for administering the two sets of procedures and laws.
- A LPA is a statutory form of power of attorney that builds on existing common law and statutory principles. Thus decisions of the courts affecting EPAs as well as practical and professional experience gained in their use will have a bearing on the use and understanding of LPAs.

---

[41]   Law Com No 231.
[42]   Mental Capacity Act 2005, Sch 4. See **CHAPTER 8**.
[43]   Mental Capacity Act 2005, s 66(1)(b).
[44]   Mental Capacity Act 2005, s 9.
[45]   See **3.109**.

- The principle requirement of the LPA is to address problems inherent in the EPA jurisdiction. It therefore needs to be measured against that standard.

NATURE OF LASTING POWERS OF ATTORNEY

Character of Lasting Powers of Attorney

3.16 A LPA is first and foremost 'a power of attorney' whose form and scope are both restricted and extended by statute. It allows the donor to confer authority on an attorney to make decisions, including decisions in circumstances where the donor no longer has capacity in relation to all or any of:

- the donor's personal welfare or specified matters concerning the donor's personal welfare; and
- the donor's property and affairs or specified matters concerning the donor's property and affairs.[46]

3.17 The essential characteristic of the LPA is that it respects the presumption contained in ss 1 and 2 of the 2005 Act, that a person must be assumed to have capacity unless it can be established that he or she lacks capacity and that capacity is only relative to the matter and at the time that capacity needs to be determined. The LPA therefore must work in tandem with the ability of the donor to make decisions for him or herself over a range or spectrum of matters for which decisions might be made. At one end of the spectrum, the donor makes decisions for him or herself, perhaps in relation to straightforward financial affairs or in respect of welfare matters such as what to eat or where to live. At the other end of the spectrum, the attorney makes decisions for the donor, perhaps in relation to more complex financial matters or when the donor's condition has deteriorated. A LPA furthermore functions, in respect of property and affairs, as an ordinary power of attorney so that the attorney may act with the implied knowledge and approval of the donor.

3.18 This holistic approach to the requirements of the donor obviates the need for an attorney to register the LPA on the onset of incapacity and thereby avoids a presumption, as happens with EPAs, that the donor is incapable of managing the full extent of his or her property and affairs.[47] The criterion for registration is not 'is the donor incapable?' but 'does the power need to be used?'. If it needs to be used, the power can be

---

[46] Mental Capacity Act 2005, s 9(1).
[47] This follows the recommendation of the Law Commission: see Law Com No 231 at 7.31.

registered by the donor or the donee. To any third party dealing with the attorney, the state of mind of the donor is irrelevant and the donor is not labelled or stigmatised as being incapable.

This approach is not followed where the power relates to welfare matters. For obvious reasons, the donor's right to make decisions over his or her own welfare takes precedence. The LPA can only be used where, in relation to the matter for which capacity to make a decision is required, the donor lacks capacity.[48]

Problems in practice

3.19   While it is obviously sensible to allow a person autonomy over their own affairs to the extent possible without making presumptions about capacity, this can cause practical difficulties. Any third party dealing with the attorney acting under a registered LPA is not 'on notice' concerning the donor's lack of capacity. This may cause problems if there are conflicting instructions or the LPA is being used fraudulently. It would, for instance, be possible for the attorney to arrange the sale of the donor's property and for the donor to say he or she does not want the property sold. If the property is then sold by the attorney and the proceeds paid into a bank account, will anyone notice if large cheques are drawn on the account and signed by the donor personally? A bank meanwhile might not notice that new and regular withdrawals are being made from the account to a friendly tradesman.

3.20   By imposing a presumption of capacity, it may well be easier for the confused and the vulnerable to make mistakes which will be harder to detect. It may therefore be likely that many LPAs will be drafted to ensure that they will only operate on the onset of incapacity.[49] Thus many donors will end up being advised to reverse the statutory presumption intended by Parliament to benefit them.

Scope of Lasting Powers of Attorney

3.21   The scope of the attorney's authority is very extensive. Legislation and cases concerning powers of attorney tend to emphasise what an attorney cannot do rather than what an attorney can do. However, the starting point is the principle that an attorney stands in the place of the donor and can do whatever the donor could do for him or herself. That seemingly limitless power is then restricted in one of four ways:

1.   *By the terms of the power itself.* The donor may limit the authority of the attorney so that the power relates only to specified matters or

---

[48]   Mental Capacity Act 2005, s 11(7)(a).
[49]   See **3.65**. Problems caused by the policy of early registration are considered in more detail at **3.79–3.80**.

operates in certain circumstances.[50] For example, a power may provide that it only relates to property and affairs or that it will only operate if the donor becomes incapable. Limitations in the form of the power are considered in more detail at **3.65** below.

2. *By common law.* There are certain personal acts that cannot be delegated to an attorney and an attorney cannot act to benefit him or herself or delegate his or her authority. These and other restrictions, including duties imposed on the attorney by law, such as a duty of care and a duty not to benefit are considered in more detail at **3.4** above.

3. *By statute.* The 2005 Act includes some crucial extensions to these restrictions. Subject to the formalities of the 2005 Act being complied with, a LPA is not revoked by the lack of capacity of the donor and in certain circumstances a power can be used to make gifts, delegate trustee functions and make decisions concerning personal welfare matters. The 2005 Act also sets out limits on the scope of the 2005 Act itself and limits on the attorney's authority.[51]

4. *By the Court.* The Court of Protection has powers to intervene in the operation of the power. The Court can cancel the power in favour of an attorney, attach conditions to the power or provide the attorney with authority to make a decision which is beyond the scope of the attorney's authority within the LPA.[52] The Court can also make decisions of its own concerning the property and affairs and welfare of the donor.[53]

Property and affairs

3.22   The 2005 Act does not specify the extent or scope of an attorney's powers over a person's property and affairs. Section 9(1) describes a LPA as 'a power of attorney' which confers authority on a donee to make decisions about all or any of the donor's property and affairs.

3.23   The formal authority granted to an attorney is similar, if more clearly defined in the 1985 Act. Where a donor grants general authority in an EPA, the power 'operates to confer, subject to the restriction imposed … and to any conditions or restrictions contained in the instrument, authority to do on behalf of the donor anything which the donor can lawfully do by an attorney'.[54] However, this authority includes the authority to make gifts and maintain others and the most basic description of what an attorney can do, is provided by s 1(2) which allows the attorney to 'maintain the donor or prevent loss to his estate'.

---

[50]   Mental Capacity Act 2005, s 9(4)(b) and see **3.65**.
[51]   Mental Capacity Act 2005, ss 27–29.
[52]   Mental Capacity Act 2005, s 23.
[53]   Mental Capacity Act 2005, ss 15–17.
[54]   Enduring Powers of Attorney Act 1985, s 3(2).

3.24   The 2005 Act does not extend the attorney's core authority beyond this. In practice, the attorney will have access to the full extent of the donor's property and affairs and have authority to administer such property and affairs. Clearly the attorney also has a fiduciary duty to the donor and their estate. But what more can he or she do with that authority? The answer is provided by the proviso that the authority conferred by the LPA is subject to s 4 and therefore to the best interests criteria laid down by the 2005 Act.[55] Thus the attorney has a duty to administer the donor's property and affairs in the donor's best interests. The donor must therefore take into account matters such as the donor's past and present wishes and feelings, beliefs and values and the other factors he or she would consider if he or she were able to do so.

3.25   The importance of the application of 'best interests' to the attorney's role is not just a re-statement of the common law duty of an agent to act in the best interests of his principal. It requires the attorney to act subjectively, in accordance with the wishes of the actual person.

The extended test of best interests requires an attorney to possess an appropriate understanding of the character and circumstances of the donor. It may though be difficult to reconcile this with an objective responsibility towards the donor's estate. For instance a donor may have been determined to live in their own home, notwithstanding a worrying degree of self-neglect. Or a donor may have been profligate or lived beyond their means. An attorney may have to make a tactful compromise between these personal circumstances and his or her responsibilities to the estate (and its preservation for the long-term benefit of the donor). The attorney may have to assume that the donor would appreciate his or her predicament as one of the 'other factors he would be likely to consider if he were able to do so'.

Power to maintain others

3.26   By contrast with the 1985 Act,[56] which refers to the maintenance of others, whereby the attorney 'may so act in relation to himself or in relation to any other person if the donor might be expected to provide for his or that person's needs respectively; and ... may do whatever the donor might be expected to do to meet those needs', the 2005 Act makes no reference to the maintenance of anyone else apart from the donor.[57] It is arguable that the attorney under a LPA has no authority to maintain anyone apart from the donor him or herself. There is no express power for the attorney to act upon any moral obligation the donor might have to maintain, for instance, a spouse or a disabled child.

---

[55]   Mental Capacity Act 2005, s 4(7) and also s 9(4).
[56]   Enduring Powers of Attorney Act 1985, s 3(4).
[57]   The extent of the 1985 Act power was illustrated in the case of *Re Cameron (deceased), Phillips v Cameron* [1999] Ch 386, [1999] 2 All ER 924, [1999] 3 WLR 394.

3.27   The Law Commission report *Mental Incapacity* took the view that the power to act in a donor's 'best interests' was more flexible and wider than the power of an attorney at common law. Because 'it requires the attorney to consider the wishes and feelings of the donor and the factors he or she would have taken into account, the attorney would in appropriate cases be quite able to meet another person's needs (including the attorney's own needs) or make seasonal or charitable gifts, while still acting within the best interests duty'.[58] However, this rather sweeping assumption is addressed by the 2005 Act in the context of gifts.[59] There is no corresponding provision addressing maintenance, and there must be some uncertainty as to whether the attorney can – or the extent to which the attorney should – act on this without the sanction of the Court of Protection.[60]

Limited power to make gifts

3.28   Section 12 of the 2005 Act restates the principle that an attorney cannot make gifts, but allows gifts to be made in certain limited circumstances. Subject to any limitation contained in the power, the donee may make gifts:[61]

> '(a) on customary occasions to persons (including himself) who are related to or connected with the donor, or
>
> (b) to any charity to whom the donor made or might have been expected to make gifts,
>
> if the value of each such gift is not unreasonable having regard to all the circumstances and, in particular, the size of the donor's estate.'

3.29   The 2005 Act therefore imposes four basic conditions on an attorney before a gift can be made:

1.   there must be no restriction in the power itself which prevents the gift from being made;
2.   the gift must be made on a 'customary occasion';
3.   an individual must be related to or connected to the donor, while a charity must be one which has benefited or might be expected to benefit from the donor; and
4.   the value of any gift must not be unreasonable having regard to all the circumstances and especially to the value of the donor's estate.

---

[58]   Law Com No 231 at 7.11.
[59]   Mental Capacity Act 2005, s 12 and see **3.28–3.32**. The draft Bill prepared by the Law Commission made no reference to gifts or to maintenance.
[60]   Mental Capacity Act 2005, s 23(4).
[61]   Mental Capacity Act 2005, s 12(2).

3.30 'Customary occasion' is defined by the 2005 Act, to allow for all types of family, seasonal or religious events which justify the making of a gift, as:[62]

'(a) the occasion or anniversary of a birth, a marriage or the formation of a civil partnership, or

(b) any other occasion on which presents are customarily given within families or among friends or associates.'

The attorney cannot therefore make a gift at a time that is not a 'customary occasion' such as the beginning or end of a tax year. For the attorney to make a valid gift as part of a tax planning exercise, it must also be of a 'customary occasion'.

3.31 In determining whether an attorney can make a gift, s 12 of the 2005 Act only requires the attorney to take account of the donor's history and likely wishes only where a gift is made to charity. This would, for instance, allow an attorney to continue an established pattern of giving, for instance maintaining standing orders to charities. However, regardless of whether gifts are made to a charity or to an individual, the attorney cannot avoid the overriding duty to act in the donor's 'best interests' and take account of matters such as the donor's past and present wishes and feelings or factors that he or she would consider if he or she had capacity.

The attorney cannot furthermore avoid his or her fiduciary duty to the donor's estate and could not make a gift which the donor could not afford to make. The gift must furthermore be reasonable having regard to the circumstances and the size of the donor's estate. It is for the attorney to exercise his or her judgment in measuring the appropriate value of a gift. There is no fixed limit as to what is reasonable or not. Different recipients may have greater or lesser needs or be more or less deserving of a gift. A wealthy donor may be able to afford a gift of several thousand pounds, although a gift of £20,000 has been treated as beyond the scope of an attorney's authority under an EPA.[63] A donor with limited capital and in receipt of benefits may, by contrast, only be able to afford a gift of a few pounds.

3.32 Where there is any doubt about the attorney's authority to make the gift or it is clear that a proposed gift goes beyond the making of the gift then the Court of Protection can authorise the gift under s 23 of the 2005 Act, which deals with the Court's powers in relation to the operation of LPAs. The Court cannot however ignore an express limitation in the power itself and allow the attorney to exceed his or her authority under

---

[62] Mental Capacity Act 2005, s 12(3).
[63] See *Re W (enduring power of attorney)* [2001] 4 All ER 88, [2001] 2 WLR 957 and in particular the comments of the judge at first instance, Jules Sher QC [2000] 1 All ER 175 at 181 and [2000] 3 WLR 45 at 51.

the power.[64] In this situation, the attorney or any other person who may apply, may request the Court to authorise a gift under s 18(1)(b) of the 2005 Act.[65]

The donor as trustee

3.33   A LPA confers the same rights as an EPA in favour of an attorney who is a trustee of land. An attorney acting under a LPA has no power to act as a trustee unless the power complies with s 25 of the Trustee Act 1925 or the provisions of s 36 of the Trustee Act 1925 apply. This latter provision saves most domestic situations where a property is owned by husband and wife under a trust for land. One of the owners, who is also a trustee for land, becomes incapable. To fulfil the 'two trustee' rule, the attorney of the incapable trustee – acting under a registered power[66] – can appoint a new trustee to act on the sale and give a valid receipt for capital monies.[67]

The donor as a litigant

3.34   A person's right or standing to conduct proceedings is governed by the relevant rules of court in which those proceedings take place. Civil proceedings in the High Court and county court are governed by the Civil Procedure Rules 1998 ('CPR').[68] Whether a person has capacity to conduct or settle proceedings is specific to the matter for which capacity is required. A person may therefore have capacity to issue and then settle proceedings even though he or she might otherwise be unable to administer his or her property and affairs.[69]

3.35   Where a person is 'a patient' for the purposes of 1983 Act, he or she is treated by the CPR as a person under a disability who must be represented by a litigation friend.[70] The litigation friend can be appointed to act by the Court of Protection[71] but if the Court of Protection is not involved in the affairs of the person, a suitable

---

[64]   See *Re R (enduring power of attorney)* [1990] Ch 647, [1990] 2 All ER 893, [1990] 2 WLR 1219.

[65]   This merely reflects the current situation where an attorney acting under an EPA is not prevented from applying to the Court of Protection under Part VII of the 1983 Act.

[66]   'Registered power' is defined as an 'Enduring Power of Attorney or Lasting Power of Attorney registered under the Mental Capacity Act 2005' (Trustee Act 1925, s 36(6C)).

[67]   Trustee Act 1925, s 36(6A).

[68]   SI 1998/3132.

[69]   *Masterman-Lister v Jewell* [2002] EWHC 417 (QB), [2002] All ER 247 (Mar); on appeal sub nom *Masterman-Lister v Jewell* [2002] EWCA Civ 1889, [2003] 3 All ER 162, [2003] 1 WLR 1511.

[70]   Civil Procedure Rules, Part 21, r 21. It is assumed that the Rules will be amended to refer to the 2005 Act.

[71]   Mental Capacity Act 2005, s 18(1)(k).

representative can nominate him or herself as litigation friend. The litigation friend must be someone capable of acting in the person's best interests with no conflict of interest in the matter and their role is limited to the proceedings in question. Thus the litigation friend may obtain a damages award but will have no authority to receive or administer that award.

An attorney acting under a LPA has no standing as an attorney to bring or defend proceedings on behalf of the donor.[72] There is therefore no change to the existing procedure whereby, if the donor lacks capacity, the attorney – if he or she wishes to act in the proceedings – must demonstrate his or her suitability to act as a litigation friend or obtain the express authority of the Court of Protection to conduct the proceedings.[73]

Welfare matters

3.36   The donor of a LPA may authorise the attorney to make decisions on his or her behalf about his or her personal welfare or specified matters concerning personal welfare. This appears at first sight an extensive power to direct matters such as where and how the donor shall live and to give or refuse consent to treatment.[74] In certain circumstances, the attorney's authority may even extend to the giving or refusing consent to life-sustaining treatment.

The principle application of this authority is to enable those providing healthcare or treatment for an incapable person to have consent to what they would propose to do in that person's best interests. A doctor performing a hip replacement or a dentist fitting a denture can be assured of having formal consent to an invasive treatment rather than having to rely on his or her own judgment about the necessity of the treatment and whether it is covered by s 5 of the 2005 Act.[75] A LPA also gives an attorney certain rights, in particular:

- a person or body determining whether a proposed act is in the best interests of the incapable person must take into account the views of, and if possible consult, the donee of the LPA (s 4(7));
- an act performed in connection with 'care or treatment' under s 5 is not authorised by that section if it conflicts with a decision of an attorney acting within the scope of his or her power (s 6(6)(a));

---

[72]   The Law Commission's draft Bill proposed giving the attorney power over 'all matters relating to the donor's property or affairs, including the conduct of legal proceedings' (cl 16(1) of the draft Bill set out as Appendix A to Law Com No 231). There is no corresponding reference in the 2005 Act.

[73]   See *Gregory v Turner* [2003] EWCA Civ 83. Although this case concerned an action conducted by an attorney acting under an EPA, the principle will be the same where a LPA is concerned.

[74]   Mental Capacity Act 2005, s 11(7)(c).

[75]   Acts in connection with care or treatment are dealt with in CHAPTER 2.

- a LPA made after an advance decision conferring authority in respect of treatment to which the advance decision relates takes precedence over the refusal of consent contained in the advance decision (s 25(2)(b)); and
- the attorney may apply to the Court of Protection for the exercise of any of its powers under the 2005 Act without seeking prior permission (s 50(1)(b)).

Limits on welfare matters

3.37   The scope of an attorney's authority in welfare matters is more limited than may at first be apparent. The principal limitations are:

- any act performed by an attorney must be in accordance with the donor's best interests (ss 1(5) and 4));
- there is no power to make decisions if the donor has capacity to make decisions for him or herself (s 11(7)(a));
- a LPA does not authorise the attorney to restrain the donor unless the attorney reasonably believes that it is necessary to prevent harm to the donor and the act of restraint is a proportionate response to the likelihood of the donor suffering harm and the seriousness of that harm (s 11(3) and (4));
- any restraint of the donor cannot deprive the donor of his or her liberty within the meaning of Art 5(1) of the Human Rights Convention (s 11(6)). This may be at odds with the power to restrain the donor which by its nature deprives the donor of his or her liberty. This will require further interpretation, especially in view of the *Bournewood* case, and it is likely that the power to 'restrain' under the 2005 Act will be interpreted very narrowly, for use in emergencies or as a temporary measure.[76] A longer-term detention of a person who cannot consent to it or detention for the purposes of treatment, may well be excluded from the 2005 Act as there is no process in the 2005 Act to protect the rights of the donor;
- the donor's authority to consent to care or treatment is subject to a valid and applicable advance decision made after the LPA;[77]
- the attorney only has authority to give or refuse consent to life-sustaining treatment if this is expressly allowed by the LPA and this authority is furthermore subject to any restrictions or conditions in the power.[78] This power of 'life and death' is considered in more detail below, but is in its turn subject to two further safeguards:

---

[76]   *HL v United Kingdom* (2004) 5 October (the Strasbourg proceedings arising out of the decision of the House of Lords in *R v Bournewood Community and Mental Health NHS Trust, ex p L* [1999] 1 AC 458 [1998] All ER 303).

[77]   Mental Capacity Act 2005, ss 11(7)(b) and 25(7).

[78]   Mental Capacity Act 2005, s 11(8).

- a person considering whether a life-sustaining treatment is in a person's best interests must not be motivated by a desire to bring about his or her death;[79] and

- the declaration in s 62 of the 2005 Act that the existing law relating to murder or manslaughter is not affected by anything contained in the 2005 Act;

- The 2005 Act confers no authority on any person or body to make decisions in respect of:

  - family relations, including consent to a marriage or civil partnership, sexual relations, divorce (based on 2 years' separation) and parental responsibilities relating to a child's welfare;[80]

  - 2005 Act matters, where medical treatment is required for mental disorder as defined by the 1983 Act;[81] and

  - voting rights where the election is for any public office or at a referendum.[82]

3.38   It is unclear therefore how useful or widespread welfare LPAs are going to be. It may be that they will serve little practical purpose beyond giving the person named by the donor an authority to act as consultee and advocate for the incapable donor, thus someone who can speak for the donor when he or she can no longer speak for him or herself. It is also possible that LPAs will become widely used (and abused) and carers will defer to attorneys making life and death decisions on behalf of incapable donors.

3.39   The provisions of the 2005 Act relating to LPAs and life-sustaining treatment are both confusing and controversial.[83] How, for instance, is the authority of an attorney to refuse consent to 'life-sustaining treatment' reconciled with the requirement that 'best interests' cannot include a desire to bring about the death of the donor? These provisions of the 2005 Act appear mutually inconsistent, but the 2005 Act does clearly allow the donor to authorise the attorney to make these decisions on his or her behalf. The only way of giving effect to this requirement is

---

[79]   Mental Capacity Act 2005, s 4(5). This was a late amendment to the Mental Capacity Bill, first referred to in a letter from the Lord Chancellor to Archbishop Smith on 14 December 2004 and subsequently incorporated in an amendment introduced in the House of Lords by Baroness Ashton of Upholland.

[80]   Mental Capacity Act 2005, s 27.

[81]   Mental Capacity Act 2005, s 28 and see also Mental Health Act 1983, s 1(2) which defines 'mental disorder' as 'mental illness, arrested or incomplete development of mind, psychopathic disorder and any other disorder or disability of mind'.

[82]   Mental Capacity Act 2005, s 29. The 2005 Act makes no reference to voting as a member of any other association such as a political party or unincorporated association.

[83]   An article in the *Daily Mail* of 8 December 2004 by Melanie Philips was headed 'A barbaric Bill that would destroy the value of life' was not untypical of some of the press coverage of the Bill at the time of its passage in the House of Commons.

to ensure that a decision to withhold treatment can be made on the basis that it is unduly burdensome or futile and not in the best interests of the donor. The motive of the attorney is to relieve pain and suffering and not primarily or exclusively to bring about the death of the patient.

3.40   The problem remains therefore that LPAs may be easy to abuse.[84] The attorney may well end up as sole arbiter of whether a refusal of a treatment is in the donor's 'best interests'. This gives rise to several potential problems:

- the 2005 Act does not address the fundamental question of who is making the decision. The attorney is still exercising his or her judgment as to what is in the donor's best interests;[85]
- doctors and other carers may find that the permission of an attorney to withdraw life-sustaining treatment removes an obligation to make an independent assessment of the donor's best wishes;
- the fiduciary character of a power of attorney is more difficult to apply to a power which relates to welfare. Many attorneys will have an obvious conflict of interest as potential beneficiaries of the donor's estate. While an attorney (who is a beneficiary) should not benefit from his or her dealings with the property and affairs of the donor, there is no equivalent safeguard to dealings with the welfare of the donor;
- a person may be deemed to lack capacity because he or she is unable to communicate a decision;[86]
- an attorney acting in respect of a donor's welfare will generally be a relative or friend, and is unlikely to be a professional person with a professional duty of care. It is unclear therefore what skill or judgment a lay attorney may be expected to exercise in making welfare decisions;
- an attorney acting in the best interests of the donor must take account of the views of anyone caring for the donor, so may be expected to act on medical advice where this is appropriate. But a decision to treat or not to treat can only be informed by medical advice. An attorney makes what he or she believes to be the right decision and is protected by the 2005 Act so long as he or she 'reasonably believes that what he does or decides is in the best interests of the person concerned'.[87]

---

[84]   The scope for abuse in the creation of LPAs is considered at **3.69**.

[85]   Much of the controversy around this question is based on the assumption that the attorney will bring about the death of the donor when the donor might not have wished that outcome. But the reverse scenario is equally valid, where the attorney refuses consent to the withdrawal of treatment which prolongs the life of a donor who has no desire to go on living.

[86]   Mental Capacity Act 2005, s 3(1)(d).

[87]   Mental Capacity Act 2005, s 4(9).

3.41 Although LPAs will be of use to some people in some circumstances, these concerns and the extent of the attorney's powers will need to be addressed carefully by donors when executing LPAs. The drafting and execution of LPAs will therefore be a relatively painstaking process, involving clear professional advice from solicitors and doctors. This will affect the costs involved and either deter potential donors from making LPAs or encourage the making of such powers without proper advice or assistance.

Form of Lasting Powers of Attorney

3.42 Any person who has reached the age of 18 and who has capacity to do so, may grant a LPA.[88] For a LPA to be effective, it must be made in a prescribed form and in a prescribed manner, comply with certain requirements as to the appointment of an attorney and must be registered.

Prescribed form

3.43 No instrument can be effective as a LPA unless it is in the prescribed form.[89] The actual form will be prescribed by statutory instrument, in the same way as the form of EPA, save that there are different prescribed forms depending on whether the power relates to personal welfare or property and affairs.

3.44 The prescribed form will provide space for the donor to write or print his or her name and address and date of birth, the names and addresses of his or her attorneys and the basis of their appointment and to set out any special conditions or restrictions in the power. The form must in particular contain a clear statement that the donor has read or has had read to him or her the relevant information explaining the form and that he or she intends the authority to make decisions where he or she no longer has capacity.[90]

3.45 As with the prescribed form of EPA, the prescribed form must contain a statement by the attorney or each of them if more than one, that the attorney has read or has had read to him or her the relevant information contained in the form and understands the duties imposed on him or her under s 1 (the principles) and s 4 (best interests).[91]

---

[88] For capacity to grant a LPA, see **3.76**.
[89] Mental Capacity Act 2005, Sch 1, Part 1. At the time of writing, draft forms have been published by the Department for Constitutional Affairs for consultation and are available at www.dca.gov.uk/consult/powerattorney.cp0106.htm#English.
[90] Mental Capacity Act 2005, Sch 1, Part 1, para 2(1)(b).
[91] Mental Capacity Act 2005, Sch 1, Part 1, para 2(1)(d).

3.46   The LPA must also indicate clearly the person or persons the donor wishes to be notified of an application to register the instrument or state that there are no such persons to be notified.[92]

Use of different prescribed forms

3.47   The same donor may give two LPAs dealing with personal welfare matters and property and affairs respectively. Different considerations apply to the requirements and content of each power, different attorneys may be appointed for different purposes and the powers may be registered at different times. For instance a donor may want a solicitor to act as an attorney in respect of property and affairs but a relative to act in respect of personal welfare matters. The former power can also be used at any time after it has been registered and without reference to the capacity of the donor; a power dealing with personal welfare matters only extends to making decisions in circumstances where the donor lacks capacity.[93]

3.48   Because different powers may be given for different purposes, there are to be two prescribed forms, one for personal welfare matters and one for property and affairs.[94]

Certificate of capacity

3.49   To safeguard the donor, the LPA must also contain a certificate given by a person of a prescribed description, who is not a donee of the power, stating that in his or her opinion, at the time the donor executes the instrument:[95]

   (a) the donor understands the purpose of the instrument and the scope of the authority given under it;

   (b) no fraud or undue pressure is being used to induce the donor to create a LPA; and

   (c) there is nothing else which would prevent a LPA from being created.[96]

---

[92]   Mental Capacity Act 2005, Sch 1, Part 1, para 2(1)(c). This is in contrast to the 1985 Act which specifies the classes of relatives that must be notified (see **3.10**).

[93]   Mental Capacity Act 2005, s 11(7)(a).

[94]   Although the 2005 Act, Sch 1, Part 1, para 1(2), allows for an instrument dealing with *both* welfare matters and property and affairs, it is unlikely that such a document would be prescribed.

[95]   The giving of the certificate is a separate act to the execution of the instrument and does not need to be contemporaneous with execution. The 2005 Act refers to 'a certificate … that … at the time when the donor executes the instrument'. Thus execution and the giving of the certificate are separate events and there is no requirement as to the length of time that passes between the two events.

[96]   Mental Capacity Act 2005, Sch 1, Part 1, para 2(1)(e). Draft LPA forms prepared by the Department of Constitutional Affairs also provide for a certificate to be given by a person

3.50   The 'prescribed description' of a person who can give a certificate of capacity is to be defined by regulations,[97] and will be set out clearly in the prescribed form. The only statutory qualification is that the certificate may not be given by a person who is named as a donee.[98] Although regulations will require such a person to be of a prescribed description, it must be assumed that such a person cannot be related to or connected with the donee.[99] However, it is expected that the class of other persons who can give a certificate will be a wide one and will not be restricted to lawyers, doctors or other professionally qualified persons as such a restriction might present a deterrent to people making LPAs. Draft forms published by the Department for Constitutional Affairs take this approach to an extreme degree and propose that a certificate can be given by any person (who is not a donee and who is not related to the donor) or a person of a prescribed description can complete the certificate of capacity.[100]

3.51   The certificate of capacity is intended to provide an important safeguard, to protect the donor from undue influence of abuse and also to avoid subsequent doubts about the validity of the power. This will therefore reinforce the presumption that already pertains to the due execution of an EPA, that a LPA which has been properly executed and contains such a certificate is a valid power.[101] A certificate of capacity will, to most persons dealing with the LPA serve as a badge of authenticity that will make it that much harder to query or object to the power. This will allow a greater scope for abuse where a certificate of capacity is procured fraudulently or without proper consideration for the importance of the subject matter. The wider the class of persons who can give a certificate of capacity, the greater the scope for misuse.

There will of course be an onus on the person giving the certificate to ensure that the donor fully comprehends the nature and effect of the power, and that onus will be greater for any person giving a certificate in a professional capacity. He or she will also need to consider carefully matter such as:[102]

---

[97]   (of no qualification or further description) who has known the donor for more than 2 years. Mental Capacity Act 2005, Sch 1, Part 1, para 1(3).

[98]   Mental Capacity Act 2005, Sch 1, Part 1, para 2(6).

[99]   Draft LPA forms prepared by the Department of Constitutional Affairs also preclude a person who is a relative, spouse or civil partner (who has lived with the donor for at least 2 years), paid carer, manager or employee of the donor's care home or named person on the power from giving such a certificate.

[100]   Persons who can give a prescribed description include a local business person or shopkeeper, registered social worker, police officer, bank or building society official, librarian, professionally qualified person, local authority councillor, civil servant, MP or MEP.

[101]   *Re W (enduring power of attorney)* [2001] Ch 609, [2001] 4 All ER 88, [2001] 2 WLR 957.

[102]   It is unclear what responsibility or duty a non-professional person has in giving a certificate of capacity. However, there is no doubt that a professional person will have a greater

- the extent of his or her instructions or retainer;[103]
- whether, if he or she is not medically qualified, medical advice is required;
- whether, if he or she is not legally qualified, legal advice is required;
- what records should be kept and for how long; and
- that if the power is given by one spouse (or civil partner) to the other, the donor in each case must be interviewed separately.

3.52　In the event that the donor does not require any person to be notified of registration of the instrument, the instrument must contain two such certificates.[104]

Defective forms

3.53　At first sight, the 2005 Act appears unequivocal about a LPA being in the prescribed form. Thus s 9(3) clearly states that an instrument which does not comply with the relevant sections 'confers no authority'.

This unequivocal assertion is however at odds with Sch 1 to the 2005 Act which deals with the formal requirements of a LPA. Paragraph 3 not only allows the Public Guardian to ignore an immaterial difference with the prescribed form, but the Court of Protection may also:[105]

'... declare that an instrument which is not in the prescribed form is to be treated as if it were, if it is satisfied that the persons executing the instrument intended it to create a lasting power of attorney.'

3.54　How these contradictory requirements will work in practice remains to be seen. If someone inadvertently creates what he or she believes to be a LPA, how defective can it be for the Court to avoid this provision? Although the latter requirement appears to be in conflict with the former, the aim of this is to enable the Court to ignore invalid or irrelevant conditions or powers written into the LPA.

---

responsibility and this will be reflected in the fee he will be obliged to charge, thereby making it more likely that LPAs will not be certified appropriately.

[103] A solicitor who prepares a document for a client needs to be satisfied that he or she understands the nature and effect of the document (see *Enduring Power of Attorney Guidelines for Solicitors* prepared by the Law Society's Mental Health and Disability Committee) and should be able to complete a certificate as part of his instructions to prepare a LPA. However, difficulties might arise if the LPA has already been executed and a certificate is given subsequently.

[104] Mental Capacity Act 2005, Sch 1, Part 1, para 2(2)(b).

[105] Mental Capacity Act 2005, Sch 1, Part 1, para 3(2).

Content

Choice of attorney

3.55 A donor who at the time the instrument is executed is 18 or over and has capacity may appoint any person or, in the case of a power relating to property and affairs, a trust corporation, to act as his or her attorney. Apart from where a trust corporation is appointed, the appointment of an attorney is personal and an attorney cannot be appointed by reference to an office or title.[106]

Where an individual is appointed then he or she must have reached 18 and must not be a bankrupt.[107] If the attorney subsequently becomes bankrupt, then his appointment as an attorney is terminated.

3.56 Clearly the choice of attorney is essential to the effective operation of a LPA. And because a LPA may be made many years before it is used, the donor needs some insurance against an attorney becoming unable to act due to death, divorce, bankruptcy, incapacity or disclaimer. The 2005 Act therefore allows the donor to appoint two or more attorneys and also allows for the appointment of successive attorneys.

More than one attorney

3.57 Section 10(4) of the 2005 Act allows the donor to appoint more than one attorney provided that the attorneys are appointed to act 'jointly' or 'jointly and severally'. The section also allows attorneys to be appointed jointly in respect of some matters and jointly and severally in respect of others. Thus a donor would be able to appoint attorneys to act jointly and severally in respect of his or her property and affairs but require them to act jointly in respect of any welfare decisions.

3.58 Where two or more attorneys are appointed *jointly*, the attorneys must act together in any act carried out under the power. For example, a contract for a care home or even a cheque drawn on the donor's bank account must be signed by both attorneys. The advantage of appointing attorneys jointly is that the attorneys must confer and co-operate with each other. Neither can act without the other's notice which provides the donor with some degree of protection. The disadvantages are that

---

[106] The Law Commission assumed that an officeholder could be appointed under existing law (Law Com No 231 at 7.21) but recommended a specific provision authorising an attorney to be described as 'the holder for the time being or a specified office or position'. This provision was not included in the 2005 Act, and contrasts with the power of the Court to appoint 'the holder for the time being or a specified office or position' as a deputy (Mental Capacity Act 2005, s 19(2)).

[107] Mental Capacity Act 2005, s 10(1).

the LPA may be cumbersome to operate in practice and that the LPA is terminated if the appointment of either attorney fails for any reason.[108]

3.59   Where two or more attorneys are appointed *jointly and severally*, each attorney may act independently of the other. Most EPAs which appoint more than one attorney to deal with a person's property and affairs provide for the attorneys being appointed jointly and severally. It is simply more practical for attorneys to work separately either with a clear division of responsibility between them or on the understanding that one will take a lead role and another will act as a spare or default attorney. However, any potential conflict or discord between the attorneys will make the power extremely difficult to operate in practice.

3.60   Whichever form of appointment is used, the instrument must make the choice clear. However, the 2005 Act not only encourages the appointment of attorneys jointly but creates a presumption in favour of their appointment jointly where the instrument does not specify how the attorneys are to be appointed.[109]

3.61   Because the donor may create more than one power, different combinations of attorneys can be appointed for different purposes or in different circumstances. A donor may, for instance, appoint his or her spouse as attorney in separate instruments in respect of welfare matters and property and affairs. The donor may then in the same instruments appoint his or her children – in default of the spouse being able to act – as attorneys *jointly* in respect of welfare matters and *jointly and severally* in respect of property and affairs.

3.62   Where a donor wishes to appoint more than one attorney, care must be taken to address the issue of how they are to act at the time the instrument is made, rather than leave matters to wishful thinking. Where one of the attorneys is a professional attorney, it will also be important for the donor to define the extent to which the professional attorney is expected to be actively involved in the administration of the donor's affairs or the supervision of the other attorney.

Successive attorneys

3.63   An attorney or attorneys cannot appoint their own successors in the same way that trustees can.[110] The difference between an attorney and a trustee is that the attorney is appointed personally in his or her own

---

[108]   Mental Capacity Act 2005, s 10(6).

[109]   This avoids the problem created by the Enduring Power of Attorney Act 1985, s 11(1), where an EPA had to be joint or jointly and severally to be valid as an EPA. An instrument that was unclear might therefore be defective. See also *Re E (enduring power of attorney)* [2001] Ch 364, [2000] 3 WLR 1974, sub nom E, *Re X v Y* [2000] 3 All ER 1004.

[110]   Mental Capacity Act 2005, s 10(8)(a).

right and owes his or her duty to the donor.[111] The 2005 Act does however allow for the appointment of successive attorneys, so that new attorneys may replace old attorneys on the failure of the earlier appointment.[112] Thus if the choice of the first attorney shall fail on say the death, divorce, bankruptcy or incapacity of that attorney, a new attorney or new attorneys can be appointed to act in that event.

3.64 Successive attorneys can be appointed in the same instrument or in different instruments. However, where attorneys are appointed as a result of a condition being satisfied, the Public Guardian will require evidence of the condition being satisfied before the instrument can be registered in favour of the substitute attorney.

Restrictions and conditions

3.65 The authority of an attorney is not only subject to the limitations imposed by the 2005 Act but also any conditions or restrictions specified in the instrument.[113] In view of the wide-ranging scope of a LPA, the donor needs to consider very carefully how the LPA can be 'tailored' to meet his or her requirements and provide the right level of compromise between function and protection. Special conditions that a donor might add, in respect of property and affairs, to the prescribed form include:

- A right to remuneration by a professional attorney. An attorney acts as a fiduciary role and should not benefit from his or her so acting without the consent of the donor. It is therefore advisable for this to be expressly provided for in the instrument.
- Authority for the delegation of investment powers to a professional fund manager. An attorney cannot generally delegate his or her functions except where he or she cannot be expected to attend to them personally.
- Authorising disclosure or safe custody of the donor's Will. A solicitor holding a Will owes a duty of confidentiality to the donor and would not normally release documents without the consent of the donor (if capable) or the Court (if incapable). An attorney may, however, need to know the contents of the Will.
- Requiring the attorney to keep accounts or to render an account to a co-attorney or to a third party such as another member of the family, a solicitor or accountant. Although an attorney has a common law duty to keep accounts, this is not always followed in practice. The Court of Protection has authority to require an

---

[111] A trust by contrast is a distinct legal entity that may need to be administered for much longer and the trustees owe their primary duty to the beneficiaries.
[112] Mental Capacity Act 2005, s 10(8). This merely confirms the common law position.
[113] Mental Capacity Act 2005, s 9(4)(b).

attorney to deliver an account, but it is unlikely that this authority will be widely exercised.[114]

- Restricting the operation of the LPA to use in specified circumstances. The LPA can be used – subject to registration – at any time by the attorney. Many donors will be unhappy with going through the formalities and expense of registration when the power only needs to be used for a limited time or function. They may also be unhappy with the prospect of the LPA being used while they are still capable. They may therefore restrict the creation of the LPA to (for example) such time as they become mentally incapable of managing their property and affairs.
- Requiring medical evidence to be supplied on an application to register the LPA. Many donors will be uncomfortable with the idea of the attorney registering and using the power without any formal medical evidence being supplied.
- Restricting the power to make gifts under s 12 of the 2005 Act by setting a maximum amount for gifts or prohibiting the making of gifts without the consent of the Court or a third party.
- Restricting the amount of capital which can be applied or limiting the value of transactions that may be entered into by the attorney.
- Confirming the revocation of an earlier LPA or EPA. One power of attorney does not automatically revoke an earlier power and there must be a clear act of revocation and the attorney under the earlier power must be notified. However, as a LPA is not created until it is registered, it is not clear whether this formality would be required where the instrument has not yet been registered. However, it must be good practice to ensure that there is a clear record of revocation of an earlier instrument.
- Requiring the consent of a third party to the disposal of a particular asset, such as the family home, heirlooms or shares in a family company.
- Restricting the scope of the LPA so that it does not apply to a particular asset, for instance that it should not apply to the sale of the family home.

Welfare restrictions

3.66   Where the welfare of the donor is concerned, the same restrictions as to when and with what evidence the LPA is created, may be applicable. However, the donor may also have strong views as to how they are treated and whether or not the LPA extends to the giving or refusing of consent to life-sustaining treatment. Special conditions might include:

---

[114]   Mental Capacity Act 2005, s 23(3)(a).

- requiring decisions to be taken in consultation with or subject to the agreement of a named individual or subject to medical evidence or advice;
- restricting the right to refuse consent to life-sustaining treatment so that it does not include the right to refuse artificial nutrition and hydration.

3.67   The danger of placing too many restrictions on a LPA is that it may make the power inflexible in practice and lead to the expense and inconvenience of involving the Court of Protection. For instance a LPA may give effect to the sensibilities of an elderly donor who is determined to stay in his or her own home and restrict the power accordingly. However, it is more important to protect the donor's interests than the convenience of the attorney. This does therefore imposes a burden on any professional adviser preparing a LPA to ensure that the adviser has sufficient knowledge of the donor's circumstances and can both address the donor's concerns without making the power prescriptive.

Named persons to be notified

3.68   The donor may specify in the power the persons to be notified of an application to register the LPA, or specifying that there are no such persons to be notified.[115] The only qualifications required by the 2005 Act are that any named person cannot be the donee of the power and that if there are no named persons then two certificates of capacity must be given.[116] The persons named by the donor must be named as individuals rather than as a class or by reference to a relationship.[117]

The right of the donor to choose the persons to be notified of the application to register the LPA differs significantly from the requirements of the 1985 Act, which requires prescribed members of a class of relatives to be notified.[118] This embodies a recommendation of the Law Commission,[119] which was critical of the statutory list of notifiable relatives which:

'... makes no acknowledgement that close and important relationships may exist outside of legal marriage and blood ties. It conflicts with the autonomy

---

[115]   Mental Capacity Act 2005, Sch 1, Part 1, para 2(1)(c).
[116]   Mental Capacity Act 2005, Sch 1, Part 1, para 2(2)(b). The certificate of capacity is considered in more detail at **3.49**.
[117]   Draft LPA forms prepared by the Department of Constitutional Affairs provide for names and addresses to be shown. However, failure to include an actual name and to refer to a relation or class such as 'my children' should not invalidate the power. See Mental Capacity Act 2005, Sch 1, Part 1, para 3(2) and **3.53** above.
[118]   Enduring Powers of Attorney Act 1985, Sch 1, Part 1, para 2(1). Safeguards in the EPA jurisdiction are considered at **3.8**.
[119]   Law Com No 231 at 7.37.

principle to require, regardless of the donor's wishes, that certain relatives must be notified of a private arrangement to govern future decision making.'

3.69   The obligation to give notice of an intention to register the power is one of the key safeguards against misuse by the donee of the power. Although the 2005 Act allows the donor to choose who is notified, it assumes that the competent donor putting his or her affairs in order and acting with a complete understanding of all the relevant factors will choose sensibly those persons who might actually be in a position to protect his or her interests in the event of abuse by the attorney. While this approach has its advantages, it also removes the benefits inherent in the statutory list. Disputes concerning EPAs often come to light when relatives are notified. Often they will continue their own disputes at the expense of the donor, but there are also many cases where the attorney is in a position of trust and confidence at the time the power is made, which may be several years before the power is used. A trusted child may subsequently have financial difficulties or have fallen out with the donor.

The donor of a LPA may be under the influence – whether malign or well-intentioned – of a particular friend or relative and avoid naming close relatives as persons to be notified.[120] It is also common for many elderly people who live alone to find that the people they trust and would like to be notified are of a similar age. No allowance is made for the passage of time and the donor's own choice may well be out of date by the time the power comes to be registered several years later.

3.70   The 2005 Act therefore replaces one flawed safeguard with another flawed safeguard. This will impose a greater burden on professional advisers to ensure that the donor makes an informed choice about the persons to be notified. If close relatives are excluded, then it needs to be established whether there are suspicious grounds for doing so. If there is no one the potential donor might wish to be notified then at the very least the donor's adviser or doctor might be named as a person to be notified.

---

[120]   Difficulties often arise where the donor has several children, some of whom live further away or abroad. For practical purposes alone the child who lives nearest has the most involvement with the donor's affairs and is appointed attorney. Under the 1985 Act the other children are notified of the registration; in most cases they may not like the preference given to the attorney, and if they object, their objections to registration are not sustained; but at least they know what is being done and in many cases, valid objections to registration arise.

CREATION OF LASTING POWER OF ATTORNEY

Stages

3.71   A LPA is made in two stages to be valid as a LPA.

Execution

3.72   The first stage is the completion and execution of the prescribed form. This involves a number of steps, which may or may not be taken at some distance in time from each other:[121]

1. The donor completes and executes the prescribed form, by signing it in the presence of a witness. Although the 2005 Act refers to the time when the donor 'executes the instrument' there is no mention in the 2005 Act to execution as a deed.[122] A power of attorney is regarded as a deed and is executed in accordance with s 1 of the Law of Property (Miscellaneous Provisions) Act 1989.[123] This principle applies to an EPA which must be signed by the donor in the presence of a witness or if by someone else at the direction of the donor then in the presence of two witnesses.[124]

2. A statement by the donee or by each donee to the effect that he or she:[125]

    '(i) has read the prescribed information or a prescribed part of it (or has had it read to him); and

    (ii) understands the duties imposed on a donee of a lasting power of attorney under sections 1 (the principles) and 4 (best interests).'

3. The certificate of capacity is signed by a person of a prescribed description confirming that in his or her opinion, at the time the donor executes the instrument:[126]

---

[121]   The 2005 Act does not require these steps to be carried out in any particular order although it is assumed that regulations will specify that the prescribed form be completed in the same sequence as the formalities are shown in Sch 1, Part 1, para 2. Thus the donor must execute the power before the attorney executes his part of the power and before the certificate of capacity can be given.

[122]   Mental Capacity Act 2005, s 9(2)(c).

[123]   Powers of Attorney Act 1971, s 1.

[124]   Enduring Power of Attorney (Prescribed Form) Regulations 1990, SI 1990/1379. It has been suggested that the requirement that there be a separate certificate of capacity obviates the need for a witness to the donor's own signature in the prescribed form of LPA. However, draft forms issued by the Department for Constitutional Affairs provide for the donor's as well as the attorney's signatures to be witnessed.

[125]   Mental Capacity Act 2005, Sch 1, para 2(1)(d).

[126]   Mental Capacity Act 2005, Sch 1, para 2(1)(e).

'(i)   the donor understands the purpose of the instrument and the scope of the authority conferred under it,

(ii)   no fraud or undue pressure is being used to induce the donor to create a lasting power of attorney, and

(iii)   there is nothing else which would prevent a lasting power of attorney from being created by the instrument.'

Creation

3.73   The second stage of the process, which 'creates' the power is its registration with the Public Guardian.[127] Thus until the LPA is actually registered, it is ineffective as a power of attorney. The registration procedure is described in more detail below.

Status

Who can give a power

3.74   A LPA can only be granted by an individual who has reached the age of 18. The donor must therefore be an individual. A company, partnership, trust corporation or a couple cannot grant a LPA.

Who can receiver a power

3.75   The donee of the power must however be an individual who is 18 or a trust corporation although a trust corporation may only act as a donee in respect of property and affairs. The only other restriction on the choice of attorney is that a person who is bankrupt cannot be appointed an attorney in respect of the donor's property and affairs. However, an attorney who is bankrupt can be appointed to act under a welfare power.

Capacity

3.76   A person's capacity to execute a LPA is specific to that matter at the material time.[128] Although the 2005 Act sets out a framework for assessing capacity, and expects a person to certify that the donor 'understands the purpose of the instrument and the scope of the authority conferred under it' it is likely that the existing case-law will assist in determining questions concerning capacity to grant a LPA.

The principle that capacity to create an EPA required a different test to that of managing property and affairs was considered in the case of *Re K, Re F*.[129] Registration of an EPA was objected to on the grounds that

---

[127]   Mental Capacity Act 2005, s 9(2)(b).
[128]   Mental Capacity Act 2005, s 2(1).
[129]   [1988] Ch 310, [1988] 1 All ER 358, [1988] 2 WLR 781.

the power had been made immediately before an application was made for its registration. Hoffman J upheld the validity of the power and set out four basic requirements as to what the donor should understand:

> '... first, if such be the terms of the power, that the attorney will be able to assume complete authority over the donor's affairs; second, if such be the terms of the power, that the attorney will in general be able to do anything with the donor's property which the donor could have done; third, that the authority will continue if the donor should be or become mentally incapable; fourth, that if he should be or become mentally incapable, the power will be irrevocable without confirmation by the court.'

3.77   As with EPAs, a properly executed LPA will create a presumption of due execution. The certificate of capacity alone places a very strong burden on anyone objecting to registration on the grounds that the power is invalid. The Public Guardian furthermore has a positive duty to register a LPA unless he or she receives a valid objection to registration within the prescribed period or an objection is made to the Court.[130] However, the Court can only revoke the power if it is satisfied that one of the limited grounds allowed by the 2005 Act has been established.[131] Thus unless the Court is satisfied that the ground for revocation has been established, it cannot prevent the LPA from being registered.

This approach is the same applied by the Court of Protection in the context of registration of EPAs.[132] The evidential burden is weighted against the objector, which in practice makes it almost impossible for the Court to revoke an EPA on the grounds of its invalidity. Unless there is clear and compelling evidence that the donor lacked capacity at the time of execution or that there was fraud or undue influence, the Court must register the EPA. The same burden of proof will apply on anyone seeking to challenge the validity of the LPA.

REGISTRATION OF LASTING POWER OF ATTORNEY

The requirement of registration

3.78   A LPA is not effective as a power of attorney unless and until it is registered with the Public Guardian in accordance with Sch 1 to the 2005 Act.[133]

---

[130]   Mental Capacity Act 2005, Sch 1, Part 2, para 5.
[131]   Mental Capacity Act 2005, s 22(3).
[132]   *Re W* [2001] Ch 609, [2001] 4 All ER 88, [2001] 2 WLR 957, [2001] 1 FLR 832.
[133]   Mental Capacity Act 2005, s 9(2)(b).

The aim of the 2005 Act is to encourage early registration of LPAs, so that the process of validation and supervision is started as soon as the power is used. A welfare power can only operate in respect of those decisions which the donor lacks capacity to make.[134] However, a power relating to property and affairs can operate – so long as it is registered – notwithstanding the capacity of the donor. This has three practical benefits:

1. It avoids misuse of the power, where as often happens with EPAs the power is used by an attorney where it should be registered with the result that the donor's interests are not protected and the attorney (who may be acting in good faith) is acting beyond the scope of his or her authority.
2. The attorney is not required to conduct a medical assessment of the donor's capacity. He or she does not need to take the responsibility for or undergo the awkwardness of asserting that a person is mentally incapable.
3. No other person is entitled to make an assessment based on the fact, that by virtue of registration, the donor is incapable of managing all his or her property and affairs. Thus the fact of registration does not give rise to a presumption of incapacity.

Problems with early registration

3.79   While the benefits of early registration of a LPA are self-evident, there are also several disadvantages. A third party dealing directly with the donor of the LPA cannot make any assumption as to the donor's lack of capacity, but must make his or her own assessment of the donor's capacity at the relevant time. While this respects the integrity of the donor, the third party's position is less clear. A bank for example cannot rely on the fact of registration to prevent the donor from using his or her account, where for instance there are large or frequent withdrawals from the account. The donor therefore may have less protection against financial abuse than the donor of an EPA.

3.80   Although the aim of the 2005 Act is to encourage early registration of LPAs, it is likely that most donors and attorneys will not follow this in practice. A capable donor may well feel stigmatised by the fact of registration but is more likely to resent the expense and inconvenience of registration as well as the sense that this restricts his or her freedom. Of course the donor can revoke the LPA but he or she must still go through the process of having the registration cancelled.[135] This may

---

[134]   Mental Capacity Act 2005, s 11(7)(a).

[135]   It is not clear from the 2005 Act on what basis registration is to be cancelled where the donor has capacity to revoke the power. The grounds on which the Public Guardian *must* cancel registration under Sch 1, para 17 do not include the revocation by the donor who has capacity to revoke the power.

cause not only inconvenience, expense, embarrassment or family discord but force the donor to demonstrate to the Court of Protection or Public Guardian that he or she is capable of revoking the power.

It is therefore likely that in the great majority of cases, LPAs will not be used and therefore registered unless and until the donor becomes or is becoming incapable of managing his or her property and affairs. It is also likely that many LPAs will contain special conditions to this effect. Thus if most LPAs are registered on incapacity, most third parties dealing with the attorney will in practice make a natural assumption that the donor lacks capacity.

Procedure for registration

3.81   The procedure for registration of a LPA is relatively straightforward, and should not therefore deter attorneys from taking on their responsibilities to register and act under the LPA. In contrast to the procedure for registration of an EPA, the application may be made by the donor as well as by the attorney.

3.82   Application to register a LPA can be made by the donor or donee or by one of two or more donees appointed to act jointly and severally. Application must be made in the prescribed form, which contains the prescribed information.[136] Although the form is to be prescribed by regulations, it will of necessity contain enough information about the donor, the donee or donees and service of notices to enable the Public Guardian to deal with the registration process. The applicant for registration will also need to submit the original LPA and a prescribed fee.[137]

3.83   Where the donor has created separate LPAs in respect of property and affairs and welfare matters, then they will need to be registered separately. It will often be the case that different attorneys are appointed for different purposes or the powers need to be registered at different times. There is therefore no obvious mechanism for registering the two powers by the same process. It is arguable that a separate fee for each process may deter attorneys from registering a LPA until the last moment.[138]

---

[136]   Mental Capacity Act 2005, Sch 1, para 4(1).
[137]   Mental Capacity Act 2005, Sch 1, para 4(3). It is expected that the fee will be higher than the present registration fee of £120 to cover the additional steps to be taken by the Public Guardian to notify the donor and donees.
[138]   The unintended consequence is in fact quite positive: a welfare LPA is only intended as a 'last resort' and may well not need to be registered. Many donors whose property and affairs are dealt with by an attorney will carry on being cared for informally without the need for intervention by an attorney. Thus a welfare power will not be registered as a matter of course on incapacity, but may be held back until there is a dispute or contentious treatment that requires the authority of an attorney to resolve.

Status of attorney prior to registration

3.84   The 2005 Act provides that a LPA is not effective until it is registered.[139] There is no transitional or temporary authority that allows the donee to take steps to act under the LPA after the application has been made but before the power has been registered.[140] Where a donor has become incapable of carrying out an act for which authority is urgently required by the donee, the donee has no ability to act under the LPA, even though an application to register the power has been made.

This apparent omission from the 2005 Act may cause difficulties for an attorney who needs to administer the donor's affairs while the power is being registered. It may be that a short delay will not prejudice the donor's interests, but the situation is more complicated if registration is delayed for perhaps several months while there is a dispute over the validity of the power or the conduct of the attorney. If the attorney requires authority in the interim, he or she must either apply to the Court of Protection for a specific order or rely on the provisions of ss 7 and 8 of the 2005 Act. Thus a donee who needs to access the donor's bank account to pay for nursing home fees must either apply to the Court of Protection for an order or spend his or her own money and be reimbursed by the donor subsequently.

3.85   Where the donee wishes to resolve any queries concerning the validity of the power, he or she can apply to the Court of Protection for a determination under s 22(2) of the 2005 Act.

Notices

3.86   The person applying to register the LPA must give notice in the prescribed form to any person named in the LPA for that purpose of the intention to register the power.[141] The form of notice and method of service will be prescribed by regulations.

3.87   The applicant is only obliged to notify the persons named in the LPA for that purpose of his intention to register the power. The Public Guardian is responsible for notifying:

- the donor where the application is made by the donee or donees; or
- the donee or donees where the application is made by the donor.[142]

---

[139]   Mental Capacity Act 2005, s 9(2)(b).

[140]   Compare the provisions of the 1985 Act, s 1(2).

[141]   Mental Capacity Act 2005, Sch 1, para 6. The rationale for notifying only named persons is dealt with at **3.69**. There is no requirement for the donee to notify any close relatives or persons involved in the care and welfare of the donor unless they have been actually named by the donor for this purpose.

[142]   Mental Capacity Act 2005, Sch 1, paras 7 and 8.

Although regulations will prescribe the manner in which a notice can be delivered and the information to be contained within a notice, the only way in which the Public Guardian can practically give notice to the donor, is by sending the notice to the donor by post.[143]

Dispensing with notice

3.88 Only the Court can direct that service of a notice on a named person be dispensed with.[144] However, the Court must first be satisfied that no useful purpose would be served by giving notice. There is no corresponding power for the Court to dispense with the requirement for the Public Guardian to notify the donor.

There is no provision in the 2005 Act which allows the person who is applying to register the LPA to dispense with the service of notice without reference to the Court. Thus if the named person cannot be located or is incapable, the Court must first agree to notice being dispensed with before the application to register the power is made.[145]

Completion of registration

3.89 Unless there is a valid objection to registration of the LPA, the Public Guardian must register the power at the end of the prescribed period.[146] There is therefore a positive duty on the Public Guardian to register the power unless there is a defect in the power or a valid objection is received.

3.90 Once the LPA is registered, the Public Guardian must notify the donor and donee of the fact of registration in a prescribed form. While it is assumed that the original LPA will be sealed and endorsed with details of the registration and returned to the applicant or his or her solicitor, s 16(1) of the 2005 Act provides authority for office copies to be conclusive evidence of the fact of registration and the contents of the power.

---

[143] Whether or not this provides the donor with any greater level of protection than a requirement to give notice in person is debatable.

[144] Mental Capacity Act 2005, Sch 1, para 10.

[145] In contrast to the donee of an EPA who does not need to notify a relative if his or her name or address is not known to the attorney and cannot reasonably ascertained or the attorney believes that the relative is under 18 or mentally incapable (Enduring Powers of Attorney Act 1985, Sch 1, para 2(2)).

[146] Mental Capacity Act 2005, Sch 1, para 5. The 1985 Act specifies a period of 5 weeks, from the date of the last notice given to a person required to be notified (s 6(4)(a)).

Objections to registration

The role of the Public Guardian

3.91   The registration authority is the Public Guardian who must register the
       LPA unless:

   - it appears to the Public Guardian that the LPA is not a valid power,
     in which case the power cannot be registered unless directed by the
     Court;[147]
   - the Court of Protection has already appointed a deputy and it
     appears to the Public Guardian that the powers conferred on the
     deputy would conflict with the powers conferred on the attorney in
     which case the power cannot be registered unless directed by the
     Court;[148]
   - it appears to the Public Guardian that there is a provision in the
     instrument which would be ineffective as part of a LPA or which
     would prevent the power from operating as a LPA, in which case
     the power must be referred to the Court for determination;[149]
   - the Public Guardian receives a notice of objection from the donee or
     named person on one of the specified grounds and it appears to the
     Public Guardian that the ground for making the objection is
     satisfied, in which case he or she must not register the power unless
     directed by the Court;[150] or
   - the Court of Protection receives a notice of objection from the
     donee or named person on one of the prescribed grounds, the Public
     Guardian must not register the power unless directed by the
     Court.[151]

Objections made to the Public Guardian

3.92   The Public Guardian's authority to refuse registration of the LPA is
       limited to cases where there is a defect in the power, which is either
       apparent from the facts or which is brought to the Public Guardian's
       attention by a named person who is objecting to registration of the

---

[147]   Mental Capacity Act 2005, Sch 1, para 11(1). For example where the power was made
       using the incorrect form or there was a technical defect in the form which prevented it from
       operating as a valid LPA.

[148]   Mental Capacity Act 2005, Sch 1, para 12.

[149]   Mental Capacity Act 2005, Sch 1, para 11(2) and (3).

[150]   Mental Capacity Act 2005, Sch 1, para 13(1) and (2). These are the narrow or technical
       grounds defined in s 13(3) and (6)(a)–(d) on which the Public Guardian can refuse to
       register the power without reference to the Court. See **3.93**.

[151]   Mental Capacity Act 2005, Sch 1, para 13(3) and (4). This part of the 2005 Act refers to
       prescribed grounds and these are not defined. It can be assumed that these are the wider or
       substantive grounds defined in s 22(3) whereby the Court can direct that the power is not to
       be registered or revoke the power.

power. Although the 2005 Act provides for the Public Guardian to be notified by means of an objection, it would be more appropriate to describe this process as a technical or procedural notice.

In these cases a LPA is either revoked or the appointment of the attorney is terminated by operation of law rather than by the intervention of the Public Guardian. The Public Guardian's role is to refuse registration of the power in these circumstances. The Court can furthermore direct the Public Guardian to register the instrument, if, for example, the appointment in favour of one attorney is terminated but continues to operate in favour of the other attorney.

3.93 The grounds on which a named person or a donee (where the application is made by the donor or the other donee) can 'object' in this way are limited to the following cases:

- insofar as the LPA relates to the property and affairs of the donor , the bankruptcy of the donor or the donee or where the donee is a trust corporation, its winding up or dissolution;[152]
- the LPA has been disclaimed by the attorney;
- the death of the donee;
- the dissolution or annulment of the donor's marriage or civil partnership between the donor and the donee (unless the power excludes revocation in these circumstances); or
- the donee lacks capacity.

If the donor objects to registration of the LPA, the Public Guardian must refuse to register the LPA unless the Court of Protection is satisfied that the donor lacks capacity to object to the registration.[153]

The role of the Court of Protection

3.94 Where a donee or a named person receives a notice of registration and objects on one of the 'prescribed grounds' the Public Guardian cannot register the LPA until directed to do so by the Court of Protection.[154] The 'prescribed grounds' on which a person can object to registration are not defined by the 2005 Act but will mirror the grounds on which the Court can revoke a power under s 22.

3.95 The Court's powers are not limited to the period of registration, but can be exercised at any time after a person has executed a power or a power has been registered as a LPA. However, an objection to registration made after the power has been registered will require the leave of the Court.[155]

---

[152] Mental Capacity Act 2005, s 13(3) and (6)(b).
[153] Mental Capacity Act 2005, Sch 1, para 14.
[154] Mental Capacity Act 2005, Sch 1, para 13(3) and (4).
[155] Mental Capacity Act 2005, s 50(2).

The Court may in such cases either refuse to register the LPA or, if the donor lacks capacity, revoke the LPA.[156] The 2005 Act does not, however, allow the Court to revoke the LPA if the donor retains capacity. Thus if the power has already been registered where the donor has capacity and the Court is satisfied that undue pressure was used to create the power, it appears that the Court cannot interfere with the donor's choice of attorney.

Whether the requirements for the creation of the power have been met

3.96   The Court can determine any question relating to whether or not any of the requirements for creating or revoking a lasting power have been met.[157] This power covers not just the formal requirements of completing and executing the power, but also covers the ability or capacity of the donor to grant the power.

3.97   Although the Court may determine any question relating to the validity of the power, where an application to register is made, the Public Guardian is obliged to register the power unless one of the grounds for objection exists. This is consistent with the 1985 Act which imposes a positive obligation to register an EPA unless a valid ground for objection is established to the satisfaction of the Court, thereby placing the evidential burden of proof on the objector.[158] The Court will assume that a LPA which has been correctly executed and which contains a certificate of capacity has been validly executed and that alone will place a strong burden of proof on the objector seeking to establish that the donor lacked capacity.

Whether the power has been revoked

3.98   The Court may determine any question relating to whether the power has been revoked or otherwise come to an end. This power enables the Court to determine whether the power has been revoked by the donor. The donor must not only demonstrate capacity to revoke the instrument, but must also communicate to the donee an intention to revoke the power.

---

[156] Mental Capacity Act 2005, s 22(4). The power to refuse registration or revoke the power is without prejudice to the Court's powers to give directions under s 22.

[157] Mental Capacity Act 2005, s 22(2).

[158] Enduring Powers of Attorney Act 1985, s 6(6) and see *Re W* [2001] 1 FLR 832.

That fraud or undue pressure was used to induce the donor to create the power

3.99 If fraud pressure is alleged, the objection will be considered very carefully with the Court expecting all available evidence to be placed before it. Although the Court of Protection has wide powers to summon witnesses and cross-examine them, it is not an appropriate venue for a detailed investigation into an alleged fraud. If the LPA has been used improperly to commit a fraud then the police should be notified and the Court may revoke the power. If fraud is merely alleged, this may merely indicate a breakdown in relations between relatives or other concerned persons.

3.100 Similar considerations arise where 'undue pressure' is alleged. Pressure may be brought which is not 'undue pressure', for instance where an elderly client is regularly advised by a solicitor or concerned relative that he or she should make a power of attorney. 'Undue pressure' is a matter of degree and requires a subjective assessment of whether the pressure was extreme or disproportionate to the extent that the donor could not have executed the power of his or her own free will.

That the donee has behaved, is behaving or proposes to behave in a way that contravenes his or her authority or contrary to the donor's best interests

3.101 The Court's power to intervene in the absence of fraud or undue influence and where the power is otherwise valid is limited to two grounds only:
1. the donee has behaved, is behaving or proposes to behave in a way that contravenes his or her authority; or
2. the donee has behaved, is behaving or proposes to behave in a way that is not or would not be in the donor's best interests.

3.102 These two grounds represent a limitation in the Court's powers to intervene in the conduct of an attorney. The first ground, where the donor contravenes his or her authority, can only cover acts which are illegal or in breach of the attorney's fiduciary duty to the donor. Thus they are acts which are actionable in their own right and for which there would be a civil or criminal remedy. For instance, an attorney who causes loss to the donor's estate may be liable to remedy the loss and an attorney who ill-treats or neglects the donor may be guilty of an offence under s 44 of the 2005 Act.

3.103 It is the second of these two grounds that is problematic in practice. The difficulty for the Court is that the Court must impose its own view of what is in the donor's 'best interests' when there is no objective measure of a person's best interests. If the attorney takes account of the factors and consults with the persons referred to in s 4, then he or she has complied with the requirements of the 2005 Act if he or she 'reasonably believes that what he does or decides is in the best interests of the person concerned'. It will take time and no doubt several cases to establish the extent of the Court's power to impose its judgment as to a person's best interests and whether it can do this without finding that the attorney has in any event exceeded the scope of his or her authority.

A person challenging a LPA on this ground also has to cross a very high evidential threshold in showing that an action (let alone a proposed action) is contrary to a person's 'best interests'. It is likely that such cases will centre around a simple argument over 'best interests' and may involve the Court making a decision on a matter such as where the donor should live rather than on the operation of the LPA.

3.104 By contrast with the 1985 Act, the Court may refuse to register an enduring power or cancel such a power if satisfied that:

> '... having regard to all the circumstances and in particular the attorney's relationship to or connection with the donor, the attorney is unsuitable to be the donor's attorney.'

The 'unsuitability' ground gives the Court more discretion to intervene in cases where it might be difficult to prove, on the balance of probabilities, that an act or proposed act is not in a person's best interests. There are also cases where an attorney is unsuitable despite ostensibly acting in the donor's best interests. For example:

- two attorneys are in conflict and both claim to be acting in the donor's best interests; or
- the attorney's financial dealings with the donor's estate give rise to a potential conflict of interest or require further investigation, even though there is no evidence or it is very difficult to prove any actual wrongdoing.

The reason for changing the basis on which the Court of Protection can intervene is that the Court's powers should be consistent with the 2005 Act generally and applied in the context of the attorney's duty to act in the best interests of the donor.[159]

Procedure

3.105 The process for objection is not defined by the 2005 Act and it is not clear whether a different process will be applied for objections dealt with by the Public Guardian and the Court of Protection. Clearly an objector will have to provide some basic information concerning the donor's and the objector's name and address, the objector's relationship

---

[159] This follows the recommendation of the Law Commission, see Law Com No 231 at 7.58.

to the donor and the grounds for the objection. However, any objection must be made within the 'prescribed period'.[160]

3.106 Because the 2005 Act separates the Court's powers from the registration process carried out by the Public Guardian, it is likely that different fees will be charged by the Court apart from the fee payable on registration.[161] This may therefore act as a deterrent to unnecessary objections which centre on a family feud rather than a genuine concern for the best interests of the donor.

3.107 Where a person wishes to make an objection, the 2005 Act does not specify any process for objection to registration. Neither is it clear whether any different procedure applies once the power has been registered. The Court's powers in relation to the validity of LPAs contained in s 22 apply before or after the power has been registered. The Court's powers in relation to EPAs are currently dealt with under the Court of Protection (Enduring Power of Attorney) Rules 2001[162] which provide for an objection made after registration being treated as an application to cancel the power. The 2005 Act does, however, require any person other than the donor or donee of the power to have permission to make an application.[163]

Powers of the Court and Public Guardian

3.108 The powers of the Court of Protection to intervene in relation to LPAs and the role of the Public Guardian in that regard are considered in more detail in **CHAPTER 4**.

ENDURING POWERS OF ATTORNEY

The future of existing powers

3.109 The 2005 Act repeals the 1985 Act and provides for a new type of power of attorney, the LPA. No new EPAs can therefore be created.[164] There will, however, remain in place countless numbers of EPAs.[165] There is no reliable record of how many EPAs have been made and

---

[160] Mental Capacity Act 2005, Sch 1, para 13(1)(b) and (3)(b).

[161] At present only one fee of £120 is charged on an application to register an EPA regardless of whether the application is straightforward or involves a long drawn-out dispute.

[162] SI 2001/825.

[163] Mental Capacity Act 2005, s 50(1) and (2).

[164] Mental Capacity Act 2005, Sch 7.

[165] There is no reliable record of how many EPAs have actually been created. Probably tens if not hundreds of thousands have been created as 'insurance policies' and remain in deed boxes and solicitors' offices across the country.

what proportion of them should be registered on the grounds that the donor lacks capacity. These EPAs which are registrable as well as the thousands which have been registered cannot be replaced by new powers of attorney. Not only does the donor lack capacity to grant a new power, but it would be contrary to public policy to require donors – who have in good faith provided for the management of their property and affairs in the event of incapacity – to go to the effort and expense of making new powers of attorney. The 2005 Act[166] therefore addresses the status of those EPAs, registered and unregistered, made before the commencement of the new 2005 Act. These transitional provisions are considered in **CHAPTER 8**.

3.110 EPAs are dealt with in more detail above and a detailed account of the rules and principles applicable to their operation is beyond the scope of this work.[167] However, practitioners will need to be able to advise on and administer two distinct types of statutory power of attorney and apply different principles and procedures to each one. There will no doubt be endless debate over whether one is better than the other, but the inevitable result will be the complexity of two different jurisdictions applicable to persons in identical circumstances. Given the difficulties faced by the Court of Protection and Public Guardianship Office in operating one jurisdiction, it must be hoped that the new Court of Protection and Public Guardian will fare better than its predecessor in the operation of two jurisdictions.

---

[166] See Mental Capacity Act 2005, Sch 4.

[167] See **3.6–3.13**. The topic is covered in greater and better detail in *Cretney & Lush on Enduring Powers of Attorney* (Jordans, 5th edn, 2001) which will remain the definitive work on the subject. See also *Heywood & Massey: Court of Protection Practice* (Sweet & Maxwell). The same law and procedure will apply to existing EPAs, only different statutory provisions will apply to their operation.

Chapter 4

Powers of the Court

Preliminary

4.1   The Mental Capacity Act 2005 ('the 2005 Act') only sets out the basic powers of the new Court of Protection and how these are to be implemented will not be known until the new Court Rules and Practice Directions have been produced. To some extent the manner in which the Court will operate and exercise its powers must therefore be a matter of speculation, but in addition to explaining the Court's powers an attempt is made here to address some of the issues that must be faced.

DECLARATIONS

Background

4.2   In regard to serious medical treatment and, more recently, welfare decisions the High Court has found it necessary to make declarations as to both capacity and then best interests when there is uncertainty or dispute over these issues in relation to an individual.[1] The High Court has had to do this under its inherent powers because the courts do not have power to make decisions on behalf of those who lack capacity.

This vacuum in the law has now been resolved by the 2005 Act which not only puts declarations on a statutory basis but also enables decisions to be made.

4.3   The civil and family courts in general struggle when doubt is raised as to the mental capacity of a party because generic judges have little experience in this area. Nevertheless, these courts must then decide whether the party is a 'patient' who needs to be represented by a suitable person and if so the implications of the lack of capacity.[2]

General powers of the court

4.4   The new Court of Protection may make declarations as to:

---

[1]   For the case-law and a further explanation reference should be made to CHAPTER 5.
[2]   This topic is covered in CHAPTER 1.

(a) whether a person has or lacks capacity to make a decision specified in the declaration;

(b) whether a person has or lacks capacity to make decisions on such matters as are described in the declaration;

(c) the lawfulness or otherwise of any act done, or yet to be done, in relation to that person.

In this respect an 'act' includes an omission and a course of conduct.[3]

Declarations as to capacity

4.5   The existing jurisdiction under the Mental Health Acts requires the present Court of Protection to make an initial decision as to whether the individual is a patient and thus within its jurisdiction. That decision is seldom reconsidered thereafter and usually a receiver is appointed to manage the patient's property and financial affairs unless there is so little involved that a short order can be made delegating everything to a suitable person without continuing supervision. The emphasis is thus on protection.

Under the new jurisdiction there will be a constant need to reassess capacity in regard to different decisions and at different times. The emphasis becomes empowerment, with protection when necessary. This power to make declarations as to capacity in regard to a particular decision or range of decisions will therefore be of considerable importance.

4.6   As the judges of the Court of Protection will be nominated from amongst circuit and district judges and sit on a regional basis, it will become possible for them to be treated as specialists in capacity issues. Colleagues can refer to them for guidance or even transfer cases to them when difficult issues as to capacity arise. This may be helpful not only for case management but also for substantive decisions. There is the potential for these judges not only to make declarations as to capacity (which may be treated as binding within particular proceedings in another court) but also to sit in a dual jurisdiction.

Declarations as to medical treatment

4.7   Although the Court may actually make decisions concerning medical treatment under its new statutory powers, it is likely that in serious or developing situations a declaration as to the lawfulness of treatment will be preferred because this delegates to the medical profession the decision as to whether treatment is appropriate in the circumstances.

For situations where the treatment will definitely be provided if it is authorised (eg non-therapeutic dental treatment or cosmetic surgery for

---

[3]   Mental Capacity Act 2005, s 15.

a learning disabled adult) there is no reason why the Court should not exercise its power to make the treatment decision.

MAKING DECISIONS AND APPOINTING DEPUTIES

Powers of the Court

4.8   If a person ('P') lacks capacity in relation to a matter or matters concerning his or her personal welfare, or his or her property and affairs, the Court is given certain powers, but these are subject to the provisions of the 2005 Act and, in particular, to s 1 (the principles) and s 4 (best interests).[4] In these situations the court may:[5]

(a) by making an order, make the decision or decisions on P's behalf in relation to the matter or matters, or

(b) appoint a person (a 'deputy') to make decisions on P's behalf in relation to the matter or matters.

An order of the Court may be varied or discharged by a subsequent order.

Making decisions

General

4.9   When deciding whether it is in P's best interests to appoint a deputy, the court must have regard (in addition to the matters mentioned in s 4[6]) to the principles that:

(a) a decision by the court is to be preferred to the appointment of a deputy to make a decision; and

(b) the powers conferred on a deputy should be as limited in scope and duration as is reasonably practicable in the circumstances.

4.10   The Court may make such further orders or give such directions, and confer on a deputy such powers or impose on him or her such duties, as it thinks necessary or expedient for giving effect to, or otherwise in connection with, an order or appointment made by it. The Court may make the order, give the directions or make the appointment on such terms as it considers are in P's best interests, even though no application is before the court for an order, directions or an appointment on those terms.

---

[4]   These are dealt with in **CHAPTER 2**.

[5]   Mental Capacity Act 2005, s 16.

[6]   This defines the concept of best interests – see generally **CHAPTER 2**.

Children

4.11   Some flexibility may be provided in regard to people under the age of
        18 years. The Lord Chancellor may by order make provision as to the
        transfer of proceedings relating to a person under 18, in such
        circumstances as are specified in the order:

        (a) from the Court of Protection to a court having jurisdiction under the
            Children Act 1989; or
        (b) from a court having jurisdiction under that Act to the Court of
            Protection.[7]

Personal welfare

4.12   The powers as respects P's personal welfare extend in particular to:[8]

        (a) deciding where P is to live;
        (b) deciding what contact, if any, P is to have with any specified
            persons;
        (c) making an order prohibiting a named person from having contact
            with P;
        (d) giving or refusing consent to the carrying out or continuation of a
            treatment by a person providing healthcare for P;
        (e) giving a direction that a person responsible for P's healthcare allow
            a different person to take over that responsibility,

        but this is subject to the restrictions on deputies set out below.

Property and affairs

4.13   The powers as respects P's property and affairs extend in particular to:[9]

        (a) the control and management of P's property;
        (b) the sale, exchange, charging, gift or other disposition of P's
            property;
        (c) the acquisition of property in P's name or on P's behalf;
        (d) the carrying on, on P's behalf, of any profession, trade or business;
        (e) the taking of a decision which will have the effect of dissolving a
            partnership of which P is a member;
        (f) the carrying out of any contract entered into by P;
        (g) the discharge of P's debts and of any of P's obligations, whether
            legally enforceable or not;
        (h) the settlement of any of P's property, whether for P's benefit or for
            the benefit of others;
        (i) the execution for P of a will;

---

[7]   Mental Capacity Act 2005, s 21.
[8]   Mental Capacity Act 2005, s 17.
[9]   Mental Capacity Act 2005, s 18.

    (j) the exercise of any power (including a power to consent) vested in P whether beneficially or as trustee or otherwise;

    (k) the conduct of legal proceedings in P's name or on P's behalf.

4.14   The powers as respects matters relating to P's property and affairs may be exercised even though P has not reached 16, if the court considers it likely that P will still lack capacity to make decisions in respect of that matter when he or she reaches 18. Once again restrictions apply to deputies as set out below.

Wills

4.15   The Court can thus, if P is an adult, make an order or give directions requiring or authorising a person ('the authorised person') to execute a will on behalf of P. The restrictions prevent this being done by a deputy or if P has not reached 18.

4.16   There are further provisions in respect of wills in Sch 2 to the 2005 Act. The will may make any provision (whether by disposing of property or exercising a power or otherwise) which could be made by a will executed by P if he or she had capacity to make it. The will must:

    (a) state that it is signed by P acting by the authorised person;

    (b) be signed by the authorised person with the name of P and his or her own name in the presence of two or more witnesses present at the same time;

    (c) be attested and subscribed by those witnesses in the presence of the authorised person; and

    (d) be sealed with the official seal of the Court.

    If a will has been so executed the Wills Act 1837 ('the 1837 Act') has effect in relation to the will as if it were signed by P by his or her own hand, except that s 9 of the 1837 Act (requirements as to signing and attestation) does not apply, and in the subsequent provisions of the 1837 Act any reference to execution in the manner required by the previous provisions is to be read as a reference to execution as stated above.

4.17   The will then has the same effect for all purposes as if P had had the capacity to make a valid will, and the will had been executed by him or her in the manner required by the 1837 Act. But this does not apply in relation to the will insofar as:

    (a) it disposes of immovable property outside England and Wales; or

    (b) it relates to any other property or matter if, when the will is executed, P is domiciled outside England and Wales, and under the law of P's domicile, any question of his or her testamentary capacity would fall to be determined in accordance with the law of a place outside England and Wales.

Settlements

4.18   Special provisions in regard to settlements are also to be found in Sch 2
        to the 2005 Act. The Court may make vesting or other orders as
        required, and may vary or revoke a settlement in certain circumstances.
        The Court may also order that investments be vested in a suitable
        curator outside England and Wales.[10]

Miscellaneous

4.19   Further provisions enable the Court to preserve the interests of others
        (eg under a will or in intestacy) in property disposed of on behalf of the
        person lacking capacity. This might involve transferring the interest to a
        replacement property. There can also be a charge imposed for P's
        benefit on property that has been improved at P's expense.[11]

Deputies

Appointment

4.20   As stated above, instead of making decisions itself the Court may
        appoint a person (a 'deputy') to make decisions on P's behalf in relation
        to matters concerning P's personal welfare, or P's property and affairs,
        or both.[12] A deputy is to be treated as P's agent in relation to anything
        done or decided by him or her within the scope of his or her
        appointment and in accordance with the 2005 Act.

Who may be appointed?

4.21   A deputy appointed by the Court must be an individual who has reached
        18, but for powers in relation to property and affairs the deputy could be
        a trust corporation. A person may not be appointed as a deputy without
        his or her consent, but the Court may appoint an individual by
        appointing the holder for the time being of a specified office or position.

        The Court may appoint two or more deputies to act jointly, jointly and
        severally, or jointly in respect of some matters and jointly and severally
        in respect of others. The Court may also appoint one or more other
        persons to succeed the existing deputy or deputies in such
        circumstances, or on the happening of such events, as may be specified
        by the Court and for such period as may be so specified.

---

[10]   Mental Capacity Act 2005, Sch 2, paras 5, 6 and 7.
[11]   Mental Capacity Act 2005, Sch 2, paras 8 and 9.
[12]   Mental Capacity Act 2005, s 19.

Control of the deputy

4.22   The Court may require a deputy:

(a) to give to the Public Guardian such security as the Court thinks fit for the due discharge of his or her functions; and

(b) to submit to the Public Guardian such reports at such times or at such intervals as the Court may direct.

Powers

4.23   The Court may confer on a deputy powers to take possession or control of all or any specified part of P's property and to exercise all or any specified powers in respect of it, including such powers of investment as the Court may determine.

The deputy is entitled to be reimbursed out of P's property for his or her reasonable expenses in discharging his or her functions and, if the Court so directs when appointing him or her, to remuneration out of P's property.

4.24   There are various restrictions on the powers of deputies appointed by the Court and indeed of the powers that the Court may give to deputies.[13] The authority conferred on a deputy is always subject to the provisions of the 2005 Act and, in particular, s 1 (the principles) and s 4 (best interests).[14]

Conditional on lack of capacity

4.25   A deputy does not have power to make a decision on behalf of P in relation to a matter if he or she knows or has reasonable grounds for believing that P has capacity in relation to the matter.

Powers that cannot be given

4.26   A deputy may not be given power:

(a) to prohibit a named person from having contact with P;

(b) to direct a person responsible for P's healthcare to allow a different person to take over that responsibility;

(c) with respect to the settlement of any of P's property, whether for P's benefit or for the benefit of others;

(d) with respect to the execution for P of a will; or

(e) with respect to the exercise of any power (including a power to consent) vested in P whether beneficially or as trustee or otherwise.

---

[13]   See Mental Capacity Act 2005, s 20.

[14]   These are dealt with in **CHAPTER 2**.

Medical treatment

4.27   A deputy may not refuse consent to the carrying out or continuation of life-sustaining treatment in relation to P.

Conflict with an attorney

4.28   A deputy may not be given power to make a decision on behalf of P which is inconsistent with a decision made, within the scope of his or her authority and in accordance with the 2005 Act, by the donee of a lasting power of attorney granted by P (or, if there is more than one donee, by any of them).

Restraint

4.29   A deputy may not do an act that is intended to restrain P unless the following four conditions are satisfied:
   1. in doing the act, the deputy is acting within the scope of an authority expressly conferred on him or her by the Court;
   2. P lacks, or the deputy reasonably believes that P lacks, capacity in relation to the matter in question;
   3. the deputy reasonably believes that it is necessary to do the act in order to prevent harm to P; and
   4. the act is a proportionate response to the likelihood of P's suffering harm, or the seriousness of that harm.

4.30   A deputy will be treated as having restrained P if he or she uses, or threatens to use, force to secure the doing of an act which P resists, or restricts P's liberty of movement, whether or not P resists, or if he or she authorises another person to do any of those things. But a deputy does more than merely restrain P if he or she deprives P of his or her liberty within the meaning of Art 5(1) of the Human Rights Convention (whether or not the deputy is a public authority).

Revocation of appointment

4.31   The Court may revoke the appointment of a deputy or vary the powers conferred on him or her if it is satisfied that the deputy:
   (a) has behaved, or is behaving, in a way that contravenes the authority conferred on him or her by the Court or is not in P's best interests, or
   (b) proposes to behave in a way that would contravene that authority or would not be in P's best interests.

How will the Court exercise these powers?

The new approach

4.32　The Court will thus have a wide range of options for decision-making on behalf of the incapacitated person ('P'). It may make supervised or non-supervised single orders, or may appoint a deputy to make all decisions or a specified range of decisions in regard to personal welfare matters and/or financial affairs. The Court will have a duty to take into account P's best interests as now defined but also to act in a way that is least restrictive of P's rights and freedom of action. The all-or-nothing approach of the past will no longer be appropriate.

There will be a desire to deal with matters so that they do not need to be repeatedly referred back to the Court, and in cases where this would be likely the appointment of a deputy may be appropriate. Conversely, if only a one-off decision is needed, perhaps about the grant of a tenancy or minor medical treatment for a person with learning disabilities, it would be unduly restrictive to appoint a deputy.

4.33　The administration is at present trying to anticipate the types of orders that judges will make and the frequency with which they will make different orders so that it can plan its procedures and allocate resources for the future, but it is only when the nominated judges start to hear cases that this will be known. Whilst the administration can indicate the types of outcome that it can best cope with, it is not in a position to dictate to judges the types of order that should be made and in what circumstances. Nevertheless, training of those nominated to sit in this jurisdiction will be essential, and an attempt will inevitably be made to discuss and achieve some consistency of approach.[15]

The bulk of this work will relate to the management of financial affairs (as at present) and in considering the range of orders that is likely to be made it is instructive to consider the existing receiverships which will inevitably continue in one form or another.

What will happen to receiverships?

The present regime

4.34　Until recently, unless a short order was appropriate, the standard outcome has been to appoint a receiver who administers the financial affairs of the patient under the supervision of the Court. This is costly and bureaucratic, and, although control over limited finances might be

---

[15]　This training will be carried out by judges through the Judicial Studies Board and must take into account the needs of the Public Guardian who will provide the administration to implement the orders that are made.

delegated to the patient, there is a reluctance by receivers to allow this in case they are later criticised. Recently there has been a tendency for the Court to adopt a less interventionist approach. The following case is an example:

> 'The patient who had recovered significant damages for a brain injury fell out with his solicitor receiver so the Public Trustee (later the Chief Executive of the Public Guardianship Office) was appointed. The patient was frustrated by the control over his spending and applied to be released from the jurisdiction. Instead the Master approved an order discharging the receiver and retaining the fund in court whilst mandating the interest to the patient and giving him the right to receive all his state benefits. The home that had been purchased for him was vested under the control of the Court.
>
> On transfer of the file from the receivership division to the "short order section" this arrangement was questioned as not meeting normal criteria. The patient then complained when he was not given access to the fund to cover debts which he had incurred. The case was referred to the regional hearing centre for resolution at an attended hearing. The Deputy Master explained to the patient how the procedure was intended to operate and that he should manage his budget so that the fund was not prematurely exhausted. The procedure was commended as being the least restrictive option and the patient was satisfied that it empowered him whilst providing necessary protection with minimum supervision. He was permitted to make infrequent applications for release of capital for specific purposes.'

The new regime

4.35   In many cases, the existing receiver will simply have to be replaced by a deputy with the same powers and there will be little more than a change of title. But where appropriate, arrangements such as that set out above are likely to be more frequent under the new jurisdiction, which favours the least restrictive approach so that a single order of the Court is preferred to the appointment of a deputy which requires the ongoing management (and supervision) of a person's affairs. The Court may also be inclined, especially in the case of professional receivers, to give them powers similar to those exercisable under lasting powers of attorney dealing with financial affairs.[16] There may even be a greater willingness to approve settlements rather than retain funds.

The key criteria will be whether the continued involvement of the Office of the Public Guardian provides added value. This may depend upon an assessment of the family and other persons involved and of the

---

[16]   The Court of Protection has already demonstrated this approach through the issue of Extended General Orders to professional receivers. These provide similar powers to those an attorney would have under an EPA save that the receiver must still provide security and submit annual accounts.

risks involved in permitting more delegation. To some extent this risk can be minimised by requiring insurance bonds to be in place.[17]

4.36 The approach to investment of funds is also likely to change with the deputy being expected to seek advice from an Independent Financial Adviser, and the special account which presently provides interest above market rates may cease to be available.

CONTROL OF LASTING POWERS OF ATTORNEY

Court's powers to intervene

General

4.37 Until the registration of a lasting power of attorney ('LPA') is revoked by a donor with capacity or by the Court on any of the specified grounds, the attorney (in the 2005 Act referred to as 'the donee') can continue to act with all the powers of an attorney subject to any restrictions and conditions contained in the power.[18] The Court, however, retains its statutory powers which are exercisable at any time, not just to revoke or cancel the power or attach conditions to the attorney's conduct, but also to guide the attorney or provide authority where the attorney requires this to carry out his or her duties under the power.[19]

4.38 All these powers which are specific to the operation of LPAs are in addition to the Court's general powers which are exercisable in respect of any matter in which a person lacks capacity, whether or not the attorney has authority to act in respect of the same matter. Thus the Court has power to make a declaration of capacity under s 15, decisions in respect of personal welfare under s 17 and decisions concerning a person's property and affairs under s 18.

In most cases, the Court will be required to exercise its powers where these are needed to supplement the attorney's powers under the LPA. For example, if the power is restricted to property and affairs the attorney may apply to the Court of Protection for a decision concerning treatment or welfare. A LPA furthermore does not authorise the attorney to make a will or settlement.

---

[17] Mental Capacity Act 2005, s 58(1)(e) allows for the Public Guardian to receive security 'which the court requires a person to give for the discharge of his functions'.
[18] See generally CHAPTER 3.
[19] These matters are considered in greater detail in CHAPTER 3.

4.39　Conflicts between the authority of the Court and the authority of the attorney should be rare. If the attorney has authority to carry out an act under the LPA then there is no need for the Court to intervene unless there are grounds for overruling the attorney, for instance if the attorney is acting contrary to the best interests of the donor. There may also be cases where the attorney simply requires the assistance of the Court to confirm that a proposed act may be carried out.

Specific powers

Creation and revocation

4.40　The Court may determine any question relating to whether the requirements for the creation of the power have been met or the power has been revoked or come to an end.[20] There is concern that although there is a prescribed form which must be adopted, the Public Guardian is to ignore an immaterial difference and the Court:

> '... may declare that an instrument which is not in the prescribed form is to be treated as if it were, if it is satisfied that the persons executing the instrument intended it to create a lasting power of attorney.'[21]

It is feared that the Office of the Public Guardian and the Court will be faced with numerous applications to permit registration of otherwise defective forms. A relaxed response would encourage a sloppy approach to these important documents, whereas refusal to register will generally result in an application for the appointment of a deputy. The imposition of a set procedure with a separate fee for these applications may resolve this dilemma.[22]

4.41　Unless a hearing is needed these applications are likely to be dealt with 'on paper' under the supervision of the senior judge in London rather than sent to regional judges. Whilst the view may be taken that in the absence of objections it is preferable to empower the donor by registering the power, how will the intention of the donor be known? Defective forms are most likely to arise where there has been no proper professional advice and these are the very situations where lack of capacity or undue pressure tends to arise. To some extent the certificate of capacity on the form provides a safeguard, but at this stage this will merely be a signature on the form. The absence of such a certificate would be a fatal defect and the Court may adopt a policy of requiring further information from the maker of the certificate before accepting a defective form.

---

[20]　Mental Capacity Act 2005, s 22(2).
[21]　Mental Capacity Act 2005, Sch 1, Part 1, para 3(2).
[22]　The fee should ensure that these applications are not subsidised by those whose applications for registration are in order.

Capacity

4.42   The Court's power to determine any question relating to whether the requirements for the creation of the power have been met will extend to whether the donor had the capacity to execute it.[23] Lack of capacity at the time of execution is often alleged in dysfunctional family cases, but the onus is on an objector to establish this and it is difficult to do so retrospectively in the absence of contemporary medical evidence. The objectors must therefore turn to one of the grounds on which registration of the power may be refused.

Registration

4.43   The Court may refuse registration or revoke an otherwise valid power if satisfied that:

1.   fraud or undue pressure was used to induce the donor to create the power;[24] or
2.   the attorney (or, if more than one, any of them) has behaved, is behaving or proposes to behave in a way that contravenes his or her authority or is not in the donor's best interests[25]

If there is more than one attorney the Court may revoke the power so far as it relates to any of them thus allowing it to be registered as regards another.[26] Presumably if fraud or undue pressure is established the whole power must fail (although the 2005 Act appears to provide otherwise), but it is not clear whether the Court is empowered to remove one misbehaving attorney under a joint power (as distinct from a joint and several power).[27]

4.44   The approach to fraud or undue pressure is unlikely to change from that now adopted in relation to enduring powers of attorney. Fraud does not require further comment, but in the case of dysfunctional families (and even where a solicitor has been involved) there is generally an objection on the basis of undue pressure in the execution of the power. There can be no objection to mere influence – it is undue pressure that is objectionable, but the boundaries may be difficult to define.[28]

The new certificate of capacity on the LPA form should assist in these cases. It will be interesting to see if the makers of these certificates attend hearings to give evidence as to the manner in which they have formed their opinion that the donor understood the purpose of the

---

[23]   Mental Capacity Act 2005, s 9(2)(c).

[24]   Mental Capacity Act 2005, s 22(3)(a).

[25]   Mental Capacity Act 2005, s 22(3)(b).

[26]   Mental Capacity Act 2005, s 22(5).

[27]   Reference should be made to the Mental Capacity Act 2005, s 10(6) in this context.

[28]   There may be no difference between 'undue pressure' and 'undue influence' in respect of which there is considerable case-law.

instrument and the scope of the authority given under it, and that execution was not induced by fraud or undue pressure.[29] If the maker is a practising solicitor it would be preferable to have taken instructions from and acted for the donor rather than simply to have provided the certificate.

4.45   In these dysfunctional family cases it will generally also be necessary for the Court to decide whether:

> '... one or more of the attorneys has behaved, is behaving or intends to behave in a way that contravenes his authority or is not in the donor's best interests.'

Even if such a finding is made there will be a discretion on the part of the Court to overlook the behaviour, taking into account all the circumstances. This differs from the equivalent ground under enduring powers of attorney, which is (and remains for those powers yet to be registered):

> '... that, having regard to all the circumstances and in particular the attorney's relationship to or connection with the donor, the attorney is unsuitable to be the donor's attorney.'

A test based on behaviour is very different from one based upon suitability, and it will be interesting to see how this change affects the conduct and outcome of these cases especially where there is implacable hostility within the family. More findings of fact may be needed and this will affect the length of hearings. If past behaviour is relied upon and the donor knew about this when the LPA was executed, it may be difficult to argue that such behaviour, or the propensity for such behaviour in the future, is not in the donor's best interests. This change demonstrates a move away from a paternalistic approach towards empowerment of the donor whose choice of attorney must be respected. It will shift the emphasis when objections are raised from suitability of the attorneys to the validity of the power and the presumption of validity may dictate the outcome in most cases. There will be cases where, despite genuine concerns as to the manner in which a LPA was procured and the intentions of the attorney, family members cannot establish an objection to registration and bringing an application to revoke the power when there has been actual misbehaviour may prove to be 'closing the stable door after the horse has bolted'.

Meaning and effect of the power

4.46   The Court may determine any question as to the meaning or the effect of the LPA (or an instrument purporting to create a LPA). The Court

---

[29]   The limited extent to which solicitors who have acted in the preparation of enduring powers of attorney are presently called to give evidence in support of the power does not provide an encouraging precedent.

may therefore clarify any uncertainty as to the form of the power or the scope of the attorney's authority.[30]

Directions to the attorney

4.47　The Court may, if the donor lacks capacity, give directions with respect to decisions the attorney has authority to make or give any consent or authorisation to act which the attorney would have to obtain from a mentally capable donor.[31] Thus an attorney who is unsure about whether he or she has authority to act can obtain prior approval from the Court before acting. An attorney who might otherwise need to obtain the consent of the donor to a proposed act, where, for instance, he or she may benefit from the act or the act is subject to the express agreement of the donor, can also obtain the prior approval of the Court.

Rendering accounts, etc

4.48　The Court may, if the donor lacks capacity, give directions to the attorney with respect to the rendering of accounts or production of records, require the attorney to supply information or produce documents,[32] and give directions with regard to remuneration or expenses.[33] These are useful powers and mirror those for enduring powers of attorney.[34]

It may be rare in practice for the Court to authorise the production of accounts whether to the Court or to a third party,[35] but the power can be useful to dispel mistrust and suspicion within families in regard to financial management. An objection to registration may be withdrawn if the Court is prepared to require basic financial disclosure to an objector whose intervention might be justifiable, and the power must then be registered. This is sometimes preferable to revocation of the power and the imposition of a professional receiver (at present) or deputy (under the new jurisdiction). There is a difficult balance to be achieved between maintaining confidentiality in regard to the donor's financial affairs which should not automatically be disclosed to family members on the onset of mental incapacity, and avoiding the suspicion and mistrust that arises when a financial manager is unduly secretive especially when all involved are potential beneficiaries of the donor's estate.

---

[30]　Mental Capacity Act 2005, s 23(1).

[31]　Mental Capacity Act 2005, s 23(2).

[32]　For example the deeds to a property or a testamentary document where it is a confidential document.

[33]　Mental Capacity Act 2005, s 23(3)(a), (b) and (c).

[34]　Enduring Powers of Attorney Act 1985, s 8(2)(c).

[35]　*Re C (Power of Attorney)* [2000] 2 FLR 1 provides one example of an account being required.

Relieving the attorney of liability

4.49   The Court has power, if the donor lacks capacity, to relieve the attorney
        wholly or partly from any liability which he or she has or may have
        incurred on account of a breach of his or her duties as attorney.[36]
        Although this power is included in the 2005 Act with those set out
        under the above heading it is fundamentally different in nature being
        retrospective in nature. Where financial shortcomings are involved it
        may be difficult to find that relief for the attorney is in the best interests
        of the donor. Where a liability has been incurred to a third party, which
        could presumably be for breach of contract or negligence, relieving the
        attorney of liability would presumably involve requiring the donor to
        provide an indemnity because this provision is not intended to take
        away the rights of third parties. Nevertheless, this provision enables the
        Court to provide relief where the donor would have done if capable.

Gifts

4.50   The Court may authorise the making of any gift which is beyond the
        scope of the attorney's limited authority under s 12(2) of the 2005 Act.[37]

Applying to the Court

4.51   A donor or an attorney under a LPA does not require permission from
        the Court to make an application for the exercise of any of its powers.[38]
        Neither does the 2005 Act appear to prevent the Court from exercising
        its powers of its own volition, for instance in response to a report made
        to it by the Public Guardian or a Visitor. However, permission is
        required for any other person to make an application. If permission is
        sought it may initially be refused 'on paper' by a nominated judge, but
        in such event the Rules should provide a right to an attended hearing
        without notice being given to other prospective parties.[39]

        There is therefore no automatic right for a close relative to apply to the
        Court if he or she is concerned that a LPA is being misused by the
        attorney and wishes the Court to intervene. While this power might be
        used to deprive concerned persons of a proper remedy, it is unlikely that
        the Court will ignore genuine concerns about the conduct of the
        attorney. However, there may be cases where a formal application is
        unnecessarily contentious and the Court may be able to obtain a report
        from the attorney and require the Public Guardian to make inquiries. In
        such cases a concerned relative or other body may make a complaint to
        the Public Guardian about the conduct of the attorney and then leave the

---

[36]   Mental Capacity Act 2005, s 23(3)(d).
[37]   Mental Capacity Act 2005, s 23(4).
[38]   Mental Capacity Act 2005, s 50(1)(c).
[39]   The Civil Procedure Rules 1998, SI 1998/3132 adopt this approach.

Public Guardian to make inquiries or take action directly or through the Court of Protection.[40]

4.52 The formalities of an application will be governed by Court of Protection Rules to be introduced pursuant to s 51(1) of the 2005 Act.

The role of the Public Guardian

4.53 The role of the Public Guardian has been considered in more detail in **CHAPTER 3** in the context of his or her principle role of registering LPAs. The Public Guardian will also be responsible for registering enduring powers of attorney ('EPAs') created before the coming into force of the 2005 Act.[41] However, the Public Guardian will have a distinct legal personality as well as an important administrative role, dealing with most routine applications to the Court of Protection.[42]

4.54 It is likely that where LPAs are concerned, the Public Guardian will be the main administrative focus for all applications and inquiries, whether contentious or non-contentious. Thus the Public Guardian will be able to determine whether applications need to be forwarded to the Court or can be addressed through correspondence by the Public Guardian.

The Public Guardian will therefore have the following statutory functions:[43]
1. establishing and maintaining a register of LPAs;
2. directing Court of Protection Visitors to visit the donee of a LPA and making reports on such matters as the Public Guardian may direct;
3. receiving reports from donees of LPAs;[44]
4. reporting to the Court of Protection on such matters as the Court requires; and
5. dealing with representations (including complaints) about the way in which a donee is exercising his or her powers.

4.55 The Secretary of State may by regulations confer other functions in connection with the 2005 Act upon the Public Guardian or make provision in connection with the discharge of his or her functions.[45] It is therefore likely that the Public Guardian's role will be developed beyond the scope of the present Public Guardianship Office, so that

---

[40] Mental Capacity Act 2005, s 58(1)(h).
[41] Mental Capacity Act 2005, Sch 4, para 4(2). See **CHAPTER 8**.
[42] The powers and responsibilities of the Public Guardian are considered in more detail in **CHAPTER 7**.
[43] Mental Capacity Act 2005, s 58.
[44] The Public Guardian receives the report but only the Court can direct a report, see ss 23(3)(a) and 49(2).
[45] Mental Capacity Act 2005, s 58.

through his or her office he or she can take a more pro-active role in monitoring the operation of LPAs. In view of the likely volume of transactions it is unlikely that there will be much scope for routine investigation, but where there are complaints or concerns are expressed about the conduct of an attorney, the Public Guardian will be able to respond and make inquiries. In most cases a call for a report from a public body such as the Public Guardian and some discrete correspondence or negotiation may be sufficient to address the particular concern. In other cases the Public Guardian will be expected to advise and involve the Court to ensure that action is taken.[46]

LIVING WITH THE NEW JURISDICTION

Overview

4.56   People who lack mental capacity fall into four broad groups:

1.   The largest group comprises elderly people who are deprived of capacity due to senile dementia, a condition that tends to be irreversible. They have enjoyed personal autonomy in the past and may have a personal income and savings that require management, but are no longer able to conduct their own lives.

2.   People with learning disabilities[47] form the second distinct group. They may never have matured to the stage where they can live a totally independent and self-supporting life, and in consequence do not have significant savings or incomes unless they have come into an inheritance.

3.   Some people are deprived of mental capacity for a period or periods of their lives due to a mental illness which might be treatable. They will need to be supported and protected when the illness is acute but at other times can make their own decisions and may be financially successful.

4.   The fourth group comprises people who have had a brain injury which affects their ability to make decisions. This is seldom treatable and may be linked with physical disabilities. Large sums of compensation may need to be managed to finance a comprehensive care plan.

Each of these groups presents different challenges as regards both financial and care management, and some people overlap these groups.

---

[46]   It is therefore likely that the Public Guardian and the Court of Protection (or at least its central registry and various nominated officers) will share the same premises so that cases can be passed from one office to another with little delay. The role of the Public Guardian is dealt with in more detail in **CHAPTER 7**.

[47]   In an educational context referred to as 'learning difficulties' and previously known as 'mental handicap'.

Those working in the new jurisdiction must be sensitive to this diversity and there can be no standard approach.

4.57 In the past the Court of Protection has only been concerned with financial management, but the new Court will have to contend with a mixture of financial and welfare issues. A nominated judge of the new Court of Protection will not be able to state, as do the Masters of the present Court, that they do not have jurisdiction over personal welfare except insofar as it is influenced by financial decisions. A single issue may be brought to the Court where there is uncertainty that must be resolved or a decision is needed to authorise some action, but any conflict over control of the individual will inevitably extend to both financial and welfare decisions.

The Law Commission identified three types of decision that may need to be made or delegated. These relate respectively to property and affairs, personal welfare and healthcare. The 2005 Act merely adopts the first two categories with healthcare falling within personal welfare. The significance of this is that it may be appropriate for these two categories to be delegated to different persons.

Property and affairs

4.58 The management of financial affairs is not a new concept for a Court of Protection and, although new statutory criteria have been imposed, in fundamental respects these do not depart from the approach that has developed over recent years. The Court will still need to adjudicate on struggles for control, whether this be the appointment of an attorney or a deputy, to approve gifts and wills and to make policy decisions in regard to large damages awards. The change will be the availability of a wider range of possible outcomes and the requirement for minimum intervention. A more personalised regime is likely to be established with more input where possible from the incapacitated individual and greater integration with welfare decisions. The pendulum has swung from protection to empowerment, but time will tell whether this creates unacceptable vulnerability.

Personal welfare

4.59 What is untried and untested is the making of personal welfare decisions especially when the need for these arises through conflict within families or between families, carers and professionals. A simple decision may have wider implications. The issue is always the best interests of the individual, but the process whereby this is addressed differs according to whether the Court is required to resolve a dispute or an uncertainty.

Healthcare

4.60   The Family Division of the High Court has become accustomed to
        identifying best interests in regard to serious medical treatment, often in
        controversial and high-profile situations. Little will change when this
        work is transferred to the new Court of Protection. The same judges will
        be nominated to hear these cases but instead of doing so under the
        inherent jurisdiction they will do so under a statutory framework. Their
        approach has already been influenced by the Law Commission
        proposals and the public debate leading up to the 2005 Act so the
        substantive law that is applied will not be radically different.[48]

        Applications relating to less serious medical treatment and healthcare
        issues that do not need to be dealt with by High Court judges will tend
        to be resolved in the same way as other personal welfare issues although
        expert medical evidence will be required. These applications will not
        necessarily result from disputes but may arise due to uncertainty, such
        as a proposal for non-therapeutic dental treatment or cosmetic surgery.

Personal care

4.61   The issues arising under this heading encompass the full range of
        decisions, from where to live and with whom to have contact down to
        holiday arrangements, mode of dress and choice of diet. Any issue that
        parents cannot agree in respect of their child with severe learning
        disabilities or siblings cannot agree in respect of their parent with
        Alzheimers has the potential to be referred to the Court. Professional
        carers may also wish to validate their plans for vulnerable individuals,
        such as participation in adventure holidays that carry some degree of
        risk.

        'Adult contact' disputes are becoming more common and at present can
        only be resolved in the High Court at disproportionate expense, but the
        seniority of that court discourages the types of application that are likely
        to become the norm for the new Court of Protection. There will
        therefore be more of these applications when the regional Court is able
        to deal with them, and there is no reason why a nominated district judge
        who spends much of his time deciding such issues in respect of children
        should not have jurisdiction.

4.62   These cases cannot be treated as litigation to be resolved on an
        adversarial basis. In some instances findings of fact will be required, but
        otherwise the hearing will be more of an inquiry with input from family,
        friends, carers and professionals – and, of course, the incapacitated

---

[48]   Since taking responsibility for the Law Commission's consultation in her former identity as
        Prof Brenda Hoggett, Lady Hale of Richmond has rapidly risen through the High Court and
        the Court of Appeal to the House of Lords carrying with her the new approach to these
        issues.

person to the extent that a contribution is meaningful. The parties may seek to bring issues before the Court yet fail to address the best interests of this person. In such cases it may be appropriate for the incapacitated person to be made a party with a litigation friend and a legal representative (unless one professional such as the Official Solicitor can act in both capacities).[49] Failing this an independent report will be required and the Visitors will often be best placed to provide this service.

A decision by the Court must be the last resort in contested cases and other forms of dispute resolution need to be made available as stepping-stones. It could be part of the role of the Public Guardian to facilitate this. Piecemeal decision-making does not enable best interests to be comprehensively addressed and a care plan will generally be required as the cornerstone if not the foundations of the process. The Court cannot provide this but can be part of the process whereby it becomes established. It is suggested that, in cases that originate through implacable hostility on the part of family or others competing for influence, judges will insist that a care plan is negotiated through multi-disciplinary care management conferences and the Court will then resolve any stumbling blocks to enable this to be finalised. Decisions on specific issues can then be made within this framework.

---

[49] Such representation may be required in any event so as not to infringe the human rights of the incapacitated person, but the manner in which the proceedings are conducted must be proportionate to the matters in issue and funding may not be available for independent legal representation.

Chapter 5

Healthcare, Advance Directives and Research

Preliminary

5.1 A number of issues arise under the Mental Capacity Act 2005 ('the Act') in regard to healthcare. First, what medical treatment should be provided for an adult who cannot make choices; secondly, how can the adult before losing capacity influence decisions about subsequent treatment; and thirdly, to what extent should medical research be permitted. These issues are considered in this Chapter. Finally, it is also appropriate to consider here the interaction between existing mental health legislation and the new Act.

MEDICAL TREATMENT

Introduction

5.2 One of the many roles of the Family Division of the High Court of Justice in England and Wales is to decide whether medical procedures should or should not be carried out on an adult who is unable to consent to the treatment in question; and this is matched by similar cases relating to children. There are three broad types of case, where medical opinion is that:

- a particular course of treatment will save life, for example a blood transfusion or a Caesarean section;[1]
- a particular procedure should be carried out to enhance the patient's quality of life or prevent physical or mental deterioration, for example a liver transplant or sterilisation;[2]
- life-prolonging treatment should either be withheld or withdrawn to allow the patient to die with dignity.[3]

---

[1] *HE v A Hospital NHS Trust* [2003] 2 FLR 408 (blood transfusion); *St George's Healthcare NHS Trust v S* [1999] Fam 26 (caesarean section).

[2] In *Re T (A Minor) (Wardship: Medical Treatment)* [1997] 1 WLR 242 (kidney transplant); *Re A (Male Sterilisation)* [2000] 1 FLR 549 and, eg, in *Re S (Adult Patient: Sterilisation)* [2001] Fam 15.

[3] *Airedale NHS Trust v Bland* [1993] AC 789.

5.3   Once the Act is in force, adult cases will be dealt with by the Court of
        Protection under its new jurisdiction.[4] The existing common law
        position will be of relevance in considering that jurisdiction and the
        particular aspects of healthcare dealt with in the Act.

The common law position

The three bases for treatment

5.4   The starting point is that any 'invasive' or 'intrusive' medical treatment
        will constitute an unlawful act unless it is authorised by statute, or it is
        done under the doctrine of necessity (see below) or with the consent of
        the person concerned. A child's parents, or a child over 16,[5] can provide
        that consent. An adult who is competent can decide for him or herself
        whether or not any treatment may be carried out on him or her and the
        court has no power to intervene, however unwise the decision may seem
        to others. An adult who is 'incompetent' cannot provide a valid consent
        to treatment and the common law has not recognised anyone else as
        having the legal power to give consent on another adult's behalf.

Court's power to authorise treatment

The demise of parens patriae

5.5   The common law has, however, from an early time allowed the High
        Court to make medical treatment decisions for children and adults
        without the mental capacity to decide for themselves. Originally the
        judges of the High Court exercised the Crown's prerogative power as
        parens patriae. This power still exists in relation to children. However,
        in relation to adults, successive Mental Health Acts, starting with the
        Mental Health Act 1959, now replaced with the Mental Health Act
        1983, have provided a comprehensive statutory code for the treatment
        of patients for their mental disorder. These Acts left no scope for the
        continued exercise of *parens patriae* powers.

The declaratory jurisdiction

5.6   The question remained open whether the courts retained any jurisdiction
        in relation to other treatment decisions which needed to be taken for

---

[4]   See **CHAPTER 2**.

[5]   Family Law Reform Act 1969, s 8 (and even if not 16, a child may be considered to be
      'Gillick' competent – *Gillick v West Norfolk and Wisbech Area Health Authority* [1986] 1
      AC 112).

adults who could not consent. This was decisively answered by the House of Lords in 1990 in the case of *In re F (Mental Patient: Sterilisation).*[6] That case has provided the foundation for much of the modern common law on this subject. The key ruling was that the High Court retained an inherent jurisdiction to make declarations as to what is lawful as being in the best interests of an incompetent adult.

An equally important relatively early ruling (in terms of this developing jurisdiction) was also provided by the House of Lords in *Airedale NHS Trust v Bland,*[7] which involved a victim of the Hillsborough football tragedy who had been diagnosed as having entered a persistent vegetative state ('PVS'). In particular, this case is authority for the lawfulness of withholding or withdrawing nutrition and hydration supplied by artificial means ('ANH') to a person in this condition.

Emerging principles

5.7 Some basic principles relating to this whole jurisdiction emerging from these two cases can be summarised as follows:

1. in the case of an incompetent adult, the principle of necessity renders lawful, despite the absence of consent, any treatment (which would otherwise be a tort at common law) a reasonable doctor would give in the best interests of the patient;[8]

2. the High Court has the power to declare whether a patient lacks competence and whether a particular treatment is lawful as being in his or her best interests;

3. that jurisdiction is based upon a determination of best interests and is not (as has emerged in the US or in some Commonwealth jurisdictions) based on the doctrine of 'substituted choice' or 'substituted judgment' of what the patient would have wanted in the circumstances facing him or her.[9]

The development of the jurisdiction

5.8 There have been many decisions and rulings since then. The jurisdiction has expanded so that it covers not only medical treatment but also other welfare-related issues, such as where someone should live or with whom they should have contact.[10] Indeed, one High Court judge commented in a recent case:

---

[6] [1990] 2 AC 1.

[7] [1993] AC 789.

[8] Ie that the treatment is 'Bolam' compliant; namely that it accords with the treatment to which a responsible body of medical practitioners would subscribe (*Bolam v Friern Hospital Management Committee* [1957] 1 WLR 582).

[9] Op cit at p 871–872.

[10] See, eg, in *Re F (Mental Patient: Sterilisation)* [1990] 2 AC 1; *Re C (Mental Patient: Contact)* [1993] 1 FLR 940; *Re F (Adult: Court's Jurisdiction)* [2000] Fam 38; and *A v A*

'… we have come a long way since the decision in *In Re F*. The courts have created and now exercise what is, in substance and reality, a jurisdiction in relation to incompetent adults which is for all practical purposes indistinguishable from its well-established *parens patriae* or wardship jurisdiction in relation to children.'

Power to grant injunctions

5.9   Even the important distinction in principle between declaring what is lawful (adult cases) and making orders (children's cases) has become blurred, as it is now well settled that injunctive relief (where permissible) in support of a declaration can be granted.[11] Doctors cannot be compelled personally to undertake a treatment they do not in their clinical judgment wish to provide, but in some circumstances the NHS Trust responsible for the treatment might be required to transfer the patient to the care of other doctors who will treat as the patient wants or in his or her best interests.[12]

Test of capacity

5.10   The common law test of capacity is issue specific to the decision in question. It depends on whether the patient fully understands the nature of the proposed medical intervention, the reasons and the consequences of submitting or not submitting to it, and can weigh these in the balance and reach and communicate a decision.[13]

The fact that a patient has been sectioned under the Mental Health Act 1983 and is subject to compulsory detention and treatment for his or her mental disorder is not determinative of whether he or she has the capacity to consent to treatment not related to that mental disorder. An example of this arose in a case that concerned a patient at Broadmoor with chronic paranoid schizophrenia and gangrene in his right foot. He was held by the Court of Appeal to have the capacity to refuse his consent to a proposed amputation of his leg and instead consent to more conservative treatment.[14]

Best interests

5.11   The approach is far wider than medical best interests so any assessment should not be restricted to the treating doctors. The court attempts to

---

Health Authority, in *Re J (a child), R (on the application of S) v Secretary of State for the Home Department* [2002] Fam 213.

11   See, eg, *A Local Authority v A* [2004] 2 WLR 926.

12   In *Re J (A Minor) (Child in Care: Medical Treatment)* [1993] Fam 15; *Re B (Consent to Treatment: Capacity)* [2002] 1 FLR 1090; and *R (Burke) v GMC and Others* [2005] QB 424 at 180–194 (per Munby J).

13   *Re: MB (Medical Treatment)* [1997] 2 FLR 426.

14   *Re: C (Adult: Refusal of Treatment)* [1994] 1 WLR 290.

reach an objective view of best interests in the light of all the relevant circumstances and evidence available to it. In addition to the medical factors, emotional and all other welfare issues have to be taken into account in deciding best interests. The Court of Appeal has said that the court should draw up a checklist of the actual benefits and disadvantages and the potential gains and losses, including physical and psychological risks and consequences, and should reach a balanced conclusion as to what is right from the point of view of the individual concerned.[15]

Practice and procedure at common law

5.12   Adult cases under the inherent jurisdiction are brought in the Family Division of the High Court, but are proceedings to which the Civil Procedure Rules 1998 ('CPR') apply. Applications are generally brought under Part 8 of CPR.[16]

The claimant should be the NHS Trust or other body responsible for the patient's care, although a claim may also be brought by a family member or other individual closely connected with the patient. The body with clinical or caring responsibility should in any event be made a party. The patient must always be a party and is usually a defendant. The Official Solicitor is generally invited to represent the incapacitated patient as litigation friend.[17] Cases may be dealt with, even 'out of hours' on an emergency basis; and when final evidence either as to capacity or best interests is not available the court may be willing to grant an interim declaration.[18] As can be seen from the citations of the various authorities, the proceedings are often anonymised so that the identity of the patient does not reach the public domain.

The need for reform

5.13   When the Law Commission first looked at reforming this area of law, the common law position was far less developed than it is now. At that time there was concern, especially among carers and service-providers, over the gaps and uncertainties in the law.[19] This particularly related to the wider welfare area, and there was much support for an overall rather

---

[15]   *Re: A (Male Sterilisation)* [2000] 1 FLR 549.

[16]   The procedure in children's cases is different. Orders may be sought in relation to a child who is a ward of court, under the Children Act 1989, or by originating summons under the inherent jurisdiction (to which the Family Proceedings Rules 1991 apply).

[17]   See the President's Practice Direction 'Declaratory Proceedings concerning Incapacitated Adults: Medical and Welfare Decisions' of 14 December 2001 and Practice Note 'Official Solicitor: Declaratory Proceedings: Medical and Welfare Decisions for Adults Who Lack Capacity' [2001] 2 FLR 158.

[18]   CPR, Part 25.1(1)(b), and see *An NHS Trust v Miss T* [2004] EWHC 1279 (Fam).

[19]   See Law Commission Consultation Paper No 128, *Mentally Incapacitated Adults and Decision-Making: A New Jurisdiction* (1993).

than piecemeal approach to reform. Once the decision was taken that this should encompass lasting powers of attorney and deputies with healthcare and welfare powers, it was clear that the legislation should deal with healthcare and welfare more generally. Indeed, the Act would have been a much less powerful instrument if its general principles were limited so as not to cover this whole area. This has given Parliament the opportunity to lay down a statutory framework and develop the common law position in a number of respects (the principal features of which are noted below).

The position under the Mental Capacity Act 2005

General

5.14   The general provisions of the Act relating to capacity, inability to make decisions, best interests, and acts in connection with care or treatment[20] will apply to medical treatment as to all other areas. Existing case-law in these areas will need to be applied with the caveat that the Act contains its own statutory definitions, which will govern future cases. It is not, however, thought that outcomes in relation to the key issues of capacity and best interests will generally be significantly altered as the statutory tests represent a codification of the position that has developed at common law since (and drawing upon) the Law Commission's proposals.

The powers of the Court of Protection

5.15   The new Court of Protection is given power either to make declarations[21] (as the High Court can now do under its inherent jurisdiction), or to issue orders making the decision on the patient's behalf.[22] In one sense this Court will start with a clean sheet and its judges will be able to develop the law in new directions in the light of the statutory framework. However, it is likely that the existing case-law will be of persuasive authority in many areas. It is open to the President of the Court of Protection to issue either Practice Directions or guidance as to the law.[23]

When should cases be brought to Court?

5.16   Existing case-law cannot be said to have totally settled the position under the inherent jurisdiction when to rely on the doctrine of necessity

---

[20]   These are to be found in ss 2–5.
[21]   Mental Capacity Act 2005, s 15.
[22]   Mental Capacity Act 2005, s 16.
[23]   Mental Capacity Act 2005, s 52.

or when to go to court, and some remaining uncertainty is likely to carry forward into the new Court of Protection jurisdiction. Those persons (doctors, etc) who act on a medical treatment decision will not incur liability if they come within s 5 of the Act (which will replace the common law doctrine of necessity). This will provide the new basis upon which the vast majority of medical treatment decisions can be taken and acted on without reference to any formal court process.

Serious justiciable issue

5.17 The court's jurisdiction (current and future) should be invoked whenever there is a serious justiciable issue requiring a decision by a court. In *D v An NHS Trust (Medical Treatment: Consent: Termination)*[24] Coleridge J observed:

> 'In cases of controversy and cases involving momentous and irrevocable decisions, the courts have treated as justiciable any genuine question as to what the best interests of a patient require or justify. In making these decisions the courts have recognised the desirability of informing those involved whether a proposed course of conduct will render them criminally or civilly liable; they have acknowledged their duty to act as a safeguard against malpractice, abuse and unjustified action; and they have recognised the desirability, in the last resort, of decisions being made by an impartial, independent tribunal.'

This covers any serious treatment decision where there is a disagreement between those involved and those close to the patient or where there are doubts or difficulties over the assessment of either the patient's capacity or best interests. The NHS Trust responsible for caring for the patient will often take the case to court to obtain a declaration which will protect it from subsequent challenge or criticism.

5.18 Case-law has also established the following categories of cases in which, irrespective of whether there are doubts or disagreements, a court application should be made.

Patients in PVS

5.19 The first identified category is, as laid down in the House of Lords in *Bland*,[25] that the withholding or withdrawal of artificial nutrition and hydration ('ANH') to patients in a persistent vegetative state ('PVS') should as a matter of practice in every case be put to the High Court for approval. This is partly a reflection of the importance of the decision to the individual but also provides a reassurance to the public as to how these decisions are taken. The President of the Family Division was given a discretion to consider whether the time has come when these

---

[24] [2004] 1 FLR 1110.
[25] *Airedale NHS Trust v Bland* [1993] AC 789.

cases do not need routinely to go to court, but this has not so far been exercised.[26]

Sterilisation

5.20   A second category of case which requires the sanction of a High Court judge is the sterilisation for contraceptive purposes of a person (whether child or adult) who cannot consent to the operation. A sterilisation procedure necessary for therapeutic as opposed to contraceptive purposes may not need an application.[27] However, if the case is at all borderline it should be referred to the court.[28] The court will need to consider, as part of its assessment of the best interests test, the likelihood of pregnancy, the damage deriving from conception and/or menstruation, and the medical and surgical techniques available, including whether any less invasive alternative would solve the problems which have been identified.[29]

Termination of pregnancy

5.21   Certain termination of pregnancy cases should also be brought to court. In *D v An NHS Trust (Medical Treatment: Consent: Termination)*, Coleridge J laid down guidelines (agreed by the President) as to when such cases should go to court, namely:

- where there is a dispute over capacity or the patient may regain capacity during her pregnancy;
- where there is a lack of unanimity amongst the medical professionals as to her best interests;
- where the procedures under s 1 of the Abortion Act 1967 have not been followed;
- where the patient, members of her immediate family, or the potential father have opposed, or expressed views inconsistent with, a termination of pregnancy; and
- where there are any other exceptional circumstances (including where this may be the patient's last chance to bear a child).

Other situations

5.22   There are two other circumstances in which a court application should be made. The first is where the medical procedure to the person lacking capacity has the primary purpose of benefiting someone else – eg a sibling. An example is bone marrow donation. To contribute to the family's welfare in this way may be in the best interests of the person

---

[26]   See [1993] AC 789 at p 874.
[27]   *Re GP (Medical Treatment)* [1992] 1 FLR 293.
[28]   *Re S (Sterilisation)* [2000] 2 FLR 389, 405.
[29]   *Re S* supra.

giving it.[30] The second is where approval in the person's overall best interests should be obtained for experimental or innovative treatment.[31]

Impact of the European Convention on Human Rights

Relevant Convention rights

5.23   The European Convention on Human Rights has been incorporated into our law by the Human Rights Act 1998 at a time when this jurisdiction has been developing. Articles with particular relevance to the substance of medical treatment cases are:

- Art 2 (right to life);
- Art 3 (not to suffer inhumane and degrading treatment); and
- Art 8 (right to a private life, including physical integrity).

The need for references to the High Court

5.24   In *Glass v UK*[32] the European Court of Human Rights at Strasbourg found the UK to be in breach of an 11-year-old's Art 8 rights in a case in which his parents were bitterly disputing the medical staff's diagnosis and proposal to provide palliative care, believing that more aggressive treatment to keep him alive should be undertaken. The hospital went ahead without referring the case to the High Court.[33] The breach was held to arise because UK law and practice, as described above, enabled a High Court application to be made and to protect his rights the NHS Trust should have applied for the Court's approval.

5.25   The withdrawal of ANH in PVS cases (where the patient has no awareness at all) requires 'as a matter of good practice' referral to the High Court, but there was no clear authority on whether or when withholding or withdrawal in any other cases, including where the patient still has some awareness, should go to court. This fell to be considered in *R (Burke) v General Medical Council and Others.*[34] At first instance Munby J ruled that the effect of *Glass* was to convert the rule of good practice into a legal obligation and there are a range of circumstances in cases involving patients not in PVS where withholding/withdrawal of ANH should not take place without prior

---

[30]   In *Re Y (Mental Patient: Bone Marrow Donation* [1997] Fam 110.

[31]   See, eg, *Simms v Simms; A v A (a child)* [2003] Fam 83.

[32]   [2004] 1 FLR 1019.

[33]   The domestic case which took place was a judicial review brought by members of the family against the NHS Trust, which was dismissed as being too blunt an instrument – see *R v Portsmouth Hospitals NHS Trust ex p Glass* [1999] 2 FLR 905.

[34]   [2005] EWCA 1003 (Court of Appeal), [2005] QB 424 (at first instance). Permission to appeal to the House of Lords has been refused.

judicial authorisation. In a list matching Coleridge J's list for abortion cases he ruled that these were where:

1. there is any doubt or disagreement as to capacity;
2. there is lack of unanimity amongst the medical professionals as to prognosis, best interests or outcome or as to whether ANH should be withheld;
3. there is evidence that the patient when competent would have wanted ANH to continue;
4. there is evidence that the patient resists or disputes the proposed withdrawal;
5. persons having a reasonable claim to have their views taken into account assert that withdrawal is contrary to the patient's wishes or not in his or her best interests.

5.26   The Court of Appeal expressly overruled Munby J on his analysis of the effect of *Glass* reaffirming, as was held to be the position in *Bland*, that the court does not authorise treatment which would otherwise be unlawful but makes a declaration as to whether or not the proposed treatment, or its withdrawal, will be lawful. The judgment of the Court states:

> 'Good practice may require medical practitioners to seek such a declaration where the legality of proposed treatment is in doubt. This is not, however, something that they are required to do as a matter of law.'

Only time will tell whether a future case analogous to the *Glass* case, but concerning the treatment of an adult, will arise and whether a claim for breach of human rights will be successful where 'good practice' has not been followed.

Withholding or withdrawing life-sustaining treatment

5.27   Given the importance accorded by both Houses of Parliament during the Bill's consideration to issues related to withholding or withdrawing life-sustaining treatment, a short commentary drawing some of the threads together is appropriate. Two of the leading cases are *Bland* and *Burke*, to which reference has already been made.

5.28   In *Bland* the House of Lords decided that, where there is no continuing duty on doctors to sustain life through medical treatment, including the provision of ANH, because of the futility of doing so in the case of a patient in PVS, it would be lawful to withhold or withdraw that treatment. It has subsequently been held that this decision is compatible with the incorporation of the European Convention on Human Rights in our law[35] and the decision has been re-affirmed in *Pretty v UK*.[36] It is

---

[35]   *NHS Trust A v H* [2002] FCR 711.
[36]   (2002) 35 EHRR 1.

the basis for the distinction in this jurisprudence between omissions and positive acts causing death.

5.29   The *Burke* case was a judicial review concerning the lawfulness of guidelines issued by the General Medical Council[37] ('GMC') and was brought by a competent adult who feared that the guidance would not adequately protect him from doctors withholding or withdrawing ANH at a time when, as a result of his wasting disease, he would need it to be kept alive. The case provided the opportunity, taken by Munby J, for a judgment covering a number of important issues, although the Court of Appeal in its judgment, allowing the GMC's appeal and setting aside the declarations made at first instance, approached the case more narrowly, finding that Mr Burke's fears are addressed by the law as it stands. The judgment of the court given in the appeal recognises that whilst the duty to keep a patient alive by administering ANH or other life-prolonging treatment is not absolute, the only exceptions are either where a competent patient refuses to receive it or where it is not considered to be in the best interests of an incompetent patient to be kept alive artificially. This latter circumstance covers patients in PVS and where the patient's continued life involves an extreme degree of pain, discomfort or indignity and he has not shown a wish to be kept alive.[38]

In relation to Mr Burke's own situation, the Court of Appeal robustly declared:

> 'Indeed, it seems to us that for a doctor deliberately to interrupt life-prolonging treatment in the face of a competent patient's expressed wish to be kept alive, with the intention of thereby terminating the patient's life, would leave the doctor with no answer to a charge of murder.'

and:

> 'Where life depends upon the continued provision of ANH there can be no question of the supply of ANH not being clinically indicated unless a clinical decision has been taken that the life in question should come to an end. That is not a decision that can lawfully be taken in the case of a competent patient who expresses the wish to remain alive.'

5.30   One of the criticisms levelled against the judgment at first instance was that it was not clear whether the judge's rulings applied only to the provision of ANH or equally to all other life-sustaining treatment. The Court of Appeal was concerned to limit the ambit of the case to the issues which arose in that case, namely whether ANH would be discontinued. There remains a question, perhaps to be answered in

---

[37]   *Withholding and Withdrawing Life-prolonging Treatments: Good Practice in Decision-making* (August 2002).

[38]   This issue also arises in severely damaged baby cases, see, eg, in *Re J (a Minor) (Wardship: Medical Treatment)* [1991] Fam 33, and more recently the Court of Appeal judgment in *Wyatt v Portsmouth Hospital NHS Trust and Charlotte Wyatt* [2005] EWCA Civ 1181.

another case, whether withholding ANH, although an aspect of medical treatment, is in any special category of life-sustaining treatment.

Bests interests at common law

5.31   The Court of Appeal in *Burke* expressly disavowed Munby J's 'test' that, when considering best interests in relation to an incompetent patient and whether to sustain life, the importance of respecting life needed to be reflected by adopting as the 'touchstone' of best interests whether or not the continuing treatment was 'intolerable' from the patient's point of view.[39] It held that the test of whether it is in the best interests of the patient to provide or continue ANH must depend on the particular circumstances. It also overturned his ruling that it is possible for a competent patient by an advance directive to require that any particular form of medical treatment, including life-sustaining treatment, be given.

Best interests under the Mental Capacity Act 2005

5.32   One aspect of the Act worthy of particular comment in relation to healthcare decisions is the definition of best interests which adopts an objective approach:[40]

> 'The person making the determination must consider all the relevant circumstances …'

It also requires more subjective factors such as the past and present wishes and feelings of the person concerned (so far as ascertainable) to be considered.[41]

5.33   The statutory definition incorporates an amalgam of factors which govern both a 'best interests' and a 'substituted judgment' approach to decision making. It will involve a careful balancing of the various considerations and, where a person has expressed views as to his or her treatment which at the time the decision needs to be made appear difficult to reconcile with 'objective' best interests (and which cannot be taken as a binding advance refusal), a judgment as to the weight to be accorded to those views will have to be made. It will be interesting to see whether a future case with similar features to those in *W Healthcare NHS Trust v KH*[42] will be decided in the same way. In this case,

---

[39]   The Court of Appeal judgment in *Wyatt* further analyses the case-law relating to whether or not an 'intolerability' test is appropriate and concludes that, whilst not a 'touchstone', it may be a valuable guide in the search for best interests. Interestingly, this judgment also suggests that the factors relevant to the treatment of adults and children may not be the same, although some statements of principle plainly apply to both.

[40]   Mental Capacity Act 2005, s 4(2).

[41]   Mental Capacity Act 2005, s 4(6).

[42]   [2005] 1 WLR 834.

concerning whether ANH should be re-instated, objective best interests and the patient's ascertainable past views did not appear to coincide. It was the unanimous medical view that the PEG tube should be re-inserted, but the family did not want this to happen since they believed that in the circumstances she would want to die. The court at first instance and on appeal decided it was in her best interests to be kept alive.

5.34   A provision introduced into the Bill at a late stage specifically related to life-sustaining treatment: [43]

> 'Where the determination relates to life-sustaining treatment [the decision-maker] must not, in considering whether the treatment is in the best interests of the person concerned, be motivated by a desire to bring about his death.'

This was introduced as a Government amendment in the House of Lords to meet concerns expressed by Archbishop Smith on behalf of the Catholic Church that the Bill as then drafted would allow discontinuance of life-sustaining treatment in circumstances in which this would be prompted by this improper motive. It does not override the decision or argument in the *Bland* case.[44] Nor does the general assurance given by s 62 in declaring that nothing in the Act is to be taken as affecting the law relating to murder, manslaughter or assisted suicide.

Practice and procedure under the Mental Capacity Act 2005

Court Rules and Practice Directions

5.35   The new Court of Protection Rules have yet to be written[45] and it is likely that Practice Directions will also be issued.[46] These will establish the procedure to be adopted in medical treatment cases.[47] They should provide answers to such matters as which judges and which regional centres will be able to undertake this work, and also who will be permitted to represent the incapacitated person in the proceedings. It also remains to be announced what legal aid provision, and to whom, will be available.

---

[43]   Mental Capacity Act 2005, s 4(5).

[44]   Reference to the parliamentary record supports this interpretation – see statement of Baroness Ashton of Upholland, *Hansard*, House of Lords Committee Stage, col 1175 (25 January 2005).

[45]   Mental Capacity Act 2005, s 51 provides for these Rules.

[46]   The President of the Court of Protection will issue these under Mental Capacity Act 2005, s 52.

[47]   As discussed at **5.12** above, these are presently dealt with by the High Court pursuant to CPR 1998 and the Practice Directions that accompany those rules. The Part 8 procedure applies and a similar approach under the new rules may be adopted.

An exclusive jurisdiction

5.36   Although the Act does not expressly state this to be the case, it must be that the new Court of Protection jurisdiction has left no room for the continuing operation of a separate High Court inherent jurisdiction in relation to adults and cases covered by the Act. In practice this means that in future only judges nominated to be judges of the Court of Protection[48] will be able to hear these cases. However, the Court of Protection will have no jurisdiction in respect of disputes where the patient has the capacity to make his or her own treatment decisions. This may result in problems where that person has fluctuating capacity, but in practice serious cases will be restricted to nominated judges from the Family Division of the High Court and it may be that such a judge will choose to sit in a dual jurisdiction.

Overlap with judicial review

5.37   The procedure described works well when those responsible for the medical care of the patient (generally an NHS Trust) either bring the proceedings to seek a decision from the court or are a party to the proceedings and are willing to abide by the result.[49] There may be cases in which the public body responsible for the treatment has already taken a decision and the question then arises how that decision can appropriately be challenged. There is existing case-law on when judicial review or a best interests application is the appropriate way to proceed.[50] When the need to proceed under both arises the current practice is for a High Court judge who is a member of the Family Division and is also a nominated judge of the Administrative Court to hear the cases. Future arrangements will need to be able to cater for a case which requires a decision under both judicial review and the new jurisdiction's principles. It will be necessary to ensure that a judge who can hear judicial review applications and is a judge of the Court of Protection will be available.

Independent mental capacity advocates

Background

5.38   One new feature of the Act, but not included in the Draft Mental Incapacity Bill as scrutinised by the Joint Parliamentary Committee, is

---

[48]   See Mental Capacity Act 2005, s 46.

[49]   See *Simms v Simms* [2003] Fam 83 where at a late stage the NHS Trust, at whose hospital it was thought that the medical procedure would take place, indicated its opposition. This led to one of the cases being re-heard in Belfast and the operation taking place there.

[50]   *A v A Health Authority* [2002] Fam 213.

the framework for the creation of the *Independent Mental Capacity Advocacy Service.* The Committee commented:

'The need for and importance of advocacy services for people affected by the Bill's provisions was reflected in the volumes of evidence we received …'

and concluded that:

'We are convinced that independent advocacy services play an essential role in assisting people with capacity problems to make and communicate decisions; helping them to enforce their rights and guard against unwarranted intrusion into their lives; providing a focus on the views and wishes of an incapacitated person in the determination of their best interests; providing additional safeguards against abuse and exploitation; and assisting in the resolution of disputes.'

It accordingly made recommendations[51] which the Government took forward in the provisions included in the Bill as subsequently presented to Parliament. When initially introduced, these were under the title of *Independent Consultee Service* but this and the associated description of functions were changed during the Bill's consideration in the House of Lords.

Establishment

5.39   The Act imposes a duty on the Secretary of State (in practice the Secretary of State for Health) in England and the Welsh Assembly in Wales to make arrangements to enable independent mental capacity advocates to be available to represent and support incapacitated persons in circumstances defined in the Act.[52] They must be designed to achieve the laudable principle that:[53]

'… a person to whom a proposed act or decision relates should, so far as practicable, be represented and supported by a person who is independent of any person who will be responsible for the act or decision.'

In discharging this duty the Secretary of State (or Welsh Assembly) may make Regulations providing for the circumstances and conditions under which such an advocate may act and as to his or her appointment.

Functions and role

5.40   Regulations may be made as to the functions of such advocates and as to the steps to be taken for the purposes of:[54]

---

[51] See paras 292–308 and recommendations 89–93, HL Paper 189-1, HC Paper 1083-1 (Session 2002–03).
[52] Mental Capacity Act 2005, s 35.
[53] Mental Capacity Act 2005, s 35(4).
[54] Mental Capacity Act 2005, s 36.

- providing support so the person whom he or she has been instructed to represent may participate as fully as possible in any relevant decision;
- obtaining and evaluating relevant information;
- ascertaining what the person's wishes and feelings would be likely to be and the beliefs and values likely to influence them;
- ascertaining what alternative courses of action are available; and
- obtaining a further medical opinion.

The regulations may also make provision as to the circumstances in which an advocate may challenge or assist in challenging a decision. Under a different regulation-making power, regulations may be made expanding the role, adjusting the obligation to make arrangements, and prescribing different circumstances in which an advocate must or may be instructed to act.[55]

The duty to instruct

NHS bodies

5.41   Once these arrangements are in place, an NHS body will be under a duty to instruct such an advocate and to take into account any information given or submissions made by that advocate before providing 'serious medical treatment' (to be defined in Regulations) when there is no one else for the provider of the treatment to discuss it with.[56] This will occur when there is neither a person in the specified list[57] who can speak for the person – namely, a person nominated by him or her, an attorney under a lasting power of attorney or pre-existing enduring power of attorney, or a deputy – nor a non-professional carer or friend whom it is appropriate to consult. If the treatment has to be provided as a matter of urgency it may be provided even though no advocate has been instructed.

5.42   A similar duty will arise where it is proposed that an incapacitated person should be accommodated in long-stay accommodation in a hospital or care home, or should transfer to another hospital or care home, where this accommodation is provided or arranged by the NHS.[58] If the accommodation is to last more than 28 days in a hospital or 8 weeks in a care home an advocate is to be instructed when there is no other person to discuss it with. The role of the advocate is again to support and represent the person concerned and any information and

---

[55] Mental Capacity Act 2005, s 41.
[56] Not being treatment regulated by Part IV of the Mental Health Act 1983. Mental Capacity Act 2005, s 37.
[57] This is set out in Mental Capacity Act 2005, s 40.
[58] Mental Capacity Act 2005, s 38.

submissions from the advocate must be taken into account. This does not apply if the accommodation arises as a result of an obligation under the Mental Health Act 1983 nor when it is being arranged as a matter of urgency.[59]

Local authorities

5.43 Matching provisions are made, and duty imposed, on a local authority in relation to long-stay accommodation arranged by that authority.[60] These apply to residential accommodation provided in accordance with s 21 or 29 of the National Assistance Act 1948 or following discharge under s 117 of the Mental Health Act 1983. The accommodation may be in a care home, nursing home, ordinary or sheltered housing, housing association or other registered social housing, or in private sector housing provided by a local authority or in hostel accommodation. Similar exceptions are made where the person concerned is required to live in the accommodation in question under the Mental Health Act 1983 or in relation to urgent placements.[61]

Powers of the advocate

5.44 Once in place an advocate under these provisions may, for the purpose of enabling him or her to carry out his or her functions:

- interview in private the person he or she has been instructed to represent; and
- examine and take copies of any health record, social services record, or care home record which the person holding the record considers may be relevant to the advocate's investigation.[62]

Comment

5.45 It can be seen that these statutory provisions are the product of work in progress. They provide the basis for the creation of an independent mental capacity advocacy service, and need to be supplemented by Regulations, at which point more of the detail will become apparent. In the course of the Bill's consideration reference was made to the advocates' being there to support the 'unbefriended' – ie where there are no family members or friends. Particular examples suggesting where this might arise included older people with dementia who have lost contact with all friends and family, or people with severe learning

---

[59] Provision is made to ensure that an advocate is involved in relation to people whose residence is initially intended to be less than the 28 days or 8 weeks if the period is later extended beyond the applicable period (s 38(4)).

[60] Mental Capacity Act 2005, s 39.

[61] Mental Capacity Act 2005, s 39 (3) and (4).

[62] Mental Capacity Act 2005, s 35(6).

disabilities or long-term mental health problems who have been in residential institutions for long periods and lack outside contacts. Potentially the scope for use of this service could go wider than that.

5.46   A number of questions arise as to how this service is to be established, organised, and funded, who will be advocates, and what provision for training will be made. The full nature and extent of the representational role also remains to be established. A consultation paper from the Department of Health has been issued which raises the following questions:

1.   how funding should be allocated;
2.   how the service should be commissioned;
3.   whether there should be national standards;
4.   what training is appropriate;
5.   how the service's independence can be maintained; and
6.   how the service should be monitored.

The consultation also canvasses whether additional functions should be given to the service and how it might be involved in an annual review for people in long-term care placements who have no family or friends. It invites comments on how to define 'serious medical treatment'. It finally asks whether there are other groups of particularly vulnerable people without capacity who may benefit from the service; and whether there are other circumstances or situations beyond serious medical treatment or care moves where the service should be provided.

THE COMPETENT ADULT – ADVANCE DECISIONS

Preliminary

5.47   In any case in which an adult is found to be competent[63] very different principles come into play. Whether, as Munby J analysed it in *Burke*, the adult is the arbiter of his own best interests or it is purely a matter of adult autonomy irrespective of best interests, the court has no basis or jurisdiction to investigate a competent adult's best interests. The principle of adult autonomy is determinative.

Particularly graphic examples of cases the High Court has considered are furnished by *Re B (Consent to Treatment: Capacity)*[64] which related to refusal to consent to continued artificial ventilation and *Re Z (An Adult: Capacity)*[65] where the individual had arranged to travel to

---

[63]   There is a presumption of competence in s.1(2) of the Mental Capacity Act 2005.
[64]   [2002] 1 FLR 109.
[65]   [2005] 2 FCR 256.

Switzerland to be assisted to commit suicide in a manner that was lawful in that country.

Advance directives at common law

Refusal of treatment

5.48   The common law has needed to consider the position of persons who are incompetent at the time a decision as to their medical treatment has to be taken but who have made an advance directive refusing that treatment. Not surprisingly, the issue soon emerged in the context of a Jehovah's Witness refusing consent to a blood transfusion;[66] and it has also been litigated in the context of a patient seeking removal of his ventilator.[67]

Essential features

5.49   Advance refusals to consent to particular treatments are an aspect of a competent adult's autonomy.[68] An advance refusal of medical treatment is to be given binding effect if, but only if:

1.   made at a time when the adult had capacity to make a decision of such a nature;
2.   intended to apply when that person is incapable;
3.   it relates to the circumstances which have arisen;
4.   the maker understood the nature and consequences of his or her decision; and
5.   there was no undue influence or coercion by a third party.

No particular form is needed, and such a refusal may be revoked in any way[69] or as a result of a change in relevant circumstances. A court will need to be satisfied the advance refusal remains valid and applicable to the particular circumstances, and if there is doubt that doubt will be resolved in favour of the preservation of life and the best interests test applied.[70] The greatest difficulty in practice can be whether from the drafting of an advance directive it can be clearly inferred that such a refusal was intended to apply in the circumstances which have arisen.[71]

---

[66]   In *Re T (Adult: Refusal of Treatment)* [1993] Fam 95; and more recently *HE v A Hospital NHS Trust* [2003] 2 FLR 408.

[67]   *Re AK (Medical Treatment: Consent)* [2001] 1 FLR 129.

[68]   Documents setting out wishes as to medical treatment were initially described as 'Living Wills'.

[69]   An advance refusal set out in a signed document may be revoked by a subsequent verbal expression of contrary wishes.

[70]   *HE v A Hospital NHS Trust* [2003] 2 FLR 408.

[71]   This may be one factor which has led to a body such as the Voluntary Euthanasia Society to offer a standard form for an advance directive refusing life-sustaining treatment; and it is possible to download a living will from www.livingwill.org.uk.

The relationship with suicide

5.50   It is settled law that whilst no one has the right to ask for and be given treatment which constitutes a positive act (such as the administration of diamorphine) to assist in their suicide, they may refuse the provision or continuation of life-sustaining treatment such as ANH even when the inevitable consequence is death.[72]

Requests for treatment

5.51   An advance directive may request rather than seek to refuse treatment. But there is no general right for a person to require, either at the time or in an advance decision, that a particular form of medical treatment be given. This has been reaffirmed by the Court of Appeal in its judgment in *Burke*.

Advance decisions under the Mental Capacity Act 2005

Recognition

5.52   The Act in ss 24 to 26 gives statutory recognition to, and governs the applicability and effect of, advance decisions to refuse specified treatments made by an adult when competent which are to have effect when the adult becomes incompetent.

A number of conditions are laid down which must be met before such a decision is to be valid and applicable. These replicate the common law position in a number of respects in relation to refusals of treatment, and in some modify it by providing additional safeguards as indicated below.

Advance refusals of treatment

5.53   These provisions of the Act in their terms only apply to advance refusals of specified treatments. It is necessary to specify the treatment which is to be refused, although this does not have to be done in medical language and can be expressed in layman's terms.[73] The circumstances in which the refusal is to apply may also be specified. Such a decision may be subsequently withdrawn or altered when the maker of the decision has capacity to do so. This need not be in writing

---

[72]   Re-affirmed in *Pretty v United Kingdom* (2002) 35 EHRR 1. In deciding whether effect must be given to an advance refusal of life-sustaining treatment it is not necessary to inquire into the motives of the person making it. The Catholic Bishops Conference of England and Wales submitted to the Court of Appeal in the *Burke* appeal that adult autonomy is limited by an inability to refuse treatment motivated by a suicidal intent. It is suggested that this is not established in existing case-law.

[73]   Mental Capacity Act 2005, s 24(1)(a) and (2).

unless the altered decision is a decision to refuse life-sustaining treatment.[74]

Advance requests for treatment

5.54   Advance requests for treatment are dealt with differently under the Act. They are treated as a relevant written statement which, if made when the person had capacity, must be considered by the decision-maker in determining best interests.[75]

Conditions for validity

5.55   To have the effect prescribed in the Act an advance decision to refuse a treatment must have been made by a person after he or she has reached the age of 18 and at a time when he or she had capacity to do so. It loses its validity if:[76]

- the person has withdrawn the decision (by any means) at a time when he or she had capacity to do so;
- he or she has created a lasting power of attorney after the decision was made in which he or she gives the donee of the power the authority to give or refuse consent to the treatment in question;
- he or she has since the decision was made acted inconsistently with that being his or her fixed intention.[77]

Applicability

5.56   An advance decision is not applicable if:[78]

- at the time the provision of the treatment is in question the person has the capacity to give or refuse consent to it;
- the treatment falls outside the treatment specified in the decision;
- any circumstances specified in the decision are absent; or
- there are reasonable grounds for believing that circumstances exist which the maker of the advance decision did not anticipate at the time of its making and which would have affected his or her decision had he or she anticipated them.

---

[74]   Mental Capacity Act 2005, s 24(5).
[75]   Mental Capacity Act 2005, s 4(6).
[76]   Mental Capacity Act 2005, s 25(2).
[77]   See *HE v A Hospital NHS Trust* [2003] 2 FLR 408 as a good example (a previous Jehovah's Witness who had become betrothed to a Muslim and was professing she would live by the principles of that faith).
[78]   Mental Capacity Act 2005, s 25(3) and (4).

Life-sustaining treatment

5.57   In addition to these conditions, there are new statutory conditions for the applicability of advance decisions refusing life-sustaining treatment. These are that:[79]

- the decision includes a statement by the maker that it is to apply to the life-sustaining treatment even if his or her life is at risk;
- the decision is in writing; and
- it is signed by or under the direction and in the presence of its maker and that signature is made or acknowledged in the presence of a witness who signs or acknowledges his or her signature in the presence of the maker of the decision.

Implications of an advance decision

Effect

5.58   A valid and applicable advance decision has effect as if the maker had made it, and had the capacity to make it, at the time the question arises whether the treatment specified in it should be carried out or continued.

       If the person providing treatment withholds or withdraws the treatment when he or she reasonably believes that an advance decision refusing the treatment exists which is valid and applicable to the treatment, he or she is protected from legal liability in doing so.[80] Conversely, a person does not incur liability for carrying out or continuing treatment unless or until he or she is satisfied that an advance decision exists which is valid and applicable to the treatment.[81]

Doubt or disagreement

5.59   If there is any doubt or disagreement over whether an advance decision exists, is valid, or is applicable to a treatment, an application can be made to the Court of Protection for it to make a declaration.[82] While a decision is being sought, those treating the person concerned are entitled to take nothing in the advance decision as preventing them providing life-sustaining treatment or doing any act they reasonably believe to be necessary to prevent a serious deterioration in the person's condition.[83]

---

[79]   Mental Capacity Act 2005, s 25(5) and (6).
[80]   Mental Capacity Act 2005, s 26(3).
[81]   Mental Capacity Act 2005, s 26(2).
[82]   Mental Capacity Act 2005, s 26(4).
[83]   Mental Capacity Act 2005, s 26(5).

The Draft Code of Practice

5.60   Chapter 8 of the Draft Code of Practice contained valuable guidance and suggestions for best practice in this area. In particular, it is suggested that:[84]

> 'It is helpful for the following information to be included in a written advance decision:
> - Full details of maker, including date of birth, home address, and any distinguishing features (so that an unconscious person, for example, might be identified).
> - Name and address of General Practitioner and whether they have a copy.
> - [Where relevant] information on where the advance decision is stored and list of people who are aware of its existence and should be contacted.
> - A statement that the decision is intended to have effect if the maker lacks capacity to make treatment decisions.
> - A clear statement of the decision, specifying the treatment to be refused and the circumstances in which the decision will apply or which will trigger a particular course of actions.
> - [Where relevant] a clear statement that the decision is intended to apply even if the treatment in question is necessary to sustain life.
> - Date the document was written (or reviewed) and, if appropriate, the time interval between creation and review.
> - The signature of witness who witnessed the maker's signature.
> - Information on the independence of witness, including details of their relationship with the maker.'

Some future issues

Striking a balance

5.61   It can be seen from the above that the statutory provisions on advance decisions are designed to strike a balance between, on the one hand, recognition of a competent adult's autonomy and, on the other, the fears expressed during the parliamentary debates on the Bill[85] that a person could be locked into an advance refusal he or she would wish to change but can no longer do so.

The alternative of a lasting power of attorney

5.62   It is a matter of individual choice whether a person wishes to plan in advance for possible future lack of capacity by indicating a refusal of

---

[84]   Draft Code of Practice, para 8.15.

[85]   See, eg, Commons *Hansard* Debates for 11 October 2004, Commons Standing Committee A for 28 October, and Lords *Hansard* Debates for 10 and 27 January 2005 and 15 and 24 March.

specified treatments. An alternative is to create a lasting power of attorney with the authority for the person chosen as donee to take healthcare decisions.

Decisions by healthcare professionals

5.63   In the absence of either an advance decision or a lasting power of attorney, decisions will be taken by the healthcare professionals in the person's best interests. A written statement which does not amount to an advance decision will be taken into account[86] but it will depend on the facts of the case at the time what the overall best interests are.[87]

5.64   Those taking treatment decisions when faced with an advance refusal of the treatment will need to take a view on the validity and applicability of the decision. For example, they will need to make an assumption as to the person's capacity at the time the decision was made (to which the statutory presumption of capacity will apply). In most instances there may be no doubt. The formalities around making an advance decision refusing life-sustaining treatment may make it easier to make this assumption in such a case. In some instances, however, where it is thought possible that the advance decision may be challenged in the future and there may be some doubt as to capacity, it may be helpful for the maker to obtain evidence confirming the person's capacity at the time.

5.65   Of greater difficulty may be (as now under the common law) whether the maker of the decision really had in mind the circumstances which have arisen and intended it to apply in those circumstances; or whether relevant circumstances have changed (eg the prospect of a new cure) which invalidate the decision. As the Draft Code of Practice suggested, particular care will need to be taken for advance decisions which do not appear to have been reviewed or updated, for instance, in the light of changes in personal circumstances or developments in medical treatment.[88]

References to the Court of Protection

5.66   It can be anticipated that there will be some issues and problems in applying these provisions in individual cases which will need to be referred to the Court of Protection.

---

[86] Mental Capacity Act 2005, s 4(6).

[87] As discussed at **5.32**, an example of a case under the existing common law in which the court accepted the evidence of family members that the patient had said she would not want to be kept alive in the circumstances but nonetheless held that her best interests were to re-instate ANH is *W Healthcare NHS Trust v KH and Others* [2005] 1 WLR 834, CA.

[88] Draft Code of Practice, para 8.35.

MEDICAL RESEARCH

Common law position

The regulation of research

5.67   It is beyond the scope of this Chapter to delve deeply into the different types of research – eg therapeutic, non-therapeutic and observational – and the volume of current learning on what is or is not permissible in accordance with modern ethical principles. There is in place a system of *Local Research Ethics Committees* and *Multi-Centre Research Ethics Committees* to regulate research carried out in an NHS body. This came into existence to relate to research involving patients who are fully informed and freely give their consent.

General principles

5.68   As a general principle it can be stated that medical research, which involves some invasion of bodily integrity on a person who is not able to consent to it, is not permissible under the existing common law, as it cannot be justified under the doctrine of necessity. A court might declare therapeutic research lawful if done in that person's best interests, although this has not been tested in court and often the point of research is not to benefit the particular individual but others who might in the future be suffering from a similar condition.

5.69   The closest the common law has come to recognising benefits to others as a factor in the best interests equation arises in the cases in which the taking of samples from one sibling for the potential benefit of another have been authorised as benefiting the child, or incapacitated adult, to contribute to the family's welfare in this way.[89] This is not a precedent justifying research. Nor is the decision in *Simms v Simms; A v A (a child)*[90] in which experimental and innovative treatment was authorised to victims of vCJD, not by way of research, but as medical treatment in their best interests as in the circumstances being the only hope for them in slowing down the decline in their condition.

Clinical Trials Regulations

5.70   Therapeutic research in the form of clinical trials on medicinal products for human use is now authorised and regulated under and in accordance with the Medicines for Human Use (Clinical Trials) Regulations 2004[91]

---

[89]   In *Re Y (Mental Patient: Bone Marrow Donation)* [1997] Fam 110.
[90]   [2003] Fam 83.
[91]   SI 2004/1031. These Regulations came into force on 1 May 2004.

made under the authority given by the *European Union Directive on Good Clinical Practice in Clinical Trials.*[92] These govern such trials in relation to both those who can provide informed consent and those who cannot, and in the latter case include the additional protections required by the Directive.

5.71   The general principles underlying these Regulations are that:

- the clinical trial must have the approval of the relevant Ethics Committee and be authorised by the appropriate Minister as licensing authority;
- the anticipated therapeutic and public health benefits must justify the risks; and
- informed consent must be given (which must be written, signed and dated) after an interview with a member of the investigating team.

5.72   The involvement of an adult who lacks capacity to consent requires the informed consent of his or her 'legal representative' and is subject to the following additional conditions:

- the research is essential to validate data obtained in clinical trials on persons able to give consent and relates directly to a life-threatening or debilitating clinical condition from which the incapacitated adult suffers;
- the trial has the potential to produce a benefit to the patient which outweighs the potential risks.

For the purposes of the Regulations, an incapacitated participant's legal representative is either:

1. a person close to the patient ('a personal legal representative'); or, where no one can act in that capacity,
2. someone such as the doctor responsible for the care of the patient or other person nominated by the healthcare provider, being someone not involved in the conduct of the trial ('a professional legal representative').

The legal representative may withdraw the subject from the trial at any time. If an adult prior to the onset of incapacity has refused to give his or her consent, he or she cannot be included as a subject.

Research authorised by the Mental Capacity Act 2005

Background

5.73   The Draft Mental Incapacity Bill presented to Parliament in June 2003 did not contain any provisions on research. The Joint Scrutiny Committee on this Bill, in response to evidence it received from the

---

[92]   Directive 2001/20/EC.

British Medical Association, the Royal College of Psychiatrists, the British Psychological Society and The Law Society, concluded that if properly regulated research involving people who may lack capacity is not possible then treatment for incapacitating disorders will not be developed. It recommended, therefore, that clauses should be included to enable strictly controlled medical research to explore the causes and consequences of mental incapacity and to develop effective treatment for such conditions. Also that these clauses should set out the key principles governing such research and the protections against exploitation or harm.[93]

5.74 As a result, provisions were included in the Mental Capacity Bill as presented to Parliament, and these were refined through various amendments made during the course of the Bill's consideration. They now form ss 30–34 of the Act.

Application of the Act

5.75 The new provisions apply to any intrusive research carried out on, or in relation to, a person who lacks capacity to consent to it other than a clinical trial subject to those Regulations (because they already make provision for trials involving participants who lack capacity). They are based upon long-standing international standards such as those laid down by the World Medical Association (originally in the Helsinki Declaration in 1964 and updated since) and in the Council of Europe Convention on Human Rights and Biomedicine.

Pre-conditions to authorisation

5.76 The pre-conditions to the authorisation of research under these provisions are, first, that the Secretary of State for Health (in relation to research in England) or the Welsh Assembly (in relation to Wales) has specified in Regulations a body (likely to be a Research Ethics Committee) as an appropriate authority to approve a research project.[94]

Secondly, such a body must have approved the research project. That approval can only be given in relation to a person who lacks capacity to consent if:[95]

- the research is connected with the person's impairing condition or its treatment;
- there are reasonable grounds for believing that research of comparable effectiveness cannot be carried out if the project is confined to persons who can consent;

---

[93] See recommendations 81–88, HL Paper 189-1, HC Paper 1083-1 (Session 2002–03).
[94] Mental Capacity Act 2005, s 30.
[95] Mental Capacity Act 2005, s 31.

- the research has the potential to benefit the person without imposing a disproportionate burden or it is intended to provide knowledge of the causes or treatment of, or the care of persons affected by, the same or a similar condition;
- in the case of research which falls only in the latter category, there are reasonable grounds for believing that the risk to the individual in taking part is negligible and anything done to that person will not interfere with his or her freedom of action or privacy in any way or be unduly invasive or restrictive; and
- there are arrangements in place to ensure the particular conditions (referred to below) will be met.

Pre-conditions relating to the individual

5.77   Before a person who lacks capacity to consent can take part in an approved research project, particular conditions relating to his or her participation must be met.

5.78   These conditions relate first to the requirement for a researcher to consult a carer (someone not professionally interested in the person's welfare) or, if a carer who is prepared to be consulted cannot be identified, a person not connected with the research project whom, in accordance with guidance to be issued by the Secretary of State (or the Welsh Assembly), the researcher has nominated as the person prepared to be consulted (eg a general practitioner or specialist engaged in the person's treatment).[96]

The regime established here is the equivalent of that provided for under the Clinical Trials Regulations outlined above. It includes provision for the consultee advising that the person concerned would not have wanted to take part, in which event that person is not to be included, or if already taking part, must be withdrawn. It also includes provision relating to treatment being provided as a matter of urgency and carrying on necessary research associated with that treatment.

5.79   Secondly, additional safeguards are provided that:

- nothing may be done in the course of the research to which the person appears to object (except where what is being done is intended to protect them or reduce their pain or discomfort) or would be contrary to any known advance decision of theirs or current statement of wishes;
- the person's interests must be assumed to outweigh those of science and society; and
- if the person lacking capacity indicates in any way that they wish to be withdrawn they must be withdrawn, as they must be if any of the

---

[96]   Mental Capacity Act 2005, s 32.

conditions for the approval of the research project cease to be met (although any treatment being given to which the research is associated may continue if there is a significant risk to health if discontinued).[97]

5.80 Regulations may be made (by the Secretary of State or the Welsh Assembly) covering the continuation of a research project in relation to a person who had consented to take part in it before these provisions were brought into force and who loses capacity to consent to continuing to take part in it before the conclusion of the project.[98]

Comment

5.81 These provisions cover the whole range of research activities which would require a person's consent if that person had capacity, which includes research involving them, their tissue or their data.[99] They steer a careful balance between allowing intrusive procedures when not necessarily of direct benefit to that person and facilitating research into an impairing condition. They are also designed to cater for situations where the research is but one aspect of the clinical or professional care of the person who lacks capacity (which will be governed by the best interests test). It remains to be seen how the Department of Health (or Welsh Assembly) is now to set about making the necessary Regulations so as to provide the basis for the operation of these provisions.

RELATIONSHIP BETWEEN THE MENTAL HEALTH AND MENTAL CAPACITY ACTS

Background

5.82 It is beyond the scope of this book to set out any detailed description or analysis of the mental health legislation, either as it exists or prospectively might be. Nevertheless, there are some interesting parallels and comparisons with the Mental Capacity Act 2005, particularly in relation to some healthcare issues discussed in this Chapter, which are worth drawing out. One of the recommendations the Joint Committee scrutinising this Bill made is that before Parliament is asked to assent to the new Mental Health Bill (see below) a clearer analysis of the interrelation between the two pieces of legislation is

---

[97] Mental Capacity Act 2005, s 33.
[98] Mental Capacity Act 2005, s 34.
[99] Research on anonymised medical data or tissue may be possible outside the terms of this Act although subject to controls under the Data Protection Act 1998 or the Human Tissue Act 2004 respectively.

presented.[100] The Government agreed that there should be clarity about the interface and undertook that the Bill and the respective Codes of Practice would seek to achieve this. So far as the mental health legislation is concerned, the exploration of this interface is done here upon the basis of the existing Mental Health Act 1983 ('the 1983 Act').

The Mental Health Act 1983

Powers of admission, detention and treatment

5.83   The 1983 Act is principally concerned with the admission of patients to hospital for assessment and treatment for their mental disorder. Mental disorder is defined in s 1(2) as:

> '... mental illness, arrested or incomplete development of mind, psychopathic disorder and any other disorder or disability of mind.'

It enables compulsory powers of detention and treatment to be used when the statutory conditions for 'sectioning' the patient are met. In the case of admission for assessment, the patient must be suffering from mental disorder of a nature or degree which warrants the detention of the patient in a hospital for assessment, and: [101]

> '... he ought to be so detained in the interests of his own health or safety or with a view to the protection of other persons.'

In the case of admission for treatment, the grounds need to be established that: [102]

> '(a) he is suffering from mental illness, severe mental impairment, psychopathic disorder or mental impairment and his mental disorder is of a nature or degree which makes it appropriate for him to receive medical treatment in a hospital; and

> (b) in the case of psychopathic disorder or mental impairment, such treatment is likely to alleviate or prevent a deterioration of his condition; and

> (c) it is necessary for the health or safety of the patient or for the protection of other persons that he should receive such treatment and it cannot be provided unless he is detained under this section.'

5.84   The 1983 Act sets out the conditions and procedures for use of these powers. These include that the application for admission (either for assessment or treatment) must be made on the recommendation in the prescribed form of two registered medical practitioners. The 1983 Act also provides for guardianship orders to be made giving a local

---

[100]   Recommendation 27 of HL Paper 79-1, HC 95-1 (Session 2004–05) and the Government's response at p 17 of Cm 6624.

[101]   Mental Health Act 1983, s 2(2).

[102]   Mental Health Act 1983, s 3(2).

authority power to require a patient in the community to reside at a specified place and attend for treatment.

Review and appeals

5.85 The 1983 Act then provides the procedures for review and appeals to the independent Mental Health Review Tribunals in relation to the use, or continued use, of the compulsory powers.

Purpose

5.86 The purpose of the 1983 Act is to provide the statutory framework for the hospital care and treatment of people for their mental disorder when they are unable or unwilling to consent to that care and treatment, and when it is necessary for that care and treatment to be given to protect themselves or others from harm.

5.87 The key point for the exercise of these powers is the inability or unwillingness of the patient who suffers from a mental disorder to consent. This encompasses people who, notwithstanding their mental disorder, have capacity to do so – and we have already seen from a case such as *Re C (Adult: Refusal of Treatment)*[103] how it is possible for someone detained under the 1983 Act to have capacity in relation to a treatment decision. Inability to consent will also include people who do not have capacity, but the question whether an individual patient has or does not have decision-making capacity is not the key determinant of whether the powers conferred by the 1983 Act should be used.

Comparisons

5.88 The Mental Capacity Act 2005 is based wholly on a capacity test. Its provisions have no application to people who have the capacity to make their own decisions. Some, who lack capacity, will not come within the definition of those for whom compulsory powers under the 1983 Act can be exercised. People with learning difficulties, for example, who may thereby not be able to give their consent to treatment, will not generally be subject to the compulsory powers of the 1983 Act, unless they are also abnormally aggressive or seriously irresponsible. Other examples are people in PVS, or anyone suffering from 'locked-in' syndrome which prevents them from communicating, or persons temporarily unconscious or drunk or under the influence of drugs.

---

[103]   [1994] 1 WLR 290; see **5.10**.

Differences

5.89   It can be seen that the differences between these two approaches are
       that:

       1. the Mental Capacity Act 2005 relates to a person's functioning –
           incapacity to make a particular decision – whereas the Mental
           Health Act 1983 relates to a person's status, as someone diagnosed
           as having a mental disorder within the meaning of the Act and
           subject to its powers;
       2. the Mental Capacity Act 2005 covers all decision-making, whereas
           the Mental Health Act 1983 is, to a very large degree, limited to
           decisions about care in hospital and medical treatment for mental
           disorder;
       3. the Mental Health Act 1983 authorises detention, but this is
           specifically excluded under the Mental Capacity Act 2005;[104]
       4. the Mental Capacity Act 2005 specifically excludes[105] anyone
           giving a patient medical treatment for mental disorder, or
           consenting to a patient being given medical treatment for mental
           disorder, if the patient is, at the relevant time, subject to the
           compulsory treatment provisions of the Mental Health Act 1983.

Overlaps

5.90   There are areas of overlap:

       1. people who are detained in hospital under the Mental Health Act
           1983 and who also lack capacity to make financial decisions may be
           subject to the provisions of the Mental Capacity Act 2005;
       2. equally, an elderly person, for example, with Alzheimer's disease,
           whose day-to-day life is managed in accordance with the provisions
           of the Mental Capacity Act 2005, may be made subject to the
           Mental Health Act 1983 if it is no longer possible to care for such a
           person at home and he or she is resisting being admitted to hospital.

Compliant patients

5.91   The great majority of people with a mental disorder are not treated
       under the 1983 Act. It has been estimated that at any point in time there
       are about 14,000 people being treated for mental disorder under the
       1983 Act. But nothing in the 1983 Act is to be treated as preventing the
       informal admission of a patient requiring treatment for mental disorder
       to any hospital or registered establishment.[106] It is estimated that there

---

[104]   See s 6 which provides the conditions under which a person may 'restrain' a person whilst
        remaining within the protection given by s 5, but this protection is not available if there is a
        deprivation of liberty.
[105]   See s 28.
[106]   Mental Health Act 1983, s 131.

are in the region of 70,000 people either in care homes or hospitals while being treated informally for their mental disorder. In their case, compulsion is not seen as necessary because they are 'compliant'. This does not give rise to any issue of particular concern when they have capacity and it is their choice. However, questions can arise as to how such patients, who may be compliant but who do not have the capacity to reach their own decisions about what is happening to them, should be dealt with. This is particularly the case so far as they are deprived of their liberty.

The 'Bournewood gap'

5.92   It is appropriate to conclude this exploration with a brief description of what has become known as the 'Bournewood gap'. This emerged out of the decision of the European Court of Human Rights in *HL v UK*.[107]

The decisions of the domestic courts

5.93   Mr HL, an autistic man, was re-admitted to the Bournewood Hospital after a period in the community with paid carers, but the decision was taken not to section him under the 1983 Act as he had not resisted admission. The ensuing dispute between the carers and the hospital over his care and treatment was first litigated in judicial review proceedings in the domestic courts. The carers lost at first instance and ultimately in the House of Lords, in the latter case basically on the ground that the circumstances were covered by the common law doctrine of necessity. This reversed the decision of the Court of Appeal, which had upheld their claim that he had been unlawfully detained.[108]

European Court of Human Rights

5.94   The case was then taken to the European Court of Human Rights. The unanimous decision was:

1. Mr HL had been deprived of his liberty contrary to Art 5(1) of the Convention;
2. that detention was arbitrary and not in accordance with a procedure prescribed by law; and
3. the procedures available to him did not comply with the requirements of Art 5(4) as there was no procedure under which he could seek a merits review of whether the conditions for his detention remained applicable.

---

[107]   Application no 45508/99, judgment on the merits given on 5 October 2004 [2004] 1 FLR 1019.

[108]   *R v Bournewood Community and Mental Health NHS Trust, ex parte L* [1999] AC 458, HL; [1998] 2 WLR 764, CA.

5.95   The specific criticisms the European Court made, and the contrast it drew between the safeguards available to a person detained under the 1983 Act and an informal patient in Mr HL's position, related to the lack of any formal procedures as to:

- who could authorise an admission;
- the reasons needing to be given for that admission (whether it was for treatment or assessment);
- the need for continuing clinical assessment and review; and
- who could represent the patient and be able to seek a review in an independent tribunal of the continued detention.

The discussion in the Court related to the position under the inherent jurisdiction as it was at the time these events occurred (1997). The enactment of the Mental Capacity Act 2005 is relevant because in some respects, notably the creation of the *Independent Mental Capacity Advocacy Service*, it deals with some of the points raised. Nevertheless, the Act was not intended to nor does it fill the gap, and the Government has recognised this.

Consultation

5.96   The Department of Health has consulted on what further measures, legislative or otherwise, are needed to fill the identified gap. This could be by way of provision in the new Mental Health Bill. The Department has indicated that, subject to the consultation response, it is inclined to adopt an approach called 'protective care'. This would be a new system to govern admission and detention procedures, reviews and appeals for people who lack capacity. It would run in parallel with the 1983 Act regime and could entail amending the Mental Capacity Act 2005 to give effect to it.

The interim position

5.97   Meanwhile, some cases may reach the courts in which an issue arises whether a best interests declaration under the inherent jurisdiction should be made governing aspects of the care and treatment of someone with mental disorder or whether the circumstances are better dealt with using 1983 Act powers. It may be possible to deal with some of these cases through a best interests application and a care plan, approved as part of the decision in that application, which contains equivalent safeguards as to review as would be available if the patient had been sectioned under the 1983 Act.

Litigation capacity

5.98   One other interface between the 1983 Act and the subject matter of this book is the test for 'litigation' capacity in cases brought in the courts (but not incorporated into the current rules relating to cases in the existing Court of Protection). Under both the CPR 1998 and the FPR 1991 the test for whether a person is a 'patient' and incapable of taking part in litigation without the support of a litigation friend (or next friend/guardian ad litem in family proceedings) is: [109]

> '... a person who by reason of mental disorder within the meaning of the Mental Health Act 1983 is incapable of managing and administering his property and affairs.'

5.99   In the light of the issue-specific nature of the test, the relevant question is whether the person can manage his or her affairs relating to the litigation.[110] It is possible, but unusual (other than in advance directive cases), for the position to be reached that the person has the capacity to reach a decision about the subject matter but not to litigate about it or *vice versa*.[111] In the medical treatment or welfare cases in the High Court under its inherent jurisdiction this test determines whether the Official Solicitor is brought in to represent the incapacitated party. It remains to be seen whether the separate test of litigation capacity will be incorporated into the new Court of Protection Rules in relation to the cases to be dealt with by this Court under the 2005 Act.

A new Mental Health Bill

5.100   At the time of writing a new Mental Health Bill has not yet been presented to Parliament. That there should be a Bill to update and replace the 1983 Act has been the Government's policy since 1998. Originally, it was thought possible that the Mental Health Bill would be considered by Parliament at more or less the same time as the Mental Capacity Bill. This did not happen.

5.101   The Department of Health has embarked upon successive consultations on a new Mental Health Bill, which have succeeded in drawing out that there are some aspects over which sharp controversy has continued. The stage has been reached that a draft Bill was published on 7 September 2004 and a Joint Parliamentary Scrutiny Committee has reported on that draft, making 107 recommendations in all.[112] The Government has announced its response to the Joint Committee's recommendations, accepting over half of them (although some areas of potential controversy are likely to remain).[113] Introduction of a Bill in the current

---

[109]   CPR, Part 21; FPR, r 9.2.
[110]   *Masterman-Lister v Brutton & Co and Jewell & Home Counties Dairies* [2002] EWCA Civ 1889, [2002] All ER (D) 297 (Dec).
[111]   For a recent discussion of this, see judgment of Munby J in *Sheffield City Council v E and another* [2005] 2 WLR 953.
[112]   HL Paper 79-1, HC Paper 95-1 (Session 2004–05).
[113]   Cm 6624 (July 2005).

session of Parliament is a Government commitment given in the Queen's Speech and the Bill is being redrafted to take account of the changes to be made following consideration of the Committee's report. The publication of a revised Bill and its introduction in Parliament was expected in the autumn of 2005 but it has not yet emerged. It is now, therefore, unlikely that a new Mental Health Bill could be enacted and brought into operation at the same time as, or shortly after, the Mental Capacity Act 2005.

Chapter 6

The Court of Protection

BACKGROUND

6.1 The present Court of Protection ('the Court') exists to protect and manage the property and financial affairs of people in England and Wales (known as 'patients') who are incapable, by reason of mental disorder, of managing and administering their own affairs.[1]

Origins of the jurisdiction

6.2 The origins of state involvement in the financial affairs of the mentally incapacitated citizen go back a long way.[2] Medieval society was based on the protection and eventual transfer of real estate, and land held in tenure by those who lacked the mental capacity to appoint or provide a competent successor risked being taken back by the sovereign. Eventually a statute recognised the existence of the Royal Prerogative but imposed limits on its operation.[3]

Distinction between 'idiots' and 'lunatics'

6.3 This law drew an important distinction between those labelled 'idiots'[4] ('natural fools from birth') and those termed 'lunatics'[5] ('sometimes of good and sound memory and understanding and sometimes not').[6] The custody of the land and persons of both belonged to the Crown and there was a prohibition against disposal of property in order that 'their heirs shall not be disinherited', but there was a difference in the treatment of any 'profits' or 'income'.

6.4 In the case of the 'idiot', the Crown took control of the estate and assumed early responsibility for his maintenance (no mention was made

---

[1] Mental Health Act 1983, s 94(2).

[2] The earliest reference is to be found in a semi-official tract known as the *De Praerogativa Regis* ('On the King's Prerogative') dating from the reign of Edward 1 (1272–1307).

[3] Statute de Prerogativa Regis, 17 Edw II (1339) St I cc 9, 10.

[4] This probably meant those who were 'mentally handicapped' (the term 'learning disability' is now used).

[5] Presumably those who today would be designated as mentally ill.

[6] David Roffe 'Madness and care in the community: a medieval perspective' (BMJ, 1995) 1708–1712.

of his household), 'contracting out' guardianship to private individuals, who paid an initial 'fine', then an annual 'rent'. But the Crown could retain any profits:

> 'The King shall have the custody of the lands of natural fools taking the profits of them without waste or destruction, and shall find them their necessaries, of whose fee soever the lands be holden; and after the death of such idiots he shall render it to their right heirs.'

'Lunatics' (also referred to as those 'whose wit had failed them') were nominally in a similar situation, in that the Crown would provide for their maintenance from their estates, but the profits of the estate would be used to care for them and their household, with any surplus being retained. When and if they returned to their right mind, and on their death, the estate would pass to their heirs:

> '... the King shall provide for the custody and sustentation of lunatics, and preserve their lands and the profits of them, for their use, when they come to their right mind: and the king shall take nothing to his own use.'

The law assumed the state of '*non compos mentis*' to be potentially transient.[7] It was thus to the lunatic's advantage to prove that his indisposition was transient whereas it was in the King's interests to establish that this was a 'lifetime' disability carrying a 'lifetime' fiat to the accrued interest.

Management of affairs

6.5   The doctrine of *negotiorum gestio*[8] was thus established at an early age. But why was the specific nature of the mental incapacity of such importance? There was no medieval welfare service and it is not suggested that this was an early form of means testing with the Crown being responsible for funding the needs of the individual over and above those which he could afford. Nor apparently was there any pooling of resources for this purpose. It was not the physical or moral welfare of these vulnerable individuals that was under consideration but their ability to preserve and pass on their inheritance. Those who regained their capacity would become aware of their rights and assert the right to peaceful enjoyment of their possessions thereby challenging the Crown. The outcome is perhaps an uneasy compromise between the Crown's interest in these possessions and the 'right' of potential beneficiaries to preserve their inheritance.

---

[7]   William Blackstone's *Commentaries on the Laws of England (1765-1769)* Book One, Chapter 8: Of the King's Revenue: Branch XVIII.

[8]   'Management of affairs' whereby a person may lawfully intervene to manage or protect the affairs of someone else who is not available to do so because of incapacity. The manager has no authorisation from the person whose affairs are managed: the authority to intervene is derived from the law itself.

'Of unsound mind so found'

Inquisitions

6.6 Until 1862 there was no provision for the administration of patients' estates unless they were persons 'of unsound mind so found by inquisition'. This jurisdiction was exercised at various times by the Lord Chancellor and other judges to whom the care and commitment of the persons and estates of persons under mental disability were granted by letters patent or warrant. In 1540 the Court of the King's Wards was created which exercised the Royal Prerogative until its abolition in the reign of Charles II. A commissioner would be appointed to investigate the matter, and a jury of local people likely to have knowledge of the circumstances. The person himself and those who knew him best were intricately involved in the process.[9]

The use of inquisition meant that a person's unsoundness of mind had to have been judicially established by inquiry, and once this had happened the patient's estate could be managed by committee. Only persons of significant wealth would justify such procedure and presumably informal steps were taken in respect of the income and assets of ordinary people.

Committees of 'the person' and 'the affairs'

6.7 It is interesting to note that by the eighteenth century there was a division between control of the person and control of their affairs. By process in the Court of Chancery it was possible to have a person's mental faculties investigated and, if found insane, a committee appointed to administer the lunatic's property. However, the potential heir was never permitted to be the committee of the person,[10] because it was in his interest that the party should die. The heir, instead, was made committee of the estate, it being in his interest by good management to preserve the value of the estate; albeit he was accountable to the Court of Chancery (and to the incapacitated person if he recovered). The need to expend the estate for the benefit of the person and the conflict of interest that thus arose was apparently not identified.

Administration without inquisition

6.8 Subsequently Commissioners in Lunacy[11] conducted jury trials as a tribunal of three. If the individual was found to be of unsound mind he would be 'taken into Chancery' and his affairs dealt with by a Master in

---

[9] CIM 1957 *Calendar of Inquisitions* IV 1377–1388 PRO. The earliest known example is that of Emma de Beston whose state of mind had become an issue in 1382 when she was alleged to have disposed of a large part of her possessions while insane. She was assessed by questions carefully linked to her experience and circumstances.

[10] The equivalent of guardianship. A committee of the person was seldom appointed.

[11] These were part-time appointments.

Chancery. In 1846 the two roles were combined and the Commissioners renamed Masters in Lunacy.[12]

The subsequent Lunacy Regulation Act 1862 rendered a formal inquisition unnecessary by introducing the concept of 'unsoundness of mind not so found'. This was applied to people whose unsoundness of mind was established to the satisfaction of the judge or Master in Lunacy, not by judicial inquiry but by medical evidence of incompetency. Potentially the procedure became available to any person with assets that needed to be administered. Full provision was made by the Lunacy Act 1890 for administration, without inquisition, of the estates of persons under mental disability. Since that time, the judicial inquiry has been abolished altogether, and a more medically oriented and informal approach has been introduced.

Assessment of capacity

Presumption of incompetence

6.9   Prior to 1959, patients who were compulsorily detained in hospital came within the jurisdiction of the court by operation of law. They were presumed incompetent to manage their affairs without any further specific inquiry into their mental condition or capacity for specific rational understanding. However, voluntary patients and mentally disordered people not living in hospital or not under guardianship were presumed competent to handle their financial interests. This presumption could be rebutted and the patient's right to manage his affairs removed, only by a finding of the judge or the Master in Lunacy of the Court of Protection.

Abolition of a status test

6.10   The Percy Commission[13] observed that a person's legal status could not of itself indicate whether he was capable of handling his own affairs. Some types of mental disorders which would justify compulsory admission 'would not necessarily affect a patient's powers of judgement in relation to financial affairs'. It concluded that:

> '... it should not be assumed in law or in administrative practice that mentally disordered patients who are admitted to hospital under compulsory powers are necessarily incapable of managing their financial affairs ... The law and administrative arrangements dealing with patient's property should not be in any way dependent on whether the patient is in hospital or not or whether a hospital patient has been admitted with or without compulsion.'

---

[12] The change of name enabled the title 'Lunacy Commissioner' to be used for new mental health functions.

[13] *Royal Commission on the Law Relating to Mental Illness and Mental Deficiency* 1957.

6.11 These recommendations were incorporated into s 101 of the Mental Health Act 1959 ('the 1959 Act') and are now to be found in s 94(2) of the Mental Health Act 1983 ('the 1983 Act'). In consequence a status test of capacity is no longer applied and, except in case of emergency, the jurisdiction of the Court can only be invoked when the Court is satisfied after considering medical evidence that the person is incapable, by reason of mental disorder, of managing and administering his or her property and affairs.[14] In many ways this is itself a status test because it is a generic test and not decision-specific. It does, however, take into account the complexity of the individual's affairs.[15]

Limitations of the jurisdiction

6.12 The 1959 Act, which was hailed as the first major overhaul of mental health legislation, also abolished the Royal Prerogative and established a completely statutory jurisdiction. It was not realised at the time that this deprived the courts of jurisdiction over personal welfare and healthcare decisions (other than in the context of treatment for a mental disorder), but this became apparent after it was held that the statutory jurisdiction of the Court of Protection only extended to financial affairs.[16]

6.13 The 1959 Act sought to answer the needs of those who required medical intervention for their mental illness alongside those whose requirements were legal intervention with their assets. The role of gatekeeper in both respects was handed to the medical profession. No longer would incapacity be decided by a jury with local knowledge of the individual concerned, and indeed, knowledge of the family. It is only in recent years that the courts have re-assumed control and look beyond the views of medical practitioners and psychiatrists when assessing mental capacity.

THE PRESENT COURT OF PROTECTION

Status

6.14 Until 1960 the jurisdiction 'in Lunacy' was in part statutory and in part dependent on the inherent jurisdiction of the Court derived from the Royal Prerogative which is often referred to as the *parens patriae*

---

[14] This person is known as a 'patient'.

[15] The Mental Capacity Act 2005 departs from this approach by providing for issue-specific determinations.

[16] *Re W* [1971] Ch 123; [1970] 2 All ER 502. See generally CHAPTER 5.

jurisdiction. Under the Lunacy Act 1890 the jurisdiction relating to the administration and management of patients' affairs was assigned to a Master in Lunacy,[17] who operated under different titles[18] until 1947 when the term Court of Protection was established. Part VIII of the 1959 Act re-established the Court of Protection and its continuing existence was confirmed by the 1983 Act, Part VII. Further jurisdiction has since been conferred on the Court by the Enduring Powers of Attorney Act 1985.

6.15   The Court of Protection is not a court as such but is an office of the Supreme Court of Judicature,[19] although in practice this is of little significance and some High Court judges are nominated to conduct its work. It is headed by the Master and situated in London. There are also about 75 Nominated Officers who are appointed by the Lord Chancellor and exercise some of the jurisdiction under the guidance of the Master who has powers of delegation.[20] The three senior ones adopt the courtesy title of Assistant Master and are given more authority including the conduct of hearings.

The Public Guardianship Office provides administrative support for the Court. It has a staff of several hundred, including those in the Judicial Support Unit who process formal applications and appeals.[21] The Court itself consists of the Master, Deputy Master and a number of Nominated Officers (including those given the courtesy title of Assistant Master).

Practice and procedure

General

6.16   The procedure of the Court is governed by the Court of Protection Rules 2001[22] ('the 2001 Rules') which are very brief compared with the Civil Procedure Rules 1998. Instead of a statement of objectives they start with an Interpretation clause in which reference is made to the Supreme Court Act 1981 for the meaning of expressions used, a 'direction' means a direction or authority given under the seal of the Court and an 'order' includes a certificate, direction or authority of the Court under

---

[17]   There were two Masters until 1922.

[18]   Initially the 'Office of the Master in Lunacy' but this was changed to the 'Management and Administration Department' in 1934 (note the abbreviation MAD).

[19]   Supreme Court Act 1981, s 1(1).

[20]   Mental Health Act 1983, ss 93(4) and 94(1). It is questionable whether and to what extent judicial powers should be delegated in this way following the Human Rights Act 1998. The Public Trustee was originally given the same powers as the Master.

[21]   Refer to **CHAPTER 7** for the historical background to the Public Guardianship Office.

[22]   SI 2001/824. This update to the existing Rules was required following the demise of the Public Trust Office and the creation of the Public Guardianship Office from 1 April 2001. The authority for the 2001 Rules is to be found in Mental Health Act 1983, s 106.

the official seal of the Court. A 'patient' is a person who is alleged to be or who the Court has reason to believe may be incapable by reason of mental disorder of managing and administering his or her property and affairs.

Exercise of jurisdiction

6.17 Under r 3 any function of the Court may be exercised by a nominated judge of the High Court, the Master or (to the extent that he is authorised) by a nominated officer. Part II (which only contains r 6) provides that this may, except where the 2001 Rules provide otherwise, be:[23]

1. without an appointment for a hearing;
2. by the Court of its own motion or at the instance or on the application of a person concerned;
3. whether or not proceedings have been commenced with respect to the patient.

Part III comprising rr 7–18 then deals with applications and hearings.

Applications

6.18 Provision is made as to the form of applications, but apart from those for the first appointment of a receiver there is considerable informality and a letter may be sufficient. The Court may allow applications to be amended at any stage,[24] and where it is urgent the Court may dispense with an application in writing. Hearings are notified by letter and may be dispensed with where it is considered that the application may properly be dealt with without one. Special rules deal with applications under the Trustee Act 1925, for settlement or a gift of a patient's property and for the execution of a will for a patient.[25]

Short orders

6.19 Rule 8 provides that where the property of the patient does not exceed a specified value[26] or it is otherwise considered appropriate, the Court may instead of appointing a receiver make a short order or direction which authorises some suitable person to deal with the patient's property or part of it, or with his or her affairs, in the manner specified. This power has been used increasingly during recent years where it is felt that intrusive supervision is not necessary. Not only may small estates be dealt with in this summary way but, for example, a tenancy may be authorised.

---

[23] Court of Protection Rules 2001, r 6.
[24] Court of Protection Rules 2001, r 51.
[25] Court of Protection Rules 2001, rr 15–18.
[26] Presently £16,000.

Persons under disability

6.20　Relatives or other persons associated with a patient may themselves
lack capacity. Rule 14 deals with applications involving 'persons under
a disability'[27] and is modelled on the former Rules of the Supreme
Court. The person must be represented by a 'next friend' if bringing the
application or by a 'guardian ad litem' if responding.[28] An order making
the appointment is not necessary unless an existing representative is to
be replaced. A written consent of the person to be appointed as
representative must be filed, and also a certificate by a solicitor acting
for the person under a disability that this person is a minor or a patient
and that the person to be appointed has no adverse interest. It follows
that a person under a disability must, through his or her representative,
initially instruct a solicitor but there seem to be no further safeguards
and the Court could allow the solicitor to withdraw thereafter.[29]

Service

6.21　Part IV (rr 19–26) deals with the service of notice of hearings and of
applications. This specifies the persons who should be given notice and
includes 'such other persons who appear to the Court to be interested as
the Court may specify'. The mode of service is prescribed and is far
from antiquated, being personal service, first-class post or document
exchange and even fax or 'other electronic means'. Service on a
solicitor who is acting for a person and substituted service are provided
for, and service on a person under a disability is to be on the parent or
guardian (for a minor) and the receiver, registered attorney or 'person
with whom he resides or in whose care he is' (for a patient).

Evidence

6.22　Part V (rr 27–36) deals with evidence. Except where the 2001 Rules
otherwise provide evidence is to be by affidavit.[30] However, the Court
may accept statements of fact or other such oral or written evidence as it
considers sufficient even if not on oath. The Court may give directions
as to how any such evidence is to be given but in general it should be
dated, signed and have numbered paragraphs. Persons who have given
written evidence may be ordered by the Court to attend and the oath
may then be administered. Written evidence should be filed in advance

---

[27]　These are minors (ie persons under 18 years of age) and 'patients' who could themselves
potentially be within the jurisdiction of the Court.

[28]　The Civil Procedure Rules 1998, Part 21 now uses the term 'litigation friend' for both.

[29]　One would expect the Court to consider whether the representative could manage without
legal assistance and to intervene if the best interests of the person under a disability are not
being addressed.

[30]　The 2001 Rules do not introduce the concept of a statement containing a certificate of truth
that now applies under the Civil Procedure Rules 1998.

although an undertaking to file the evidence may be sufficient. Evidence that has been used may subsequently be used in any other proceedings in the Court relating to the same patient and, if authorised by the Court, in proceedings in other specified courts.

Hearings

6.23　Part VI of the 2001 Rules deals with hearings and Part IX with additional Court control including requiring the attendance of witnesses. Where appropriate the Master should refer matters to a judge but may give any necessary directions for the purpose, and a judge may refer any question back to the Master for inquiry and report.[31]

Accommodation

6.24　Applications are to be heard in chambers unless, in the case of an application before a judge, the judge otherwise directs.[32] This approach is outdated, being based upon the former distinction between hearings in 'open court' (a courtroom with the public admitted) or 'in chambers' (a courtroom but with the public excluded). The relevant distinction is now between hearings in public and in private. The decision whether to conduct proceedings in the judge's chambers or a courtroom will be influenced by the requirements of the case and the facilities available. Chambers are preferred for a more relaxed, intimate hearing but may be too small to accommodate all who need to attend. There is now a trend, especially in the family courts and for district judges, towards multi-purpose hearing rooms. The Master has a private hearing room and the present Deputy Master uses his chambers which accommodate up to 16 people but moves to an adjacent courtroom if necessary.

Attendance

6.25　The Court determines which persons are to be permitted to attend any part of a hearing, although it will be obvious that certain persons need to attend. Even these persons may be excluded for part of a hearing. It is interesting to note that the Court may require two or more persons to be separately represented where a legal representative purports to act for both of them, because in the civil courts this is generally left to the Solicitors' Code for Professional Conduct.

Witnesses

6.26　The Court may allow or direct any person to take out a witness summons requiring the person named in it to attend before the Court

---

[31]　This mirrors the procedure in Chancery and Insolvency proceedings in the High Court.
[32]　This inevitably means a High Court judge.

and give oral evidence or produce any document. The application for the summons must then be supported by a statement giving relevant information and stating the grounds on which it is made. The summons must be served a reasonable time before the time fixed for the attendance and conduct money must be tendered.

Control of proceedings

6.27   The Court has wide powers under r 49 to require persons having conduct of proceedings to explain delay or other causes of dissatisfaction and to make orders for expediting proceedings. It may direct any person to make any application or carry out directions and even appoint the Official Solicitor (with his or her consent) to act as solicitor for a patient.

The Court may also under r 50 require a patient to attend at a specified time and place for examination by the Master, a Visitor or any medical practitioner. These are valuable powers which enable the Court to identify and address the actual needs of the patient and similar powers will be even more important under the new, wider jurisdiction.

Outcomes

6.28   Part XI (rr 54–55) deals with the rights of persons aggrieved by a decision of the Court and Part VIII (rr 45–47) deals with enforcement.

Reviews and appeals

6.29   Where a decision is made without an attended hearing, any person who is aggrieved may apply to the Court within 14 days to have the decision reviewed by the Court.[33] The Court may then confirm or revoke the previous decision or make any other order that it thinks fit, but if still aggrieved the person may within 14 days apply for an attended hearing.

6.30   Any person who is aggrieved by the decision of the Court made at an attended hearing may appeal within 14 days, and procedures are then prescribed. Appeals are heard by nominated High Court judges of the Chancery or Family Division although it appears that all are now nominated and deputy judges sometimes hear appeals.[34]

---

[33]   This does not apply to decisions about the remission or postponement of fees.

[34]   The concept of appeals being dealt with by a deputy High Court judge who sits part time and is otherwise a practising barrister who might appear before the Master is open to criticism.

Enforcement

6.31 Every order, certificate, direction or authority of the Court which is drawn up will be sealed and filed. A 'slip rule' allows for clerical mistakes in orders or directions or other errors to be corrected.[35] Enforcement procedures are to be issued out of the Central Office of the Supreme Court. It is possible that the Public Guardian will instigate enforcement proceedings, although where there has been a dispute it is more likely that the other party to the proceedings will take steps to enforce the outcome.

Fees and costs

Court fees

6.32 The Court charges fees which are usually paid out of the estate of the patient,[36] or by the donor in the case of a registered enduring power of attorney.[37] A policy of full costs recovery applies which means that the books should be balanced on an annual basis. These fees are intended to reflect the actual cost of the service provided and during recent years there has been an attempt to prevent the cross-subsidy between various aspects of the work of the Public Guardianship Office that previously existed.

6.33 The Court has power to remit or postpone the payment of the whole or part of any fee where:[38]

1. in its opinion hardship might otherwise be caused to the patient or to his or her dependents or in any other case where the circumstances are exceptional; or
2. the cost of calculation and collection would be disproportionate to the amount involved.

To this extent there is an external subsidy. These powers are discretionary and not subject to review or appeal, but in response to criticism the Public Guardianship Office (which exercises this power through the Nominated Officers) has recently published general guidelines on fee remission. The Court remains willing to consider circumstances of hardship that do not fall within the published criteria.

---

[35] Court of Protection Rules 2001, r 52.

[36] Court of Protection Rules 2001, Part XVII, rr 76–83. The fees are specified in an Appendix which is updated at intervals.

[37] Court of Protection (Enduring Power of Attorney) Rules 2001, SI 2001/825, Part VI, r 26. The fees are specified in a Schedule which is updated at intervals.

[38] Court of Protection Rules 2001, r 83. Court of Protection (Enduring Power of Attorney) Rules 2001, r 26A. These rules make the decision a judicial one, but under the new jurisdiction the power will be given to the administration (as in the county courts).

Any application for fee remission or postponement is made in writing to the Public Guardianship Office.

Legal costs

6.34   Part XVIII (rr 84–89) deals with costs. All costs incurred in relation to proceedings in the Court of Protection are at the discretion of the Court, which may order them to be paid out of the estate of the patient (or donor in the case of an enduring power of attorney), or by an applicant, objector or any other person attending or taking part in the proceedings. Unlike proceedings in the civil courts, costs do not automatically follow the event and the Court has an unlimited discretion to make whatever order it considers that the justice of the case requires. In exercising its discretion the Court must have regard to all the circumstances of the case, including the relationship between the parties, their conduct, their respective means and the amount of costs involved.

Where an application is made in good faith, supported by medical evidence, in the best interests of the donor and without any personal motive, the applicant is generally entitled to his or her costs, even if he or she is unsuccessful. However, in cases where the Court considers an objection or application to have been made in bad faith, frivolous, malicious, vexatious or motivated by self-interest, it may order the applicant or objector to pay some or all of the costs. Similarly where a person places him or herself in a hostile position to the donor, or where his or her conduct results in the costs of the proceedings being more expensive than they might otherwise have been, the Court may consider it appropriate to penalise them as to costs.[39]

6.35   The usual order is that the costs of the parties be subject to detailed assessment on the standard basis[40] and paid from the estate. This has been approved by the President of the Family Division in a recent appeal following objections to the registration of an enduring power of attorney,[41] and a decision of Deputy Master Ashton in the following terms has also been upheld on appeal:[42]

> 'An enquiry was not unreasonable … whistle blowers should not be discouraged when the affairs of vulnerable adults are involved … I am not willing to condemn this objector in costs so all costs must be borne by the estate … that is the price to pay for supervision of this nature.'

6.36   There is a range of procedures available to approve the costs including fixed costs and assessment of costs (the option of agreed costs was

---

[39]   *Re Cathcart* [1893] 1 Ch 466.
[40]   The Master directed with effect from 1 April 2005 that this be changed from the indemnity basis.
[41]   *Re Livesey*, Dame Elizabeth Butler-Sloss (unreported) 19 December 2002.
[42]   *Re Jefferson*, Neuberger J (unreported) 17 February 2003.

abolished in 2004). The procedures of the civil courts have now been adopted but with modifications.[43] The costs actually charged by solicitors must be approved by the Court before being paid from the funds of a patient and in this respect summary assessment is not allowed but the Court may order the patient to pay a fixed contribution towards the costs of a party.

The regional Court of Protection

Background

6.37   Although in the early days Inquisitions took place throughout the country and involved local people who knew the alleged patient, since its creation the Court of Protection has sat in London despite having a jurisdiction extending to England and Wales. Recently the Master has conducted some fund management hearings in the area where the patient resides and even at the patient's home. There are substantial advantages in this because the home visit better informs the Master, but this is not generally an economical use of Court time and there are other vulnerabilities.[44]

Law Commission proposals.

6.38   Following an extensive consultation[45] the Law Commission proposed that a reconstituted Court of Protection with jurisdiction over incapacity matters should have a regional presence, with designated judges throughout the country dealing with hearings locally. These specially trained judges could be called upon to take mental incapacity cases alongside their ordinary work and where appropriate sit in a dual jurisdiction. Thus a local district judge whose daily work includes resolving disputes over broken relationships and the welfare of children could resolve disputes and uncertainty concerning the personal needs of incapacitated adults, with High Court judges tackling serious healthcare decisions. This would be done under the umbrella of a London-based Court of Protection which would retain its existing financial jurisdiction.

After further consultation the Lord Chancellor published the Government's proposals in October 1999 in the Report *Making Decisions* and these included a new Court of Protection with a regional

---

[43]   The costs provisions of the Civil Procedure Rules 1998 have been incorporated in the 2001 Rules by reference subject to certain modifications.

[44]   The Master will be attending alone and without recording facilities.

[45]   This is outlined in **CHAPTER 1**. The proposal of a tribunal for some types of case was rejected.

presence. It thus became current policy to make the Court of Protection more accessible to the public by providing it with a regional presence.

Pressures for change

6.39 The Court of Protection was not readily accessible to those in the North of England and other parts of the country. The cost to parties of travelling to and staying in London for a hearing can be prohibitive and may represent a denial of justice to those involved. In addition, solicitors in the provinces were discouraged from gaining 'hands-on' experience of the work of the Court by attending hearings and therefore less able to give well-informed advice to their clients.

Concerns were also expressed that the Master was the only human rights compliant judge of the Court,[46] as the Assistant Masters who take some of the hearings do not have a judicial appointment.[47] This could cause problems if there was a case that the Master could not hear or if he or she was unable to sit for an extended period. It also limited the scope for coping with variations in workload which could result in unacceptable delay.

6.40 In consequence it was proposed that even before the implementation of a new mental incapacity jurisdiction a few district judges based at carefully selected locations (eg one on each Circuit) should be appointed as Deputy Masters to hear locally cases that were referred to them by the Master. There would then be a structure in place to cope with any new jurisdiction that was introduced. The post of Deputy Master of the Court of Protection had been created by the 1959 Act, but ceased to exist on the retirement of the then Deputy Master in 1982, and is not mentioned in the 1983 Act. However, s 91 of the Supreme Court Act 1981 permitted the Lord Chancellor to appoint deputy judges if he considered that it was expedient to do so in order to facilitate the disposal of the business of the court. Any person so acting would have all the jurisdiction of a person permanently appointed to the office in which he or she was acting. There was no reason why this procedure should not be adopted in respect of the Master of the Court of Protection.

---

[46] Apart from the nominated High Court judges. The official view is that only the decision that an individual is a patient requires a judicial determination, but other disputes within this jurisdiction may possibly engage the human rights of the patient and members of the family or civil partners.

[47] The term Assistant Master is a courtesy title and they are in reality legally qualified civil servants in the Department of Constitutional Affairs who are 'nominated officers' under the 1983 Act, s 93(4).

The Preston pilot

6.41 The *Preston Regional Pilot* which commenced on 1 October 2001 was a first attempt to implement this proposal. District Judge Ashton was appointed a part-time Deputy Master of the Court of Protection for a 6-month trial period to hear any case where it was more convenient for the parties to attend Preston Combined Court Centre in Lancashire. Parties were given the option of appearing at this venue and were asked to complete questionnaires for an evaluation. A 'protocol' was agreed, a monitoring exercise set up and standard letters and forms produced. There was a good working relationship from the inception and matters soon became routine. Apart from fine-tuning the initial procedures have continued throughout and have not caused any serious problems.[48]

The trial proved successful and the appointment was confirmed for a 5-year term. A Northern Court of Protection operating as a 'satellite' of the central court in London was thus established and on certain days in each month[49] hearings take place at Preston Combined Court Centre. These are contested hearings (mainly disputes over enduring powers of attorney and the choice of receiver) and fund management hearings for large damages awards, but statutory wills and applications to be discharged from the jurisdiction due to recovery have also been heard.

The pilot district judge

6.42 District Judge Ashton had for many years been actively interested in issues surrounding decision-making and mental capacity. Prior to full-time judicial appointment in 1992 he was for more than 25 years a solicitor in a practice dealing predominantly with older clients and gained experience of working with the Court of Protection. He was a former member of the Law Society's *Mental Health and Disability Committee* and in the early 1990s a member of the *Joint Committee of the Law Society, the Court of Protection and the Public Trust Office*.

It was fortuitous that he was also an enthusiastic user of technology in the courts who was piloting the use of e-mail for applications by solicitors with orders being made 'online' under the PREMA pilot.[50] A desktop computer networked to the Government Secure Intranet ('GSI') had already been provided with a personal e-mail address and access through MS Outlook. Experience has shown that this facility is essential for a judge to function in a regional court because it provides an efficient means of communication with the Court of Protection and the

---

[48] As anticipated, a case did arise in London which the Master could not hear and was not suitable for an Assistant Master. The Deputy Master was able to hear this in London thereby avoiding the need to involve a nominated High Court judge at first instance.

[49] Presently every Thursday.

[50] Preston E-Mail Applications (PREMA), part of the *Modernising the Civil Courts* programme.

Public Guardianship Office in London. Also, a regional hearing is of little value if the outcome and any guidance given is not fully recorded and this record placed on the file maintained at the Public Guardianship Office. Where no local administrative support is available the ability and willingness of the judge to prepare detailed notes and draft orders is essential.

The pilot Court

6.43 Preston County Court and District Registry of the High Court of Justice has jurisdiction in civil, family, bankruptcy and Chancery cases (being a civil trial centre but not a care centre). It is based at the Preston Combined Court Centre, which was built during the 1990s and has modern facilities with full disability access. Telephone conference and video-link facilities are available.

The four district judges each have their own chambers but courtrooms are available and regularly used by them. There is scope for lists to be exchanged on short notice and for cases to be swapped during the course of the day, so this provides flexibility. The Diary Manager who controls the sittings of judges and availability of courtrooms on the Group is based at the Court. If it is necessary for a district judge to take a hearing at a different venue on the Group (or even on the Circuit) that can be arranged through the Diary Manager (by swapping the day's list if necessary with another district judge). Deputies are brought in to cover lists when needed.

6.44 Hearings usually take place in the district judge's chambers but a courtroom is available if more than 15 people need to be accommodated. The Deputy Master has made it clear that if necessary due to the infirmity of a party or witness he is prepared to sit at another court on the Northern Circuit or even at a different venue (eg a residential care or nursing home) but this has not arisen to date and circumstances justifying this will be rare. He has, however, for several fund management hearings attended at the home of the patient in the vicinity of Preston[51] when the patient was being cared for there by parents (of whom one was the receiver) and found this to be particularly beneficial.

Further developments

6.45 This link with the civil and family courts has led to the cross-fertilisation of ideas and resulted in more local practitioners becoming familiar with the work of this specialised but nonetheless essential jurisdiction. The Master and Deputy Master are in regular contact and hold a monthly meeting by video link to discuss current issues. Based

---

[51] This has included addresses conveniently between his own home in Cumbria and Preston.

on experience at Preston the Court of Protection in London has introduced the recording of hearings and telephone conferences, and attendance may now be by video link for hearings in London or Preston.

Procedure

6.46 No one approaches the Deputy Master or Preston Court directly although last-minute documents may be lodged there prior to hearings. All the administration remains with the Public Guardianship Office in London but electronic communication has proved effective with arrangements being made and information transferred by e-mail over a secure government network.[52] The Master identifies cases referred to him that may be suitable for a Northern hearing, completes an information form on his computer and adds a case summary. This is sent as an e-mail attachment to the case officers involved and to the Deputy Master who checks that he can take the case[53] and sends his response by e-mail to all recipients of the original messages. The response may include a date and time for a telephone conference (if solicitors are involved) or for a full hearing with a time estimate. Directions given at that stage generally relate to disclosure of documents and witness statements, but a report by a General or Medical Visitor may be requested and the patient is generally invited to attend the hearing unless unable to contribute or this would be detrimental to health. The Public Guardianship Office then notifies the parties of the directions and listing arrangements, and deals with any communications in the interim. If necessary the Deputy Master or his own court staff communicate with parties or their solicitors locally but this is not encouraged because time and resources are limited and all communications should be recorded in the file maintained by the Public Guardianship Office.

6.47 The file is sent by the case officer at the Public Guardianship Office to Preston Combined Court Centre by courier a week before the hearing so that it may be read by the Deputy Master, and it is returned as soon as possible after the hearing with a print of the Deputy Master's signed Notes and Judgment or draft Order.[54] Hearings are usually recorded and the tapes preserved for a period in case a transcript is requested. It is the policy of the Deputy Master to hand a print of his Notes taken on computer during the hearing to the parties before they leave but if this is

---

[52] The Public Guardianship Office is on a different e-mail system from that used by the judges, but both are within the GSI.

[53] Ie that he does not know the parties, etc.

[54] The Notes and Judgment are also sent to the Public Guardianship Office ('PGO') as an e-mail attachment as soon as available so that those responsible for the file are kept fully up to date, and this is copied to the Master so that he may monitor the judicial activity at his satellite court.

not possible (eg because judgment is reserved) the Public Guardianship Office is directed to send a copy to them or they are sent a copy direct by e-mail.

If a hearing is adjourned the file may be retained at Preston until after the final hearing unless it is needed for action to be taken in the interim by the Public Guardianship Office. With the development of electronic files[55] it is hoped that for some cases it may become unnecessary for the paper file to be sent to the regional Court.[56]

6.48   The result is a neatly packaged judicial decision following a hearing at a venue convenient to the parties with little (if any) additional cost to the Public Guardianship Office. The Deputy Master does not then become involved in the case again unless there are queries or a further hearing is required.

An evaluation of the present Court of Protection

Overview

6.49   It will be seen from the above outline that the Rules provide only the most basic structure for the conduct of applications and hearings, and much is left to the discretion of the Master, Deputy Master or Assistant Master dealing with the case. In view of the nature of the work involved this may be beneficial, but this should not be assumed and an evaluation of any shortcomings may be helpful before a replacement jurisdiction is introduced. The views and perspective of those dealing with the Court are as important in this respect as those of persons working within the Court.

The lack of guidance to practitioners or the parties themselves as to the submission of applications and preparation for or conduct of hearings coupled with no requirement for active case management may be seen as an obstacle to justice. Recently telephone conferences have been introduced for the purpose of giving directions before an attended hearing, but these are only appropriate where each party is represented by a solicitor. There are also problems caused by the large number of litigants in person who are unfamiliar with court procedures although the Enduring Power of Attorney Team does send out a brochure to those involved in hearings.

6.50   It cannot be over-emphasised that the issues that have to be tackled in the Court of Protection are very different from those in the civil courts

---

[55]   These are only available for enduring power of attorney cases at present.

[56]   At the present time it is not possible for LINK (the system used by HM Courts Service and judges) to access MERIS (the PGO system) directly but the prospect of this is being investigated.

although a parallel may be drawn with proceedings relating to the welfare of children. Whilst a paternalistic approach is acceptable when considering the best interests of children because parents are entitled to influence their upbringing, it must be avoided for adults. The Court of Protection is concerned to identify and safeguard the best interests of incapacitated adults rather than to impose what other persons think is best for them, and will be influenced more by the previous lifestyle and any expressed wishes of the individual. However, it only has power to do this through the management and administration of the individual's property and financial affairs.

Categories of case

6.51　Few applications are contested and the Master has a very heavy paperwork caseload although some of this is delegated to the Assistant Masters and nominated officers. It is essential that the smooth flow of this work is not impaired by the fact that a small proportion of applications become contentious.

There are some 6,000 applications each year under the 1983 Act. Most are for powers to be delegated (eg the appointment of a receiver)[57] and the rest are for short orders (in low value cases), for authority to commence or settle litigation, for permission to expend or invest money (eg purchase of a home) or for the making of a gift or the execution of a statutory will. The procedures for dealing with these applications should be simple with a minimum of formality.

Attended hearings

Dispute resolution

6.52　It is only when there is disagreement or conflict resulting in the need for an attended hearing that more prescriptive Rules are required to regulate the conduct of the parties involved. This may arise in six situations, namely where:

1. there is uncertainty as to whether an individual is a patient within the jurisdiction of the Court and this must be resolved;
2. there is a dispute as to who should be appointed to act as receiver;
3. there is an unresolved challenge to the registration of an enduring power of attorney;
4. a receiver or registered attorney is not satisfied with the extent of any authority given or restriction imposed;
5. family, carers or other persons concerned with the welfare of a patient are in dispute; and
6. an application is made for a statutory will, gift or settlement.

---

[57]　About 4,200 each year.

Policymaking

6.53   Attended hearings may also be required for the setting of broad policy
where substantial compensation has been awarded for brain injury and
are most common following clinical negligence claims. Awards of over
£1m are the norm and these may now be four or five times this sum. It
is helpful to all concerned to have an initial fund management hearing
as soon as possible after the damages award has been finalised or
become certain. Experience shows that there is seldom any conflict. The
family, who may have been the carers to date and contemplate the
continued provision of a care environment, are anxious to have
authoritative guidance as to how they should handle the funding. There
may be an enhancement in their own standard of living and judicial
approval to this assuages any feeling of guilt in a context where earning
capacity is otherwise impaired.

6.54   These hearings are called 'attendances' and are generally friendly and
constructive. The Master will look to the heads of loss in the civil claim
as pointers to what should be considered but will not seek to impose
these on the family. It is more appropriate to concentrate upon what is
achievable with the personal and financial resources available whilst
keeping an eye on the future when intensive family care may no longer
be available. Headings that are discussed include:

1. the provision of a suitable home and modifications to meet
    disability needs;
2. transport (usually a personal vehicle which can accommodate any
    disability needs);
3. the monthly personal and household budget;
4. care provision and funding;
5. holidays;
6. disability aids and appliances (including computers);
7. the retention by the parents or family carers of a personal stake in
    the housing market where the shared home is purchased by the
    patient.

Investment policy must also be determined for the contingency fund
available after the provision of a home, although in some cases there
will be an index linked tax-free annuity for the life of the patient from a
structured settlement.

THE NEW COURT OF PROTECTION

Preliminary

6.55   In the Mental Capacity Act 2005 and hence the paragraphs that follow,
references are made to the Lord Chancellor who was given various

powers. These references must be interpreted in the light of the Constitutional Reforms that overlapped with the Act before Parliament, so an overview of the impact of those reforms is needed.[58]

Constitutional Reform

6.56 In June 2003 abolition of the office of Lord Chancellor was announced as part of a suite of constitutional reforms which also includes the establishment of an independent Judicial Appointments Commission and a new Supreme Court. The overall aim of these reforms is to put the relationship between the executive, legislature and judiciary on a modern footing, respecting the separation of powers between the three. On 26 January 2004 the Government announced proposals which included the transfer of the Lord Chancellor's judiciary-related functions, and these were effected within the reforms by the Constitutional Reform Act 2005.[59]

Judiciary-related functions

6.57 Following concerns expressed by the judiciary a Concordat was established between the Lord Chancellor and the Lord Chief Justice.[60] So far as is relevant to the new mental capacity jurisdiction the roles become as follows. The Lord Chancellor is:

- under a duty to ensure that there is an efficient and effective system to support the carrying on of the business of the courts in England and Wales, as set out in Part 1 of the Courts Act 2003;[61]
- accountable to Parliament for the overall efficiency and effectiveness of the administration of the court system, including the proper use of public resources voted by Parliament;
- responsible for ensuring that the public interest is served in decisions taken on matters affecting the judiciary in relation to the administration of justice;
- responsible for supporting the judiciary in enabling them to fulfil their functions for dispensing justice.

---

[58] The relevant consequential amendments are yet to be made by statutory instrument under the Constitutional Reform Act 2005.

[59] The title Lord Chancellor was to be abolished in favour of Secretary of State for Constitutional Affairs but the Bill was amended to retain that title although the role and functions of the office are substantively recast.

[60] The Concordat is 'an essential tool for protecting the independence of the judiciary, as a blueprint governing the relations between the judiciary and the government for the long-term and as providing a much-needed, non-contentious way of appointing and disciplining the judiciary', per Lord Woolf CJ.

[61] This includes the provision and allocation of resources which include financial, material and human resources.

The Lord Chief Justice is responsible for ensuring that appropriate structures are in place to ensure the well-being of and training and provision of guidance for the judiciary, and for the deployment of individual members of the judiciary and the allocation of work within the courts.

Deployment of judges

6.58   The Lord Chancellor, in consultation with the Lord Chief Justice, is responsible for the efficient and effective administration of the court system including setting the framework for the organisation of the courts system (such as geographical and functional jurisdictional boundaries). This includes determining the number of judges required for each jurisdiction and region and the number required at each level of the judiciary; also the provision of the courts, their location and sitting times and consequent administrative staffing to meet the expected business requirement.

6.59   The majority of judicial appointments will fall within the remit of the Judicial Appointments Commission ('JAC'). The Lord Chief Justice is responsible, after consulting the Lord Chancellor, for determining which individual judge should be assigned to which court and the authorisation of individual members of the judiciary to sit in particular levels of court. Also for deciding the level of judge appropriate to hear particular classes of case (including the issuing of Practice Directions in that regard) and the nominations of judges to particular posts including those that provide judicial leadership not formal promotion.

Rules and Practice Directions

6.60   In general, functions relating to the allowing of procedural Rules of Court remain with the Lord Chancellor. The making of such rules and Practice Directions will rest with the relevant rule committees where such a committee exists, and otherwise will be exercised by the Lord Chief Justice, with the concurrence of the Lord Chancellor.[62]

Judicial training

6.61   The Lord Chief Justice is responsible for the provision and sponsorship of judicial training within the resources provided by the Lord Chancellor, but responsibility for assessing the need for and providing training of professional judicial office-holders remains with the Judicial Studies Board ('JSB').

---

[62]   The Mental Capacity Act 2005 makes no provision for a Rules Committee.

Status of the new Court

6.62 Part 2 of the Mental Capacity Act 2005 comprising ss 45 to 56 deals with the creation of the new Court of Protection and its powers.

Name and venue

6.63 The Act creates a new superior court of record with an official seal known as the Court of Protection. The present office of the Supreme Court called the Court of Protection will then cease to exist. The functions of the new Court are described in **CHAPTER 4**.

The Court will have a central office and registry at a place appointed by the Lord Chancellor and may sit at any place in England and Wales, on any day and at any time. The Lord Chancellor may designate as additional registries of the Court any District Registry of the High Court and any county court office.[63]

The judges

6.64 The Act also provides that, subject to Court of Protection rules which have yet to be created, the jurisdiction of the new Court will be exercisable by a number of judges nominated for that purpose by the Lord Chancellor.[64] The judges who may be nominated are the President of the Family Division, the Vice-Chancellor,[65] puisne judges of the High Court,[66] circuit judges and district judges.[67]

President and Senior Judge

6.65 The President of the Family Division, Sir Mark Potter, has been appointed as the first President of the Court of Protection and the Vice-Chancellor Sir Andrew Morritt (soon to be the Chancellor of the High Court) as Vice-President.[68] Similarly one of the nominated judges will be appointed to be Senior Judge of the Court of Protection, having such administrative functions in relation to the Court as the Lord Chancellor

---

[63] In this context references to the Lord Chancellor should be interpreted as being with the concurrence of the Lord Chief Justice pursuant to the constitutional reforms.

[64] The references in this and the following paragraph to the Lord Chancellor may be interpreted as being to the Lord Chief Justice after consulting the Lord Chancellor on the basis that the judges will be 'ticketed' according to need and suitability, although it remains possible that nomination will mean appointment by the JAC – see the Constitutional Reforms.

[65] This is the Senior Judge of the Chancery Division whose title under the Constitutional Reforms is being changed to the Chancellor of the High Court.

[66] Note that this is no longer reserved to judges of the Family or Chancery Division.

[67] The Court of Protection Rules may make provision for delegation to nominated officers.

[68] Mental Capacity Act 2005, s 46. The President of the Family Division and the Vice-Chancellor were respectively appointed to these new roles in October 2005.

may direct. This is similar to the position of the present Master whose appointment would provide much needed continuity and introduce his considerable experience to the new Court.[69]

Powers

6.66　The Court will have in connection with its jurisdiction the same powers, rights, privileges and authority as the High Court.[70] Office copies of orders made, directions given or other instruments issued by the court and sealed with its official seal are to be admissible in all legal proceedings as evidence of the originals without further proof.[71]

Interim orders and directions

6.67　The Court may, pending the determination of an application to it in relation to a person make an order or give directions in respect of any matter if:[72]

(a) there is reason to believe that this person lacks capacity in relation to the matter,

(b) the matter is one to which its powers under this Act extend, and

(c) it is in the person's best interests to make the order, or give the directions, without delay.

Power to call for reports

6.68　The Court may, where in proceedings brought in respect of a person it is considering a question relating to that person:[73]

(a) require a report to be made to it by the Public Guardian or by a Court of Protection Visitor; or

(b) require a local authority, or an NHS body,[74] to arrange for a report to be made by one of its officers or employees, or such other person as the authority, or the NHS body, considers appropriate.

The report must deal with such matters relating to the person, and be made in writing or orally, as the court may direct.[75]

---

[69]　The present Master is Denzil Lush and the previous Master was Mrs A B (Biddy) Macfarlane. Both are well known for their contribution to the work of the existing Court of Protection.

[70]　Law of Property Act 1925, s 204 (orders of High Court conclusive in favour of purchasers) will apply in relation to orders and directions of the court as it applies to orders of the High Court.

[71]　Mental Capacity Act 2005, s 47.

[72]　Mental Capacity Act 2005, s 48.

[73]　Mental Capacity Act 2005, s 49.

[74]　As defined in s 148 of the Health and Social Care (Community Health and Standards) Act 2003.

[75]　Court of Protection Rules may specify matters which, unless the Court directs otherwise, must also be dealt with in the report.

6.69 When preparing a report the Public Guardian or a Court of Protection Visitor[76] may, at all reasonable times, examine and take copies of any health record, any record of, or held by, a local authority and compiled in connection with a social services function, and any record held by a person registered under Part II of the Care Standards Act 2000 so far as the record relates to the person. When making a visit the Public Guardian or a Court of Protection Visitor may interview the person in private.

A Special Visitor when making a visit may, if the court so directs, carry out in private a medical, psychiatric or psychological examination of the person's capacity and condition.

Practice and procedure

Court of Protection Rules

6.70 The Lord Chancellor is empowered to make Rules of Court with respect to the practice and procedure of the court.[77] The Court of Protection Rules may, in particular, make provision:

(a) as to the manner and form in which proceedings are to be commenced;

(b) as to the persons entitled to be notified of, and be made parties to, the proceedings;

(c) for the allocation, in such circumstances as may be specified, of any specified description of proceedings to a specified judge or to specified descriptions of judges;

(d) for the exercise of the jurisdiction of the Court, in such circumstances as may be specified, by its officers or other staff;

(e) for enabling the Court to appoint a suitable person (who may, with his or her consent, be the Official Solicitor) to act in the name of, or on behalf of, or to represent the person to whom the proceedings relate;

(f) for enabling an application to the Court to be disposed of without a hearing;

(g) for enabling the Court to proceed with, or with any part of, a hearing in the absence of the person to whom the proceedings relate;

(h) for enabling or requiring the proceedings or any part of them to be conducted in private and for enabling the Court to determine who is

---

[76] The status and role of the Public Guardian and the Visitors is considered in **Chapter 7**.

[77] Mental Capacity Act 2005, s 51. The reference to the Lord Chancellor should be interpreted as being to the Lord Chief Justice with the concurrence of the Lord Chancellor. There is no provision for a Rules Committee.

to be admitted when the Court sits in private and to exclude specified persons when it sits in public;

(i) as to what may be received as evidence (whether or not admissible apart from the rules) and the manner in which it is to be presented;

(j) for the enforcement of orders made and directions given in the proceedings.

The Rules may, instead of providing for any matter, refer to provision made or to be made about that matter by directions. They may also make different provision for different areas.

Practice Directions

6.71 The President of the Court of Protection may, with the concurrence of the Lord Chancellor, give directions as to the practice and procedure of the court. No such directions may be given by anyone else without the approval of the President and the Lord Chancellor, but this does not prevent the President from giving directions which contain guidance as to law or making judicial decisions.[78]

Applications

Forms

6.72 It is necessary for the forms used by the present Court of Protection to be reviewed and entirely rewritten so as to be fit for purpose and align with other court forms. The forms should identify where any party has impairments or potential difficulty in understanding or communicating in the court so that reasonable adjustments to the procedures can then be made to accommodate any special needs.

Who may apply

6.73 It has in the past been found necessary to control those who may bring applications to the Court. Genuine applications must not be discouraged but there needs to be a screening process to prevent those who seek to interfere without justification from causing inconvenience and expense to others. A procedure similar to that under the Children Act 1989 is being adopted whereby certain categories of person have a right to apply but others must obtain permission from the Court.[79]

No permission is required for an application to the Court for the exercise of any of its powers under the Mental Capacity Act 2005 by the following:

(a) a person who lacks, or is alleged to lack, capacity;

---

[78] Mental Capacity Act 2005, s 52. The references to the Lord Chancellor may be interpreted as being to the Lord Chief though with the concurrence of the Lord Chancellor.

[79] Mental Capacity Act 2005, s 50.

(b) if such a person has not reached 18, anyone with parental responsibility[80] for him or her;

(c) the donor or a donee of a lasting power of attorney to which the application relates;

(d) a deputy appointed by the Court for a person to whom the application relates; or

(e) a person named in an existing order of the Court, if the application relates to the order.

Permission to apply

6.74 Subject to the Court of Protection Rules[81] permission is required for any other application to the Court. In deciding whether to grant permission the Court must, in particular, have regard to:

(a) the applicant's connection with the person to whom the application relates;

(b) the reasons for the application;

(c) the benefit to the person to whom the application relates of a proposed order or directions; and

(d) whether the benefit can be achieved in any other way.

It is likely that most applications for permission to pursue a full application will be dealt with on paper (ie without an attended hearing) but there will be a right to be heard in the event that permission is refused.

Rights of appeal

6.75 The Act provides some flexibility as to how appeals may be dealt with.[82] Having stated that an appeal lies to the Court of Appeal from any decision of the Court of Protection, it is further enacted that the Court of Protection Rules may provide that an appeal from the decision of a court officer,[83] district judge or circuit judge lies to a prescribed higher judge of the Court of Protection. These higher judges are identified according to the status of the first instance judge.

Thus the appeal hierarchy is likely to be as follows:

(a) from a court officer to a district judge or circuit judge;

(b) from a district judge or circuit judge to a High Court judge who is nominated to sit in the Court of Protection (including the President of the Family Division or the Vice-Chancellor);

(c) from a High Court judge to the Court of Appeal.

---

[80] This has the same meaning as in the Children Act 1989.

[81] Also to para 20(2) of Sch 3 to the Act (declarations relating to private international law).

[82] Mental Capacity Act 2005, s 53.

[83] An officer as provided for under s 51(2)(d) – see above. This is the new term for what used to be called 'nominated officers'.

Although appeals could be from nominated district judges to nominated circuit judges it is unlikely that this will be the procedure.

Permission to appeal

6.76 The Court of Protection Rules may also provide that permission is required to appeal in specified cases. Further provision will then be made as to the judge entitled to grant permission and any requirements to be satisfied before permission is granted, and as to any considerations to be taken into account in relation to granting or refusing permission to appeal.[84]

Where a higher judge of the Court makes a decision on an appeal, no appeal may be made to the Court of Appeal from that decision unless the Court of Appeal considers that the appeal would raise an important point of principle or practice, or there is some other compelling reason for the Court of Appeal to hear it.

Fees and costs

Fees

6.77 It has been Government policy that the existing Court of Protection be self-funding, raising its income from court fees, although some subsidy is necessary for those who cannot afford the fees. It is likely that such subsidy will have to be enhanced and increased for the new enlarged jurisdiction because many applications will relate to situations where there is no money available or involved.

6.78 The Lord Chancellor may with the consent of the Treasury by order prescribe fees payable in respect of anything dealt with by the Court.[85] Such order may contain provision as to scales or rates of fees, exemptions from and reductions in fees and remission of fees in whole or in part. Before making an order the Lord Chancellor must consult the President and Vice-President and the Senior Judge of the Court of Protection. Such steps as are reasonably practicable must then be taken to bring information about fees to the attention of persons likely to have to pay them. The fees will be recoverable summarily as a civil debt.

Costs

6.79 The costs of and incidental to all proceedings in the Court of Protection are in its discretion but the Rules will make detailed provision for regulating those costs.[86] It is likely that parts of the Civil Procedure Rules 1998 will be incorporated so as to introduce provisions for

---

[84] Mental Capacity Act 2005, s 53(4).
[85] Mental Capacity Act 2005, s 54. Following the constitutional reforms this remains the responsibility of the Lord Chancellor.
[86] Mental Capacity Act 2005, s 55.

summary and detailed assessment. There may also be prescribed scales of costs to be paid to legal or other representatives, but the adoption of agreed costs for certain legal work such as conveyancing raises issues as to whether an officer of the Court (as distinct from a judge) should have authority to agree costs and, if so, how such an officer should be trained.

6.80   The Court will have full power to determine by whom and to what extent the costs are to be paid and will be given power, in any proceedings, to disallow costs or order the legal or other representatives[87] concerned to meet the whole or part of any wasted costs. 'Wasted costs' means any costs incurred by a party:

(a) as a result of any improper, unreasonable or negligent act or omission on the part of any legal or other representative or any employee of such a representative; or

(b) which, in the light of any such act or omission occurring after they were incurred, the Court considers it is unreasonable to expect that party to pay.

This enables unreasonable conduct by representatives to be controlled by costs sanctions.

General

6.81   Court of Protection Rules may make provision:[88]

(a) as to the way in which, and funds from which, fees and costs are to be paid;

(b) for charging fees and costs upon the estate of the person to whom the proceedings relate;

(c) for the payment of fees and costs within a specified time of the death of the person to whom the proceedings relate or the conclusion of the proceedings.

A charge on the estate of a person created by this provision does not cause any interest of the person in any property to fail or determine or to be prevented from recommencing.

Challenges ahead

Overview

6.82   Hitherto the Court of Protection has been the Cinderella of the judicial system, little known and under-recognised despite its extensive jurisdiction. This will change with generic judges becoming involved,

---

[87]   This expression means any person exercising a right of audience or right to conduct litigation on behalf of a party to proceedings.

[88]   Mental Capacity Act 2005, s 56.

the regional presence and the acquisition of jurisdiction for declarations previously dealt with by the High Court. There will also be more interdependence between the civil and family courts and the Court of Protection once it is no longer restricted to financial affairs. There is an important distinction between the way the current Court of Protection operates (ie declaring someone to be a 'patient' and taking over responsibility for his or her property and affairs) and the future, where the issue is whether a Deputy should be appointed, subject to supervision by the Public Guardian, or a specific decision taken on behalf of the incapacitated person. This difference in approach has consequences in terms of the appropriate, and Human Rights Act 1998 compliant, procedures to be adopted.

How different is the Court of Protection from other courts? Which functions are truly judicial? How many judges should be nominated to the Court and where will they be deployed? On what basis will the different levels of the judiciary be allocated cases? What procedural rules will be appropriate? How will hearings be conducted and what human rights issues arise? To what extent and in what manner will judgments be reported? What right will individuals have to disclosure of information held about them by the Court? What should be the relationship between the new Court of Protection and the Public Guardian? To what extent will the legal profession become involved and who will fund the non-money cases? When should cases be publicly funded? These are all questions that must now be faced.

The new Court

The judges

6.83   There will be a supervising resident judge effectively replacing the present Master and the courtesy title of 'Master' will not be retained for this post. A small number of existing circuit and district judges will be authorised to sit in the new jurisdiction[89] and it appears that they will be nominated by the Lord Chief Justice.[90] They will on these occasions retain their existing titles and not be described as Deputy Master.[91] It is likely that one district or circuit judge will initially be nominated for

---

[89]   In Scotland the new jurisdiction was given to every sheriff but this has not proved to be ideal because some have little experience or interest in the jurisdiction and a close working relationship with the Public Guardian has not developed.

[90]   This already happens for public law care work under the Children Act 1989 although a large number of district and circuit judges are involved. It is unlikely that they will be appointed by the JAC under the constitutional reforms.

[91]   In the existing regional Court at Preston cases are listed before 'District Judge Ashton sitting as Deputy Master of the Court of Protection'.

each Region[92] and further appointments will then be made according to demand.

High Court judges will also be nominated to the Court to deal with serious healthcare decisions (mainly sterilisation of learning disabled adults and 'end of life' decisions) in place of the declarations of best interest that they presently make in the High Court under the inherent jurisdiction. The nominated High Court judges will deal with appeals from the circuit and district judges. Further appeals will be to the Court of Appeal and thence to the House of Lords (or the new Supreme Court).

Allocation of cases

6.84 The 2001 Act contemplates that three levels of the judiciary will be nominated to the Court. In the civil and family jurisdiction of the High Court and county courts the Rules and Practice Directions allocate cases between these levels.[93] Will the new Court of Protection function with three tiers? It is suggested that it would be difficult and result in considerable problems in the deployment of judges if the new incapacity jurisdiction was administered in this way. Existing experience shows that there is no identifiable middle tier for allocation to circuit judges and cases may in any event overlap any tiers that are created. It is to be hoped that the roles of circuit and district judges will be interchangeable and that nominations to the Court will be made according to availability and suitability.

Administration

6.85 Hitherto there has been a close relationship between the Court of Protection and the Public Guardianship Office to the extent that it can be difficult to identify which is responding, but the establishment of the Public Guardian with an office and a statutory role makes this less appropriate. A policy decision was needed as to whether the Office of the Public Guardian or an independent body would provide the administration for the new Court of Protection. There are significant advantages and disadvantages with each option and a compromise has been reached whereby there will be separate but shared administrative functions.[94]

The Court may need to be more independent but must still make uncontested decisions in an efficient manner whilst being shielded from

---

[92] In April 2005 the term Region replaced the historical term Circuit. The administration of the courts is divided into Regions.

[93] Circuit judges (unlike district judges) do not sit in the High Court unless specifically authorised to do so on a case-by-case basis under s 9 of the Supreme Court Act 1981.

[94] This topic is considered in **CHAPTER 7** which deals with the role of the new Public Guardian.

trivial disputes with its resources being reserved for those cases that really need judicial intervention. The Rules may provide or the Court may direct that mediation must be attempted before a reference to the Court, and the Public Guardian will be well placed to facilitate this, but how relevant is it to negotiate a compromise between parties when neither may be addressing the best interests of the incapacitated individual? Some judicial oversight may still be required.

6.86   Other fundamental issues arise which must now be addressed. To what extent should a case officer at the Office of the Public Guardian control the process of decision-making? At what stage does an issue require judicial intervention? Should there be restrictions on the right of access to the Court and who will be the gatekeeper? Who should be the parties? How extensive should case-management be and should this be imposed by the Rules, Practice Directions or Court Orders? When is a hearing needed? To what extent is there a public interest in hearings and how is this balanced against the right to privacy?

Some of these issues may be resolved by the process of regionalisation. Intractable cases will increasingly be referred by the Senior Judge to nominated judges who spend most of their time in other courts handling civil and family cases. They will introduce case management and trial procedures based upon their more diverse experience and will be independent of any links that may exist between the Court and the Public Guardian. They will also have to conduct their hearings in a manner that is compatible with the expectations of local practitioners who are not familiar with any peculiarities of the Court. But in contentious cases the judges and practitioners will look to the new Court of Protection Rules and Practice Directions for guidance and these must not be found wanting.

Training and support

6.87   The present Deputy Master has described himself as 'a satellite trying not to go out of orbit'. In view of the specialist and developing nature of this work it is essential that the nominated judges who sit in the regions are not left to their own devices but are supported individually and collectively and that there develops a cadre of judges who communicate with one another.[95] They should be able to maintain regular contact by e-mail with the Senior Judge who will act as coordinator but should also meet with each other at intervals. They will initially need training because the jurisdiction of the Court of Protection is very different in both nature and application from that of the civil and family courts and a discrete area of law must be understood and applied. Some 'in house'

---

[95]   Collective communication is very effective within the judicial e-mail network.

training will be provided informally and newly nominated judges may be invited to sit in on hearings before the Senior Judge.

The Judicial Studies Board ('JSB') has the expertise and resources to structure and coordinate the training requirement and is charged with that role under the constitutional reforms. A residential training course may be appropriate for all judges initially nominated to the jurisdiction, but the training itself should be judicially led.[96] Given the time now available before planned implementation in April 2007 and the need to identify and nominate suitable judges before any training can commence, it is likely that the regionalised Court will be established in stages after implementation although an approach has already been made to the JSB about the training requirements.

Regionalisation

6.88   The selection of venues and judges will be crucial to the success of comprehensive regionalisation of the new Court of Protection. Having a centralised administration with satellite courts raises many problems. To a large extent these have been tackled in the Preston pilot[97] and workable solutions have been devised. Communication by e-mail has been very effective and the main problems have proved to be access to the case file,[98] uncertainty amongst parties and solicitors as to where to send documents and delay in receiving documents sent at a late stage to the Public Guardianship Office. There is a lack of administrative support because HM Courts Service staff have hitherto had no involvement with the Public Guardianship Office. Experience has shown that these difficulties can be overcome and leads to the following recommendations.

The Court

6.89   The desirable features are:

    (a) a court with several full-time district judges unless a resident circuit judge is appointed, so as to achieve flexibility with listing hearings;

    (b) adequately sized chambers with availability of courtrooms when a larger than normal number of people will attend the hearing;

    (c) good access for people with impaired mobility (eg in wheelchairs);

    (d) availability of telephone conference and video link facilities;

    (e) access to a computer networked to the GSI (preferably in the judge's chambers).

---

[96]   This is the policy adopted for all judicial training.

[97]   This is described in **6.41**.

[98]   A courier service has been established.

The nominated Judge

6.90   A full-time district judge has been found best placed to fulfil the role of Deputy Master because of the judicial lifestyle and range of work. District judges are based in chambers at particular courts where they hear civil and family cases so the facilities that they have available are well suited to Court of Protection hearings. Their experience in handling small claims cases which generally involve unrepresented parties encourage a more informal style, and they are accustomed to handling a large volume of family cases which include disputes relating to the welfare of children and resolving ancillary relief claims.[99] By contrast, most circuit judges spend the bulk of their time sitting on criminal cases. However, a circuit judge who is based in the designated court for most of the week and sits in civil and/or family cases but not crime could cope equally well. The following criteria should be taken into account in selection:

(a) an interest in and aptitude for work involving persons with impaired mental capacity (including an abundance of patience and tolerance);

(b) preferably some experience of the work of the Court of Protection but certainly a willingness to learn a new jurisdiction (there is a steep learning curve);

(c) a computer user who can cope with e-mails and is willing to prepare notes and judgments in MS Word on the computer;

(d) willingness to travel to and if necessary stay in London for visits to the PGO and the Court of Protection;

(e) willingness to travel to other courts and venues within the Region when required.

Contact with the legal profession

6.91   One of the advantages of regionalisation is that more provincial solicitors and barristers will appear before the 'local' Court of Protection and thereby gain experience with which they may better advise their clients. It is to be hoped that the nominated judges will develop relationships with local firms who undertake this field of practice and make themselves available to give lectures to or attend seminars arranged by professional organisations[100] or charities.[101]

---

[99]   These relate to the financial settlement following divorce.

[100]   Solicitors for the Elderly now has a large number of members and functions on a regional basis, as does Headway (the brain injury association). STEP (the Society of Trust and Estate Practitioners) also covers this area of work.

[101]   Eg Age Concern, MENCAP, MIND.

Procedural issues

General

6.92 The Court of Protection Rules 2001 and their predecessors are extremely brief and leave much to judicial discretion. This may be appropriate for a jurisdiction of this nature where the objective is to address the best interests of the incapacitated person rather than personal disputes between members of their families, carers and other concerned persons. But it is not easy for practitioners to know how they should prepare or conduct their cases. These uncertainties are displayed at almost every hearing and extend to identifying the persons who may attend and participate in the hearing. The Court is anxious not to exclude any person with a legitimate interest but also conscious that personal information concerning the incapacitated individual is to be discussed and there should not be any unnecessary intrusion into this person's right to privacy. The human rights of family (especially spouses, children and siblings) and civil partners must now be respected as well as those of the incapacitated individual.

6.93 How formal should hearings be, and will this change under the new jurisdiction? Options include the formality of a courtroom trial, the relative informality of a chambers hearing or a round the table conference. Will the proceedings be recorded?[102] To what extent will telephone conferences and video links be utilised as part of the hearing process?[103] Should evidence be taken on oath? Should the public be admitted and (anonymised) case reports be published, or will it be a contempt to publish information about the hearing?[104]

These are not issues that appear to have troubled the Court of Protection in the past but they became highlighted with the introduction of the Preston pilot. A judge who was accustomed to hearing cases and resolving disputes in a different climate found himself asking these questions and the generic judges who are nominated to the new Court of Protection will inevitably seek authoritative guidance.

Transfer of cases

6.94 In the case of a mentally incapacitated person under the age of 18 years the Lord Chancellor may by order make provision as to transfer of

---

[102] This is always to be preferred, if only to protect the judge from allegations of inappropriate behaviour by a disaffected party.

[103] There should be consistency so these facilities need to be available at all regional hearing centres.

[104] If all hearings continue to be held in private with no reporting there is little opportunity for practitioners to gain experience in the new jurisdiction and, perhaps of equal importance, for the public to be aware of how decisions are made by the Court on behalf of incapacitated adults.

proceedings from the Court of Protection to a court with jurisdiction under the Children Act 1989, or vice versa.[105]

Types of case

6.95   A degree of flexibility in the procedures is essential because the various categories of case that come before the Court require very different treatment. There is a world of difference between contested hearings involving a seriously dysfunctional family and fund management meetings intended to reassure hesitant receivers (henceforth to be deputies). The categories based on experience in the present Court of Protection can be identified in general terms as follows and could be used to allocate cases to a Track for case management:

Fund management – Hearings to make policy decisions in regard to the investment and application of substantial funds arising from compensation awards. These take the form of a conference involving concerned members of the family and care professionals although financial advisers and solicitors may attend. There is little need for prior directions and any uncertainty as to who should attend or documentation to be produced can be resolved by correspondence.

Specific authorities and issues – Most applications for authority to make gifts and execute statutory wills and to resolve uncertainty (eg as to assessment of capacity) are non-contentious but a hearing may be needed and, unless there is a need for evidence to be taken in an adversarial climate, a procedure is required that imposes minimum stress and expense on those involved. It is sufficient that the essential background facts are identified and viewpoints exchanged before everyone with a legitimate interest is afforded the opportunity of attending a hearing.

Contested applications – Many attended hearings resolve disputes between members of the family or concerned persons as to the welfare of the incapacitated individual. The issue may be whether an enduring power of attorney should be registered, who should be appointed receiver, or whether an attorney or receiver should be replaced. In a large proportion of these case the contestants had fallen out with one another long before and the dispute over control is symptomatic of a dysfunctional family, although legal and factual issues may need to be determined. Some degree of case management is required so that the hearing is manageable but it may be possible for the Court to steer the parties to a consensus or make a decision after a hearing lasting no more than 2 hours.

Serious allegations or complex issues – Cases do arise where the Court must make significant findings of fact (eg as to the conduct of

---

a party) and a full trial is then unavoidable. This requires active case management.

Rules and Practice Directions

6.96 Little consideration has yet been given to the content of the new Rules and Practice Directions and significant policy issues will have to be addressed. The existing Rules leave matters very much in the discretion of the Court and may not be human rights compliant for certain types of hearing. Contested hearings in the Court of Protection should not become litigation between individuals because it is the best interests of the patient that are being addressed. Yet on occasion the Court may need to make findings of fact relating to the conduct of a party and a human rights compliant trial is then required. Certainly there is now an expectation of greater disclosure before any final hearing and case management is the norm in both civil and family proceedings.[106]

6.97 Although it is anticipated that the new Rules will draw upon the current Civil Procedure Rules 1998 and may even incorporate parts of those Rules by reference, aspects of the rather dated Family Proceedings Rules 1991 may be a more appropriate model in view of the nature of the work.[107] It is to be hoped that the Rules will commence with the overriding objective. They must then cover matters such as:

- the Court's general case-management powers;
- who may issue applications and in what circumstances (including any steps that must first be taken to resolve the matter);
- the form of applications and any permitted responses;
- the serving of documents and notices, including the manner of service and who should be served;
- the evidence that may be admitted and the form in which it is introduced;
- disclosure of documents;
- exchange of witness statements;
- the use of expert evidence;
- representation of parties (or those involved);
- persons under a disability (whether children or patients);
- hearings of proceedings;
- the award and assessment of costs;

---

[106] See Civil Procedure Rules 1998 and Family Proceedings Rules 1991 and associated Practice Directions.

[107] The Family Proceedings Rules 1991 are not a complete code but continue to rely upon the former Rules of the Supreme Court 1965 and County Court Rules 1981 in the form that they existed before the Civil Procedure Rules 1998 superseded them.

- the entry and enforcement of orders;

- appeals, including whether permission is required, time limits and procedural requirements.

6.98   In order to avoid inadequate or excessive case management it may be helpful for the Rules to stipulate different procedures according to which Track a case is allocated to either by the Senior Judge when it is referred to a regional judge for a hearing or by the regional judge when asked to undertake responsibility for the case. An alternative is for the Rules to provide that the Senior Judge or the regional judge to whom the case is referred will give directions as to the procedure to be adopted. A wide range of model directions could be available which the judge can adopt with such variations as may be desired including the setting of a timetable.[108] The Directions Order issued to the parties can be produced by the judge from a template held on his or her computer or by the administration following completion by the judge of a tick-box form.

Parties

6.99   The Court of Protection addresses the best interests of vulnerable incapacitated individuals so will not be concerned to resolve disputes between members of the family which may have continued for years and resurface in the context of a struggle for control over the incapacitated member. This has implications as to who is, or may be, party to the proceedings. In this respect the Court of Protection differs from the civil courts whose purpose is to resolve disputes between parties who select themselves. The approach is more akin to the family courts when addressing the best interests of children.[109] In reality the Court is often called upon to make a decision following an application by a party and will only do so after giving other persons with a relevant interest the opportunity to state their case. Treating these persons as parties introduces an unnecessarily adversarial approach to the hearing, yet those persons may expect this.

6.100 There is an issue as to whether the incapacitated person to whom the proceedings relate[110] should also be made a party and in that event a representative such as the litigation friend in civil proceedings would be required. It is suggested that a procedure such as that adopted in private law proceedings under the Children Act 1989 would be appropriate.

---

[108] It is contemplated by Mental Capacity Act 2005, s 51(3) that the Rules will provide for this. The directions may presumably be general or made by judges on a case-by-case basis.

[109] The Family Proceedings Rules 1991 specify who may bring proceedings and who shall be parties. Other persons must seek the permission of the court to become involved.

[110] Previously called a 'patient' but this terminology is not being continued because it is the consequence of a status test and the new jurisdiction is decision-specific.

The Court could be given power to make this person a party if this was thought necessary, usually when none of the other parties appeared to be addressing the best interests of this person and the Court wished to have further input. However, this raises the question as to how such representation is to be funded especially in cases where the issue does not concern financial affairs. In regard to healthcare decisions the High Court presently ensures that this person is a party and the Official Solicitor is frequently appointed as the representative.

Conduct of hearings

6.101 A procedure similar to that for the small claims track under the Civil Procedure Rules 1998 is all that is required for many hearings which may be conducted informally in the judge's chambers, with an inquisitorial approach being adopted. In these cases it may not be necessary to identify parties to the proceedings as long as everyone with a legitimate interest is given the opportunity to attend. Only those cases where significant findings of fact are required will necessitate a formal trial with an adversarial approach, the parties being identified in advance and evidence being given on oath. The difference of judicial approach will not be a problem to a district judge but those involved need to know in advance which form is to be adopted

Findings of fact

6.102 There are occasions when findings of fact need to be made as to the conduct of individuals but this is not the primary purpose of the proceedings and the existence of conflict may of itself dictate that the involvement of an independent outsider is required. Four situations may be identified under the present regime where findings of fact are required, namely where:

1. there is doubt as to mental capacity, which may relate to the execution of an enduring power of attorney or management of property and affairs;

2. allegations are made of significant financial defalcations. The Court will need to follow this up in case it is appropriate for money to be recovered, but it is more likely that a receiver will be appointed who is suitably qualified to investigate and make representations to the Court;

3. it appears to the Court that an attorney or receiver has acted in a responsible manner and the attempt to interfere may be completely devoid of merit. There may be longer-term advantages in making findings and, if necessary, having a protective order from the Court

that the person who has provoked the issue may be marginalised in the future;[111]

4. there are objections to the registration of an enduring power of attorney on the ground that the attorney is unsuitable. The Court should confirm the appointment of the person chosen by the donor unless adverse findings are made, but the onus of proof is on the objector.

Costs

6.103 The costs of proceedings under the Children Act 1989 are generally borne by the parents unless they are publicly funded (which is often the case). In regard to financial management in the Court of Protection it is usually the 'patient' who has to bear the costs out of the funds that are being managed, although where one party has acted unreasonably that party may be ordered to pay some or all of the costs. Who will pay the costs under the new jurisdiction where the incapacitated adult does not have personal funds?

The workload

Volume of cases

6.104 There will be a wider range of cases under the new jurisdiction because this relates not only to financial management but also to social welfare and healthcare – in fact the entire range of personal decision-making for adults who lack capacity. In consequence there will be an increased volume of cases for the new Court of Protection to cope with. Estimates of the extent of this increase differ but much depends upon how accessible the Court makes itself to parties who wish to pursue disputes or clarify their rights or those of an incapacitated person.

The present unmet need for a decision-making body is likely to emerge. The Court will no doubt develop techniques for dealing with this, for example referring welfare and healthcare issues initially to multi-disciplinary case conferences, but even then some of the more intransigent cases will be referred back to the Court. It will be necessary for a particular judge to retain and control a case once it is referred to him or her.

Complexity of cases

6.105 Cases will also become more complex because there will be an extended range of outcomes and when dealing with financial affairs the Court will not, as at present, be entitled to step aside from welfare issues on the ground that it has no jurisdiction. More people will

---

[111] Orders have been made to stem the activities of persistent troublemakers in this way.

potentially be involved because those entitled to be consulted as part of a best interests determination include 'anyone engaged in caring for the person or interested in his welfare'.[112] In addition the assessment of capacity will be more demanding because this is not only decision-specific but may need to be constantly reassessed for those whose capacity fluctuates. Lack of public funding will result in a high proportion of unrepresented parties.

Cases under the new jurisdiction

6.106 The following are examples of situations that may need to be dealt with under the new jurisdiction but are not encountered by the existing Court of Protection. They illustrate the need for local dispute resolution by a nominated district or circuit judge as to the best interests of the person lacking capacity.

Care dispute – Dispute between a son and daughter who live some distance apart as to which residential care or nursing home their mother should move to. She has Alzheimer's disease and is incapable of participating in the decision but has adequate funds to meet the fees.

Contact disputes –

(a) A daughter from an Asian background has married outside her ethnic origins and adopted a way of life that results in her being cut off by her family. She still wishes to visit her learning disabled brother but the family prevent this.

(b) Older parents with a learning disabled son became involved in a bitter divorce which results in father being excluded from the matrimonial home where mother continues to care for this son. A daughter who has sided with father is then denied access to her brother.

There may be a preliminary issue as to whether they have capacity to decide whom they wish to have contact with. This means that the Court will decide this first and only proceed to a best interests inquiry if capacity to make the decision is lacking.

Activities – A charity providing outdoor adventure holidays for adults with learning disabilities wishes to take an individual on a mountaineering course but mother (who may be over-protective) thinks it is too dangerous and objects. Care workers and a personal advocate wish to support this opportunity for personal development. The charity seeks reassurance that this is in the best interests of the individual so that they would only be vulnerable to legal

---

[112] Mental Capacity Act 2005, s 4(7).

proceedings if negligent (and not irrespective of fault in the event of an accident).[113]

Education – Father wants the 19-year-old son with severe learning disabilities to attend a residential training college and has arranged funding. Mother prefers him to live with her but has made no arrangements for his daytime activities. The local authority has offered a place at the local training centre and is very concerned that mother will not allow him to attend. A local nominated judge could see the parties, consider welfare reports and make a decision (if an attempt at mediation did not result in the deadlock being resolved).

Minor medical decisions – Parents wish to arrange for their 23-year-old daughter with Downs Syndrome to have some dental treatment which will improve her appearance but is not otherwise necessary. She appears to want this treatment but there is doubt as to whether she can legally consent so the dentist is unwilling to proceed perhaps because there is some element of risk. A local nominated judge could resolve this.

Medical intervention – Parents are concerned that it is proposed to remove the teeth of their incapacitated son who presents challenging behaviour and is biting everything and everyone in the local authority home where he is cared for. They wish to oppose this decision before it is implemented and encourage other methods of behaviour control but receive no support from those responsible for his care. A local nominated judge could provide the necessary intervention by addressing the best interests of the son.[114]

Sexual relationships – Care workers are concerned as to whether a resident with learning disabilities being supported in a group living arrangement is competent to enter into a sexual relationship with another resident. They seek a declaration from the Court.[115]

Integration with other courts

Judicial support

6.107 Historically there has been little liaison between the Court of Protection and the civil or family courts, although there are occasions when one must refer to the other. When a few generic judges spread throughout the country are nominated to sit in the Court of Protection there will be more integration of an informal nature, with judicial colleagues seeking support and guidance on capacity issues. Cases with a capacity

---

[113] This type of activity may well be covered under Mental Capacity Act 2005, s 5 and not require Court of Protection authority.

[114] It is hoped that this type of activity will be covered under Mental Capacity Act 2005, s 5 but an application to the Court might be made in case of doubt.

[115] The Court does not have power to consent on a person's behalf to a sexual relationship – Mental Capacity Act 2005, s 27(1)(b).

element[116] may be transferred to, or listed before, the local nominated judge because of their additional expertise.[117] For example:

Ancillary relief – Following a divorce between an elderly couple financial claims are made which include the future of the former matrimonial home. At an FDR (financial dispute resolution hearing) the husband makes proposals under which the wife may remain in the home for life. The lawyers involved agree that these proposals are more beneficial to the wife than she is likely to achieve at a contested hearing. She cannot grasp the implications and refuses to accept. The district judge is in a dilemma because if she persists in refusing the offer she is in danger of paying all the costs and losing the home. He questions whether she lacks mental capacity and should be treated as a 'patient' with a 'next friend' appointed to conduct the proceedings on her behalf (often the Official Solicitor), but she refuses to be medically examined. *A nominated district judge to whom the case is transferred could tackle all the issues and resolve them locally with minimum delay and expense.*

Possession – A landlord or mortgagee brings a possession claim for non-payment of sums due and the elderly tenant or mortgagor attends but appears confused and unable to cope. Doubts arise as to mental capacity and the judge is in great difficulty knowing how to proceed. If this defendant is a 'patient' a litigation friend must be appointed but a separate application would have to be made to the Court of Protection for the appointment of a receiver. *The case could be referred to a nominated judge who could deal with the capacity issue, the need for practical support and the merits of the possession claim all in the same series of hearings, invoking the jurisdiction of the Court of Protection if necessary.*

Contract – A local shopkeeper sues a customer with learning disabilities who has been placed 'in the community' for non-payment of bills for normal provisions. Support from social services (who set up this living arrangement) has evaporated with everyone passing the buck. *A district judge dealing with the matter as a 'small claim' will be in difficulty, but could pass the case to a nominated judge who would have the powers (under a dual jurisdiction if necessary) and experience to deal with it.*

---

[116] Note that the concept of a 'patient' still applies under the civil and family jurisdictions, but under the mental capacity jurisdiction people are not stigmatised in that way and the issue is whether they lack capacity in regard to the decision in question.

[117] These are unexpected consequences of the Preston pilot. It should be emphasised that the existing procedures are adequate but involving a judge with greater experience of mental capacity issues can be helpful.

Dual jurisdiction

6.108 There are situations where it might be helpful for a nominated judge to
sit in a dual capacity, namely in the Court of Protection and also the
civil or family court. The following are examples that are not
encountered by the existing Court of Protection but illustrate both the
need for local dispute resolution and an overlap with the existing role of
the civil or family courts:

   (a) Following a divorce between elderly parents there is a dispute as to
   which parent is to continue to care for their 40-year-old mentally
   disabled child and the future of the matrimonial home may depend
   on this. *A nominated district judge could simultaneously deal with
   the care issue under the new jurisdiction and the ancillary relief
   claims in the county court, these being interdependent.*[118]

   (b) There is a dispute between parents relating to contact by father to
   their two children, one of whom has learning disabilities but is by
   now an adult. *An application in the county court under the Children
   Act 1989 relating to the younger child could be linked with an
   application to the Court of Protection in respect of the older child
   and heard together by a nominated district judge.*

   (c) Older parents with a learning disabled adult son became involved in
   a bitter divorce which results in father being excluded from the
   matrimonial home where mother continues to care for the son. A
   daughter who has sided with father is then denied access to her
   brother and seeks to establish that it is in his best interests to see her
   on a regular basis. *A nominated district judge could resolve the
   issue under the new jurisdiction in the context of the divorce
   proceedings thereby having an overview of the whole family
   situation.*

   (d) A local authority has made a decision about the placement of an
   incapacitated adult, and it may be necessary, if that decision is to be
   challenged, to proceed both by way of proceedings for judicial
   review and a best interests claim under the new Court of Protection
   jurisdiction. *A nominated High Court judge could deal with both
   matters together.*

6.109 At present any settlement of a claim by a patient for whom a receiver
has already been appointed must be approved first by the Court of
Protection and then referred to the court in which the claim is
proceeding for approval. Whilst it may be convenient to merge the two
approvals, it has been felt that there are advantages in maintaining the
two different viewpoints. The extent to which the new Court of
Protection will be involved under the new jurisdiction is not yet clear.

---

[118] If the child had not yet attained his majority the residence and ancillary relief claims would
have been amalgamated in the county court.

Conflict

6.110 Caution must be exercised because a conflict of roles may arise. An example is the following issue over a past care award:[119]

> 'By the time a Hillsborough victim recovered his damages the mother who cared for him had died. A sum of over £80,000 (which was needed by the patient) was awarded for gratuitous past care and three children would inherit mother's share on intestacy including the patient. The sister wished the patient to retain this sum especially as mother had received support from a charity, but the brother obtained Letters of Administration to mother's estate and demanded the sum in that capacity. This raised an issue as to the terms of the "trust" upon which the patient received the past care award. Did mother have a legal entitlement and did this survive her death?
>
> The Deputy Master considered referring the case to a Chancery High Court Judge who could resolve the trust issue at the same hearing, but concluded that this would create a conflict of roles. The jurisdiction of the Court of Protection was merely to decide whether payment should be authorised (this being the decision that the patient would have made). On the basis that there was serious doubt as to legal entitlement and that it would be in the patient's best interests to retain the money, the Deputy Master refused payment and directed that (subject to counsel's advice) any Chancery proceedings instituted by the brother as administrator should be defended.'

Access to justice

Background

A change of culture

6.111 There has been a change of culture in the civil and family courts during the past decade. Proceedings not only have to be fair, but also seen as fair and it is the view of the public that is relevant rather than that of lawyers. No longer are litigants expected to cope with the court process and denied access to justice if unable to do so. There is an expectation, in a diverse and multi-cultural society, that judges will ensure that there is effective communication with all manner of persons and take into account their personal attributes and beliefs. This is the art of *Judgecraft* on which judges receive training through the Judicial Studies Board ('JSB').

An *Equal Treatment Advisory Committee* of the JSB[120] ensures that all training courses include this topic and has produced an *Equal Treatment*

---

[119] Such awards are frequently included in the damages awarded to brain damaged claimants, but following a compromise settlement it is not always easy to identify the amount or how the total sum should be apportioned between different carers.

[120] The author of this chapter is a member of that Committee.

Bench Book which is supplied to all judges and tribunal chairmen.[121] This identifies potential problem areas, offers information and guidance, and then concentrates upon the following areas of particular concern:

1. minority ethnic communities;
2. belief systems (different religions);
3. gender issues;
4. disability;
5. children; and
6. sexual orientation.

The issues of unrepresented parties and social exclusion are also addressed. Equal access to justice is not assured if people are too frightened to attend a hearing or unable to cope when they get there.

6.112 Any court that seeks to protect and empower those who have mental impairments must set a good example to other courts and tribunals in ensuring equal access to justice, and the establishment of a new Court of Protection is an opportunity to get things right from the start.[122]

Discrimination

6.113 There must be no discrimination in the delivery of legal services. A person who cannot cope with the facilities and procedures of the courts and the administration is as entitled to justice as those who have no such difficulty. It is fundamental to the delivery of justice that those involved are able to appear before and communicate with the relevant court or tribunal. It is equally important that judges understand what those who appear before them are endeavouring to say and that they in turn understand what the judge and any advocates are saying and have an adequate opportunity to consider this. Any misunderstanding may impair justice and it is not sufficient to say that this is the failing of the individual who must take the consequences – it is the responsibility of the court to ensure that communication is effective.

6.114 A further development is that those who appear before the courts are no longer expected to cope with whatever facilities happen to be available. The special needs of those with disabilities must be addressed in an effective way both by the administration in regard to the facilities made available and by the judge in the manner in which hearings are conducted. All courts and tribunals must comply with the Disability

---

[121] This is available on the JSB website: www.jsboard.co.uk/etac/etbb/index.htm.

[122] The Mental Capacity Bill team set the standard for the Department for Constitutional Affairs by producing various documents in easy read format for their stakeholders with learning difficulties prior to Royal Assent. They also worked closely with the Disability Rights Commission and various representative disability groups.

Discrimination Act 1995 and also ensure that the human rights of those who become involved in the justice system are respected.[123]

It follows that courts and tribunals must be accessible to those who appear before them. This is not merely a question of access to the building or the provision of disabled facilities within the courtroom, but also of proximity.

Unrepresented parties

6.115 Some litigants seek to represent themselves rather than instruct a lawyer[124] and everybody of full age and capacity is entitled to do so. This may be because they cannot afford a solicitor, distrust lawyers or believe that they will be better at putting their case across.

Disadvantages

6.116 Those who do exercise this right find that they are operating in an alien environment because the courts have not traditionally been receptive to their needs:

> 'All too often the litigant in person is regarded as a problem for judges and for the court system rather than a person for whom the system of civil justice exists.'[125]

They are likely to experience feelings of fear, ignorance, anger, frustration and bewilderment. Their cases will tend to dominate their thoughts and they will feel at a disadvantage. The aim of the judge should be to ensure that the parties leave with the sense that they have been listened to and had a fair hearing – whatever the outcome.

6.117 Disadvantages stem from a lack of knowledge of the law and court procedure. For many their perception of the court environment will be based on what they have seen on the television and in films. They:

- are likely to be unfamiliar with the language and specialist vocabulary of legal proceedings;
- have little knowledge of the procedures involved and find it difficult to apply the rules even if they do read them;
- tend to lack objectivity and emotional distance from their case;
- may not be skilled in advocacy and are unlikely to be able to undertake cross-examination or to test the evidence of an opponent;
- may be confused about the presentation of evidence;

---

[123] Before the European Convention on Human Rights became enforceable it was the principles of 'natural justice' that were invoked.

[124] Traditionally known as 'litigants in person'.

[125] Lord Woolf, *Access to Justice*, Interim Report, June 1995.

- are unlikely to understand the relevance of law and regulations to their own problem, or to know how to challenge a decision that they believe to be wrong.

The aim must be to ensure that unrepresented parties understand what is going on and what is expected of them at all stages of the proceedings. The court is therefore under an obligation to ensure that:

1. the process is (or has been) explained to them in a manner that they can understand;
2. they have access to appropriate information through books or websites;
3. they are informed about what is expected of them in ample time for them to comply; and
4. wherever possible they are given sufficient time according to their needs.

Personal assistance

6.118 A litigant who cannot arrange legal representation may request that someone be permitted to 'quietly assist' at the hearing (the role of the *McKenzie friend*). The court can refuse this and will do so if the friend is unsuitable.[126] Such assistance is less likely to be needed at a hearing in the Court of Protection because a more informal approach is adopted and the judge is more likely to provide explanations and assistance.

Alternatively the litigant may request that someone speak for him or her (known as a *lay representative*). There is no right of audience but the court has a discretion to allow such representation and it may be in the interests of justice to do so.[127] The litigant should normally justify the request and be present in court when personal interests are involved.[128] The doubt about the status of an attorney under a power of attorney has recently been resolved – there is still no right of audience.[129]

---

[126] The 'friend' may be seeking to provide general advocacy services or pursuing a separate agenda the pursuit of which is not in the best interests of the litigant.

[127] Advocacy rights may be granted under the Courts and Legal Services Act 1990, s 27(2)(c) – see also Civil Procedure Rules 1998, PD27, para 3.2; Lay Representatives (Right of Audience) Order 1999, SI 1999/1225.

[128] *Clarkson v Gilbert & ors* (2000) *The Times*, July 4, CA; *Izzo v Phillip Ross & Co* (2001) *The Times*, August 9.

[129] If this is an enduring power of attorney enquiry should be made as to whether it has been registered with the Public Guardianship Office, because if it has the litigant may be a patient who needs a litigation friend.

Physical and sensory impairments

Hearings

6.119 There is a Directory of courts with disabled facilities and, when it is known that a party or witness has a physical impairment, arrangements should be made for any hearing to take place where there are appropriate facilities. These may extend beyond wheelchair access to the existence of disabled toilets and the loop system for those with hearing impairments. Ideally every regional venue of the Court of Protection will have suitable facilities but if these are not adequate for a particular hearing consideration should be given to conducting the hearing at a more suitable venue. When necessary justice should be taken to those who are unable to come to the court and the examination of a witness or even part of a hearing may take place elsewhere, for example in a residential care home or mental hospital. A video link may assist where an infirm party cannot travel far.[130]

6.120 It may be appropriate to arrange hearings at particular times, keep them shorter or take more frequent breaks. Allowance should be made for the need to attend a toilet, take medication or otherwise recover concentration. This may result in a longer time estimate for the hearing.

Interpreters

6.121 Interpreters are provided for a party or witness who does not speak the language of the court or has a hearing impairment, and the court must arrange one if the party cannot. Other communication difficulties may need to be addressed in a similar manner.[131] The interpreter should not be simply a relative or friend but needs to be independent and fully conversant with the individual's preferred method of communication. A witness will only need an interpreter whilst giving evidence but a party may need one before, during and after the hearing. The interpreter should be provided with breaks at regular intervals.

Mental incapacity

6.122 All courts encounter adults who lack the capacity to conduct the proceedings. It is necessary for this condition to be defined by the rules and identified by the court, and then for special procedures to apply to enable the proceedings to continue in a human rights compliant way.

---

[130] The President of the Family Division adopted both these procedures in the recent 'right to die' case of *Re B* when she attended at the hospital and then continued by video link.

[131] The special measures directions introduced by the Youth Justice and Criminal Evidence Act 1999, Part II to assist vulnerable and intimidated witnesses to give evidence in criminal proceedings refer to communicators rather than just language interpreters. These include the use of *intermediaries* and *communication aids*.

Rule 14 of the Court of Protection Rules 2001 deals with applications involving 'persons under a disability'[132] and is modelled on the former Rules of the Supreme Court. The person must be represented by a 'next friend' if bringing the application or by a 'guardian ad litem' if responding. The Civil Procedure Rules 1998, Part 21 now use the term 'litigation friend' for both and it is likely that the new Court of Protection Rules will do the same.

---

[132] These are minors (ie persons under 18 years of age) and 'patients' who could themselves potentially be within the jurisdiction of the Court.

Chapter 7

The Public Guardian and Supporting Services

BACKGROUND

The administration

7.1   The existing Court of Protection depends heavily upon the support that it receives from its administrative arm. This is presently the Public Guardianship Office whose responsibilities extend across the whole of England and Wales, whereas separate arrangements exist for Scotland and Northern Ireland. In the first instance this office must support the Court in the same way that Her Majesty's Courts Service supports all other courts,[1] but that is only a small part of its functions.

7.2   The administration also provides services to promote the financial and social well-being of clients who are not able to manage their financial affairs because of mental incapacity (known as 'patients'). The incapacity may be related to an illness suffered by some older people (eg dementia), or the result of an accident or negligence (brain injury) or of mental illness (eg schizophrenia). Some people with learning difficulties may also be clients depending on the nature or extent of their financial affairs. Most patients fall into the first of these categories, but by reason of their age the average duration of these files in the office is between 2 and 3 years. A significant 'core business' is now developing of brain injured patients with substantial awards who, because of improvements in healthcare, may live for a normal life span.

Support is provided for the families and advisers of the person who is incapable, often after someone has applied to the Court of Protection to manage the incapacitated person's financial affairs. When the Court has considered the application, it may appoint someone, called a Receiver, to manage and administer the person's financial affairs whilst they are unable to do so themselves. The administration thus assists and supports

---

[1]   Until April 2005 the Court Service administered the High Court of Justice, the county courts and the Crown Courts whilst magistrates' courts were administered by 42 separate committees, but all has now been merged into HM Courts Service.

the Receiver in completing his or her duties and works with the Receiver to promote the best interests of the person with mental incapacity (the Protection function).

7.3   Sometimes the administration will act as Receiver through a designated official (the Receivership function). This occurs only as a last resort when the Court of Protection can find no one else willing or suitable to become the Receiver. The staff will then be involved on a daily basis in the client's financial and legal affairs. As a result, the administrative arm may develop and maintain very close working relationships with its clients, their families, carers and any other people or organisations involved in their welfare.

7.4   There have been several changes during recent years.

The Public Trust Office

Nature

7.5   On 2 January 1987 the Receivership and Protection Divisions of the Court became part of a new department known as the Public Trust Office ('PTO').[2] There was also transferred to this department two other parts of the Lord Chancellor's Department concerned with private money, namely the Public Trustee Office and the Court Funds Office. The head of this department was an official known as both the Accountant General of the Supreme Court and the Public Trustee.

The PTO became an Executive Agency in July 1994 and in 2000 employed some 580 staff and had annual administrative running costs of £21m. The Court of Protection remained a separate body wholly dependent upon the PTO.

7.6   The new PTO was thus an amalgam of four separate functions only two of which related to mental incapacity, namely:

1. the Public Trustee, whose office was established in 1906, acted as an executor or trustee and could be appointed by individuals, the court or trustees. By 2000 the current caseload of the *Trust Division* was 1,750 but diminishing and client funds amounted to £711m (the Official Solicitor also had a similar function);

2. the *Receivership Division* which managed the financial affairs of incapacitated people who had no one else suitable to do so, with the Public Trustee acting as receiver (there were some 2,800 cases in early 2000 and client funds of £252m);

3. the *Protection Division* which supervised receivers appointed by the Court of Protection (the caseload in 2000 was 22,000 with client

---

[2]   Public Trustee and Administration of Funds Act 1986.

funds of £1.78bn) and also registered enduring powers of attorney ('EPAs') (the Enduring Power of Attorney Team registers about three times as many enduring powers as there are receivers appointed);

4. the *Court Funds Office* (first so named in 1975), which administered funds held in court for whatever purpose (about £2.47bn in 2000) and had accumulated substantial unclaimed balances (about £33m).

It proved to be an unsatisfactory partnership. There was an expectation that the Office would perform to certain standards, but it was also expected to be self-financing which stifled development and produced the injustice of cross-subsidy.

Demise of the PTO

Quinquennial Review

7.7   In 1999 the PTO was criticised by both the National Audit Office and the Public Accounts Committee[3] for failing to ensure that a large proportion of receivers submitted annual accounts and failing to ensure, through its visits programme, that patients' funds were being used for their benefit. It was also criticised for serious weaknesses in financial and management information across its activities. An administrative *Quinquennial Review* in November 1999 then proposed that the Office should be dismantled and those services that were still required delivered through other organisations and private sector suppliers. In particular:

- enduring powers of attorney should be registered at the Official Solicitor's Office;
- the tasks of receiver and trustee be delegated to local panel solicitors with problem cases being taken over by the Official Solicitor;
- there be a 'partnership' with local authorities whereby someone from the authority be appointed for a patient in their care;
- the work of the *Protection Division* be transferred to the Official Solicitor's Office;
- visiting of patients (and receivers) be undertaken by the Benefits Agency, local authorities and charities under service level agreements;
- the Inland Revenue interview receivers and monitor their accounts;
- the *Court Funds Office* services be reduced and transferred to the Court Service.

---

[3]   Committee of Public Accounts, Thirty-Fifth Report, Session 1998–99.

A Director of Change was appointed in the absence of the Public Trustee who resigned, and receivers and solicitors witnessed a downturn in the service provided as experienced staff became involved in the process of change and the remainder struggled on with the workload in a demoralised state.

7.8   There were serious concerns amongst professionals involved. It was unclear what, if anything, would replace the PTO and it was foreseen that when a new decision-making jurisdiction was introduced there would be the need for an administrative and supervisory body which could have developed from the existing PTO. With its break-up there would be the need to create a new organisation from scratch and it would be preferable to build on and develop the existing organisation. The concerns were summarised in the following article then published in *The Times*:[4]

'Demise of Public Trust Office would be "a disaster"?

The Public Trust Office (PTO) may not be everyone's favourite institution. But do we want to see it scrapped and its functions delegated to a variety of bodies? The office exists to provide protective oversight of the financial affairs of people mentally incapable of managing for themselves (known as "patients"). But a recent review of its work since it achieved agency status in 1994 has raised a question mark over its future: the review found it had not performed as well as expected and recommended radical reform.

The review was led by Anne Chant, a senior civil servant on secondment from the Department of Social Security. The report to the Lord Chancellor in November highlighted the problems of neglect and proposed reform, including dismantling the PTO and delivery of key services through other organisations and private sector suppliers. It concluded that there was a basic problem: the conflict between an increasing workload and meeting the need to be self-financing.

But the team ignored the obvious remedy – giving the PTO adequate resources. When an administrative body is failing there are three options – new management and pump-priming funding; handing over some or all of the functions to other bodies; or denying the need for those functions. It is the assumption that the second must be adopted and the willingness to rely on the third, without adequate consultation, that causes concern. The impression from the Report is that the overriding objective is to break up the PTO and sell off its building, which backs on to Lincoln's Inn Fields, rather than provide a better service for mentally vulnerable people.

The Public Trustee acts as receiver in case of need through the *Receivership Division* and as an executor or trustee through the *Trust Division*. The recommendation that these tasks be delegated to local panel solicitors, with problem cases being taken over by the Official Solicitor, has much to commend it – provided that there is control over the cost and those who undertake these responsibilities are suitably qualified. The proposal of a "partnership" with local authorities in which somebody from the authority

---

[4]   22 February 2000, by District Judge Gordon Ashton.

is appointed for a patient in their care overlooks the conflict of interest when the care-planner and funder has control of the individual's finances.

The *Protection Division* supervises all other receivers and registers enduring powers of attorney. The need to move the latter task to the Official Solicitor's Office is not self evident – that office would have to recruit staff and create systems that could equally well be implemented within a properly staffed and funded PTO.

The idea that visiting of receivers and patients should be undertaken by the Benefits Agency and local authorities ignores the fact that the receiver will want to ensure that these bodies meet their own obligations. Also worrying is the suggestion that the Inland Revenue be involved in advising receivers and monitoring their accounts. Would automatic disclosure to the tax authorities of the affairs of a wealthy man who becomes mentally incapable survive a challenge under the Human Rights Act 1998?

The *Court Funds Office* administers money held in court. The Report suggests that this service is not needed and demands that the Senior Master of the Queen's Bench Division maintains a personal oversight of awards to minors, overlooking the fact that this is also a function of 380 district judges. The team also proposed that this discretion be removed in cases below £10,000 and that a trust approach be favoured. These are surely matters for the courts. Given the enormous sums involved it should be possible for an efficient self-funding system to be maintained. The fact that "unclaimed balances" amount to £33 million shows the inadequacy of administration over past years.

Dealing with adults who lack capacity and their families and carers requires special expertise and this is best concentrated in one place. More oversight will be required when the Lord Chancellor acts on the Law Commission's mental incapacity proposals, yet the Review does not seem to address future requirements.

… The review is likely to dictate the approach adopted by the Director of Change who reports to the Lord Chancellor this month. The Law Society must not be seduced by the prospect of work being delegated to solicitors into overlooking the impact of these proposals. Consultation is essential. The reforms are based on administrative convenience and may affect the fundamental human rights of individuals concerned.'

Consultation

7.9   The outcome was a consultation paper *Making Changes: The Future of the Public Trust Office* (April 2000) followed by a Report *The Way Forward* (December 2000). This represented a major shift from the previous administrative proposals and heralded 'ongoing and extensive' consultation linked with the *Making Decisions* policy proposals which were then receiving serious consideration.[5] The Lord Chancellor stated the policy as follows:

---

[5]   These followed Law Commission recommendations and are considered in CHAPTER 1.

'I am seeking to create a centre of excellence in service provision for the mentally incapacitated in this area. My prime concern is to protect the vulnerable while avoiding intrusive State intervention where it is not necessary.'

A centre of excellence was indeed what was needed. The problem remained how to achieve this, but at least the professionals involved could look beyond the long neglected and marginalised Public Trust Office to a new administrative body that would concentrate on the needs of incapacitated adults.

7.10   The Trust functions were to be co-located with the office of the Official Solicitor[6] and Court Funds transferred to the Court Service. There was no reason why these should be retained by the new body. The remaining Protection and Receivership functions which directly related to adults who lack mental capacity[7] were to be performed by the new body[8] which would include a unit for the registration of EPAs. This was to be reformed with an emphasis on:

1.   pre-appointment procedures to assist in appointing the right receiver;
2.   providing greater assistance to receivers;
3.   extending visiting services with more visits and better targeting;
4.   providing more support in the completion of accounts;
5.   finding suitable receivers to avoid last resort work;
6.   eliminating the present cross-subsidy of fees.[9]

Other planned changes included the setting up of a *Strategic Investment Board* to oversee all clients' funds, a series of regional *Open Days* for receivers providing support and information, and a newsletter for receivers called *Reaching Out*. There was also to be a new website: www.guardianship.gov.uk.

The Public Guardianship Office

Launch of the PGO

7.11   Everything happened very quickly and from 1 April 2001 the Public Trust Office ceased to exist and its mental incapacity functions were transferred to the new Public Guardianship Office ('PGO') which is an executive agency of the Department for Constitutional Affairs. The

---

6   This became the Office of the Official Solicitor and Public Trustee.
7   This includes minors who are unlikely to have capacity when they attain their majority.
8   Provisionally named the Mental Incapacity Support Unit, but that name was much criticised.
9   The Office is expected to be self-financing and derives its income from the fees charged to clients, but remission of fees may take place on a discretionary basis so some public subsidy is required.

PGO is thus now the administrative arm of the Court of Protection responsible for implementing the Court's decisions.

Initially the PGO occupied the premises of the former Public Trust Office at Stewart House, Kingsway, London but a move soon took place to new premises at Archway Tower in North London. The PGO may now be contacted at:

Archway Tower
2 Junction Road
London N19 5SZ
DX 141150 Archway 2
Tel: 0845 330 2900 (local call rate)
Fax: 0870 739 5780 (UK callers)
Or   020 7151 7531 (callers outside UK)
E-mail: custserv@guardianship.gsi.gov.uk
Website: www.guardianship.gov.uk/

7.12   The PGO's focus is on overseeing the work of receivers who are appointed by the Court to look after the financial affairs of people who have lost, or never had, mental capacity. These are either lay people, for example a close relative, or a professional, usually a solicitor, or an officer from a local authority. The Chief Executive of the PGO was appointed as receiver in place of the former Public Trustee in a small number of cases (now less than 250), and in a handful of cases has since been appointed as a receiver of last resort.

The PGO also implements the Court's function of registering enduring powers of attorney but the Court's oversight of an attorney differs from that of a receiver in that the client's choice of attorney was made when the client had capacity. Once registered, an attorney does not have to submit accounts to the Court unless expressly required and the donor is not usually visited by one of the Visitors so there is no continuing involvement unless a dispute arises.

Progress

7.13   The PGO had a difficult beginning and the standard of service declined further with a proliferation of complaints mainly concerning delay or inattention. This was contributed to by the departure of experienced members of staff, the move to the new office outside Central London, an unsatisfactory telephone call system, the reorganisation of case officers into larger teams and inaccessible file storage. The office was in danger of imploding.

7.14   The 'Change Programme' led to an implant of new management and ideas which began to bear fruit. The following changes were initially made:

1. a new Customer Services Division was created;
2. an Independent Complaints Examiner was appointed;
3. a new senior management team was put in place;
4. a Consultative Forum was established;
5. Receiver's Forums were to take place;
6. Open Days were planned when clients could meet their case worker;
7. the cross-subsidy of fees was to be eliminated;
8. all cases with capital under £10,000 were to be reviewed.

The Mission statement

7.15 The PGO now states that its Mission is:

(a) to work with the families, friends, carers and others from the professional and not-for-profit sectors to promote the finances and well-being of people with mental incapacity;

(b) to provide a responsive and accessible service, designed to meet the individual needs of our many different clients and their representatives,

and that its Vision is 'Financial protection and a better life for all who need its services'. The Values which shape the way the PGO does business and help to achieve the vision of financial protection and a better life for all who need these services are expressed as follows:

Customer focus – Putting the needs of our clients and customers first.

Achievement – Results count. This means taking responsibility for resolving issues for our clients and customers.

Professionalism – Being effective and responsible, and ensuring we have the skills to do the job.

Collaboration – Working in partnership with each other, with stakeholders, and working with common purpose.

Valuing people – Recognising each person as a unique individual.

Forward looking – Being progressive, innovative and flexible.

It is likely that this approach will be adopted by the new administrative arm to be set up under the Mental Capacity Act 2005.

The Consultative Forum

7.16 One of the new initiatives prior to the launch of the PGO was the formation of a Consultative Forum, a body comprising representatives of 'stakeholders' that had regular meetings and whose role was to advise on the Change Programme. Members included representatives of Action on Elder Abuse, Age Concern, Alzheimer's Disease Society, Carers National Association, Headway, MENCAP, MIND, The Royal College of Psychiatrists, and The Law Society.[10] A representative of the

---

[10] District Judge Gordon Ashton, the Deputy Master, represents the judiciary.

General Visitors subsequently joined the Forum. The Forum continues to meet four times each year and the present Terms of Reference are:

'To maintain a forum for continuing dialogue with user representatives that reflects the PGO's diverse client base.

To work in partnership with the PGO – identifying problems and solutions.

To discuss key issues in mental incapacity and decision-making policy development with DCA representatives.

To assist the PGO in planning for likely future enhancements in the jurisdiction of the Court of Protection.

To ensure that important issues are addressed and are client focused.'

7.17 In the early years discussions concentrated upon the continued failings in performance of the PGO and the fire-fighting that was taking place to contain this. With the improvement in service delivery a change of climate has become apparent and members now contribute to new initiatives and plans for the implementation of the new jurisdiction. The breadth of experience and perspective within the Forum is a valuable resource to the senior executives at the PGO and the members are able to provide feedback to their organisations.

National Audit Office Report

7.18 There was a more positive Report on the PGO by the National Audit Office in June 2005.[11] This found that:

'Since its creation in 2001, the Public Guardianship Office has improved the quality of information it receives on the stewardship of the financial affairs of people who lose mental capacity. It has begun to target its scrutiny, reducing the regulatory burden on some receivers deemed to be a lower risk, and in some cases where the client has assets less than £16,000 in value. The Public Guardianship Office needs, however, to do more to target its resources, focusing on those cases where the risk of mismanagement or financial abuse are greatest. It should also make it easier for people to report concerns about potential exploitation.'

The Report recognised that, with over 24,000 receivership cases to supervise, the resources that could be devoted to scrutinising each case are necessarily limited, but recommended more effective targeting of resources and making better use of the information available to help direct scrutiny.

7.19 The PGO has sought to improve its knowledge of the nature of the risks it is trying to regulate by commissioning research, and collects a variety of information on individual cases. The Office currently lacks an overall picture of the circumstances in which abuse or mismanagement most

---

[11] *Public Guardianship Office: protecting and promoting the financial affairs of people who lose mental capacity*, Report by the Comptroller and Auditor General, HC 27 2005–06, ISBN: 0102932786.

often occurs, how instances of mismanagement or abuse have been detected, and whether its regulatory controls are effective in detecting and remedying these problems. The Report recommends that the PGO should build on its recent establishment of an investigation team by improving procedures for receiving, evaluating and following up potential concerns that come to its attention. An inability to access case information quickly when receivers and others call with queries, and delays in dealing with some transactions are identified. The continuing lack of an electronic case management system[12] was stated to be inhibiting improvement and efficiency.

7.20   The PGO has recognised that public awareness of the services it provides is limited and put a marketing strategy in place in April 2004 to raise its profile with other organisations and the public. In January 2005 it began to roll out a marketing programme across England and Wales. The Report recommends that the PGO should continue to raise its profile and make it easier for people to report concerns. Relatives, friends, social workers and other professionals are, in many instances, well placed to spot the first signs of potential mismanagement or financial abuse but are not sufficiently aware of the PGO's role in reporting concerns.

7.21   When presenting this Report the Head of the National Audit Office commented:

> 'The Public Guardianship Office must do more ... to target its scrutiny at the cases presenting the greatest risks. It should also make sure that a larger proportion of the public and professionals know about its work and how to report concerns. The vulnerable people who rely on the Public Guardianship Office to protect their financial affairs deserve the best possible service.'

A critical analysis

7.22   In 2005 a project team within the PGO concluded a critical analysis of all office functions and its conclusions are likely to influence the delivery of services under the new jurisdiction. The test being applied is to establish what 'added value' any particular function may provide for the client or his or her family/carers, and whether there is any other appropriate agency which is better placed to provide the service or afford the protection required. It was recognised that there must be better interdepartmental coordination and more effective co-operation in achieving the best outcomes for the incapacitated adults.

7.23   After being settled for many years it is now considered that the relationship with receivers and families needs to be revised. The process

---

[12]   A planned system was cancelled in 2003 after difficulties in implementation.

in receivership cases has been seen as a source of dissatisfaction for customers and adding little of value. The initial forms are complex and demanding, being time consuming to complete at what is generally a stressful time. Accessing the required financial information when there is no authority to do so can be a problem. There is then a long delay before an Order is issued causing a hiatus in financial management. A new procedure is to be introduced which will:

1. utilise simpler application forms;
2. make provision for more 'up front' processing (a bond for a fixed amount and advance notice to the patient);
3. speed up the process of appointment;
4. simplify the First Order by focusing on the powers that are immediately needed including authority to investigate and report back to the Court;
5. introduce a management plan to provide the basis for more proactive engagement between the Court, PGO and receiver.

The management plan which is to be prepared by the receiver will be required 3 months after appointment and will relate to the forthcoming year. It will set out what monies are needed and why, and (subject to an assets threshold) be accompanied by written advice from an Independent Financial Adviser. When the management plan is lodged the receiver will indicate what further powers or authorities are desired. The case will then be considered on its own merits with supervisory and regulatory provisions being applied according to a risk assessment. A 'one size fits all' approach will thus no longer be adopted. Professional receivers will be further empowered and the one case lay receiver will be subject to closer scrutiny whilst receiving more support.

Other jurisdictions

7.24   There is a difference of approach to the need for and the services provided by a Public Guardian in the separate jurisdictions of the UK and Ireland.

Scotland

7.25   The Adults with Incapacity (Scotland) Act 2000 ('the 2000 Act') introduced a new jurisdiction for Scotland. This established with effect from 2 April 2001 a Public Guardian based in Falkirk with supervisory and support functions. He has published a useful range of forms, precedents and guidance notes.[13] There is also a Mental Welfare Commission which was established in 1960 and has been given additional functions under the 2000 Act. Lessons are to be learnt from the fact that the Court's jurisdiction was given to every sheriff, some of

---

[13]   These are available on the website: www.scotcourts.gov.uk.

whom have little knowledge of this area of law, and there is no direct link between the Public Guardian and the courts, which has resulted in conflict on some occasions.

A 2-year review of the operation of this legislation was commissioned by the Scottish Executive in 2002 and the Report *Learning from Experience* was published in the Autumn of 2004. In broad terms the 2000 Act was considered to be meeting its central aims, but there was concern about lack of publicity and knowledge as to how it may benefit incapacitated adults and their carers. The take-up rate was considerably lower than had been anticipated and the jurisdiction was proving costly and over complex in parts. The court process was seen as intimidating. The need for a financial manager of last resort has been highlighted and options being considered include local authorities, the Office of the Public Guardian, the voluntary sector and a combination of these.

Northern Ireland

7.26   There is at present no equivalent of a Public Guardian in Northern Ireland. The functions of the Court of Protection and Public Guardianship Office in England and Wales are carried out by the Office of Care and Protections which is led by Master Brian Hall who has judicial status. An assessment is presently being made of future needs and the additional functions which might be assigned to a Public Guardian. There is concern about a single organisation being both regulator and provider and a desire to relinquish last resort work. An advocacy service would be welcomed with a cadre of advocates to take on legal representation unless the Official Solicitor was engaged for this. The availability of funding is a crucial issue.

Ireland

7.27   There is no equivalent of the Public Guardian in the Republic of Ireland and any intervention by the courts is based on the Wardship jurisdiction exercised by the President of the High Court who has medical visitors at his disposal. There is a need for modernising legislation although some lawyers consider that the present system works adequately and it is unlikely that a comprehensive new jurisdiction will be introduced in the foreseeable future. The Office of the General Solicitor for Minors and Wards of Court assists the Court.

THE PUBLIC GUARDIAN

7.28   The legislation[14] establishes a new a statutory office holder to be appointed by the Lord Chancellor known as the Public Guardian.

Office of the Public Guardian

7.29   The Lord Chancellor may, after consulting the Public Guardian, provide him or her with such officers and staff, or enter into such contracts with other persons for the provision (by them or their subcontractors) of officers, staff or services, as the Lord Chancellor thinks necessary for the proper discharge of the Public Guardian's functions. Any functions of the Public Guardian may, to the extent authorised by him or her, be performed by any of his or her officers. So the Office of the Public Guardian, which may well be abbreviated to 'OPG', is itself recognised by and funded under the authority of Parliament.[15]

Functions

7.30   The Public Guardian will have the following basic functions:[16]

1.   establishing and maintaining a register of lasting powers of attorney;
2.   establishing and maintaining a register of orders appointing deputies;
3.   supervising deputies appointed by the Court;
4.   directing a Court of Protection Visitor to visit (i) a donee of a lasting power of attorney, (ii) a deputy appointed by the Court, or (iii) the person granting the power of attorney or for whom the deputy is appointed, and to make a report to the Public Guardian on such matters as he or she may direct;
5.   receiving security which the Court requires a person to give for the discharge of his or her functions;
6.   receiving reports from donees of lasting powers of attorney and deputies appointed by the Court;
7.   reporting to the Court on such matters relating to proceedings under the Mental Capacity Act 2005 as the Court requires;
8.   dealing with representations (including complaints) about the way in which a donee of a lasting power of attorney or a deputy appointed by the Court is exercising his or her powers; and
9.   publishing, in any manner the Public Guardian thinks appropriate, any information he or she thinks appropriate about the discharge of his or her functions.

---

[14]   Mental Capacity Act 2005, s 57.
[15]   Mental Capacity Act 2005, s 57(4), (5).
[16]   Mental Capacity Act 2005, s 58.

These functions (with the exception of the final one) may be discharged in co-operation with any other person who has functions in relation to the care or treatment of the incapacitated person. It is intended that the Public Guardian will work closely with organisations such as local authorities and NHS Trusts.

7.31   The Lord Chancellor may by Regulations make provision conferring on the Public Guardian other functions in connection with the Mental Capacity Act 2005 or in connection with the discharge by the Public Guardian of his or her functions. In particular Regulations may make provision as to:[17]

- the giving of security by deputies appointed by the Court and the enforcement and discharge of security so given;
- the fees which may be charged by the Public Guardian;
- the way in which, and funds from which, such fees are to be paid;
- exemptions from and reductions in such fees;
- remission of such fees in whole or in part;
- the making of reports to the Public Guardian by deputies appointed by the Court and others who are directed by the court to carry out any transaction for a person who lacks capacity.

This provides considerable scope for development of the operation and services of the PGO as experience is gained under the new jurisdiction. This list does not include the PGO's present function of acting as receiver of last resort, consistent with the desire within the PGO to relinquish that role.

Powers

7.32   For the purpose of enabling him or her to carry out his or her functions, the Public Guardian may, at all reasonable times, examine and take copies of any health record, any record of (or held by) a local authority and compiled in connection with a social services function, and any record held by a person registered under Part II of the Care Standards Act 2000 so far as the record relates to the client. The Public Guardian may also for that purpose interview the incapacitated person in private.

Annual Report

7.33   The Public Guardian must make an annual report to the Lord Chancellor about the discharge of his or her functions.[18]

---

[17]   Mental Capacity Act 2005, s 58(3), (4).
[18]   Mental Capacity Act 2005, s 60.

Public Guardian Board

7.34 There is to be a new body known as the Public Guardian Board whose duty is to scrutinise and review the way in which the Public Guardian discharges his or her functions and to make such recommendations to the Lord Chancellor about that matter as it thinks appropriate.[19] The Lord Chancellor must, in discharging his functions in regulating the Public Guardian, give due consideration to recommendations made by the Board.

The members of the Board will be appointed by the Lord Chancellor and will comprise at least one judge of the new Court of Protection and at least four members who are persons appearing to the Lord Chancellor to have appropriate knowledge or experience of the work of the Public Guardian. Members will hold and vacate office in accordance with the terms of the instrument appointing them and receive such payments by way of reimbursement of expenses, allowances and remuneration as the Lord Chancellor may determine.[20]

7.35 The Lord Chancellor may by Regulations make provision as to:[21]

- the appointment of members of the Board (and, in particular, the procedures to be followed in connection with appointments);
- the selection of one of the members to be the chairman;
- the term of office of the chairman and members;
- their resignation, suspension or removal;
- the procedure of the Board (including quorum);
- the validation of proceedings in the event of a vacancy among the members or a defect in the appointment of a member.

Annual report

7.36 The Board must make an annual report to the Lord Chancellor about the discharge of its functions.[22]

Challenges ahead

7.37 Whilst the PGO forms the embryo of an administrative and supervisory body that could serve us well when we have the new incapacity jurisdiction and the recent reforms will inevitably be carried forward, a change of culture is also required. The Office of the Public Guardian is fundamentally different in status and functions from its predecessor despite a similarity of name. It will have a statutory existence with

---

[19]   Mental Capacity Act 2005, s 59.
[20]   In consequence of the Constitutional Reform Act 2005 the members of the Board will be appointed by the Lord Chief Justice.
[21]   Mental Capacity Act 2005, s 59(6).
[22]   Mental Capacity Act 2005, s 59(9).

supervisory and regulatory functions and may (or may not) be the administrative arm of the Court of Protection.[23] This cannot be emphasised too strongly and it is hoped that the Public Guardian (through his senior staff to whom he can delegate his powers) will act fearlessly and independently, becoming a mediator and problem solver as well as performing administrative functions.

The new role

7.38   The Public Guardian has three distinct and sometimes conflicting roles: administrative, supervisory and policymaking. He or she must:

1. be a supporter of patients and their families and carers;
2. be an ally of good attorneys and managers;
3. be an enemy of abusers and a channel for whistle-blowers;
4. develop the right public image and educate the public by promoting his or her services;
5. monitor standards in decision-making for vulnerable adults that everyone is expected to follow;
6. establish procedures for investigating allegations of abuse;
7. work with local authorities and other agencies.

The new Office of the Public Guardian must achieve its purpose of becoming a 'centre of excellence in service provision for the mentally incapacitated'. Partnerships must be developed with social services and health authorities and agencies and also those charitable organisations working in this area.

Dispute resolution

7.39   There is a new role that must be actively developed, namely that of dispute resolution. This will run in tandem with the new emphasis on ADR[24] in the civil courts save that the OPG may wish to establish its own dispute resolution procedures in addition to being a facilitator for services provided by outside agencies. This will be dealt with in the Codes of Practice. But it must not be overlooked that the objective is to address the best interests of the incapacitated individual rather than resolve disputes between other persons especially when these persons are not addressing this individual's welfare. In the case of many dysfunctional families the issue becomes control over rather than the welfare of the vulnerable member and involving an outsider may be the appropriate solution.

---

[23]   See **7.47**.

[24]   Alternative Dispute Resolution.

Investigating abuse

7.40   An Investigations Unit has recently been established at the PGO and lessons are being learnt as to how this may best function. It is likely that this will form the basis of a similar Unit within the OPG. Internal procedures for referring cases have to be developed and other procedures agreed for external referrals. Publicity will be necessary if this is to function effectively and a dedicated helpline may be required. Cases may be referred by Adult Protection Officers in local authorities and the PGO is presently working with the Association of Directors of Social Services on a Working Protocol. In the future referrals will extend beyond financial abuse and include other forms of abuse but the OPG will only be able to carry out its own investigation where the individual lacks mental capacity. In some instances a new manager will be appointed and instructed to take appropriate action.

Use of technology

7.41   This will only be achieved if the Office becomes a trail-blazer in the use of technology. A willingness to do this has already been demonstrated. The existing PGO already has a much-improved website, it is ahead of HM Courts Service in the development of electronic filing and the staff communicate with one another by secure e-mail. There is even a willingness to communicate with receivers, solicitors and others by e-mail although security issues have yet to be fully addressed. A policy for use of video links has also being developed with a published list of access venues.

Partnerships

7.42   Following up the progress made by the PGO, the OPG will wish to take over the partnerships that have been established with other organisations and bodies and to develop further partnerships. These include working arrangements with voluntary organisations, the Law Society, the Department for Work and Pensions, the Department of Health, HM Revenue & Customs, the police, the Criminal Records Bureau, the Citizen's Advice Bureau and the financial sector.

Regionalisation

7.43   Regional access to the Office would be helpful because those who need its services often have difficulty coping with a remote service provider in London. In this area of work personal contact is beneficial, as demonstrated by the increasingly valuable service being provided by the Visitors in supporting both patients and receivers. Although regional offices may not be justified, regional 'nodes' (or points of contact) and the deployment of travelling officers could be piloted and developed in the light of experience.[25] There is an increasing tendency for the Visitors to overlap with and even trespass on the role of case officers whereas their original function was to report to the Court. It may be better to improve the contact between case officers and receivers by enabling regional officers to make more personal visits and reserve the more specialist services of the Visitors to those cases where these are needed.

In the same way as the Probate Registries maintain a presence in certain county courts premises on specified days, staff from the Office of the Public Guardian could operate part-time regional offices perhaps at the courts where Deputy Masters sit. A network of access points could develop throughout England and Wales concentrating on those areas where there is a high incidence of involvement with the Court of Protection.

Funding

7.44   Although the Public Guardian appears to have inherited the objective of full cost recovery in regard to all basic functions, this will be harder to achieve in a jurisdiction which extends beyond cases where there is money to be administered. The need for waiver of fees on hardship grounds in more cases will exacerbate the shortfall in fee income. This problem has yet to be addressed but it is hoped that lack of resources will not frustrate access to justice under the new jurisdiction.

7.45   A similar problem arises in respect of legal representation. Historically Legal Aid has never been available for applications to or hearings before the Court of Protection. In consequence there is no legal representation in a high proportion of cases. A new dividing line will have to be drawn with cases previously dealt with by the High Court now being absorbed within the Court of Protection's jurisdiction.[26]

Relationship with the Court of Protection

7.46   It follows that the new Court of Protection will deal with disputes that require a hearing and be the ultimate decision-maker when matters cannot be resolved by the Public Guardian. The Court will also retain a considerable volume of paper-based decision-making much of which may be delegated to nominated officers although they should not determine disputes that require judicial involvement. Recourse to the Court should be regarded as a last resort. The extent to which the Public Guardian may ultimately act on his or her own initiative will be dictated

---

[25]   The success of the regional Court of Protection in Preston has already demonstrated what can be achieved.

[26]   These are applications for declaratory relief, eg in medical treatment cases. See generally **CHAPTER 5**.

by decisions of the Court of Protection on references and appeals, and no doubt by the High Court in the event of judicial reviews. But the OPG will have a more authoritative role than the present PGO.

7.47 This enhanced role for the Public Guardian does lead to a change in the relationship with the Court of Protection. If the OPG is to act independently from the Court of Protection should it also administer the Court in the same way as HM Courts Service administers the civil courts? There is a need to demonstrate the distinction between administrative and judicial functions and to maintain judicial independence, yet there are significant advantages in maintaining a link between the Court and the OPG. Even where there is no dispute an order of the Court is generally required, and this is the reality in the overwhelming majority of cases. Any nominated officers of the future who are given judicial powers should be independent of the OPG.

It may be significant that the list of functions conferred by the Mental Capacity Act 2005 does not expressly include the PGO's present function of processing originating applications to the new Court of Protection, although the Lord Chancellor may yet by regulation confer this additional function on the Public Guardian. Is it envisaged that there will be two separate organisations, perhaps in separate offices, with the Court having its own administrative staff? The Master has identified a need to 'disentangle the close relationship that currently exists between the Court of Protection and the PGO in a way that achieves a proper distinction between the two organisations, whilst retaining the positive aspects of the present close working arrangements' but the Chief Executive of the PGO has concerns as to how that close relationship may be maintained. The solution may be reliance in contentious cases upon the nominated judges who do operate quite independently, with the Senior Judge based in the same office building being the administrative link.

COURT OF PROTECTION VISITORS

Background [27]

Historical

7.48 The office of Visitor dates from the Lunatics' Visitors Act 1833 which authorised the Lord Chancellor to appoint two physicians and a barrister to visit patients at least once a year – more often, if necessary – and to

---

[27] The material under this heading relies on articles written by Denzil Lush, Master of the Court of Protection.

superintend, inspect and report on their care and treatment.[28] Under the Lunacy Regulation Act 1853 the Masters in Lunacy became *ex officio* Visitors.[29] The first Visitors were paid an annual salary, but only worked part-time and were allowed to remain in private practice. The Lunacy Regulation Act 1862 required them to visit on a full-time basis and increased their salary to compensate. Consequently, the post became both lucrative and prestigious and attracted some of the leading psychiatrists of the day.

7.49   Until 1981 all visits to Court of Protection patients were carried out by the Medical and Legal Visitors. The majority of these visits required a combination of social work, public relations and plain common sense, and did not warrant the expense of being made by an eminent psychiatrist or leading counsel. So, with effect from 1 October 1981, the Lord Chancellor created a panel of lay General Visitors, membership of which was initially drawn from the welfare officers in his own department.[30] The Medical Visitors and Legal Visitor subsequently ceased to be full-time employees of the Lord Chancellor's Department, and now make their visits on an ad hoc basis. In March 2000 there were six General Visitors each covering a particular region of England and Wales.

The present regime

7.50   If the Court considers that a patient should be visited for any reason, it sends one of the Lord Chancellor's Visitors and there is a strategy to ensure that visits are carried out in the most suitable cases. The visits are usually carried out at the patient's place of residence, but the Visitors do not have automatic rights of entry and inspection although anyone who obstructs a visit commits an offence.[31] There are presently three panels whose qualifications and functions are defined in the Mental Health Act 1983 ('the 1983 Act'):[32]

1. Medical Visitors;
2. Legal Visitors (though usually there has only been one at any time); and
3. General Visitors.

---

[28]   3 & 4 Will IV, c 36. The Lunatics' Visitors Act 1833 also introduced a system of percentage, whereby patients were required to pay a percentage of their clear annual income to the court, in order to fund the Visitors' salaries. This is the origin of the present fee structure in the Court of Protection.

[29]   This provision can now be found in the Mental Health Act 1983, s 103(7). The Master occasionally visits patients in their own home.

[30]   Supreme Court Act 1981, s 144.

[31]   Mental Health Act 1983, s 129. This is also a contempt of court.

[32]   In ss 102 and 103 respectively.

The 1983 Act also provides that:[33]

> '... every visit ... shall be made by a General Visitor unless, in a case where it appears to the judge that it is in the circumstances essential for the visit to be made by a Visitor with medical of legal qualifications, the judge directs that the visit shall be made by a Medical or a Legal Visitor.'

and the Court of Protection Rules 2001 make further provision.[34]

Medical Visitors

7.51   A Medical Visitor must be a 'registered medical practitioner who appears to the Lord Chancellor to have special knowledge and experience of cases of mental disorder'.[35] There are currently six and between them they conduct about 100 visits each year. They are all senior consultant psychiatrists, mostly retired or semi-retired and some also sit as medical members of Mental Health Review Tribunals. Each Medical Visitor covers a particular region of England and Wales, roughly approximating to the former court Circuits, but there are reserve Visitors who can be called upon when necessary. A report made in their official capacity cannot be requested by anyone other than the Court of Protection[36] – not even the county court or High Court – and they are independent, unbiased experts with no personal interest (other than a purely professional interest) in the outcome of their reports.

7.52   The reports by Medical Visitors address the particular issues they have been asked to investigate. Their principal function is to assess an individual's:

- capacity to manage and administer their property and financial affairs, either on entry into the jurisdiction or exit from it;
- capacity to create or revoke an enduring power of attorney, which nearly always requires a retrospective assessment; and
- testamentary capacity.

These visits are only commissioned where other medical evidence is conflicting, unsatisfactory, or non-existent. The Medical Visitors also report on a variety of other matters which the court may wish to consider before taking action, for example a patient's life expectancy, which may be helpful for setting an investment strategy, or deciding whether an intended lifetime gift is likely to be effective for Inheritance Tax purposes.

7.53   The Medical Visitors may carry out a medical examination of the patient in private and are entitled to the production of any medical

---

[33]   Section 103(3). A Visitor may interview a patient in private – s 103(5).
[34]   Court of Protection Rules 2001, r 67.
[35]   Mental Health Act 1983, s 102(3)(a).
[36]   Ie a Master or nominated judge.

records relating to the patient,[37] and inasmuch as there is one, the standard format of their report is:

1. the reason for the visit;
2. information and records studied;
3. the patient's history;
4. clinical examination;
5. opinion.

7.54   Occasionally a medical visit is abortive because the patient either refuses to admit the Visitor into his or her home, or is no longer available. Nevertheless, even though a visit is abortive, it may still be possible for the Court to accept jurisdiction on the basis of the Visitor's examination of the patient's medical records alone. The Court has an emergency jurisdiction which enables it to intervene if it has *reason to believe* that a person may be incapable, by reason of mental disorder, of managing and administering his or her property and affairs, and it is of the opinion that it is *necessary* to make immediate provision in respect of that person's affairs.[38]

The Legal Visitor

7.55   The Legal Visitor must be a lawyer with a 10-year general qualification within the meaning of s 71 of the Courts and Legal Services Act 1990.[39] His or her main function is to advise the Medical and General Visitors, and indeed the Court itself, on any questions of law, evidence and procedure arising out of the visits. It is unusual, though not unprecedented, for him or her to carry out a visit personally.

General Visitors

7.56   The General Visitors regard themselves as 'the eyes and the ears of the court, and the voice of the patient'. The purpose of their visits is to enable the Court and the PGO to assess whether a patient's needs are being properly addressed and to alert them to any action needed to bring about improvements. Their reports may cover, for example, how money has actually been expended; the patient's or donor's present wishes and feelings, so far as they are ascertainable, as to who should manage their property and financial affairs during their incapacity; whether a proposed course of action is likely to be in a patient's best interests; the suitability of a patient's accommodation; whether a patient requires residential care or specialist nursing care.

---

[37]   Mental Health Act 1983, s 103(6).
[38]   Mental Health Act 1983, s 98.
[39]   Mental Health Act 1983, s 102(3)(b) (as amended).

Additionally, the Visitors can show patients, receivers and carers that the Court and the PGO are interested in their welfare and are ready to discuss any particular difficulties or concerns. In most cases they are the only face-to-face contact a patient or receiver has with the authorities. Their routine reports follow a set format:

1. A brief summary of the case.
2. Accommodation. The Visitor is required to give: (i) a description of the patient's accommodation including staff attitudes and/or comments on family arrangements; (ii) details on the costs of extras, or contributions to household finances; and (iii) the cost of particular requirements.
3. Visitors. In other words, who comes to see the patient; what is their relationship to or connection with the patient; how frequently do they visit; and what interest do they show in the patient's welfare?
4. The patient's needs at the time of the visit.
5. Care: namely, (i) the arrangements for care and attention; (ii) the degree of attention required; and (iii) the patient's progress over the last 6 to 12 months.
6. Co-operation from the receiver. What degree of co-operation is received in payment of charges and provision of extras and what degree of general interest is shown?
7. The patient's condition: (i) physical; (ii) mental; and (iii) material.
8. Whether the case needs to be brought to anyone's attention. For example, the patient's GP or the local social services.
9. Recommendations for further visits. Whether they should be annual or less frequent, or whether the patient's name can safely be removed from the Visitors' Permanent List.
10. Whether a visit by a Medical Visitor is advisable.
11. Further comments, such as: overall care; present and future problems for the Court of Protection; and possible action.

7.57 Occasionally, a General Visitor is asked to carry out a special visit when a particular problem arises. For example:

- where the relationship between a patient and his or her receiver, carers or family is strained or appears to have broken down completely;
- where a receiver is behaving in a manner or proposing a course of action which the Court has reason to believe may not be in the patient's best interests;
- to assist in resolving some particular difficulty with the Court or the PGO, for example, expenditure, accounts or investment strategy.

Enduring powers of attorney

7.58   Although there is provision[40] for the donors of enduring powers of attorney to be visited, in practice they are never visited by the General Visitors.[41] This is principally because the philosophy underlying the Enduring Powers of Attorney Act 1985 is that there should be minimal public intervention in the operation of the enduring powers of attorney scheme. The Law Commission has suggested that:[42]

> '... apart from the registration procedure, we would regard court involvement in the running of any given EPA as very much more the exception than the rule. This would underline the essential distinction to be drawn between the court's functions under Part VII of the Mental Health Act 1983 on the one hand and those under the EPA scheme on the other. Under the former, the court has a continuing responsibility to supervise the receiver: under the latter the responsibility would be firmly vested in the attorney and the court would only be involved if a problem arose.'

Confidentiality of reports

The legal position

7.59   The Visitors' reports are confidential: their contents cannot be disclosed to anyone unless authorised by the Court of Protection.[43] However, the Court may at its discretion allow the report, or part of it, to be disclosed and in that event there are provisions for written questions to be submitted.[44] The General Visitors are reluctant to have their reports routinely disclosed because this may inhibit their comments, but one way round this is for them to include an addendum with these confidential comments which is not disclosed.

It has been held that in some cases, though not all, the principles of natural justice must prevail over the Court of Protection's paternalistic jurisdiction.[45] In initial applications for the appointment of a receiver and in applications to determine proceedings, where the ultimate issue is whether an individual should either become or remain subject to the jurisdiction, the Court should lean towards disclosing the Visitor's report, and the individual should be permitted to test the report by putting questions to the Visitor. The Court should only withhold

---

[40]   Enduring Powers of Attorney Act 1985, s 10(1)(a) and (2).

[41]   The donor of an enduring power of attorney may be visited by one of the Medical Visitors when there is a conflict of evidence as to whether the donor had the capacity to create or revoke an enduring power, or whether an application to register the power is premature.

[42]   *The Incapacitated Principal*, Law Com No 122, Cmnd 8977 (HMSO, July 1983) para 4.78.

[43]   Mental Health Act 1983, s 103(8). Any unauthorised disclosure is an offence. This goes further than the rules in relation to reports by CAFCASS Reporters in children cases which may only be disclosed to the parties and their legal advisers.

[44]   Court of Protection Rules 2001, r 29.

[45]   *Re WLW* [1972] Ch 456, Goff J.

disclosure where it feels that this would better serve the best interests of the alleged patient. In all other cases, the judge should only direct disclosure if he or she sees a positive advantage in so doing, either in the interest of the patient generally, or because he or she feels it would assist the judge himself in the exercise of his or her functions.

Recent recommendations

7.60 In 2001 the Master issued a direction, having in mind the Freedom of Information and Data Protection legislation, that the default position should be that copies of reports could be supplied to receivers and clients on request.[46] This direction has never taken effect and the position is now being reviewed. At the annual Conference of the General Visitors in September 2003 various concerns were articulated including:

1. if a client expressed dissatisfaction with a receiver who subsequently saw the report, the receiver might treat the client adversely as a result;
2. disclosure should be managed sensitively because the routine copying of reports to receivers might damage relationships between those involved;
3. disclosure might forewarn a receiver that corrective action was being planned;
4. clients regard their relationship with the Visitor as confidential and believe that only the Court will read the report.

It has been recommended that the existing procedure be retained but revised so that where no action is required following a visit a pro forma letter is sent to the receiver confirming this. Where action is required the receiver will become aware in any event. Any request by the client or receiver for a copy of the report should be referred to the Court which may direct that instead of an entire copy only a summary is provided, or a relevant extract. Visitors should mark reports where they feel that disclosure would not be in the best interests of the client and the Court will have due regard to this view when deciding whether to authorise disclosure. Disclosure of the entire report will be the norm except when it contains comments about a third party.

General recommendations

7.61 The National Audit Office has been critical of the way that Visitors have in the past been deployed and the consequent recommendations are likely to influence the arrangements made under the new

---

[46] The Deputy Master has since expressed the view, consistent with the position with CAFCASS reports in children cases, that other than in exceptional circumstances he is reluctant to rely upon any Report that has not been disclosed to the parties and that to do so without justification may make any decision vulnerable to an appeal.

jurisdiction. A report in 1994 recommended 'strengthening the planning, frequency and conduct of visits to help ensure proper use of patients' monies and greater attention to their individual circumstances and needs'.[47] The Public Accounts Committee, which considered that report, concluded:[48]

> 'We believe that there are fundamental benefits in regular visits to patients, carried out by sympathetic and well-trained staff who are properly briefed on the patient's circumstances. We therefore consider it unacceptable that so few private receivership patients are visited each year, and that many will never be visited at all. We are surprised that visits which do take place are undertaken by officials whose main job is to look after the welfare of employees of the Lord Chancellor's Department. We regard this as clearly unsatisfactory and do not believe these arrangements give this task sufficient priority.'

7.62   A second report in 1999 resulted in the following recommendations being made:[49]

1.   publicly advertise Visitor work, so that applicants with wider experience of dealing with people with mental incapacity are able to apply;

2.   improve its monitoring of visits to Public Trustee receivership patients and ensure that visits are made to all patients each year unless, exceptionally, the patient's circumstances do not warrant a visit;

3.   improve its management information on patients to be visited, the required frequency of visits, and actual visits made in order to provide assurance to management that visit requirements for individual patients are being met;

4.   assess whether, for patients removed from the visit list, adequate trigger points exist to keep the position under review so that they are returned promptly to the list where changes in personal circumstances are such that visits should be resumed;

5.   consider whether current arrangements for visiting are the most appropriate, or whether alternative arrangements, perhaps involving local organisations, with appropriate quality controls, or the appointment of additional Visitors would enable more local delivery of visits;

6.   monitor whether Visitors are applying the guidance on repeat visits consistently;

7.   improve and computerise its management information on visits to patients to ensure that visits are concentrated on patients with the

---

[47]   *Looking After the Financial Affairs of People with Mental Incapacity* (NAO, 1994) p 42, para 6.10.

[48]   HC 39, Session 1993–94, para 40.

[49]   *Protecting the Welfare of People with Mental Incapacity* (NAO, 1999) p 3, para 9.

greatest need and investigate the reasons for the wide differences in visiting rates across regions; and

8. ensure that Visitors have up-to-date and adequate briefing on patients' circumstances to ensure that patients receive maximum benefit from visits.

Interim reform

7.63 The PGO has made strenuous efforts to comply with these recommendations. The Visiting programme is now delivered through a network of self-employed, regionally based Visitors. The number has been increased to 17 and recruitment is by open competition according to set criteria concentrating on candidates with social services, welfare and mental health backgrounds followed by a training programme. In its second year of existence the PGO arranged some 7,000 visits compared with 1,800 in the penultimate year of the Public Trust Office. Yet even with this expansion in the number of visits, clients up until 2004–05 had been visited on average only once every 5 years, unless more frequent visits were judged appropriate by the Court, visitor or caseworker.

The visits that did take place were also better targeted under guidelines laid down as to the purpose of the visit. All cases where the PGO acts as receiver of last resort are now visited, new cases are targeted, repeat visits are made where this has previously been recommended and special visits are made where the Court requests this. Urgent visits may also be arranged where annual accounts have been outstanding for some time or fraud is suspected.

Purpose of visits

7.64 Initially the Court and the PGO agreed that the purpose of a visit to a client was to:

- confirm that their affordable needs are being met and where they are not to recommend what expenditure might be considered;
- establish whether or not the client's circumstances reflect financial information supplied by the receiver and to report any discrepancies;
- provide an opportunity for the client to communicate in person with a representative of the office and where appropriate pass on the Client's views;
- advise on the client's views generally and inform case management;
- comment on any issues raised in their briefing.

More recently the following new comprehensive purpose has been defined:

'To provide an independent assessment of the client's circumstances and to help the PGO and the Court decide what further can be done to promote the client's well-being.'

It is significant that in practice the General Visitor has become a valuable source of assistance and encouragement for receivers in their role of addressing the best interests of the patient.

7.65   An internal *Review on the effectiveness of visits carried out by the Lord Chancellor's Visitors* was completed in February 2004 and produced a series of recommendations intended to achieve the following benefits:

1. transparent terms and conditions for the Visitors;
2. agreed standards of performance for Visitors, expressed through a formal agreement with the PGO;
3. a formalised system for monitoring Visitor's performance;
4. a process for obtaining qualitative feedback on the value of visits to customers and for collecting and recording evidence to demonstrate the effectiveness of visits;
5. clear policies and processes for arranging visits, disclosing reports and Visitor's safety;
6. a formal process for reviewing fees.

The way that the Visitors operate at present is likely to shape the Visitors Service under the new jurisdiction save that there will no longer be such emphasis on the financial aspects.

The new regime

Appointment

7.66   For the purpose of the new jurisdiction there will be two panels of Court of Protection Visitors[50] appointed by the Lord Chancellor: a panel of Special Visitors and a panel of General Visitors.[51] They are appointed to carry out visits and produce reports as directed by the Court and the Public Guardian in much the same way as at present although the brief may be wider. There is not seen to be the need for a Legal Visitor under the new regime.

Special Visitors

7.67   A Special Visitor must be a registered medical practitioner (or appear to the Lord Chancellor to have other suitable qualifications or training), and must also appear to the Lord Chancellor to have special knowledge of and experience in cases of impairment of or disturbance in the functioning of the mind or brain.

---

[50] This title will replace 'Lord Chancellor's Visitors'.
[51] Mental Capacity Act 2005, s 61.

General Visitors

7.68 A General Visitor need not have a medical qualification. Visitors may be appointed for such term and subject to such conditions, and may be paid such remuneration and allowances, as the Lord Chancellor may determine. It is assumed that these criteria will be laid down and published and that the appointment of Visitors will be by open competition rather than private invitation.

Powers

7.69 For the purpose of carrying out their functions under the Mental Capacity Act 2005 in relation to a person who lacks capacity, Court of Protection Visitors may, at all reasonable times, examine and take copies of:[52]

(a) any health record;

(b) any record of, or held by, a local authority and compiled in connection with a social services function; and

(c) any record held by a person registered under Part 2 of the Care Standards Act 2000 so far as the record relates to the person who lacks capacity.

A Court of Protection Visitor may also for that purpose interview the person who lacks capacity in private.

7.70 A completely reconstituted Court of Protection will acquire jurisdiction over personal welfare and healthcare decisions affecting mentally incapacitated adults, in addition to the Court's present jurisdiction over their property and financial affairs. Accordingly, the Medical Visitors may be required to report on matters relating to where a patient should live, and whether a decision should be made to withhold or withdraw medical treatment.

THE OFFICIAL SOLICITOR

Status and function

7.71 The Official Solicitor is an officer of the Supreme Court appointed by the Lord Chancellor under s 90 of the Supreme Court Act 1981. His main function is to represent parties to proceedings who are without capacity, deceased or unascertained when no other suitable person or agency is able and willing to do so. The purpose is to prevent a possible denial of justice and safeguard the welfare, property or status of the party. Such proceedings may be in the county court, High Court or Court of Protection. He usually becomes formally involved when

---

[52] Mental Capacity Act 2005, s 61(5)–(6).

appointed by the Court, and he may act as his own solicitor, or instruct a private firm of solicitors to act for him.

Once the Constitutional Reform Act 2005 is brought into effect and the new Supreme Court is created the current Supreme Court will be no longer so called and the title will be changed to 'Official Solicitor to the Senior Courts'.[53]

7.72   The Official Solicitor can be contacted at:

81 Chancery Lane
London WC2A 1DD
DX 141150 London/Chancery Lane WC2
Tel: 020 7911 7127
Fax: 020 7911 7105
E-mail: enquiries@offsol.gsi.gov.uk
Website: www.offsol.demon.co.uk

Background

7.73   The development of the functions of the Official Solicitor's office date back to the eighteenth century. The state has always recognised the need for representation of an incapacitated person when a benevolent relative or friend cannot be found to act on his or her behalf. This function was undertaken on behalf of the Crown as *parens patriae* in various ways. The present office of the Official Solicitor to the Supreme Court of Judicature was created by an Order of the Lord Chancellor on 6 November 1875 under the power given to him by s 84 of the Supreme Court of Judicature Act 1873 to appoint officers to serve the Supreme Court generally. It was not until 1981 that this became a statutory office and was renamed the Official Solicitor to the Supreme Court.

7.74   The distinct office of the Public Trustee was created under the Public Trustee Act 1906. Since then trustee services have become more readily available in the private sector so the Public Trustee has tended to become a trustee of last resort. In the early 1980s the Court of Protection was relocated within the Public Trustee Office which later became known as the Public Trust Office. Subsequently the Public Trustee was given the additional responsibilities of acting as receiver of last resort, performing judicial functions as authorised by the Court of Protection Rules and dealing with the registration of enduring powers of attorney.

7.75   The offices of the Official Solicitor and the Public Trustee were co-located from 1 April 2001 when the trust division of the Public Trust Office was abolished and some of the Official Solicitor's work was

---

[53]   Constitutional Reform Act 2005, Sch 11, para 26.

transferred to CAFCASS.[54] Although both are now housed in one office building they continue to have separate corporate functions and the Public Trustee is not involved in mental capacity issues. Functionally the Official Solicitor is part of the judicial system of England and Wales (that is, excluding Scotland and Northern Ireland), while the Public Trustee is a separate and independent statutory body, and both are appointed by the Lord Chancellor.

The present office

7.76 The office is currently administered as part of the Department for Constitutional Affairs. The Official Solicitor and Public Trustee is Laurence Oates, a barrister, and his deputy is Edward Solomons, a solicitor. There are around 166 staff, of whom 15 are lawyers. The staff are civil servants who specialise in particular areas of the work.[55] About 110 of the staff are caseworkers, all of whom have access to in-house legal advice where appropriate, and some of whom have the conduct of cases under the direct supervision of the lawyers.

In 2004–05 the Official Solicitor took on 425 new civil cases (representing either a child or adult under disability), and over 800 new family cases (mostly representing an adult).

7.77 Both the Official Solicitor and the Public Trustee have such powers and perform such duties as may be conferred on them by statute and by Rules of Court, and, in the case of the Official Solicitor, also at common law.

7.78 The Official Solicitor's role in Court proceedings is recognised by the court Rules,[56] and the Court of Protection Rules 2001 and Practice Directions make specific provision for his involvement.[57] By way of guidance he has issued Practice Notes dealing with medical and welfare decisions for incapacitated adults[58] (including sterilisation[59]) and permanent vegetative state ('PVS') cases.[60]

---

[54] This followed the *Quinquennial review of the Public Trust Office* in 1999.

[55] Part of the work of the Official Solicitor is covered in **Chapter 5**.

[56] See the Civil Procedure Rules 1998, rr 21.4–21.7, and 21PD-002, para 3.6 and the Family Proceedings Rules 1991, r 9.5(1)(a).

[57] Rule 11 allows the Court to request him to make an application, r 13 enables the Court to represent the patient, r 49(2) allows him to act in place of any solicitor when the Court of Protection is dissatisfied and rr 67 or 68 enables the Court to request him to make inquiries and report back.

[58] Practice Note: *Medical and Welfare Decisions for Adults* ([2001] 2 FLR 158 and Practice Note (Family Division: Incapacitated Adults) (2002) *The Times*, January 4).

[59] Practice Note: *Sterilisation Cases* ([2001] 2 FLR 163).

[60] Practice Note: *PVS cases* ([2001] 2 FLR 165).

Vision statement

7.79   The vision statement of the Official Solicitor's office is:

> '... to be an organisation delivering high quality customer focused legal services for vulnerable persons, where those services need to be provided by the public sector ...'

or, in summary, to achieve justice for those who need its services.

Acceptance policy

7.80   The Official Solicitor requires evidence of incapacity (or a judicial determination of incapacity) before he can accept appointment to represent a party to Court proceedings. He operates a 'last resort' acceptance policy, namely that he will only accept appointment when there is no other suitable and willing person who could be appointed. Once appointed as litigation friend (or next friend/guardian ad litem in family proceedings) he will decide whether the solicitor's role is handled in-house or external solicitors are instructed. He operates to a fixed budget and has to consider how his costs in litigation to which he may become a party are to be funded. Depending on the circumstances, this may be out of the patient's own estate, where external solicitors are used their costs may be met through public funding where available, or he can seek an undertaking as to costs, or an order for all or some of his costs, from another party to the litigation.

The incapacity work of the Official Solicitor

Giving advice

7.81   Inquiries are frequently made by the judiciary and members of the legal profession. Other members of the general public are usually encouraged to obtain the advice of their own solicitor, or perhaps consult their local Citizens' Advice Bureau.

Representing adults who lack capacity

7.82   An Order of the Court, directing the Official Solicitor to act as a legal representative in a civil court case for a person under disability, will either be made with his prior consent, or will only take effect if his consent is obtained. The Official Solicitor needs to be satisfied that his involvement in the case will be consistent with the *Vision Statement* of his office, and in appropriate cases he will also require security that his charges and expenses will be met before agreeing to act.

It is desirable that the Official Solicitor be consulted about any proposed application which seeks his involvement in any proceedings before a court in England and Wales. However, he is unable to act as solicitor to individual members of the general public as though he were a solicitor in private practice, nor will he respond to inquiries from individuals who are seeking free legal advice for their own benefit.

Assisting the civil and family courts

7.83 The Official Solicitor may also be called on to give confidential advice to judges, to instruct counsel to appear before a judge to assist the court as advocate to the Court, or to investigate any matter on which the Court needs a special report.[61] A common enquiry requested is to ascertain the mental capacity of a party to proceedings before the Court. A special report may be requested by the Court from the Official Solicitor when the judge feels he needs help to ascertain facts or information relevant to the case which would not otherwise be made available to the Court. It is probably a contempt of court to interfere with an investigation by the Official Solicitor.

Assisting the Court of Protection

7.84 Subject to his consent, the Official Solicitor may be asked to bring an application or represent a patient in any proceedings.[62] He is frequently asked to assist the Court in applications for statutory wills or authority to make gifts or other dispositions. He will usually be appointed to represent the patient because the receiver or attorney has a personal interest in the outcome. This work is undertaken in-house and costs are generally payable from the patient's estate. Where he acts in-house both as litigation friend and solicitor in medical treatment cases current practice is that he may be awarded half his costs from the NHS Trust seeking the Court's decision and his assistance in that process.[63]

Adult Medical and Welfare Declarations

7.85 The Official Solicitor represents mentally disordered adults, and sometimes acts as adviser to the Court, at the hearings of applications concerning, for example, the sterilisation of women suffering from severe learning disabilities, or the withdrawal of life-sustaining treatment (PVS cases). Other applications may be made concerning a wide range of welfare disputes, usually in respect of residence and contact matters, when there is a serious justiciable issue requiring a decision by the Court.

---

[61] Known as a *Harbin v Masterman* inquiry (1896 1 Ch 351).

[62] Court of Protection Rules 2001, rr 11 and 13.

[63] Recently blessed as a proper exercise of a court's discretion by Munby J in *X NHS Trust v J (by her litigation friend the Official Solicitor)* [2005] EWHC 1273 (Fam). See generally CHAPTER 5.

Other jurisdictions

7.86   Although there should be a clear definition of the range of services to be
        provided by the Official Solicitor, there is a diversity of services
        available in the jurisdictions of the UK and Ireland.

Scotland

7.87   There is no equivalent of the Official Solicitor in Scotland and the
        Office of the Public Guardian has no recourse to a professional legal
        service other than in response to its own departmental administrative
        requirements. This is proving to be a significant disadvantage.

Northern Ireland

7.88   The Official Solicitor based in Belfast has two legal officers and a staff
        of eight which includes four caseworkers. She acts as Controller of last
        resort, *amicus* to the Court where required, a general overseer and
        investigator and representative for persons under legal disability[64] in
        civil court proceedings. The workload is heavy and financial resources
        restricted. Costs are sought where feasible but there is no full costs
        recovery because this could obstruct access to justice for those who
        need the services. Proposals include contracting out certain work to an
        accredited panel of solicitors and transferring children work elsewhere
        leaving financial oversight, representation of patients and court
        assistance as core functions.

Ireland

7.89   The equivalent in the Republic of Ireland is the *Office of the General
        Solicitor for Minors and Wards of Court* situated in Dublin. Its origins
        lie in Chancery practice but it was brought within the public service in
        1969. There is no equivalent of the Public Guardian. The General
        Solicitor may assist the High Court to arrange medical examinations,
        act as *guardian ad litem* of a Ward (or a minor) and act as a *Committee
        of the Estate* (or *of the Person*) of last resort. In many ways this latter
        role appears similar to that of a social worker but with a legal or
        administrative bias and legal services may be provided. There is a very
        heavy caseload for the Office but a lack of support from a multi-
        disciplinary team, and although the institutions where Wards were
        placed have now been closed down there are no resources available for
        those now living in the community.

---

64   This includes both patients and children.

The future

7.90   Some fundamental questions must be asked as to the role of the Official Solicitor under the new jurisdiction. Is he to be the patient's representative in all, or only some, of the cases which will go to the Court of Protection? If the latter, what is the dividing line between those cases in which the patient should be represented by the Official Solicitor and those in which other arrangements are acceptable? Is there a clear demarcation between his role and that which the independent mental capacity advocacy service could be expanded to fulfil? When the Official Solicitor does act, should he conduct all the work in-house through his own staff or to what extent can his office send the work out to approved external solicitors? How should his costs of acting be met? It is unclear whether once the Mental Capacity Act 2005 is in force there is a role for a state body to be appointed as deputy of last resort, and, if so, which body that is to be?

7.91   A possible question is who should represent the Public Guardian in Court of Protection proceedings to justify or explain a stance he has taken? It might be appropriate that the Official Solicitor should be instructed as it could be unacceptable for the Public Guardian to become a party as such. However, this could conflict with the need for independent representation of the incapacitated individual. It is not yet known how this potential conflict will be resolved.

Chapter 8

Miscellaneous

ENDURING POWERS – TRANSITIONAL (SCH 4)

8.1   The Mental Capacity Act 2005 ('the 2005 Act') repeals the Enduring Powers of Attorney Act 1985 ('the 1985 Act') so no new enduring powers of attorney ('EPAs') can be created.[1] There remain in place countless numbers of EPAs, some already registered but perhaps the majority unregistered and held in deed boxes and solicitors' offices across the country as 'insurance policies' in case of future incapacity. The registered EPAs cannot be replaced by new lasting powers of attorney ('LPAs') because the donors will invariably lack capacity to grant a new power. Although it may be prudent for those who have already executed an enduring power to replace this with a new lasting power, many simply will not do so and it would be contrary to public policy to require donors – who have in good faith provided for the management of their property and affairs in the event of incapacity – to go to the effort and expense of making new LPAs. The status of these EPAs, registered and unregistered, has therefore been addressed.

8.2   Schedule 4 to the 2005 Act provides for the recognition and operation of EPAs made before the commencement of the Act. Although the 1985 Act is repealed, all EPAs made prior to the commencement of the 2005 Act will remain effective and operate as EPAs. The provisions of Sch 4 replicate the provisions of the 1985 Act. The 2005 Act therefore confirms that an EPA is a power of attorney, which has been executed in the prescribed form and which is not revoked on the onset of incapacity provided it is registered with the Public Guardian.[2] The attorney must, as soon as is practicable, make an application to register the EPA if he or she has reason to believe that the donor is or is

---

[1]   Mental Capacity Act 2005, Sch 7.

[2]   This preserves, for existing EPAs, a 'diagnostic threshold' which has to be attained before the power can be registered and, as a result, a presumption that the donor is incapable of managing his or her property and affairs. Section 1 of the 2005 Act does not therefore apply (Sch 4, para 1(1)).

becoming mentally incapable.[3] The attorney must furthermore notify a prescribed class of relatives before applying to register the LPA.

8.3   EPAs are dealt with in more detail in **CHAPTER 3** and a detailed account of the rules and principles applicable to their operation is beyond the scope of this work.[4] However, practitioners will need to be able to advise on and administer two distinct types of statutory power of attorney and apply different principles and procedures to each one. There will no doubt be endless debate over whether one is better than the other, but the inevitable result will be the complexity of two different jurisdictions applicable to persons in identical circumstances.

TRANSITIONAL PROVISIONS (SCH 5)

8.4   Schedule 5 to the 2005 Act[5] deals with transitional provisions and savings in two Parts. Part 1 covers the repeal of Part VII of the Mental Health Act 1983 (which established the jurisdiction of the present Court of Protection) and Part 2 covers the repeal of the 1985 Act (which established EPAs).

Mental Health Act 1983, Part VII

8.5   A receiver under the former regime is in effect to be converted into a deputy under the new jurisdiction from its commencement but with the same functions as he or she had as receiver. Application may be made to the Court to end the appointment, to make a decision not authorised or for the Court to exercise its powers. Any existing order or appointment, direction or authority will continue to have effect despite the repeal of Part VII.

Any pending application for the exercise of a power under Part VII is to be treated, insofar as a corresponding power is exercisable as an application for the exercise of that power.[6] An appeal which has not been determined will continue to be dealt with under the former regime. All fees and other payments which, having become due, have not been

---

[3]   Mental Capacity Act 2005, Sch 7, Part 2, para 4(1). Part 8 defines 'mentally incapable' in the context of the management of the donor's property and affairs.

[4]   The topic is covered in greater and better detail in *Cretney & Lush on Enduring Powers of Attorney* (Jordans, 5th edn, 2001) which will remain the definitive work on the subject. See also *Heywood & Massey Court of Protection Practice* (Sweet & Maxwell). The same law and procedure will apply to existing EPAs, only different statutory provisions will apply to their operation.

[5]   Section 66(4) of the 2005 Act.

[6]   An application for the appointment of a receiver will be treated as an application for the appointment of a deputy.

paid are to be paid to the new Court of Protection after the commencement day.

8.6   The records of the former Court of Protection will be treated as records of the new Court of Protection and the Public Guardian for the purpose of exercising any of his or her functions will have access thereto. The new Court of Protection Rules may provide that former receivers must continue to render accounts.

Enduring Powers of Attorney Act 1985

8.7   Any order or determination made, or other thing done, under the 1985 Act will continue to have effect under the new jurisdiction from its commencement and insofar as it could have been done under Sch 4[7] will be so treated. Any instrument registered under the 1985 Act is to be treated as having been registered by the Public Guardian under Sch 4.

Any pending application for the exercise of a power under the 1985 Act will be treated, insofar as a corresponding power is exercisable under Sch 4, as an application for the exercise of that power. Special provisions apply to powers given by trustees. An appeal which has not been determined will continue to be dealt with under the former regime.

INTERNATIONAL PROTECTION OF ADULTS (SCH 3)

The Convention on the International Protection of Adults

8.8   The *Hague Convention on Private International Law* seeks to establish international agreements to reduce conflicts of law and to lay down rules to determine jurisdiction and related matters. Under its auspices the *Convention on the International Protection of Adults* was concluded on 13 January 2000. It applies to the protection in international situations of 'adults who, by reason of an impairment or insufficiency of their personal faculties, are not in a position to protect their interests'.[8]

Objects

8.9   The objects of the Convention are set out in Art 1(2):

'(a) to determine the State whose authorities have jurisdiction to take measures directed to the protection of the person or property of the adult;

---

7   See above.
8   For the text of the Convention see www.hcch.net.

(b) to determine which law is applied by such authorities in exercising their jurisdiction;

(c) to determine the law applicable to representation of the adult;

(d) to provide for the recognition and enforcement of such measures of protection in all Contracting States; and

(e) to establish such co-operation between the authorities of the Contracting States as may be necessary to achieve the purposes of the Convention.'

Rationale

8.10   The rationale behind the making of the Convention was that the ageing of the world's population, combined with greater international mobility, has created the need for improved international protection for vulnerable adults through legal regulation and international co-operation. Whilst the law has been reformed relating to the protection of incapable adults in a number of national systems (of which the 2005 Act in England and Wales is the latest example), it was recognised that the issues of protection do not stop at state borders. In particular, the increasing tendency for retired persons to move to warmer countries, leaving the bulk of their property behind, sometimes acquiring a home in the new country and sometimes making advance arrangements for their care or representation in the event of incapacity, made it essential to have clear rules specifying which national authorities are competent to take any necessary protective measures.

Commencement

8.11   The Convention is not yet in force, requiring at least three countries to have ratified or acceded to it before that can happen. So far only the UK has ratified, and that is only in relation to Scotland.[9] By making provision for it in Sch 3 to the 2005 Act[10] the UK will be able to give effect to and ratify the Convention in relation to England and Wales. The provisions of the Schedule are intended to be compatible with Sch 3 to the Adults with Incapacity (Scotland) Act 2000, which gave effect to the Convention there.

The Schedule provides private international law rules to govern jurisdictional issues between Scotland and England and Wales irrespective of whether the Convention is in force.

---

[9]   Instrument of ratification of 1 April 2003.
[10]   See s 63 of and Sch 3 to the 2005 Act.

The legal provisions

Protective measures

8.12   The Schedule adopts the Convention definition of adults with incapacity[11] and applies it to any person who has reached 16. The 'protective measures' within the scope of its provisions are any of the following:[12]

'(a) the determination of incapacity and the institution of a protective regime;

(b)   placing an adult under the protection of an appropriate authority;

(c)   guardianship, curatorship or any corresponding system;

(d)   the designation and functions of a person having charge of an adult's person or property, or representing or otherwise helping him;

(e)   placing an adult in a place where protection can be provided;

(f)   administering, conserving or disposing of an adult's property; or

(g)   authorising a specific intervention for the protection of the person or property of an adult.'

These cover the range of different possible interventions adopted in the laws of the different countries involved in the preparation of the Convention. They include more developed systems of adult guardianship and the powers of Public Guardians and/or Public Trustees; our domestic equivalent to 'curators' are receivers, to be replaced under the 2005 Act by deputies.

Jurisdiction

8.13   Under the Convention the country of habitual residence has the primary right to exercise jurisdiction. As a secondary rule, presence will suffice for urgent and temporary measures, in relation to refugees and displaced persons, and where property is located. The state of nationality may take jurisdiction, but this is subordinate to any measure taken by the state of habitual residence. The state of habitual residence can, with the agreement of the receiving state, transfer jurisdiction to another state connected with the adult.[13]

---

[11]   See **8.3** above.

[12]   Mental Capacity Act 2005, Sch 3, para 5.

[13]   Effect is given to these principles so far as the law of England and Wales is concerned by paras 7–10 of Sch 3.

Applicable law

8.14   The state with jurisdiction will apply its own law but may instead choose to apply the law of another state with which the adult has a connection.

A special rule is created in relation to incapacity planning tools such as our enduring or lasting powers of attorney (which the laws of some states permit but others do not). The maker may alternatively designate the law of the state of which he or she is a national, in which he or she was formerly habitually resident, or in which property of his or hers is located. Article 16 provides that where such powers of representation are not exercised in a manner to guarantee the protection of the person or property of the adult, the country having jurisdiction may take measures withdrawing or modifying those powers, but where it does so it should take into consideration to the extent possible the law chosen by the donor of those powers.

8.15   Accordingly, the court in England and Wales is given the power to apply the law of a country other than England and Wales if it thinks that the matter has a substantial connection with that country. Where a protective measure is to be implemented in another country, the conditions of implementation are governed by the law of that other country. Mandatory provisions of the law of England and Wales are to be taken to apply, irrespective of any system of law which would otherwise apply, and the court is not required to apply any provision of another country's law if that would be manifestly contrary to public policy.[14]

Recognition and enforcement

8.16   Parties to the Convention are required to recognise measures taken under the Convention, subject to specific fairly narrow grounds of refusal. An interested person can require a ruling on whether a particular measure taken in another state is recognised. The requested state is bound by the findings of fact and of the merits taken in the originating state.

8.17   A protective measure is to be recognised in England and Wales if taken under the law of the country of habitual residence, and, in relation to a measure taken under the law of any other country in which the Convention is in force, if that country had jurisdiction under the Convention. The court in England and Wales is entitled to disregard the measure if in a non-urgent case the adult was not given the opportunity to be heard and this amounted to a breach of natural justice; and also if manifestly contrary to public policy, inconsistent with a mandatory

---

[14]   The special rules relating to LPAs and equivalent instruments are in paras 13–16.

provision of our law or inconsistent with a protective measure subsequently taken or recognised here. As required by the Convention, provision is also made that a declaration may be obtained as to whether a protective measure taken under the law of any other country is recognised and enforceable.[15]

Co-operation

8.18 Each contracting state is required to designate a Central Authority to co-operate with each other to achieve the purposes of the Convention, and in England and Wales the functions of the Central Authority are exercisable by the Lord Chancellor.[16] In addition to the duties required of Central Authorities, the Convention places duties on a contracting state's 'competent authorities'. So far as these duties fall to the courts, effect has been given to them by the Schedule as described above.

Specific duties are placed upon public authorities in relation to cross-border placement or adults in danger. A public authority proposing to place an adult in an establishment in a Convention country outside England and Wales must consult an appropriate authority in that other country; and where a public authority is aware that that an adult who is in serious danger and in relation to whom protective measures are in existence or could be taken has become resident in another Convention country, it must notify the appropriate authority in that country of the danger and the measures taken or under consideration.[17]

Certificates

8.19 The authorities of a contracting state where a protective measure has been taken may give a certificate to a person such as a guardian, attorney or other legally authorised representative indicating the capacity that person has and the powers conferred on him or her. That certificate issued by an authority in a Convention country is to be taken, unless the contrary is shown, as proof of the matters contained in it.[18]

Comment

8.20 These provisions will, when in force, cater for cross-border issues which can increasingly occur. Here are two examples:

1. A senior citizen resident in England acquires a second home in, say, Spain. If he becomes incapacitated and a receiver or deputy is appointed here, that representative would have to gain a separate

---

[15] Mental Capacity Act 2005, Sch 3, paras 19–25.
[16] It is unlikely that this will become the Lord Chief Justice pursuant to the Constitutional Reform Act 2005.
[17] Mental Capacity Act 2005, Sch 3, paras 26–29.
[18] Mental Capacity Act 2005, Sch 3, para 30.

authority in Spain before he could dispose of the Spanish property. If the Convention is in force, and Spain has acceded to it, that would not be necessary.

2. A person from, say, British Colombia, has under applicable provincial law made a healthcare representation agreement appointing a healthcare proxy. If that citizen is injured here and unable to consent to medical treatment, under the Convention the Canadian proxy would have the legal authority to give substitute consent.

The provisions are a useful clarification of the private international law rules which are to apply, particularly as between England and Wales and Scotland, even if the Convention is not in force. As yet there is no indication when the requisite three states will ratify it to enable it to come into force.

CONSEQUENTIAL AMENDMENTS AND REPEALS (SCHS 6 AND 7)

8.21 It is inevitable that there is a long list of minor and consequential amendments to earlier legislation and these are to be found in Sch 6 to the 2005 Act. They date from the Fines and Recoveries Act 1833 and include amendments to the following legislation:

Administration of Estates Act 1925Trustee Act 1925

Law of Property Act 1925

National Assistance Act 1948, s 49

Intestates' Estates Act 1952

Variation of Trusts Act 1958

Administration of Justice Act 1960

Compulsory Purchase Act 1965

Industrial and Provident Societies Act 1965

Leasehold Reform Act 1967

Medicines Act 1968

Family Law Reform Act 1969

Local Authority Social Services Act 1970

Local Government Act 1972

Matrimonial Causes Act 1973

Consumer Credit Act 1974

Sale of Goods Act 1979

Limitation Act 1980, s 38

Mental Health Act 1983

Insolvency Act 1986

Public Trustee and Administration of Funds Act 1986

Child Support Act 1991

Social Security Administration Act 1992

Leasehold Reform, Housing and Urban Development Act 1993

Disability Discrimination Act 1995

Trusts of Land and Appointment of Trustees Act 1996

Adoption and Children Act 2002

Licensing Act 2003

8.22 In addition, specific repeals of earlier legislation are to be found in Sch 7 to the 2005 Act. The following wholesale repeals are noteworthy:

Enduring Powers of Attorney Act 1985

Mental Health Act 1983, Part VII

Mental Capacity Act 2005

2005 Chapter 9

PART 1
PERSONS WHO LACK CAPACITY

The principles

1 The principles

(1) The following principles apply for the purposes of this Act.

(2) A person must be assumed to have capacity unless it is established that he lacks capacity.

(3) A person is not to be treated as unable to make a decision unless all practicable steps to help him to do so have been taken without success.

(4) A person is not to be treated as unable to make a decision merely because he makes an unwise decision.

(5) An act done, or decision made, under this Act for or on behalf of a person who lacks capacity must be done, or made, in his best interests.

(6) Before the act is done, or the decision is made, regard must be had to whether the purpose for which it is needed can be as effectively achieved in a way that is less restrictive of the person's rights and freedom of action.

Preliminary

2 People who lack capacity

(1) For the purposes of this Act, a person lacks capacity in relation to a matter if at the material time he is unable to make a decision for himself in relation to the matter because of an impairment of, or a disturbance in the functioning of, the mind or brain.

(2) It does not matter whether the impairment or disturbance is permanent or temporary.

(3) A lack of capacity cannot be established merely by reference to–
    (a)   a person's age or appearance, or
    (b)   a condition of his, or an aspect of his behaviour, which might lead others to make unjustified assumptions about his capacity.

(4) In proceedings under this Act or any other enactment, any question whether a person lacks capacity within the meaning of this Act must be decided on the balance of probabilities.

(5) No power which a person ('D') may exercise under this Act–
    (a)   in relation to a person who lacks capacity, or
    (b)   where D reasonably thinks that a person lacks capacity,

is exercisable in relation to a person under 16.

(6) Subsection (5) is subject to section 18(3).

3 Inability to make decisions

(1) For the purposes of section 2, a person is unable to make a decision for himself if he is unable–

    (a)   to understand the information relevant to the decision,

    (b)   to retain that information,

    (c)   to use or weigh that information as part of the process of making the decision, or

    (d)   to communicate his decision (whether by talking, using sign language or any other means).

(2) A person is not to be regarded as unable to understand the information relevant to a decision if he is able to understand an explanation of it given to him in a way that is appropriate to his circumstances (using simple language, visual aids or any other means).

(3) The fact that a person is able to retain the information relevant to a decision for a short period only does not prevent him from being regarded as able to make the decision.

(4) The information relevant to a decision includes information about the reasonably foreseeable consequences of–

    (a)   deciding one way or another, or

    (b)   failing to make the decision.

4 Best interests

(1) In determining for the purposes of this Act what is in a person's best interests, the person making the determination must not make it merely on the basis of–

    (a)   the person's age or appearance, or

    (b)   a condition of his, or an aspect of his behaviour, which might lead others to make unjustified assumptions about what might be in his best interests.

(2) The person making the determination must consider all the relevant circumstances and, in particular, take the following steps.

(3) He must consider–

    (a)   whether it is likely that the person will at some time have capacity in relation to the matter in question, and

    (b)   if it appears likely that he will, when that is likely to be.

(4) He must, so far as reasonably practicable, permit and encourage the person to participate, or to improve his ability to participate, as fully as possible in any act done for him and any decision affecting him.

(5) Where the determination relates to life-sustaining treatment he must not, in considering whether the treatment is in the best interests of the person concerned, be motivated by a desire to bring about his death.

(6) He must consider, so far as is reasonably ascertainable–

    (a)   the person's past and present wishes and feelings (and, in particular, any relevant written statement made by him when he had capacity),

(b)   the beliefs and values that would be likely to influence his decision if he had capacity, and

(c)   the other factors that he would be likely to consider if he were able to do so.

(7) He must take into account, if it is practicable and appropriate to consult them, the views of–

(a)   anyone named by the person as someone to be consulted on the matter in question or on matters of that kind,

(b)   anyone engaged in caring for the person or interested in his welfare,

(c)   any donee of a lasting power of attorney granted by the person, and

(d)   any deputy appointed for the person by the court,

as to what would be in the person's best interests and, in particular, as to the matters mentioned in subsection (6).

(8) The duties imposed by subsections (1) to (7) also apply in relation to the exercise of any powers which–

(a)   are exercisable under a lasting power of attorney, or

(b)   are exercisable by a person under this Act where he reasonably believes that another person lacks capacity.

(9) In the case of an act done, or a decision made, by a person other than the court, there is sufficient compliance with this section if (having complied with the requirements of subsections (1) to (7)) he reasonably believes that what he does or decides is in the best interests of the person concerned.

(10) 'Life-sustaining treatment' means treatment which in the view of a person providing health care for the person concerned is necessary to sustain life.

(11) 'Relevant circumstances' are those–

(a)   of which the person making the determination is aware, and

(b)   which it would be reasonable to regard as relevant.

5 Acts in connection with care or treatment

(1) If a person ('D') does an act in connection with the care or treatment of another person ('P'), the act is one to which this section applies if–

(a)   before doing the act, D takes reasonable steps to establish whether P lacks capacity in relation to the matter in question, and

(b)   when doing the act, D reasonably believes–

(i)   that P lacks capacity in relation to the matter, and

(ii)   that it will be in P's best interests for the act to be done.

(2) D does not incur any liability in relation to the act that he would not have incurred if P–

(a)   had had capacity to consent in relation to the matter, and

(b)   had consented to D's doing the act.

(3) Nothing in this section excludes a person's civil liability for loss or damage, or his criminal liability, resulting from his negligence in doing the act.

(4) Nothing in this section affects the operation of sections 24 to 26 (advance decisions to refuse treatment).

6 Section 5 acts: limitations

(1) If D does an act that is intended to restrain P, it is not an act to which section 5 applies unless two further conditions are satisfied.

(2) The first condition is that D reasonably believes that it is necessary to do the act in order to prevent harm to P.

(3) The second is that the act is a proportionate response to–
    (a)   the likelihood of P's suffering harm, and
    (b)   the seriousness of that harm.

(4) For the purposes of this section D restrains P if he–
    (a)   uses, or threatens to use, force to secure the doing of an act which P resists, or
    (b)   restricts P's liberty of movement, whether or not P resists.

(5) But D does more than merely restrain P if he deprives P of his liberty within the meaning of Article 5(1) of the Human Rights Convention (whether or not D is a public authority).

(6) Section 5 does not authorise a person to do an act which conflicts with a decision made, within the scope of his authority and in accordance with this Part, by–
    (a)   a donee of a lasting power of attorney granted by P, or
    (b)   a deputy appointed for P by the court.

(7) But nothing in subsection (6) stops a person–
    (a)   providing life-sustaining treatment, or
    (b)   doing any act which he reasonably believes to be necessary to prevent a serious deterioration in P's condition,

while a decision as respects any relevant issue is sought from the court.

7 Payment for necessary goods and services

(1) If necessary goods or services are supplied to a person who lacks capacity to contract for the supply, he must pay a reasonable price for them.

(2) 'Necessary' means suitable to a person's condition in life and to his actual requirements at the time when the goods or services are supplied.

8 Expenditure

(1) If an act to which section 5 applies involves expenditure, it is lawful for D–
    (a)   to pledge P's credit for the purpose of the expenditure, and
    (b)   to apply money in P's possession for meeting the expenditure.

(2) If the expenditure is borne for P by D, it is lawful for D–
    (a)   to reimburse himself out of money in P's possession, or
    (b)   to be otherwise indemnified by P.

(3) Subsections (1) and (2) do not affect any power under which (apart from those subsections) a person–
    (a)   has lawful control of P's money or other property, and
    (b)   has power to spend money for P's benefit.

Lasting powers of attorney

9 Lasting powers of attorney

(1) A lasting power of attorney is a power of attorney under which the donor ('P') confers on the donee (or donees) authority to make decisions about all or any of the following–

    (a)   P's personal welfare or specified matters concerning P's personal welfare, and

    (b)   P's property and affairs or specified matters concerning P's property and affairs,

and which includes authority to make such decisions in circumstances where P no longer has capacity.

(2) A lasting power of attorney is not created unless–

    (a)   section 10 is complied with,

    (b)   an instrument conferring authority of the kind mentioned in subsection (1) is made and registered in accordance with Schedule 1, and

    (c)   at the time when P executes the instrument, P has reached 18 and has capacity to execute it.

(3) An instrument which–

    (a)   purports to create a lasting power of attorney, but

    (b)   does not comply with this section, section 10 or Schedule 1,

confers no authority.

(4) The authority conferred by a lasting power of attorney is subject to–

    (a)   the provisions of this Act and, in particular, sections 1 (the principles) and 4 (best interests), and

    (b)   any conditions or restrictions specified in the instrument.

10 Appointment of donees

(1) A donee of a lasting power of attorney must be–

    (a)   an individual who has reached 18, or

    (b)   if the power relates only to P's property and affairs, either such an individual or a trust corporation.

(2) An individual who is bankrupt may not be appointed as donee of a lasting power of attorney in relation to P's property and affairs.

(3) Subsections (4) to (7) apply in relation to an instrument under which two or more persons are to act as donees of a lasting power of attorney.

(4) The instrument may appoint them to act–

    (a)   jointly,

    (b)   jointly and severally, or

    (c)   jointly in respect of some matters and jointly and severally in respect of others.

(5) To the extent to which it does not specify whether they are to act jointly or jointly and severally, the instrument is to be assumed to appoint them to act jointly.

(6) If they are to act jointly, a failure, as respects one of them, to comply with the requirements of subsection (1) or (2) or Part 1 or 2 of Schedule 1 prevents a lasting power of attorney from being created.

(7) If they are to act jointly and severally, a failure, as respects one of them, to comply with the requirements of subsection (1) or (2) or Part 1 or 2 of Schedule 1–

    (a)   prevents the appointment taking effect in his case, but

    (b)   does not prevent a lasting power of attorney from being created in the case of the other or others.

(8) An instrument used to create a lasting power of attorney–

    (a)   cannot give the donee (or, if more than one, any of them) power to appoint a substitute or successor, but

    (b)   may itself appoint a person to replace the donee (or, if more than one, any of them) on the occurrence of an event mentioned in section 13(6)(a) to (d) which has the effect of terminating the donee's appointment.

11 Lasting powers of attorney: restrictions

(1) A lasting power of attorney does not authorise the donee (or, if more than one, any of them) to do an act that is intended to restrain P, unless three conditions are satisfied.

(2) The first condition is that P lacks, or the donee reasonably believes that P lacks, capacity in relation to the matter in question.

(3) The second is that the donee reasonably believes that it is necessary to do the act in order to prevent harm to P.

(4) The third is that the act is a proportionate response to–

    (a)   the likelihood of P's suffering harm, and

    (b)   the seriousness of that harm.

(5) For the purposes of this section, the donee restrains P if he–

    (a)   uses, or threatens to use, force to secure the doing of an act which P resists, or

    (b)   restricts P's liberty of movement, whether or not P resists,

or if he authorises another person to do any of those things.

(6) But the donee does more than merely restrain P if he deprives P of his liberty within the meaning of Article 5(1) of the Human Rights Convention.

(7) Where a lasting power of attorney authorises the donee (or, if more than one, any of them) to make decisions about P's personal welfare, the authority–

    (a)   does not extend to making such decisions in circumstances other than those where P lacks, or the donee reasonably believes that P lacks, capacity,

    (b)   is subject to sections 24 to 26 (advance decisions to refuse treatment), and

    (c)   extends to giving or refusing consent to the carrying out or continuation of a treatment by a person providing health care for P.

(8) But subsection (7)(c)–

    (a)   does not authorise the giving or refusing of consent to the carrying out or continuation of life-sustaining treatment, unless the instrument contains express provision to that effect, and

    (b)   is subject to any conditions or restrictions in the instrument.

12 Scope of lasting powers of attorney: gifts

(1) Where a lasting power of attorney confers authority to make decisions about P's property and affairs, it does not authorise a donee (or, if more than one, any of them) to dispose of the donor's property by making gifts except to the extent permitted by subsection (2).

(2) The donee may make gifts–
- (a) on customary occasions to persons (including himself) who are related to or connected with the donor, or
- (b) to any charity to whom the donor made or might have been expected to make gifts,

if the value of each such gift is not unreasonable having regard to all the circumstances and, in particular, the size of the donor's estate.

(3) 'Customary occasion' means–
- (a) the occasion or anniversary of a birth, a marriage or the formation of a civil partnership, or
- (b) any other occasion on which presents are customarily given within families or among friends or associates.

(4) Subsection (2) is subject to any conditions or restrictions in the instrument.

13 Revocation of lasting powers of attorney etc.

(1) This section applies if–
- (a) P has executed an instrument with a view to creating a lasting power of attorney, or
- (b) a lasting power of attorney is registered as having been conferred by P,

and in this section references to revoking the power include revoking the instrument.

(2) P may, at any time when he has capacity to do so, revoke the power.

(3) P's bankruptcy revokes the power so far as it relates to P's property and affairs.

(4) But where P is bankrupt merely because an interim bankruptcy restrictions order has effect in respect of him, the power is suspended, so far as it relates to P's property and affairs, for so long as the order has effect.

(5) The occurrence in relation to a donee of an event mentioned in subsection (6)–
- (a) terminates his appointment, and
- (b) except in the cases given in subsection (7), revokes the power.

(6) The events are–
- (a) the disclaimer of the appointment by the donee in accordance with such requirements as may be prescribed for the purposes of this section in regulations made by the Lord Chancellor,
- (b) subject to subsections (8) and (9), the death or bankruptcy of the donee or, if the donee is a trust corporation, its winding-up or dissolution,
- (c) subject to subsection (11), the dissolution or annulment of a marriage or civil partnership between the donor and the donee,
- (d) the lack of capacity of the donee.

(7) The cases are–
- (a) the donee is replaced under the terms of the instrument,

(b)   he is one of two or more persons appointed to act as donees jointly and severally in respect of any matter and, after the event, there is at least one remaining donee.

(8) The bankruptcy of a donee does not terminate his appointment, or revoke the power, in so far as his authority relates to P's personal welfare.

(9) Where the donee is bankrupt merely because an interim bankruptcy restrictions order has effect in respect of him, his appointment and the power are suspended, so far as they relate to P's property and affairs, for so long as the order has effect.

(10) Where the donee is one of two or more appointed to act jointly and severally under the power in respect of any matter, the reference in subsection (9) to the suspension of the power is to its suspension in so far as it relates to that donee.

(11) The dissolution or annulment of a marriage or civil partnership does not terminate the appointment of a donee, or revoke the power, if the instrument provided that it was not to do so.

14 Protection of donee and others if no power created or power revoked

(1) Subsections (2) and (3) apply if–
(a)   an instrument has been registered under Schedule 1 as a lasting power of attorney, but
(b)   a lasting power of attorney was not created,

whether or not the registration has been cancelled at the time of the act or transaction in question.

(2) A donee who acts in purported exercise of the power does not incur any liability (to P or any other person) because of the non-existence of the power unless at the time of acting he–
(a)   knows that a lasting power of attorney was not created, or
(b)   is aware of circumstances which, if a lasting power of attorney had been created, would have terminated his authority to act as a donee.

(3) Any transaction between the donee and another person is, in favour of that person, as valid as if the power had been in existence, unless at the time of the transaction that person has knowledge of a matter referred to in subsection (2).

(4) If the interest of a purchaser depends on whether a transaction between the donee and the other person was valid by virtue of subsection (3), it is conclusively presumed in favour of the purchaser that the transaction was valid if–
(a)   the transaction was completed within 12 months of the date on which the instrument was registered, or
(b)   the other person makes a statutory declaration, before or within 3 months after the completion of the purchase, that he had no reason at the time of the transaction to doubt that the donee had authority to dispose of the property which was the subject of the transaction.

(5) In its application to a lasting power of attorney which relates to matters in addition to P's property and affairs, section 5 of the Powers of Attorney Act 1971 (c 27) (protection where power is revoked) has effect as if references to revocation included the cessation of the power in relation to P's property and affairs.

(6) Where two or more donees are appointed under a lasting power of attorney, this section applies as if references to the donee were to all or any of them.

General powers of the court and appointment of deputies

15 Power to make declarations

(1) The court may make declarations as to–

    (a)   whether a person has or lacks capacity to make a decision specified in the declaration;

    (b)   whether a person has or lacks capacity to make decisions on such matters as are described in the declaration;

    (c)   the lawfulness or otherwise of any act done, or yet to be done, in relation to that person.

(2) 'Act' includes an omission and a course of conduct.

16 Powers to make decisions and appoint deputies: general

(1) This section applies if a person ('P') lacks capacity in relation to a matter or matters concerning–

    (a)   P's personal welfare, or

    (b)   P's property and affairs.

(2) The court may–

    (a)   by making an order, make the decision or decisions on P's behalf in relation to the matter or matters, or

    (b)   appoint a person (a 'deputy') to make decisions on P's behalf in relation to the matter or matters.

(3) The powers of the court under this section are subject to the provisions of this Act and, in particular, to sections 1 (the principles) and 4 (best interests).

(4) When deciding whether it is in P's best interests to appoint a deputy, the court must have regard (in addition to the matters mentioned in section 4) to the principles that–

    (a)   a decision by the court is to be preferred to the appointment of a deputy to make a decision, and

    (b)   the powers conferred on a deputy should be as limited in scope and duration as is reasonably practicable in the circumstances.

(5) The court may make such further orders or give such directions, and confer on a deputy such powers or impose on him such duties, as it thinks necessary or expedient for giving effect to, or otherwise in connection with, an order or appointment made by it under subsection (2).

(6) Without prejudice to section 4, the court may make the order, give the directions or make the appointment on such terms as it considers are in P's best interests, even though no application is before the court for an order, directions or an appointment on those terms.

(7) An order of the court may be varied or discharged by a subsequent order.

(8) The court may, in particular, revoke the appointment of a deputy or vary the powers conferred on him if it is satisfied that the deputy–

(a)   has behaved, or is behaving, in a way that contravenes the authority conferred on him by the court or is not in P's best interests, or

(b)   proposes to behave in a way that would contravene that authority or would not be in P's best interests.

17 Section 16 powers: personal welfare

(1) The powers under section 16 as respects P's personal welfare extend in particular to–

(a)   deciding where P is to live;

(b)   deciding what contact, if any, P is to have with any specified persons;

(c)   making an order prohibiting a named person from having contact with P;

(d)   giving or refusing consent to the carrying out or continuation of a treatment by a person providing health care for P;

(e)   giving a direction that a person responsible for P's health care allow a different person to take over that responsibility.

(2) Subsection (1) is subject to section 20 (restrictions on deputies).

18 Section 16 powers: property and affairs

(1) The powers under section 16 as respects P's property and affairs extend in particular to–

(a)   the control and management of P's property;

(b)   the sale, exchange, charging, gift or other disposition of P's property;

(c)   the acquisition of property in P's name or on P's behalf;

(d)   the carrying on, on P's behalf, of any profession, trade or business;

(e)   the taking of a decision which will have the effect of dissolving a partnership of which P is a member;

(f)   the carrying out of any contract entered into by P;

(g)   the discharge of P's debts and of any of P's obligations, whether legally enforceable or not;

(h)   the settlement of any of P's property, whether for P's benefit or for the benefit of others;

(i)   the execution for P of a will;

(j)   the exercise of any power (including a power to consent) vested in P whether beneficially or as trustee or otherwise;

(k)   the conduct of legal proceedings in P's name or on P's behalf.

(2) No will may be made under subsection (1)(i) at a time when P has not reached 18.

(3) The powers under section 16 as respects any other matter relating to P's property and affairs may be exercised even though P has not reached 16, if the court considers it likely that P will still lack capacity to make decisions in respect of that matter when he reaches 18.

(4) Schedule 2 supplements the provisions of this section.

(5) Section 16(7) (variation and discharge of court orders) is subject to paragraph 6 of Schedule 2.

(6) Subsection (1) is subject to section 20 (restrictions on deputies).

19 Appointment of deputies

(1) A deputy appointed by the court must be–
- (a) an individual who has reached 18, or
- (b) as respects powers in relation to property and affairs, an individual who has reached 18 or a trust corporation.

(2) The court may appoint an individual by appointing the holder for the time being of a specified office or position.

(3) A person may not be appointed as a deputy without his consent.

(4) The court may appoint two or more deputies to act–
- (a) jointly,
- (b) jointly and severally, or
- (c) jointly in respect of some matters and jointly and severally in respect of others.

(5) When appointing a deputy or deputies, the court may at the same time appoint one or more other persons to succeed the existing deputy or those deputies–
- (a) in such circumstances, or on the happening of such events, as may be specified by the court;
- (b) for such period as may be so specified.

(6) A deputy is to be treated as P's agent in relation to anything done or decided by him within the scope of his appointment and in accordance with this Part.

(7) The deputy is entitled–
- (a) to be reimbursed out of P's property for his reasonable expenses in discharging his functions, and
- (b) if the court so directs when appointing him, to remuneration out of P's property for discharging them.

(8) The court may confer on a deputy powers to–
- (a) take possession or control of all or any specified part of P's property;
- (b) exercise all or any specified powers in respect of it, including such powers of investment as the court may determine.

(9) The court may require a deputy–
- (a) to give to the Public Guardian such security as the court thinks fit for the due discharge of his functions, and
- (b) to submit to the Public Guardian such reports at such times or at such intervals as the court may direct.

20 Restrictions on deputies

(1) A deputy does not have power to make a decision on behalf of P in relation to a matter if he knows or has reasonable grounds for believing that P has capacity in relation to the matter.

(2) Nothing in section 16(5) or 17 permits a deputy to be given power–
- (a) to prohibit a named person from having contact with P;
- (b) to direct a person responsible for P's health care to allow a different person to take over that responsibility.

(3) A deputy may not be given powers with respect to–

(a)   the settlement of any of P's property, whether for P's benefit or for the benefit of others,

(b)   the execution for P of a will, or

(c)   the exercise of any power (including a power to consent) vested in P whether beneficially or as trustee or otherwise.

(4) A deputy may not be given power to make a decision on behalf of P which is inconsistent with a decision made, within the scope of his authority and in accordance with this Act, by the donee of a lasting power of attorney granted by P (or, if there is more than one donee, by any of them).

(5) A deputy may not refuse consent to the carrying out or continuation of life-sustaining treatment in relation to P.

(6) The authority conferred on a deputy is subject to the provisions of this Act and, in particular, sections 1 (the principles) and 4 (best interests).

(7) A deputy may not do an act that is intended to restrain P unless four conditions are satisfied.

(8) The first condition is that, in doing the act, the deputy is acting within the scope of an authority expressly conferred on him by the court.

(9) The second is that P lacks, or the deputy reasonably believes that P lacks, capacity in relation to the matter in question.

(10) The third is that the deputy reasonably believes that it is necessary to do the act in order to prevent harm to P.

(11) The fourth is that the act is a proportionate response to–

(a)   the likelihood of P's suffering harm, or

(b)   the seriousness of that harm.

(12) For the purposes of this section, a deputy restrains P if he–

(a)   uses, or threatens to use, force to secure the doing of an act which P resists, or

(b)   restricts P's liberty of movement, whether or not P resists,

or if he authorises another person to do any of those things.

(13) But a deputy does more than merely restrain P if he deprives P of his liberty within the meaning of Article 5(1) of the Human Rights Convention (whether or not the deputy is a public authority).

21 Transfer of proceedings relating to people under 18

The Lord Chancellor may by order make provision as to the transfer of proceedings relating to a person under 18, in such circumstances as are specified in the order–

(a)   from the Court of Protection to a court having jurisdiction under the Children Act 1989 (c 41), or

(b)   from a court having jurisdiction under that Act to the Court of Protection.

Powers of the court in relation to lasting powers of attorney

22 Powers of court in relation to validity of lasting powers of attorney

(1) This section and section 23 apply if–

(a)   a person ('P') has executed or purported to execute an instrument with a view to creating a lasting power of attorney, or

(b)   an instrument has been registered as a lasting power of attorney conferred by P.

(2) The court may determine any question relating to–

(a)   whether one or more of the requirements for the creation of a lasting power of attorney have been met;

(b)   whether the power has been revoked or has otherwise come to an end.

(3) Subsection (4) applies if the court is satisfied–

(a)   that fraud or undue pressure was used to induce P–

      (i)   to execute an instrument for the purpose of creating a lasting power of attorney, or

      (ii)   to create a lasting power of attorney, or

(b)   that the donee (or, if more than one, any of them) of a lasting power of attorney–

      (i)   has behaved, or is behaving, in a way that contravenes his authority or is not in P's best interests, or

      (ii)   proposes to behave in a way that would contravene his authority or would not be in P's best interests.

(4) The court may–

(a)   direct that an instrument purporting to create the lasting power of attorney is not to be registered, or

(b)   if P lacks capacity to do so, revoke the instrument or the lasting power of attorney.

(5) If there is more than one donee, the court may under subsection (4)(b) revoke the instrument or the lasting power of attorney so far as it relates to any of them.

(6) 'Donee' includes an intended donee.

23 Powers of court in relation to operation of lasting powers of attorney

(1) The court may determine any question as to the meaning or effect of a lasting power of attorney or an instrument purporting to create one.

(2) The court may–

(a)   give directions with respect to decisions–

      (i)   which the donee of a lasting power of attorney has authority to make, and

      (ii)   which P lacks capacity to make;

(b)   give any consent or authorisation to act which the donee would have to obtain from P if P had capacity to give it.

(3) The court may, if P lacks capacity to do so–

(a)   give directions to the donee with respect to the rendering by him of reports or accounts and the production of records kept by him for that purpose;

(b)   require the donee to supply information or produce documents or things in his possession as donee;

(c)   give directions with respect to the remuneration or expenses of the donee;

(d)   relieve the donee wholly or partly from any liability which he has or may have incurred on account of a breach of his duties as donee.

(4) The court may authorise the making of gifts which are not within section 12(2) (permitted gifts).

(5) Where two or more donees are appointed under a lasting power of attorney, this section applies as if references to the donee were to all or any of them.

Advance decisions to refuse treatment

24 Advance decisions to refuse treatment: general

(1) 'Advance decision' means a decision made by a person ('P'), after he has reached 18 and when he has capacity to do so, that if–
   (a)   at a later time and in such circumstances as he may specify, a specified treatment is proposed to be carried out or continued by a person providing health care for him, and
   (b)   at that time he lacks capacity to consent to the carrying out or continuation of the treatment,

the specified treatment is not to be carried out or continued.

(2) For the purposes of subsection (1)(a), a decision may be regarded as specifying a treatment or circumstances even though expressed in layman's terms.

(3) P may withdraw or alter an advance decision at any time when he has capacity to do so.

(4) A withdrawal (including a partial withdrawal) need not be in writing.

(5) An alteration of an advance decision need not be in writing (unless section 25(5) applies in relation to the decision resulting from the alteration).

25 Validity and applicability of advance decisions

(1) An advance decision does not affect the liability which a person may incur for carrying out or continuing a treatment in relation to P unless the decision is at the material time–
   (a)   valid, and
   (b)   applicable to the treatment.

(2) An advance decision is not valid if P–
   (a)   has withdrawn the decision at a time when he had capacity to do so,
   (b)   has, under a lasting power of attorney created after the advance decision was made, conferred authority on the donee (or, if more than one, any of them) to give or refuse consent to the treatment to which the advance decision relates, or
   (c)   has done anything else clearly inconsistent with the advance decision remaining his fixed decision.

(3) An advance decision is not applicable to the treatment in question if at the material time P has capacity to give or refuse consent to it.

(4) An advance decision is not applicable to the treatment in question if–
   (a)   that treatment is not the treatment specified in the advance decision,
   (b)   any circumstances specified in the advance decision are absent, or

(c)   there are reasonable grounds for believing that circumstances exist which P did not anticipate at the time of the advance decision and which would have affected his decision had he anticipated them.

(5) An advance decision is not applicable to life-sustaining treatment unless–
(a)   the decision is verified by a statement by P to the effect that it is to apply to that treatment even if life is at risk, and
(b)   the decision and statement comply with subsection (6).

(6) A decision or statement complies with this subsection only if–
(a)   it is in writing,
(b)   it is signed by P or by another person in P's presence and by P's direction,
(c)   the signature is made or acknowledged by P in the presence of a witness, and
(d)   the witness signs it, or acknowledges his signature, in P's presence.

(7) The existence of any lasting power of attorney other than one of a description mentioned in subsection (2)(b) does not prevent the advance decision from being regarded as valid and applicable.

26 Effect of advance decisions

(1) If P has made an advance decision which is–
(a)   valid, and
(b)   applicable to a treatment,

the decision has effect as if he had made it, and had had capacity to make it, at the time when the question arises whether the treatment should be carried out or continued.

(2) A person does not incur liability for carrying out or continuing the treatment unless, at the time, he is satisfied that an advance decision exists which is valid and applicable to the treatment.

(3) A person does not incur liability for the consequences of withholding or withdrawing a treatment from P if, at the time, he reasonably believes that an advance decision exists which is valid and applicable to the treatment.

(4) The court may make a declaration as to whether an advance decision–
(a)   exists;
(b)   is valid;
(c)   is applicable to a treatment.

(5) Nothing in an apparent advance decision stops a person–
(a)   providing life-sustaining treatment, or
(b)   doing any act he reasonably believes to be necessary to prevent a serious deterioration in P's condition,

while a decision as respects any relevant issue is sought from the court.

Excluded decisions

27 Family relationships etc.

(1) Nothing in this Act permits a decision on any of the following matters to be made on behalf of a person–
(a)   consenting to marriage or a civil partnership,
(b)   consenting to have sexual relations,

(c)   consenting to a decree of divorce being granted on the basis of two years' separation,

(d)   consenting to a dissolution order being made in relation to a civil partnership on the basis of two years' separation,

(e)   consenting to a child's being placed for adoption by an adoption agency,

(f)   consenting to the making of an adoption order,

(g)   discharging parental responsibilities in matters not relating to a child's property,

(h)   giving a consent under the Human Fertilisation and Embryology Act 1990 (c 37).

(2) 'Adoption order' means–

(a)   an adoption order within the meaning of the Adoption and Children Act 2002 (c 38) (including a future adoption order), and

(b)   an order under section 84 of that Act (parental responsibility prior to adoption abroad).

28 Mental Health Act matters

(1) Nothing in this Act authorises anyone–

(a)   to give a patient medical treatment for mental disorder, or

(b)   to consent to a patient's being given medical treatment for mental disorder,

if, at the time when it is proposed to treat the patient, his treatment is regulated by Part 4 of the Mental Health Act.

(2) 'Medical treatment', 'mental disorder' and 'patient' have the same meaning as in that Act.

29 Voting rights

(1) Nothing in this Act permits a decision on voting at an election for any public office, or at a referendum, to be made on behalf of a person.

(2) 'Referendum' has the same meaning as in section 101 of the Political Parties, Elections and Referendums Act 2000 (c 41).

Research

30 Research

(1) Intrusive research carried out on, or in relation to, a person who lacks capacity to consent to it is unlawful unless it is carried out–

(a)   as part of a research project which is for the time being approved by the appropriate body for the purposes of this Act in accordance with section 31, and

(b)   in accordance with sections 32 and 33.

(2) Research is intrusive if it is of a kind that would be unlawful if it was carried out–

(a)   on or in relation to a person who had capacity to consent to it, but

(b)   without his consent.

(3) A clinical trial which is subject to the provisions of clinical trials regulations is not to be treated as research for the purposes of this section.

(4) 'Appropriate body', in relation to a research project, means the person, committee or other body specified in regulations made by the appropriate authority as the appropriate body in relation to a project of the kind in question.

(5) 'Clinical trials regulations' means–
- (a) the Medicines for Human Use (Clinical Trials) Regulations 2004 (S.I. 2004/1031) and any other regulations replacing those regulations or amending them, and
- (b) any other regulations relating to clinical trials and designated by the Secretary of State as clinical trials regulations for the purposes of this section.

(6) In this section, section 32 and section 34, 'appropriate authority' means–
- (a) in relation to the carrying out of research in England, the Secretary of State, and
- (b) in relation to the carrying out of research in Wales, the National Assembly for Wales.

31 Requirements for approval

(1) The appropriate body may not approve a research project for the purposes of this Act unless satisfied that the following requirements will be met in relation to research carried out as part of the project on, or in relation to, a person who lacks capacity to consent to taking part in the project ('P').

(2) The research must be connected with–
- (a) an impairing condition affecting P, or
- (b) its treatment.

(3) 'Impairing condition' means a condition which is (or may be) attributable to, or which causes or contributes to (or may cause or contribute to), the impairment of, or disturbance in the functioning of, the mind or brain.

(4) There must be reasonable grounds for believing that research of comparable effectiveness cannot be carried out if the project has to be confined to, or relate only to, persons who have capacity to consent to taking part in it.

(5) The research must–
- (a) have the potential to benefit P without imposing on P a burden that is disproportionate to the potential benefit to P, or
- (b) be intended to provide knowledge of the causes or treatment of, or of the care of persons affected by, the same or a similar condition.

(6) If the research falls within paragraph (b) of subsection (5) but not within paragraph (a), there must be reasonable grounds for believing–
- (a) that the risk to P from taking part in the project is likely to be negligible, and
- (b) that anything done to, or in relation to, P will not–
  - (i) interfere with P's freedom of action or privacy in a significant way, or
  - (ii) be unduly invasive or restrictive.

(7) There must be reasonable arrangements in place for ensuring that the requirements of sections 32 and 33 will be met.

32 Consulting carers etc.

(1) This section applies if a person ('R')–

(a)   is conducting an approved research project, and

(b)   wishes to carry out research, as part of the project, on or in relation to a person ('P') who lacks capacity to consent to taking part in the project.

(2) R must take reasonable steps to identify a person who–

(a)   otherwise than in a professional capacity or for remuneration, is engaged in caring for P or is interested in P's welfare, and

(b)   is prepared to be consulted by R under this section.

(3) If R is unable to identify such a person he must, in accordance with guidance issued by the appropriate authority, nominate a person who–

(a)   is prepared to be consulted by R under this section, but

(b)   has no connection with the project.

(4) R must provide the person identified under subsection (2), or nominated under subsection (3), with information about the project and ask him–

(a)   for advice as to whether P should take part in the project, and

(b)   what, in his opinion, P's wishes and feelings about taking part in the project would be likely to be if P had capacity in relation to the matter.

(5) If, at any time, the person consulted advises R that in his opinion P's wishes and feelings would be likely to lead him to decline to take part in the project (or to wish to withdraw from it) if he had capacity in relation to the matter, R must ensure–

(a)   if P is not already taking part in the project, that he does not take part in it;

(b)   if P is taking part in the project, that he is withdrawn from it.

(6) But subsection (5)(b) does not require treatment that P has been receiving as part of the project to be discontinued if R has reasonable grounds for believing that there would be a significant risk to P's health if it were discontinued.

(7) The fact that a person is the donee of a lasting power of attorney given by P, or is P's deputy, does not prevent him from being the person consulted under this section.

(8) Subsection (9) applies if treatment is being, or is about to be, provided for P as a matter of urgency and R considers that, having regard to the nature of the research and of the particular circumstances of the case–

(a)   it is also necessary to take action for the purposes of the research as a matter of urgency, but

(b)   it is not reasonably practicable to consult under the previous provisions of this section.

(9) R may take the action if–

(a)   he has the agreement of a registered medical practitioner who is not involved in the organisation or conduct of the research project, or

(b)   where it is not reasonably practicable in the time available to obtain that agreement, he acts in accordance with a procedure approved by the appropriate body at the time when the research project was approved under section 31.

(10) But R may not continue to act in reliance on subsection (9) if he has reasonable grounds for believing that it is no longer necessary to take the action as a matter of urgency.

33 Additional safeguards

(1) This section applies in relation to a person who is taking part in an approved research project even though he lacks capacity to consent to taking part.

(2) Nothing may be done to, or in relation to, him in the course of the research–
   (a) to which he appears to object (whether by showing signs of resistance or otherwise) except where what is being done is intended to protect him from harm or to reduce or prevent pain or discomfort, or
   (b) which would be contrary to–
      (i) an advance decision of his which has effect, or
      (ii) any other form of statement made by him and not subsequently withdrawn,

of which R is aware.

(3) The interests of the person must be assumed to outweigh those of science and society.

(4) If he indicates (in any way) that he wishes to be withdrawn from the project he must be withdrawn without delay.

(5) P must be withdrawn from the project, without delay, if at any time the person conducting the research has reasonable grounds for believing that one or more of the requirements set out in section 31(2) to (7) is no longer met in relation to research being carried out on, or in relation to, P.

(6) But neither subsection (4) nor subsection (5) requires treatment that P has been receiving as part of the project to be discontinued if R has reasonable grounds for believing that there would be a significant risk to P's health if it were discontinued.

34 Loss of capacity during research project

(1) This section applies where a person ('P')–
   (a) has consented to take part in a research project begun before the commencement of section 30, but
   (b) before the conclusion of the project, loses capacity to consent to continue to take part in it.

(2) The appropriate authority may by regulations provide that, despite P's loss of capacity, research of a prescribed kind may be carried out on, or in relation to, P if–
   (a) the project satisfies prescribed requirements,
   (b) any information or material relating to P which is used in the research is of a prescribed description and was obtained before P's loss of capacity, and
   (c) the person conducting the project takes in relation to P such steps as may be prescribed for the purpose of protecting him.

(3) The regulations may, in particular,–
   (a) make provision about when, for the purposes of the regulations, a project is to be treated as having begun;
   (b) include provision similar to any made by section 31, 32 or 33.

Independent mental capacity advocate service

35 Appointment of independent mental capacity advocates

(1) The appropriate authority must make such arrangements as it considers reasonable to enable persons ('independent mental capacity advocates') to be available to represent and support persons to whom acts or decisions proposed under sections 37, 38 and 39 relate.

(2) The appropriate authority may make regulations as to the appointment of independent mental capacity advocates.

(3) The regulations may, in particular, provide–
  (a)   that a person may act as an independent mental capacity advocate only in such circumstances, or only subject to such conditions, as may be prescribed;
  (b)   for the appointment of a person as an independent mental capacity advocate to be subject to approval in accordance with the regulations.

(4) In making arrangements under subsection (1), the appropriate authority must have regard to the principle that a person to whom a proposed act or decision relates should, so far as practicable, be represented and supported by a person who is independent of any person who will be responsible for the act or decision.

(5) The arrangements may include provision for payments to be made to, or in relation to, persons carrying out functions in accordance with the arrangements.

(6) For the purpose of enabling him to carry out his functions, an independent mental capacity advocate–
  (a)   may interview in private the person whom he has been instructed to represent, and
  (b)   may, at all reasonable times, examine and take copies of–
    (i)   any health record,
    (ii)   any record of, or held by, a local authority and compiled in connection with a social services function, and
    (iii) any record held by a person registered under Part 2 of the Care Standards Act 2000 (c 14),

which the person holding the record considers may be relevant to the independent mental capacity advocate's investigation.

(7) In this section, section 36 and section 37, 'the appropriate authority' means–
  (a)   in relation to the provision of the services of independent mental capacity advocates in England, the Secretary of State, and
  (b)   in relation to the provision of the services of independent mental capacity advocates in Wales, the National Assembly for Wales.

36 Functions of independent mental capacity advocates

(1) The appropriate authority may make regulations as to the functions of independent mental capacity advocates.

(2) The regulations may, in particular, make provision requiring an advocate to take such steps as may be prescribed for the purpose of–
  (a)   providing support to the person whom he has been instructed to represent ('P') so that P may participate as fully as possible in any relevant decision;

(b)   obtaining and evaluating relevant information;

(c)   ascertaining what P's wishes and feelings would be likely to be, and the beliefs and values that would be likely to influence P, if he had capacity;

(d)   ascertaining what alternative courses of action are available in relation to P;

(e)   obtaining a further medical opinion where treatment is proposed and the advocate thinks that one should be obtained.

(3) The regulations may also make provision as to circumstances in which the advocate may challenge, or provide assistance for the purpose of challenging, any relevant decision.

37 Provision of serious medical treatment by NHS body

(1) This section applies if an NHS body–

(a)   is proposing to provide, or secure the provision of, serious medical treatment for a person ('P') who lacks capacity to consent to the treatment, and

(b)   is satisfied that there is no person, other than one engaged in providing care or treatment for P in a professional capacity or for remuneration, whom it would be appropriate to consult in determining what would be in P's best interests.

(2) But this section does not apply if P's treatment is regulated by Part 4 of the Mental Health Act.

(3) Before the treatment is provided, the NHS body must instruct an independent mental capacity advocate to represent P.

(4) If the treatment needs to be provided as a matter of urgency, it may be provided even though the NHS body has not been able to comply with subsection (3).

(5) The NHS body must, in providing or securing the provision of treatment for P, take into account any information given, or submissions made, by the independent mental capacity advocate.

(6) 'Serious medical treatment' means treatment which involves providing, withholding or withdrawing treatment of a kind prescribed by regulations made by the appropriate authority.

(7) 'NHS body' has such meaning as may be prescribed by regulations made for the purposes of this section by–

(a)   the Secretary of State, in relation to bodies in England, or

(b)   the National Assembly for Wales, in relation to bodies in Wales.

38 Provision of accommodation by NHS body

(1) This section applies if an NHS body proposes to make arrangements–

(a)   for the provision of accommodation in a hospital or care home for a person ('P') who lacks capacity to agree to the arrangements, or

(b)   for a change in P's accommodation to another hospital or care home,

and is satisfied that there is no person, other than one engaged in providing care or treatment for P in a professional capacity or for remuneration, whom it would be appropriate for it to consult in determining what would be in P's best interests.

(2) But this section does not apply if P is accommodated as a result of an obligation imposed on him under the Mental Health Act.

(3) Before making the arrangements, the NHS body must instruct an independent mental capacity advocate to represent P unless it is satisfied that–
  (a)   the accommodation is likely to be provided for a continuous period which is less than the applicable period, or
  (b)   the arrangements need to be made as a matter of urgency.

(4) If the NHS body–
  (a)   did not instruct an independent mental capacity advocate to represent P before making the arrangements because it was satisfied that subsection (3)(a) or (b) applied, but
  (b)   subsequently has reason to believe that the accommodation is likely to be provided for a continuous period–
     (i)   beginning with the day on which accommodation was first provided in accordance with the arrangements, and
     (ii)   ending on or after the expiry of the applicable period,

it must instruct an independent mental capacity advocate to represent P.

(5) The NHS body must, in deciding what arrangements to make for P, take into account any information given, or submissions made, by the independent mental capacity advocate.

(6) 'Care home' has the meaning given in section 3 of the Care Standards Act 2000 (c 14).

(7) 'Hospital' means–
  (a)   a health service hospital as defined by section 128 of the National Health Service Act 1977 (c 49), or
  (b)   an independent hospital as defined by section 2 of the Care Standards Act 2000.

(8) 'NHS body' has such meaning as may be prescribed by regulations made for the purposes of this section by–
  (a)   the Secretary of State, in relation to bodies in England, or
  (b)   the National Assembly for Wales, in relation to bodies in Wales.

(9) 'Applicable period' means–
  (a)   in relation to accommodation in a hospital, 28 days, and
  (b)   in relation to accommodation in a care home, 8 weeks.

39 Provision of accommodation by local authority

(1) This section applies if a local authority propose to make arrangements–
  (a)   for the provision of residential accommodation for a person ('P') who lacks capacity to agree to the arrangements, or
  (b)   for a change in P's residential accommodation,

and are satisfied that there is no person, other than one engaged in providing care or treatment for P in a professional capacity or for remuneration, whom it would be appropriate for them to consult in determining what would be in P's best interests.

(2) But this section applies only if the accommodation is to be provided in accordance with–
  (a)   section 21 or 29 of the National Assistance Act 1948 (c 29), or
  (b)   section 117 of the Mental Health Act,

as the result of a decision taken by the local authority under section 47 of the National Health Service and Community Care Act 1990 (c 19).

(3) This section does not apply if P is accommodated as a result of an obligation imposed on him under the Mental Health Act.

(4) Before making the arrangements, the local authority must instruct an independent mental capacity advocate to represent P unless they are satisfied that–
  (a)   the accommodation is likely to be provided for a continuous period of less than 8 weeks, or
  (b)   the arrangements need to be made as a matter of urgency.

(5) If the local authority–
  (a)   did not instruct an independent mental capacity advocate to represent P before making the arrangements because they were satisfied that subsection (4)(a) or (b) applied, but
  (b)   subsequently have reason to believe that the accommodation is likely to be provided for a continuous period that will end 8 weeks or more after the day on which accommodation was first provided in accordance with the arrangements,

they must instruct an independent mental capacity advocate to represent P.

(6) The local authority must, in deciding what arrangements to make for P, take into account any information given, or submissions made, by the independent mental capacity advocate.

40 Exceptions

Sections 37(3), 38(3) and (4) and 39(4) and (5) do not apply if there is–
  (a)   a person nominated by P (in whatever manner) as a person to be consulted in matters affecting his interests,
  (b)   a donee of a lasting power of attorney created by P,
  (c)   a deputy appointed by the court for P, or
  (d)   a donee of an enduring power of attorney (within the meaning of Schedule 4) created by P.

41 Power to adjust role of independent mental capacity advocate

(1) The appropriate authority may make regulations–
  (a)   expanding the role of independent mental capacity advocates in relation to persons who lack capacity, and
  (b)   adjusting the obligation to make arrangements imposed by section 35.

(2) The regulations may, in particular–
  (a)   prescribe circumstances (different to those set out in sections 37, 38 and 39) in which an independent mental capacity advocate must, or circumstances in which one may, be instructed by a person of a prescribed description to represent a person who lacks capacity, and
  (b)   include provision similar to any made by section 37, 38, 39 or 40.

(3) 'Appropriate authority' has the same meaning as in section 35.

Miscellaneous and supplementary

42 Codes of practice

(1) The Lord Chancellor must prepare and issue one or more codes of practice–
- (a)   for the guidance of persons assessing whether a person has capacity in relation to any matter,
- (b)   for the guidance of persons acting in connection with the care or treatment of another person (see section 5),
- (c)   for the guidance of donees of lasting powers of attorney,
- (d)   for the guidance of deputies appointed by the court,
- (e)   for the guidance of persons carrying out research in reliance on any provision made by or under this Act (and otherwise with respect to sections 30 to 34),
- (f)   for the guidance of independent mental capacity advocates,
- (g)   with respect to the provisions of sections 24 to 26 (advance decisions and apparent advance decisions), and
- (h)   with respect to such other matters concerned with this Act as he thinks fit.

(2) The Lord Chancellor may from time to time revise a code.

(3) The Lord Chancellor may delegate the preparation or revision of the whole or any part of a code so far as he considers expedient.

(4) It is the duty of a person to have regard to any relevant code if he is acting in relation to a person who lacks capacity and is doing so in one or more of the following ways–
- (a)   as the donee of a lasting power of attorney,
- (b)   as a deputy appointed by the court,
- (c)   as a person carrying out research in reliance on any provision made by or under this Act (see sections 30 to 34),
- (d)   as an independent mental capacity advocate,
- (e)   in a professional capacity,
- (f)   for remuneration.

(5) If it appears to a court or tribunal conducting any criminal or civil proceedings that–
- (a)   a provision of a code, or
- (b)   a failure to comply with a code,

is relevant to a question arising in the proceedings, the provision or failure must be taken into account in deciding the question.

(6) A code under subsection (1)(d) may contain separate guidance for deputies appointed by virtue of paragraph 1(2) of Schedule 5 (functions of deputy conferred on receiver appointed under the Mental Health Act).

(7) In this section and in section 43, 'code' means a code prepared or revised under this section.

43 Codes of practice: procedure

(1) Before preparing or revising a code, the Lord Chancellor must consult–
- (a)   the National Assembly for Wales, and
- (b)   such other persons as he considers appropriate.

(2) The Lord Chancellor may not issue a code unless–

    (a)   a draft of the code has been laid by him before both Houses of Parliament, and

    (b)   the 40 day period has elapsed without either House resolving not to approve the draft.

(3) The Lord Chancellor must arrange for any code that he has issued to be published in such a way as he considers appropriate for bringing it to the attention of persons likely to be concerned with its provisions.

(4) '40 day period', in relation to the draft of a proposed code, means–

    (a)   if the draft is laid before one House on a day later than the day on which it is laid before the other House, the period of 40 days beginning with the later of the two days;

    (b)   in any other case, the period of 40 days beginning with the day on which it is laid before each House.

(5) In calculating the period of 40 days, no account is to be taken of any period during which Parliament is dissolved or prorogued or during which both Houses are adjourned for more than 4 days.

44 Ill-treatment or neglect

(1) Subsection (2) applies if a person ('D')–

    (a)   has the care of a person ('P') who lacks, or whom D reasonably believes to lack, capacity,

    (b)   is the donee of a lasting power of attorney, or an enduring power of attorney (within the meaning of Schedule 4), created by P, or

    (c)   is a deputy appointed by the court for P.

(2) D is guilty of an offence if he ill-treats or wilfully neglects P.

(3) A person guilty of an offence under this section is liable–

    (a)   on summary conviction, to imprisonment for a term not exceeding 12 months or a fine not exceeding the statutory maximum or both;

    (b)   on conviction on indictment, to imprisonment for a term not exceeding 5 years or a fine or both.

PART 2
THE COURT OF PROTECTION
AND THE PUBLIC GUARDIAN

The Court of Protection

45 The Court of Protection

(1) There is to be a superior court of record known as the Court of Protection.

(2) The court is to have an official seal.

(3) The court may sit at any place in England and Wales, on any day and at any time.

(4) The court is to have a central office and registry at a place appointed by the Lord Chancellor.

(5) The Lord Chancellor may designate as additional registries of the court any district registry of the High Court and any county court office.

(6) The office of the Supreme Court called the Court of Protection ceases to exist.

46 The judges of the Court of Protection

(1) Subject to Court of Protection Rules under section 51(2)(d), the jurisdiction of the court is exercisable by a judge nominated for that purpose by–
    (a)   the Lord Chancellor, or
    (b)   a person acting on the Lord Chancellor's behalf.

(2) To be nominated, a judge must be–
    (a)   the President of the Family Division,
    (b)   the Vice-Chancellor,
    (c)   a puisne judge of the High Court,
    (d)   a circuit judge, or
    (e)   a district judge.

(3) The Lord Chancellor must–
    (a)   appoint one of the judges nominated by virtue of subsection (2)(a) to (c) to be President of the Court of Protection, and
    (b)   appoint another of those judges to be Vice-President of the Court of Protection.

(4) The Lord Chancellor must appoint one of the judges nominated by virtue of subsection (2)(d) or (e) to be Senior Judge of the Court of Protection, having such administrative functions in relation to the court as the Lord Chancellor may direct.

Supplementary powers

47 General powers and effect of orders etc.

(1) The court has in connection with its jurisdiction the same powers, rights, privileges and authority as the High Court.

(2) Section 204 of the Law of Property Act 1925 (c 20) (orders of High Court conclusive in favour of purchasers) applies in relation to orders and directions of the court as it applies to orders of the High Court.

(3) Office copies of orders made, directions given or other instruments issued by the court and sealed with its official seal are admissible in all legal proceedings as evidence of the originals without any further proof.

48 Interim orders and directions

The court may, pending the determination of an application to it in relation to a person ('P'), make an order or give directions in respect of any matter if–
    (a)   there is reason to believe that P lacks capacity in relation to the matter,
    (b)   the matter is one to which its powers under this Act extend, and
    (c)   it is in P's best interests to make the order, or give the directions, without delay.

49 Power to call for reports

(1) This section applies where, in proceedings brought in respect of a person ('P') under Part 1, the court is considering a question relating to P.

(2) The court may require a report to be made to it by the Public Guardian or by a Court of Protection Visitor.

(3) The court may require a local authority, or an NHS body, to arrange for a report to be made–
    (a)   by one of its officers or employees, or
    (b)   by such other person (other than the Public Guardian or a Court of Protection Visitor) as the authority, or the NHS body, considers appropriate.

(4) The report must deal with such matters relating to P as the court may direct.

(5) Court of Protection Rules may specify matters which, unless the court directs otherwise, must also be dealt with in the report.

(6) The report may be made in writing or orally, as the court may direct.

(7) In complying with a requirement, the Public Guardian or a Court of Protection Visitor may, at all reasonable times, examine and take copies of–
    (a)   any health record,
    (b)   any record of, or held by, a local authority and compiled in connection with a social services function, and
    (c)   any record held by a person registered under Part 2 of the Care Standards Act 2000 (c 14),

so far as the record relates to P.

(8) If the Public Guardian or a Court of Protection Visitor is making a visit in the course of complying with a requirement, he may interview P in private.

(9) If a Court of Protection Visitor who is a Special Visitor is making a visit in the course of complying with a requirement, he may if the court so directs carry out in private a medical, psychiatric or psychological examination of P's capacity and condition.

(10) 'NHS body' has the meaning given in section 148 of the Health and Social Care (Community Health and Standards) Act 2003 (c 43).

(11) 'Requirement' means a requirement imposed under subsection (2) or (3).

Practice and procedure

50 Applications to the Court of Protection

(1) No permission is required for an application to the court for the exercise of any of its powers under this Act–
    (a)   by a person who lacks, or is alleged to lack, capacity,
    (b)   if such a person has not reached 18, by anyone with parental responsibility for him,
    (c)   by the donor or a donee of a lasting power of attorney to which the application relates,
    (d)   by a deputy appointed by the court for a person to whom the application relates, or

(e) by a person named in an existing order of the court, if the application relates to the order.

(2) But, subject to Court of Protection Rules and to paragraph 20(2) of Schedule 3 (declarations relating to private international law), permission is required for any other application to the court.

(3) In deciding whether to grant permission the court must, in particular, have regard to–
- (a) the applicant's connection with the person to whom the application relates,
- (b) the reasons for the application,
- (c) the benefit to the person to whom the application relates of a proposed order or directions, and
- (d) whether the benefit can be achieved in any other way.

(4) 'Parental responsibility' has the same meaning as in the Children Act 1989 (c 41).

51 Court of Protection Rules

(1) The Lord Chancellor may make rules of court (to be called 'Court of Protection Rules') with respect to the practice and procedure of the court.

(2) Court of Protection Rules may, in particular, make provision–
- (a) as to the manner and form in which proceedings are to be commenced;
- (b) as to the persons entitled to be notified of, and be made parties to, the proceedings;
- (c) for the allocation, in such circumstances as may be specified, of any specified description of proceedings to a specified judge or to specified descriptions of judges;
- (d) for the exercise of the jurisdiction of the court, in such circumstances as may be specified, by its officers or other staff;
- (e) for enabling the court to appoint a suitable person (who may, with his consent, be the Official Solicitor) to act in the name of, or on behalf of, or to represent the person to whom the proceedings relate;
- (f) for enabling an application to the court to be disposed of without a hearing;
- (g) for enabling the court to proceed with, or with any part of, a hearing in the absence of the person to whom the proceedings relate;
- (h) for enabling or requiring the proceedings or any part of them to be conducted in private and for enabling the court to determine who is to be admitted when the court sits in private and to exclude specified persons when it sits in public;
- (i) as to what may be received as evidence (whether or not admissible apart from the rules) and the manner in which it is to be presented;
- (j) for the enforcement of orders made and directions given in the proceedings.

(3) Court of Protection Rules may, instead of providing for any matter, refer to provision made or to be made about that matter by directions.

(4) Court of Protection Rules may make different provision for different areas.

52 Practice directions

(1) The President of the Court of Protection may, with the concurrence of the Lord Chancellor, give directions as to the practice and procedure of the court.

(2) Directions as to the practice and procedure of the court may not be given by anyone other than the President of the Court of Protection without the approval of the President of the Court of Protection and the Lord Chancellor.

(3) Nothing in this section prevents the President of the Court of Protection, without the concurrence of the Lord Chancellor, giving directions which contain guidance as to law or making judicial decisions.

53 Rights of appeal

(1) Subject to the provisions of this section, an appeal lies to the Court of Appeal from any decision of the court.

(2) Court of Protection Rules may provide that where a decision of the court is made by–
- (a) a person exercising the jurisdiction of the court by virtue of rules made under section 51(2)(d),
- (b) a district judge, or
- (c) a circuit judge,

an appeal from that decision lies to a prescribed higher judge of the court and not to the Court of Appeal.

(3) For the purposes of this section the higher judges of the court are–
- (a) in relation to a person mentioned in subsection (2)(a), a circuit judge or a district judge;
- (b) in relation to a person mentioned in subsection (2)(b), a circuit judge;
- (c) in relation to any person mentioned in subsection (2), one of the judges nominated by virtue of section 46(2)(a) to (c).

(4) Court of Protection Rules may make provision–
- (a) that, in such cases as may be specified, an appeal from a decision of the court may not be made without permission;
- (b) as to the person or persons entitled to grant permission to appeal;
- (c) as to any requirements to be satisfied before permission is granted;
- (d) that where a higher judge of the court makes a decision on an appeal, no appeal may be made to the Court of Appeal from that decision unless the Court of Appeal considers that–
  - (i) the appeal would raise an important point of principle or practice, or
  - (ii) there is some other compelling reason for the Court of Appeal to hear it;
- (e) as to any considerations to be taken into account in relation to granting or refusing permission to appeal.

Fees and costs

54 Fees

(1) The Lord Chancellor may with the consent of the Treasury by order prescribe fees payable in respect of anything dealt with by the court.

(2) An order under this section may in particular contain provision as to–
- (a) scales or rates of fees;
- (b) exemptions from and reductions in fees;

(c)   remission of fees in whole or in part.

(3) Before making an order under this section, the Lord Chancellor must consult–
    (a)   the President of the Court of Protection,
    (b)   the Vice-President of the Court of Protection, and
    (c)   the Senior Judge of the Court of Protection.

(4) The Lord Chancellor must take such steps as are reasonably practicable to bring information about fees to the attention of persons likely to have to pay them.

(5) Fees payable under this section are recoverable summarily as a civil debt.

55 Costs

(1) Subject to Court of Protection Rules, the costs of and incidental to all proceedings in the court are in its discretion.

(2) The rules may in particular make provision for regulating matters relating to the costs of those proceedings, including prescribing scales of costs to be paid to legal or other representatives.

(3) The court has full power to determine by whom and to what extent the costs are to be paid.

(4) The court may, in any proceedings–
    (a)   disallow, or
    (b)   order the legal or other representatives concerned to meet,

the whole of any wasted costs or such part of them as may be determined in accordance with the rules.

(5) 'Legal or other representative', in relation to a party to proceedings, means any person exercising a right of audience or right to conduct litigation on his behalf.

(6) 'Wasted costs' means any costs incurred by a party–
    (a)   as a result of any improper, unreasonable or negligent act or omission on the part of any legal or other representative or any employee of such a representative, or
    (b)   which, in the light of any such act or omission occurring after they were incurred, the court considers it is unreasonable to expect that party to pay.

56 Fees and costs: supplementary

(1) Court of Protection Rules may make provision–
    (a)   as to the way in which, and funds from which, fees and costs are to be paid;
    (b)   for charging fees and costs upon the estate of the person to whom the proceedings relate;
    (c)   for the payment of fees and costs within a specified time of the death of the person to whom the proceedings relate or the conclusion of the proceedings.

(2) A charge on the estate of a person created by virtue of subsection (1)(b) does not cause any interest of the person in any property to fail or determine or to be prevented from recommencing.

The Public Guardian

57 The Public Guardian

(1) For the purposes of this Act, there is to be an officer, to be known as the Public Guardian.

(2) The Public Guardian is to be appointed by the Lord Chancellor.

(3) There is to be paid to the Public Guardian out of money provided by Parliament such salary as the Lord Chancellor may determine.

(4) The Lord Chancellor may, after consulting the Public Guardian–
  (a)   provide him with such officers and staff, or
  (b)   enter into such contracts with other persons for the provision (by them or their sub-contractors) of officers, staff or services,

as the Lord Chancellor thinks necessary for the proper discharge of the Public Guardian's functions.

(5) Any functions of the Public Guardian may, to the extent authorised by him, be performed by any of his officers.

58 Functions of the Public Guardian

(1) The Public Guardian has the following functions–
  (a)   establishing and maintaining a register of lasting powers of attorney,
  (b)   establishing and maintaining a register of orders appointing deputies,
  (c)   supervising deputies appointed by the court,
  (d)   directing a Court of Protection Visitor to visit–
      (i)   a donee of a lasting power of attorney,
      (ii)   a deputy appointed by the court, or
      (iii) the person granting the power of attorney or for whom the deputy is appointed ('P'),

   and to make a report to the Public Guardian on such matters as he may direct,
  (e)   receiving security which the court requires a person to give for the discharge of his functions,
  (f)   receiving reports from donees of lasting powers of attorney and deputies appointed by the court,
  (g)   reporting to the court on such matters relating to proceedings under this Act as the court requires,
  (h)   dealing with representations (including complaints) about the way in which a donee of a lasting power of attorney or a deputy appointed by the court is exercising his powers,
  (i)   publishing, in any manner the Public Guardian thinks appropriate, any information he thinks appropriate about the discharge of his functions.

(2) The functions conferred by subsection (1)(c) and (h) may be discharged in co-operation with any other person who has functions in relation to the care or treatment of P.

(3) The Lord Chancellor may by regulations make provision–
  (a)   conferring on the Public Guardian other functions in connection with this Act;

(b)   in connection with the discharge by the Public Guardian of his functions.

(4) Regulations made under subsection (3)(b) may in particular make provision as to–
   (a)   the giving of security by deputies appointed by the court and the enforcement and discharge of security so given;
   (b)   the fees which may be charged by the Public Guardian;
   (c)   the way in which, and funds from which, such fees are to be paid;
   (d)   exemptions from and reductions in such fees;
   (e)   remission of such fees in whole or in part;
   (f)   the making of reports to the Public Guardian by deputies appointed by the court and others who are directed by the court to carry out any transaction for a person who lacks capacity.

(5) For the purpose of enabling him to carry out his functions, the Public Guardian may, at all reasonable times, examine and take copies of–
   (a)   any health record,
   (b)   any record of, or held by, a local authority and compiled in connection with a social services function, and
   (c)   any record held by a person registered under Part 2 of the Care Standards Act 2000 (c 14),

so far as the record relates to P.

(6) The Public Guardian may also for that purpose interview P in private.

59 Public Guardian Board

(1) There is to be a body, to be known as the Public Guardian Board.

(2) The Board's duty is to scrutinise and review the way in which the Public Guardian discharges his functions and to make such recommendations to the Lord Chancellor about that matter as it thinks appropriate.

(3) The Lord Chancellor must, in discharging his functions under sections 57 and 58, give due consideration to recommendations made by the Board.

(4) The members of the Board are to be appointed by the Lord Chancellor.

(5) The Board must have–
   (a)   at least one member who is a judge of the court, and
   (b)   at least four members who are persons appearing to the Lord Chancellor to have appropriate knowledge or experience of the work of the Public Guardian.

(6) The Lord Chancellor may by regulations make provision as to–
   (a)   the appointment of members of the Board (and, in particular, the procedures to be followed in connection with appointments);
   (b)   the selection of one of the members to be the chairman;
   (c)   the term of office of the chairman and members;
   (d)   their resignation, suspension or removal;
   (e)   the procedure of the Board (including quorum);
   (f)   the validation of proceedings in the event of a vacancy among the members or a defect in the appointment of a member.

(7) Subject to any provision made in reliance on subsection (6)(c) or (d), a person is to hold and vacate office as a member of the Board in accordance with the terms of the instrument appointing him.

(8) The Lord Chancellor may make such payments to or in respect of members of the Board by way of reimbursement of expenses, allowances and remuneration as he may determine.

(9) The Board must make an annual report to the Lord Chancellor about the discharge of its functions.

60 Annual report

(1) The Public Guardian must make an annual report to the Lord Chancellor about the discharge of his functions.

(2) The Lord Chancellor must, within one month of receiving the report, lay a copy of it before Parliament.

Court of Protection Visitors

61 Court of Protection Visitors

(1) A Court of Protection Visitor is a person who is appointed by the Lord Chancellor to–
    (a)   a panel of Special Visitors, or
    (b)   a panel of General Visitors.

(2) A person is not qualified to be a Special Visitor unless he–
    (a)   is a registered medical practitioner or appears to the Lord Chancellor to have other suitable qualifications or training, and
    (b)   appears to the Lord Chancellor to have special knowledge of and experience in cases of impairment of or disturbance in the functioning of the mind or brain.

(3) A General Visitor need not have a medical qualification.

(4) A Court of Protection Visitor–
    (a)   may be appointed for such term and subject to such conditions, and
    (b)   may be paid such remuneration and allowances,

as the Lord Chancellor may determine.

(5) For the purpose of carrying out his functions under this Act in relation to a person who lacks capacity ('P'), a Court of Protection Visitor may, at all reasonable times, examine and take copies of–
    (a)   any health record,
    (b)   any record of, or held by, a local authority and compiled in connection with a social services function, and
    (c)   any record held by a person registered under Part 2 of the Care Standards Act 2000 (c 14),

so far as the record relates to P.

(6) A Court of Protection Visitor may also for that purpose interview P in private.

PART 3
MISCELLANEOUS AND GENERAL

Declaratory provision

62 Scope of the Act

For the avoidance of doubt, it is hereby declared that nothing in this Act is to be taken to affect the law relating to murder or manslaughter or the operation of section 2 of the Suicide Act 1961 (c 60) (assisting suicide).

Private international law

63 International protection of adults

Schedule 3–
    (a)   gives effect in England and Wales to the Convention on the International Protection of Adults signed at the Hague on 13th January 2000 (Cm. 5881) (in so far as this Act does not otherwise do so), and
    (b)   makes related provision as to the private international law of England and Wales.

General

64 Interpretation

(1) In this Act–
    'the 1985 Act' means the Enduring Powers of Attorney Act 1985 (c 29),
    'advance decision' has the meaning given in section 24(1),
    'the court' means the Court of Protection established by section 45,
    'Court of Protection Rules' has the meaning given in section 51(1),
    'Court of Protection Visitor' has the meaning given in section 61,
    'deputy' has the meaning given in section 16(2)(b),
    'enactment' includes a provision of subordinate legislation (within the meaning of the Interpretation Act 1978 (c 30)),
    'health record' has the meaning given in section 68 of the Data Protection Act 1998 (c 29) (as read with section 69 of that Act),
    'the Human Rights Convention' has the same meaning as 'the Convention' in the Human Rights Act 1998 (c 42),
    'independent mental capacity advocate' has the meaning given in section 35(1),
    'lasting power of attorney' has the meaning given in section 9,
    'life-sustaining treatment' has the meaning given in section 4(10),
    'local authority' means–
        (a)   the council of a county in England in which there are no district councils,
        (b)   the council of a district in England,
        (c)   the council of a county or county borough in Wales,
        (d)   the council of a London borough,
        (e)   the Common Council of the City of London, or
        (f)   the Council of the Isles of Scilly,
    'Mental Health Act' means the Mental Health Act 1983 (c 20),

'prescribed', in relation to regulations made under this Act, means prescribed by those regulations,

'property' includes any thing in action and any interest in real or personal property,

'public authority' has the same meaning as in the Human Rights Act 1998,

'Public Guardian' has the meaning given in section 57,

'purchaser' and 'purchase' have the meaning given in section 205(1) of the Law of Property Act 1925 (c 20),

'social services function' has the meaning given in section 1A of the Local Authority Social Services Act 1970 (c 42),

'treatment' includes a diagnostic or other procedure,

'trust corporation' has the meaning given in section 68(1) of the Trustee Act 1925 (c 19), and

'will' includes codicil.

(2) In this Act, references to making decisions, in relation to a donee of a lasting power of attorney or a deputy appointed by the court, include, where appropriate, acting on decisions made.

(3) In this Act, references to the bankruptcy of an individual include a case where a bankruptcy restrictions order under the Insolvency Act 1986 (c 45) has effect in respect of him.

(4) 'Bankruptcy restrictions order' includes an interim bankruptcy restrictions order.

65 Rules, regulations and orders

(1) Any power to make rules, regulations or orders under this Act–
  (a) is exercisable by statutory instrument;
  (b) includes power to make supplementary, incidental, consequential, transitional or saving provision;
  (c) includes power to make different provision for different cases.

(2) Any statutory instrument containing rules, regulations or orders made by the Lord Chancellor or the Secretary of State under this Act, other than–
  (a) regulations under section 34 (loss of capacity during research project),
  (b) regulations under section 41 (adjusting role of independent mental capacity advocacy service),
  (c) regulations under paragraph 32(1)(b) of Schedule 3 (private international law relating to the protection of adults),
  (d) an order of the kind mentioned in section 67(6) (consequential amendments of primary legislation), or
  (e) an order under section 68 (commencement),

is subject to annulment in pursuance of a resolution of either House of Parliament.

(3) A statutory instrument containing an Order in Council under paragraph 31 of Schedule 3 (provision to give further effect to Hague Convention) is subject to annulment in pursuance of a resolution of either House of Parliament.

(4) A statutory instrument containing regulations made by the Secretary of State under section 34 or 41 or by the Lord Chancellor under paragraph 32(1)(b) of Schedule 3 may not be made unless a draft has been laid before and approved by resolution of each House of Parliament.

66 Existing receivers and enduring powers of attorney etc.

(1) The following provisions cease to have effect–
    (a)   Part 7 of the Mental Health Act,
    (b)   the Enduring Powers of Attorney Act 1985 (c 29).

(2) No enduring power of attorney within the meaning of the 1985 Act is to be created after the commencement of subsection (1)(b).

(3) Schedule 4 has effect in place of the 1985 Act in relation to any enduring power of attorney created before the commencement of subsection (1)(b).

(4) Schedule 5 contains transitional provisions and savings in relation to Part 7 of the Mental Health Act and the 1985 Act.

67 Minor and consequential amendments and repeals

(1) Schedule 6 contains minor and consequential amendments.

(2) Schedule 7 contains repeals.

(3) The Lord Chancellor may by order make supplementary, incidental, consequential, transitional or saving provision for the purposes of, in consequence of, or for giving full effect to a provision of this Act.

(4) An order under subsection (3) may, in particular–
    (a)   provide for a provision of this Act which comes into force before another provision of this Act has come into force to have effect, until the other provision has come into force, with specified modifications;
    (b)   amend, repeal or revoke an enactment, other than one contained in an Act or Measure passed in a Session after the one in which this Act is passed.

(5) The amendments that may be made under subsection (4)(b) are in addition to those made by or under any other provision of this Act.

(6) An order under subsection (3) which amends or repeals a provision of an Act or Measure may not be made unless a draft has been laid before and approved by resolution of each House of Parliament.

68 Commencement and extent

(1) This Act, other than sections 30 to 41, comes into force in accordance with provision made by order by the Lord Chancellor.

(2) Sections 30 to 41 come into force in accordance with provision made by order by–
    (a)   the Secretary of State, in relation to England, and
    (b)   the National Assembly for Wales, in relation to Wales.

(3) An order under this section may appoint different days for different provisions and different purposes.

(4) Subject to subsections (5) and (6), this Act extends to England and Wales only.

(5) The following provisions extend to the United Kingdom–
    (a)   paragraph 16(1) of Schedule 1 (evidence of instruments and of registration of lasting powers of attorney),
    (b)   paragraph 15(3) of Schedule 4 (evidence of instruments and of registration of enduring powers of attorney).

(6) Subject to any provision made in Schedule 6, the amendments and repeals made by Schedules 6 and 7 have the same extent as the enactments to which they relate.

69 Short title

This Act may be cited as the Mental Capacity Act 2005.

SCHEDULE 1
LASTING POWERS OF ATTORNEY: FORMALITIES

Section 9

PART 1
MAKING INSTRUMENTS

General requirements as to making instruments

1 (1) An instrument is not made in accordance with this Schedule unless–
    (a)   it is in the prescribed form,
    (b)   it complies with paragraph 2, and
    (c)   any prescribed requirements in connection with its execution are satisfied.

(2) Regulations may make different provision according to whether–
    (a)   the instrument relates to personal welfare or to property and affairs (or to both);
    (b)   only one or more than one donee is to be appointed (and if more than one, whether jointly or jointly and severally).

(3) In this Schedule–
    (a)   'prescribed' means prescribed by regulations, and
    (b)   'regulations' means regulations made for the purposes of this Schedule by the Lord Chancellor.

Requirements as to content of instruments

2 (1) The instrument must include–
    (a)   the prescribed information about the purpose of the instrument and the effect of a lasting power of attorney,
    (b)   a statement by the donor to the effect that he–
        (i)   has read the prescribed information or a prescribed part of it (or has had it read to him), and
        (ii)   intends the authority conferred under the instrument to include authority to make decisions on his behalf in circumstances where he no longer has capacity,
    (c)   a statement by the donor–
        (i)   naming a person or persons whom the donor wishes to be notified of any application for the registration of the instrument, or

(ii)   stating that there are no persons whom he wishes to be notified of any such application,

(d)   a statement by the donee (or, if more than one, each of them) to the effect that he–

     (i)   has read the prescribed information or a prescribed part of it (or has had it read to him), and

     (ii)   understands the duties imposed on a donee of a lasting power of attorney under sections 1 (the principles) and 4 (best interests), and

(e)   a certificate by a person of a prescribed description that, in his opinion, at the time when the donor executes the instrument–

     (i)   the donor understands the purpose of the instrument and the scope of the authority conferred under it,

     (ii)   no fraud or undue pressure is being used to induce the donor to create a lasting power of attorney, and

     (iii)   there is nothing else which would prevent a lasting power of attorney from being created by the instrument.

(2) Regulations may–

(a)   prescribe a maximum number of named persons;

(b)   provide that, where the instrument includes a statement under sub-paragraph (1)(c)(ii), two persons of a prescribed description must each give a certificate under sub-paragraph (1)(e).

(3) The persons who may be named persons do not include a person who is appointed as donee under the instrument.

(4) In this Schedule, 'named person' means a person named under sub-paragraph (1)(c).

(5) A certificate under sub-paragraph (1)(e)–

(a)   must be made in the prescribed form, and

(b)   must include any prescribed information.

(6) The certificate may not be given by a person appointed as donee under the instrument.

Failure to comply with prescribed form

3 (1) If an instrument differs in an immaterial respect in form or mode of expression from the prescribed form, it is to be treated by the Public Guardian as sufficient in point of form and expression.

(2) The court may declare that an instrument which is not in the prescribed form is to be treated as if it were, if it is satisfied that the persons executing the instrument intended it to create a lasting power of attorney.

PART 2
REGISTRATION

Applications and procedure for registration

4 (1) An application to the Public Guardian for the registration of an instrument intended to create a lasting power of attorney–

(a)   must be made in the prescribed form, and

(b)   must include any prescribed information.

(2) The application may be made–

(a)   by the donor,

(b)   by the donee or donees, or

(c)   if the instrument appoints two or more donees to act jointly and severally in respect of any matter, by any of the donees.

(3) The application must be accompanied by–

(a)   the instrument, and

(b)   any fee provided for under section 58(4)(b).

(4) A person who, in an application for registration, makes a statement which he knows to be false in a material particular is guilty of an offence and is liable–

(a)   on summary conviction, to imprisonment for a term not exceeding 12 months or a fine not exceeding the statutory maximum or both;

(b)   on conviction on indictment, to imprisonment for a term not exceeding 2 years or a fine or both.

5 Subject to paragraphs 11 to 14, the Public Guardian must register the instrument as a lasting power of attorney at the end of the prescribed period.

Notification requirements

6 (1) A donor about to make an application under paragraph 4(2)(a) must notify any named persons that he is about to do so.

(2) The donee (or donees) about to make an application under paragraph 4(2)(b) or (c) must notify any named persons that he is (or they are) about to do so.

7 As soon as is practicable after receiving an application by the donor under paragraph 4(2)(a), the Public Guardian must notify the donee (or donees) that the application has been received.

8 (1) As soon as is practicable after receiving an application by a donee (or donees) under paragraph 4(2)(b), the Public Guardian must notify the donor that the application has been received.

(2) As soon as is practicable after receiving an application by a donee under paragraph 4(2)(c), the Public Guardian must notify–

(a)   the donor, and

(b)   the donee or donees who did not join in making the application,

that the application has been received.

9 (1) A notice under paragraph 6 must be made in the prescribed form.

(2) A notice under paragraph 6, 7 or 8 must include such information, if any, as may be prescribed.

Power to dispense with notification requirements

10 The court may–

(a)   on the application of the donor, dispense with the requirement to notify under paragraph 6(1), or

(b)   on the application of the donee or donees concerned, dispense with the requirement to notify under paragraph 6(2),

if satisfied that no useful purpose would be served by giving the notice.

Instrument not made properly or containing ineffective provision

11 (1) If it appears to the Public Guardian that an instrument accompanying an application under paragraph 4 is not made in accordance with this Schedule, he must not register the instrument unless the court directs him to do so.

(2) Sub-paragraph (3) applies if it appears to the Public Guardian that the instrument contains a provision which–
    (a)   would be ineffective as part of a lasting power of attorney, or
    (b)   would prevent the instrument from operating as a valid lasting power of attorney.

(3) The Public Guardian–
    (a) must apply to the court for it to determine the matter under section 23(1), and
    (b) pending the determination by the court, must not register the instrument.

(4) Sub-paragraph (5) applies if the court determines under section 23(1) (whether or not on an application by the Public Guardian) that the instrument contains a provision which–
    (a)   would be ineffective as part of a lasting power of attorney, or
    (b)   would prevent the instrument from operating as a valid lasting power of attorney.

(5) The court must–
    (a)   notify the Public Guardian that it has severed the provision, or
    (b)   direct him not to register the instrument.

(6) Where the court notifies the Public Guardian that it has severed a provision, he must register the instrument with a note to that effect attached to it.

Deputy already appointed

12 (1) Sub-paragraph (2) applies if it appears to the Public Guardian that–
    (a)   there is a deputy appointed by the court for the donor, and
    (b)   the powers conferred on the deputy would, if the instrument were registered, to any extent conflict with the powers conferred on the attorney.

(2) The Public Guardian must not register the instrument unless the court directs him to do so.

Objection by donee or named person

13 (1) Sub-paragraph (2) applies if a donee or a named person–
    (a)   receives a notice under paragraph 6, 7 or 8 of an application for the registration of an instrument, and
    (b)   before the end of the prescribed period, gives notice to the Public Guardian of an objection to the registration on the ground that an event mentioned in section 13(3) or (6)(a) to (d) has occurred which has revoked the instrument.

(2) If the Public Guardian is satisfied that the ground for making the objection is established, he must not register the instrument unless the court, on the application of the person applying for the registration—

    (a)   is satisfied that the ground is not established, and

    (b)   directs the Public Guardian to register the instrument.

(3) Sub-paragraph (4) applies if a donee or a named person—

    (a)   receives a notice under paragraph 6, 7 or 8 of an application for the registration of an instrument, and

    (b)   before the end of the prescribed period—

        (i)   makes an application to the court objecting to the registration on a prescribed ground, and

        (ii)   notifies the Public Guardian of the application.

(4) The Public Guardian must not register the instrument unless the court directs him to do so.

Objection by donor

14 (1) This paragraph applies if the donor—

    (a)   receives a notice under paragraph 8 of an application for the registration of an instrument, and

    (b)   before the end of the prescribed period, gives notice to the Public Guardian of an objection to the registration.

(2) The Public Guardian must not register the instrument unless the court, on the application of the donee or, if more than one, any of them—

    (a)   is satisfied that the donor lacks capacity to object to the registration, and

    (b)   directs the Public Guardian to register the instrument.

Notification of registration

15 Where an instrument is registered under this Schedule, the Public Guardian must give notice of the fact in the prescribed form to—

    (a)   the donor, and

    (b)   the donee or, if more than one, each of them.

Evidence of registration

16 (1) A document purporting to be an office copy of an instrument registered under this Schedule is, in any part of the United Kingdom, evidence of—

    (a)   the contents of the instrument, and

    (b)   the fact that it has been registered.

(2) Sub-paragraph (1) is without prejudice to—

    (a)   section 3 of the Powers of Attorney Act 1971 (c 27) (proof by certified copy), and

    (b)   any other method of proof authorised by law.

PART 3
CANCELLATION OF REGISTRATION AND NOTIFICATION OF SEVERANCE

17 (1) The Public Guardian must cancel the registration of an instrument as a lasting power of attorney on being satisfied that the power has been revoked–
- (a) as a result of the donor's bankruptcy, or
- (b) on the occurrence of an event mentioned in section 13(6)(a) to (d).

(2) If the Public Guardian cancels the registration of an instrument he must notify–
- (a) the donor, and
- (b) the donee or, if more than one, each of them.

18 The court must direct the Public Guardian to cancel the registration of an instrument as a lasting power of attorney if it–
- (a) determines under section 22(2)(a) that a requirement for creating the power was not met,
- (b) determines under section 22(2)(b) that the power has been revoked or has otherwise come to an end, or
- (c) revokes the power under section 22(4)(b) (fraud etc.).

19 (1) Sub-paragraph (2) applies if the court determines under section 23(1) that a lasting power of attorney contains a provision which–
- (a) is ineffective as part of a lasting power of attorney, or
- (b) prevents the instrument from operating as a valid lasting power of attorney.

(2) The court must–
- (a) notify the Public Guardian that it has severed the provision, or
- (b) direct him to cancel the registration of the instrument as a lasting power of attorney.

20 On the cancellation of the registration of an instrument, the instrument and any office copies of it must be delivered up to the Public Guardian to be cancelled.

PART 4
RECORDS OF ALTERATIONS IN REGISTERED POWERS

Partial revocation or suspension of power as a result of bankruptcy

21 If in the case of a registered instrument it appears to the Public Guardian that under section 13 a lasting power of attorney is revoked, or suspended, in relation to the donor's property and affairs (but not in relation to other matters), the Public Guardian must attach to the instrument a note to that effect.

Termination of appointment of donee which does not revoke power

22 If in the case of a registered instrument it appears to the Public Guardian that an event has occurred–
- (a) which has terminated the appointment of the donee, but
- (b) which has not revoked the instrument,

the Public Guardian must attach to the instrument a note to that effect.

Replacement of donee

23 If in the case of a registered instrument it appears to the Public Guardian that the donee has been replaced under the terms of the instrument the Public Guardian must attach to the instrument a note to that effect.

Severance of ineffective provisions

24 If in the case of a registered instrument the court notifies the Public Guardian under paragraph 19(2)(a) that it has severed a provision of the instrument, the Public Guardian must attach to it a note to that effect.

Notification of alterations

25 If the Public Guardian attaches a note to an instrument under paragraph 21, 22, 23 or 24 he must give notice of the note to the donee or donees of the power (or, as the case may be, to the other donee or donees of the power).

SCHEDULE 2
PROPERTY AND AFFAIRS: SUPPLEMENTARY PROVISIONS

Section 18(4)

Wills: general

1 Paragraphs 2 to 4 apply in relation to the execution of a will, by virtue of section 18, on behalf of P.

Provision that may be made in will

2 The will may make any provision (whether by disposing of property or exercising a power or otherwise) which could be made by a will executed by P if he had capacity to make it.

Wills: requirements relating to execution

3 (1) Sub-paragraph (2) applies if under section 16 the court makes an order or gives directions requiring or authorising a person ('the authorised person') to execute a will on behalf of P.

(2) Any will executed in pursuance of the order or direction–
    (a)   must state that it is signed by P acting by the authorised person,
    (b)   must be signed by the authorised person with the name of P and his own name, in the presence of two or more witnesses present at the same time,
    (c)   must be attested and subscribed by those witnesses in the presence of the authorised person, and
    (d)   must be sealed with the official seal of the court.

Wills: effect of execution

4 (1) This paragraph applies where a will is executed in accordance with paragraph 3.

(2) The Wills Act 1837 (c 26) has effect in relation to the will as if it were signed by P by his own hand, except that–

    (a)   section 9 of the 1837 Act (requirements as to signing and attestation) does not apply, and

    (b)   in the subsequent provisions of the 1837 Act any reference to execution in the manner required by the previous provisions is to be read as a reference to execution in accordance with paragraph 3.

(3) The will has the same effect for all purposes as if–

    (a)   P had had the capacity to make a valid will, and

    (b)   the will had been executed by him in the manner required by the 1837 Act.

(4) But sub-paragraph (3) does not have effect in relation to the will–

    (a)   in so far as it disposes of immovable property outside England and Wales, or

    (b)   in so far as it relates to any other property or matter if, when the will is executed–

        (i)   P is domiciled outside England and Wales, and

        (ii)   the condition in sub-paragraph (5) is met.

(5) The condition is that, under the law of P's domicile, any question of his testamentary capacity would fall to be determined in accordance with the law of a place outside England and Wales.

Vesting orders ancillary to settlement etc.

5 (1) If provision is made by virtue of section 18 for–

    (a)   the settlement of any property of P, or

    (b)   the exercise of a power vested in him of appointing trustees or retiring from a trust,

the court may also make as respects the property settled or the trust property such consequential vesting or other orders as the case may require.

(2) The power under sub-paragraph (1) includes, in the case of the exercise of such a power, any order which could have been made in such a case under Part 4 of the Trustee Act 1925 (c 19).

Variation of settlements

6 (1) If a settlement has been made by virtue of section 18, the court may by order vary or revoke the settlement if–

    (a)   the settlement makes provision for its variation or revocation,

    (b)   the court is satisfied that a material fact was not disclosed when the settlement was made, or

    (c)   the court is satisfied that there has been a substantial change of circumstances.

(2) Any such order may give such consequential directions as the court thinks fit.

Vesting of stock in curator appointed outside England and Wales

7 (1) Sub-paragraph (2) applies if the court is satisfied–

(a) that under the law prevailing in a place outside England and Wales a person ('M') has been appointed to exercise powers in respect of the property or affairs of P on the ground (however formulated) that P lacks capacity to make decisions with respect to the management and administration of his property and affairs, and

(b) that, having regard to the nature of the appointment and to the circumstances of the case, it is expedient that the court should exercise its powers under this paragraph.

(2) The court may direct–

(a) any stocks standing in the name of P, or

(b) the right to receive dividends from the stocks,

to be transferred into M's name or otherwise dealt with as required by M, and may give such directions as the court thinks fit for dealing with accrued dividends from the stocks.

(3) 'Stocks' includes–

(a) shares, and

(b) any funds, annuity or security transferable in the books kept by any body corporate or unincorporated company or society or by an instrument of transfer either alone or accompanied by other formalities,

and 'dividends' is to be construed accordingly.

Preservation of interests in property disposed of on behalf of person lacking capacity

8 (1) Sub-paragraphs (2) and (3) apply if–

(a) P's property has been disposed of by virtue of section 18,

(b) under P's will or intestacy, or by a gift perfected or nomination taking effect on his death, any other person would have taken an interest in the property but for the disposal, and

(c) on P's death, any property belonging to P's estate represents the property disposed of.

(2) The person takes the same interest, if and so far as circumstances allow, in the property representing the property disposed of.

(3) If the property disposed of was real property, any property representing it is to be treated, so long as it remains part of P's estate, as if it were real property.

(4) The court may direct that, on a disposal of P's property–

(a) which is made by virtue of section 18, and

(b) which would apart from this paragraph result in the conversion of personal property into real property,

property representing the property disposed of is to be treated, so long as it remains P's property or forms part of P's estate, as if it were personal property.

(5) References in sub-paragraphs (1) to (4) to the disposal of property are to–

(a) the sale, exchange, charging of or other dealing (otherwise than by will) with property other than money;

(b) the removal of property from one place to another;

(c) the application of money in acquiring property;

(d)   the transfer of money from one account to another;

and references to property representing property disposed of are to be construed accordingly and as including the result of successive disposals.

(6) The court may give such directions as appear to it necessary or expedient for the purpose of facilitating the operation of sub-paragraphs (1) to (3), including the carrying of money to a separate account and the transfer of property other than money.

9 (1) Sub-paragraph (2) applies if the court has ordered or directed the expenditure of money–
(a)   for carrying out permanent improvements on any of P's property, or
(b)   otherwise for the permanent benefit of any of P's property.

(2) The court may order that–
(a)   the whole of the money expended or to be expended, or
(b)   any part of it,

is to be a charge on the property either without interest or with interest at a specified rate.

(3) An order under sub-paragraph (2) may provide for excluding or restricting the operation of paragraph 8(1) to (3).

(4) A charge under sub-paragraph (2) may be made in favour of such person as may be just and, in particular, where the money charged is paid out of P's general estate, may be made in favour of a person as trustee for P.

(5) No charge under sub-paragraph (2) may confer any right of sale or foreclosure during P's lifetime.

Powers as patron of benefice

10 (1) Any functions which P has as patron of a benefice may be discharged only by a person ('R') appointed by the court.

(2) R must be an individual capable of appointment under section 8(1)(b) of the 1986 Measure (which provides for an individual able to make a declaration of communicant status, a clerk in Holy Orders, etc. to be appointed to discharge a registered patron's functions).

(3) The 1986 Measure applies to R as it applies to an individual appointed by the registered patron of the benefice under section 8(1)(b) or (3) of that Measure to discharge his functions as patron.

(4) 'The 1986 Measure' means the Patronage (Benefices) Measure 1986 (No. 3).

SCHEDULE 3
INTERNATIONAL PROTECTION OF ADULTS

Section 63

PART 1
PRELIMINARY

Introduction

1 This Part applies for the purposes of this Schedule.

The Convention

2 (1) 'Convention' means the Convention referred to in section 63.

(2) 'Convention country' means a country in which the Convention is in force.

(3) A reference to an Article or Chapter is to an Article or Chapter of the Convention.

(4) An expression which appears in this Schedule and in the Convention is to be construed in accordance with the Convention.

Countries, territories and nationals

3 (1) 'Country' includes a territory which has its own system of law.

(2) Where a country has more than one territory with its own system of law, a reference to the country, in relation to one of its nationals, is to the territory with which the national has the closer, or the closest, connection.

Adults with incapacity

4 'Adult' means a person who–
  (a)   as a result of an impairment or insufficiency of his personal faculties, cannot protect his interests, and
  (b)   has reached 16.

Protective measures

5 (1) 'Protective measure' means a measure directed to the protection of the person or property of an adult; and it may deal in particular with any of the following–
  (a)   the determination of incapacity and the institution of a protective regime,
  (b)   placing the adult under the protection of an appropriate authority,
  (c)   guardianship, curatorship or any corresponding system,
  (d)   the designation and functions of a person having charge of the adult's person or property, or representing or otherwise helping him,
  (e)   placing the adult in a place where protection can be provided,
  (f)   administering, conserving or disposing of the adult's property,
  (g)   authorising a specific intervention for the protection of the person or property of the adult.

(2) Where a measure of like effect to a protective measure has been taken in relation to a person before he reaches 16, this Schedule applies to the measure in so far as it has effect in relation to him once he has reached 16.

Central Authority

6 (1) Any function under the Convention of a Central Authority is exercisable in England and Wales by the Lord Chancellor.

(2) A communication may be sent to the Central Authority in relation to England and Wales by sending it to the Lord Chancellor.

PART 2
JURISDICTION OF COMPETENT AUTHORITY

Scope of jurisdiction

7 (1) The court may exercise its functions under this Act (in so far as it cannot otherwise do so) in relation to–
  - (a) an adult habitually resident in England and Wales,
  - (b) an adult's property in England and Wales,
  - (c) an adult present in England and Wales or who has property there, if the matter is urgent, or
  - (d) an adult present in England and Wales, if a protective measure which is temporary and limited in its effect to England and Wales is proposed in relation to him.

(2) An adult present in England and Wales is to be treated for the purposes of this paragraph as habitually resident there if–
  - (a) his habitual residence cannot be ascertained,
  - (b) he is a refugee, or
  - (c) he has been displaced as a result of disturbance in the country of his habitual residence.

8 (1) The court may also exercise its functions under this Act (in so far as it cannot otherwise do so) in relation to an adult if sub-paragraph (2) or (3) applies in relation to him.

(2) This sub-paragraph applies in relation to an adult if–
  - (a) he is a British citizen,
  - (b) he has a closer connection with England and Wales than with Scotland or Northern Ireland, and
  - (c) Article 7 has, in relation to the matter concerned, been complied with.

(3) This sub-paragraph applies in relation to an adult if the Lord Chancellor, having consulted such persons as he considers appropriate, agrees to a request under Article 8 in relation to the adult.

Exercise of jurisdiction

9 (1) This paragraph applies where jurisdiction is exercisable under this Schedule in connection with a matter which involves a Convention country other than England and Wales.

(2) Any Article on which the jurisdiction is based applies in relation to the matter in so far as it involves the other country (and the court must, accordingly, comply with any duty conferred on it as a result).

(3) Article 12 also applies, so far as its provisions allow, in relation to the matter in so far as it involves the other country.

10 A reference in this Schedule to the exercise of jurisdiction under this Schedule is to the exercise of functions under this Act as a result of this Part of this Schedule.

PART 3
APPLICABLE LAW

Applicable law

11 In exercising jurisdiction under this Schedule, the court may, if it thinks that the matter has a substantial connection with a country other than England and Wales, apply the law of that other country.

12 Where a protective measure is taken in one country but implemented in another, the conditions of implementation are governed by the law of the other country.

Lasting powers of attorney, etc.

13 (1) If the donor of a lasting power is habitually resident in England and Wales at the time of granting the power, the law applicable to the existence, extent, modification or extinction of the power is–
    (a)   the law of England and Wales, or
    (b)   if he specifies in writing the law of a connected country for the purpose, that law.

(2) If he is habitually resident in another country at that time, but England and Wales is a connected country, the law applicable in that respect is–
    (a)   the law of the other country, or
    (b)   if he specifies in writing the law of England and Wales for the purpose, that law.

(3) A country is connected, in relation to the donor, if it is a country–
    (a)   of which he is a national,
    (b)   in which he was habitually resident, or
    (c)   in which he has property.

(4) Where this paragraph applies as a result of sub-paragraph (3)(c), it applies only in relation to the property which the donor has in the connected country.

(5) The law applicable to the manner of the exercise of a lasting power is the law of the country where it is exercised.

(6) In this Part of this Schedule, 'lasting power' means–
    (a)   a lasting power of attorney (see section 9),
    (b)   an enduring power of attorney within the meaning of Schedule 4, or
    (c)   any other power of like effect.

14 (1) Where a lasting power is not exercised in a manner sufficient to guarantee the protection of the person or property of the donor, the court, in exercising jurisdiction under this Schedule, may disapply or modify the power.

(2) Where, in accordance with this Part of this Schedule, the law applicable to the power is, in one or more respects, that of a country other than England and Wales, the court must, so far as possible, have regard to the law of the other country in that respect (or those respects).

15 Regulations may provide for Schedule 1 (lasting powers of attorney: formalities) to apply with modifications in relation to a lasting power which comes within paragraph 13(6)(c) above.

Protection of third parties

16 (1) This paragraph applies where a person (a 'representative') in purported exercise of an authority to act on behalf of an adult enters into a transaction with a third party.

(2) The validity of the transaction may not be questioned in proceedings, nor may the third party be held liable, merely because–
  (a)   where the representative and third party are in England and Wales when entering into the transaction, sub-paragraph (3) applies;
  (b)   where they are in another country at that time, sub-paragraph (4) applies.

(3) This sub-paragraph applies if–
  (a)   the law applicable to the authority in one or more respects is, as a result of this Schedule, the law of a country other than England and Wales, and
  (b)   the representative is not entitled to exercise the authority in that respect (or those respects) under the law of that other country.

(4) This sub-paragraph applies if–
  (a)   the law applicable to the authority in one or more respects is, as a result of this Part of this Schedule, the law of England and Wales, and
  (b)   the representative is not entitled to exercise the authority in that respect (or those respects) under that law.

(5) This paragraph does not apply if the third party knew or ought to have known that the applicable law was–
  (a)   in a case within sub-paragraph (3), the law of the other country;
  (b)   in a case within sub-paragraph (4), the law of England and Wales.

Mandatory rules

17 Where the court is entitled to exercise jurisdiction under this Schedule, the mandatory provisions of the law of England and Wales apply, regardless of any system of law which would otherwise apply in relation to the matter.

Public policy

18 Nothing in this Part of this Schedule requires or enables the application in England and Wales of a provision of the law of another country if its application would be manifestly contrary to public policy.

PART 4
RECOGNITION AND ENFORCEMENT

Recognition

19 (1) A protective measure taken in relation to an adult under the law of a country other than England and Wales is to be recognised in England and Wales if it was taken on the ground that the adult is habitually resident in the other country.

(2) A protective measure taken in relation to an adult under the law of a Convention country other than England and Wales is to be recognised in England and Wales if it was taken on a ground mentioned in Chapter 2 (jurisdiction).

(3) But the court may disapply this paragraph in relation to a measure if it thinks that–
    (a)   the case in which the measure was taken was not urgent,
    (b)   the adult was not given an opportunity to be heard, and
    (c)   that omission amounted to a breach of natural justice.

(4) It may also disapply this paragraph in relation to a measure if it thinks that–
    (a)   recognition of the measure would be manifestly contrary to public policy,
    (b)   the measure would be inconsistent with a mandatory provision of the law of England and Wales, or
    (c)   the measure is inconsistent with one subsequently taken, or recognised, in England and Wales in relation to the adult.

(5) And the court may disapply this paragraph in relation to a measure taken under the law of a Convention country in a matter to which Article 33 applies, if the court thinks that that Article has not been complied with in connection with that matter.

20 (1) An interested person may apply to the court for a declaration as to whether a protective measure taken under the law of a country other than England and Wales is to be recognised in England and Wales.

(2) No permission is required for an application to the court under this paragraph.

21 For the purposes of paragraphs 19 and 20, any finding of fact relied on when the measure was taken is conclusive.

Enforcement

22 (1) An interested person may apply to the court for a declaration as to whether a protective measure taken under the law of, and enforceable in, a country other than England and Wales is enforceable, or to be registered, in England and Wales in accordance with Court of Protection Rules.

(2) The court must make the declaration if–
    (a)   the measure comes within sub-paragraph (1) or (2) of paragraph 19, and
    (b)   the paragraph is not disapplied in relation to it as a result of sub-paragraph (3), (4) or (5).

(3) A measure to which a declaration under this paragraph relates is enforceable in England and Wales as if it were a measure of like effect taken by the court.

Measures taken in relation to those aged under 16

23 (1) This paragraph applies where–

    (a)   provision giving effect to, or otherwise deriving from, the Convention in a country other than England and Wales applies in relation to a person who has not reached 16, and

    (b)   a measure is taken in relation to that person in reliance on that provision.

(2) This Part of this Schedule applies in relation to that measure as it applies in relation to a protective measure taken in relation to an adult under the law of a Convention country other than England and Wales.

Supplementary

24 The court may not review the merits of a measure taken outside England and Wales except to establish whether the measure complies with this Schedule in so far as it is, as a result of this Schedule, required to do so.

25 Court of Protection Rules may make provision about an application under paragraph 20 or 22.

PART 5
CO-OPERATION

Proposal for cross-border placement

26 (1) This paragraph applies where a public authority proposes to place an adult in an establishment in a Convention country other than England and Wales.

(2) The public authority must consult an appropriate authority in that other country about the proposed placement and, for that purpose, must send it–

    (a)   a report on the adult, and

    (b)   a statement of its reasons for the proposed placement.

(3) If the appropriate authority in the other country opposes the proposed placement within a reasonable time, the public authority may not proceed with it.

27 A proposal received by a public authority under Article 33 in relation to an adult is to proceed unless the authority opposes it within a reasonable time.

Adult in danger etc.

28 (1) This paragraph applies if a public authority is told that an adult–

    (a)   who is in serious danger, and

    (b)   in relation to whom the public authority has taken, or is considering taking, protective measures,

is, or has become resident, in a Convention country other than England and Wales.

(2) The public authority must tell an appropriate authority in that other country about–

    (a)   the danger, and

    (b)   the measures taken or under consideration.

29 A public authority may not request from, or send to, an appropriate authority in a Convention country information in accordance with Chapter 5 (co-operation) in relation to an adult if it thinks that doing so–
  (a)   would be likely to endanger the adult or his property, or
  (b)   would amount to a serious threat to the liberty or life of a member of the adult's family.

PART 6
GENERAL

Certificates

30 A certificate given under Article 38 by an authority in a Convention country other than England and Wales is, unless the contrary is shown, proof of the matters contained in it.

Powers to make further provision as to private international law

31 Her Majesty may by Order in Council confer on the Lord Chancellor, the court or another public authority functions for enabling the Convention to be given effect in England and Wales.

32 (1) Regulations may make provision–
  (a)   giving further effect to the Convention, or
  (b)   otherwise about the private international law of England and Wales in relation to the protection of adults.

(2) The regulations may–
  (a)   confer functions on the court or another public authority;
  (b)   amend this Schedule;
  (c)   provide for this Schedule to apply with specified modifications;
  (d)   make provision about countries other than Convention countries.

Exceptions

33 Nothing in this Schedule applies, and no provision made under paragraph 32 is to apply, to any matter to which the Convention, as a result of Article 4, does not apply.

Regulations and orders

34 A reference in this Schedule to regulations or an order (other than an Order in Council) is to regulations or an order made for the purposes of this Schedule by the Lord Chancellor.

Commencement

35 The following provisions of this Schedule have effect only if the Convention is in force in accordance with Article 57–
  (a)   paragraph 8,
  (b)   paragraph 9,
  (c)   paragraph 19(2) and (5),
  (d)   Part 5,
  (e)   paragraph 30.

SCHEDULE 4
PROVISIONS APPLYING TO EXISTING
ENDURING POWERS OF ATTORNEY

Section 66(3)

PART 1
ENDURING POWERS OF ATTORNEY

Enduring power of attorney to survive mental incapacity of donor

1 (1) Where an individual has created a power of attorney which is an enduring power within the meaning of this Schedule–

  (a)   the power is not revoked by any subsequent mental incapacity of his,

  (b)   upon such incapacity supervening, the donee of the power may not do anything under the authority of the power except as provided by sub-paragraph (2) unless or until the instrument creating the power is registered under paragraph 13, and

  (c)   if and so long as paragraph (b) operates to suspend the donee's authority to act under the power, section 5 of the Powers of Attorney Act 1971 (c 27) (protection of donee and third persons), so far as applicable, applies as if the power had been revoked by the donor's mental incapacity,

and, accordingly, section 1 of this Act does not apply.

(2) Despite sub-paragraph (1)(b), where the attorney has made an application for registration of the instrument then, until it is registered, the attorney may take action under the power–

  (a)   to maintain the donor or prevent loss to his estate, or

  (b)   to maintain himself or other persons in so far as paragraph 3(2) permits him to do so.

(3) Where the attorney purports to act as provided by sub-paragraph (2) then, in favour of a person who deals with him without knowledge that the attorney is acting otherwise than in accordance with sub-paragraph (2)(a) or (b), the transaction between them is as valid as if the attorney were acting in accordance with sub-paragraph (2)(a) or (b).

Characteristics of an enduring power of attorney

2 (1) Subject to sub-paragraphs (5) and (6) and paragraph 20, a power of attorney is an enduring power within the meaning of this Schedule if the instrument which creates the power–

  (a)   is in the prescribed form,

  (b)   was executed in the prescribed manner by the donor and the attorney, and

  (c)   incorporated at the time of execution by the donor the prescribed explanatory information.

(2) In this paragraph, 'prescribed' means prescribed by such of the following regulations as applied when the instrument was executed–

(a)   the Enduring Powers of Attorney (Prescribed Form) Regulations 1986 (S.I. 1986/126),

(b)   the Enduring Powers of Attorney (Prescribed Form) Regulations 1987 (S.I. 1987/1612),

(c)   the Enduring Powers of Attorney (Prescribed Form) Regulations 1990 (S.I. 1990/1376),

(d)   the Enduring Powers of Attorney (Welsh Language Prescribed Form) Regulations 2000 (S.I. 2000/289).

(3) An instrument in the prescribed form purporting to have been executed in the prescribed manner is to be taken, in the absence of evidence to the contrary, to be a document which incorporated at the time of execution by the donor the prescribed explanatory information.

(4) If an instrument differs in an immaterial respect in form or mode of expression from the prescribed form it is to be treated as sufficient in point of form and expression.

(5) A power of attorney cannot be an enduring power unless, when he executes the instrument creating it, the attorney is–

(a)   an individual who has reached 18 and is not bankrupt, or

(b)   a trust corporation.

(6) A power of attorney which gives the attorney a right to appoint a substitute or successor cannot be an enduring power.

(7) An enduring power is revoked by the bankruptcy of the donor or attorney.

(8) But where the donor or attorney is bankrupt merely because an interim bankruptcy restrictions order has effect in respect of him, the power is suspended for so long as the order has effect.

(9) An enduring power is revoked if the court–

(a)   exercises a power under sections 16 to 20 in relation to the donor, and

(b)   directs that the enduring power is to be revoked.

(10) No disclaimer of an enduring power, whether by deed or otherwise, is valid unless and until the attorney gives notice of it to the donor or, where paragraph 4(6) or 15(1) applies, to the Public Guardian.

Scope of authority etc. of attorney under enduring power

3 (1) If the instrument which creates an enduring power of attorney is expressed to confer general authority on the attorney, the instrument operates to confer, subject to–

(a)   the restriction imposed by sub-paragraph (3), and

(b)   any conditions or restrictions contained in the instrument,

authority to do on behalf of the donor anything which the donor could lawfully do by an attorney at the time when the donor executed the instrument.

(2) Subject to any conditions or restrictions contained in the instrument, an attorney under an enduring power, whether general or limited, may (without obtaining any consent) act under the power so as to benefit himself or other persons than the donor to the following extent but no further–

(a)   he may so act in relation to himself or in relation to any other person if the donor might be expected to provide for his or that person's needs respectively, and

(b)   he may do whatever the donor might be expected to do to meet those needs.

(3) Without prejudice to sub-paragraph (2) but subject to any conditions or restrictions contained in the instrument, an attorney under an enduring power, whether general or limited, may (without obtaining any consent) dispose of the property of the donor by way of gift to the following extent but no further–

(a)   he may make gifts of a seasonal nature or at a time, or on an anniversary, of a birth, a marriage or the formation of a civil partnership, to persons (including himself) who are related to or connected with the donor, and

(b)   he may make gifts to any charity to whom the donor made or might be expected to make gifts,

provided that the value of each such gift is not unreasonable having regard to all the circumstances and in particular the size of the donor's estate.

PART 2
ACTION ON ACTUAL OR IMPENDING INCAPACITY OF DONOR

Duties of attorney in event of actual or impending incapacity of donor

4 (1) Sub-paragraphs (2) to (6) apply if the attorney under an enduring power has reason to believe that the donor is or is becoming mentally incapable.

(2) The attorney must, as soon as practicable, make an application to the Public Guardian for the registration of the instrument creating the power.

(3) Before making an application for registration the attorney must comply with the provisions as to notice set out in Part 3 of this Schedule.

(4) An application for registration–

(a)   must be made in the prescribed form, and

(b)   must contain such statements as may be prescribed.

(5) The attorney–

(a)   may, before making an application for the registration of the instrument, refer to the court for its determination any question as to the validity of the power, and

(b)   must comply with any direction given to him by the court on that determination.

(6) No disclaimer of the power is valid unless and until the attorney gives notice of it to the Public Guardian; and the Public Guardian must notify the donor if he receives a notice under this sub-paragraph.

(7) A person who, in an application for registration, makes a statement which he knows to be false in a material particular is guilty of an offence and is liable–

(a)   on summary conviction, to imprisonment for a term not exceeding 12 months or a fine not exceeding the statutory maximum or both;

(b)   on conviction on indictment, to imprisonment for a term not exceeding 2 years or a fine or both.

(8) In this paragraph, 'prescribed' means prescribed by regulations made for the purposes of this Schedule by the Lord Chancellor.

PART 3
NOTIFICATION PRIOR TO REGISTRATION

Duty to give notice to relatives

5 Subject to paragraph 7, before making an application for registration the attorney must give notice of his intention to do so to all those persons (if any) who are entitled to receive notice by virtue of paragraph 6.

6 (1) Subject to sub-paragraphs (2) to (4), persons of the following classes ('relatives') are entitled to receive notice under paragraph 5–
  (a)   the donor's spouse or civil partner,
  (b)   the donor's children,
  (c)   the donor's parents,
  (d)   the donor's brothers and sisters, whether of the whole or half blood,
  (e)   the widow, widower or surviving civil partner of a child of the donor,
  (f)   the donor's grandchildren,
  (g)   the children of the donor's brothers and sisters of the whole blood,
  (h)   the children of the donor's brothers and sisters of the half blood,
  (i)   the donor's uncles and aunts of the whole blood,
  (j)   the children of the donor's uncles and aunts of the whole blood.

(2) A person is not entitled to receive notice under paragraph 5 if–
  (a)   his name or address is not known to the attorney and cannot be reasonably ascertained by him, or
  (b)   the attorney has reason to believe that he has not reached 18 or is mentally incapable.

(3) Except where sub-paragraph (4) applies–
  (a)   no more than 3 persons are entitled to receive notice under paragraph 5, and
  (b)   in determining the persons who are so entitled, persons falling within the class in sub-paragraph (1)(a) are to be preferred to persons falling within the class in sub-paragraph (1)(b), those falling within the class in sub-paragraph (1)(b) are to be preferred to those falling within the class in sub-paragraph (1)(c), and so on.

(4) Despite the limit of 3 specified in sub-paragraph (3), where–
  (a)   there is more than one person falling within any of classes (a) to (j) of sub-paragraph (1), and
  (b)   at least one of those persons would be entitled to receive notice under paragraph 5,

then, subject to sub-paragraph (2), all the persons falling within that class are entitled to receive notice under paragraph 5.

7 (1) An attorney is not required to give notice under paragraph 5–
  (a)   to himself, or
  (b)   to any other attorney under the power who is joining in making the application,

even though he or, as the case may be, the other attorney is entitled to receive notice by virtue of paragraph 6.

(2) In the case of any person who is entitled to receive notice by virtue of paragraph 6, the attorney, before applying for registration, may make an application to the court to be dispensed from the requirement to give him notice; and the court must grant the application if it is satisfied–

    (a)   that it would be undesirable or impracticable for the attorney to give him notice, or

    (b)   that no useful purpose is likely to be served by giving him notice.

Duty to give notice to donor

8 (1) Subject to sub-paragraph (2), before making an application for registration the attorney must give notice of his intention to do so to the donor.

(2) Paragraph 7(2) applies in relation to the donor as it applies in relation to a person who is entitled to receive notice under paragraph 5.

Contents of notices

9 A notice to relatives under this Part of this Schedule must–

    (a)   be in the prescribed form,

    (b)   state that the attorney proposes to make an application to the Public Guardian for the registration of the instrument creating the enduring power in question,

    (c)   inform the person to whom it is given of his right to object to the registration under paragraph 13(4), and

    (d)   specify, as the grounds on which an objection to registration may be made, the grounds set out in paragraph 13(9).

10 A notice to the donor under this Part of this Schedule–

    (a)   must be in the prescribed form,

    (b)   must contain the statement mentioned in paragraph 9(b), and

    (c)   must inform the donor that, while the instrument remains registered, any revocation of the power by him will be ineffective unless and until the revocation is confirmed by the court.

Duty to give notice to other attorneys

11 (1) Subject to sub-paragraph (2), before making an application for registration an attorney under a joint and several power must give notice of his intention to do so to any other attorney under the power who is not joining in making the application; and paragraphs 7(2) and 9 apply in relation to attorneys entitled to receive notice by virtue of this paragraph as they apply in relation to persons entitled to receive notice by virtue of paragraph 6.

(2) An attorney is not entitled to receive notice by virtue of this paragraph if–

    (a)   his address is not known to the applying attorney and cannot reasonably be ascertained by him, or

    (b)   the applying attorney has reason to believe that he has not reached 18 or is mentally incapable.

Supplementary

12 Despite section 7 of the Interpretation Act 1978 (c 30) (construction of references to service by post), for the purposes of this Part of this Schedule a notice given by post is to be regarded as given on the date on which it was posted.

PART 4
REGISTRATION

Registration of instrument creating power

13 (1) If an application is made in accordance with paragraph 4(3) and (4) the Public Guardian must, subject to the provisions of this paragraph, register the instrument to which the application relates.

(2) If it appears to the Public Guardian that–
- (a)   there is a deputy appointed for the donor of the power created by the instrument, and
- (b)   the powers conferred on the deputy would, if the instrument were registered, to any extent conflict with the powers conferred on the attorney,

the Public Guardian must not register the instrument except in accordance with the court's directions.

(3) The court may, on the application of the attorney, direct the Public Guardian to register an instrument even though notice has not been given as required by paragraph 4(3) and Part 3 of this Schedule to a person entitled to receive it, if the court is satisfied–
- (a)   that it was undesirable or impracticable for the attorney to give notice to that person, or
- (b)   that no useful purpose is likely to be served by giving him notice.

(4) Sub-paragraph (5) applies if, before the end of the period of 5 weeks beginning with the date (or the latest date) on which the attorney gave notice under paragraph 5 of an application for registration, the Public Guardian receives a valid notice of objection to the registration from a person entitled to notice of the application.

(5) The Public Guardian must not register the instrument except in accordance with the court's directions.

(6) Sub-paragraph (7) applies if, in the case of an application for registration–
- (a)   it appears from the application that there is no one to whom notice has been given under paragraph 5, or
- (b)   the Public Guardian has reason to believe that appropriate inquiries might bring to light evidence on which he could be satisfied that one of the grounds of objection set out in sub-paragraph (9) was established.

(7) The Public Guardian–
- (a)   must not register the instrument, and
- (b)   must undertake such inquiries as he thinks appropriate in all the circumstances.

(8) If, having complied with sub-paragraph (7)(b), the Public Guardian is satisfied that one of the grounds of objection set out in sub-paragraph (9) is established–

(a)   the attorney may apply to the court for directions, and

(b)   the Public Guardian must not register the instrument except in accordance with the court's directions.

(9) A notice of objection under this paragraph is valid if made on one or more of the following grounds–

(a)   that the power purported to have been created by the instrument was not valid as an enduring power of attorney,

(b)   that the power created by the instrument no longer subsists,

(c)   that the application is premature because the donor is not yet becoming mentally incapable,

(d)   that fraud or undue pressure was used to induce the donor to create the power,

(e)   that, having regard to all the circumstances and in particular the attorney's relationship to or connection with the donor, the attorney is unsuitable to be the donor's attorney.

(10) If any of those grounds is established to the satisfaction of the court it must direct the Public Guardian not to register the instrument, but if not so satisfied it must direct its registration.

(11) If the court directs the Public Guardian not to register an instrument because it is satisfied that the ground in sub-paragraph (9)(d) or (e) is established, it must by order revoke the power created by the instrument.

(12) If the court directs the Public Guardian not to register an instrument because it is satisfied that any ground in sub-paragraph (9) except that in paragraph (c) is established, the instrument must be delivered up to be cancelled unless the court otherwise directs.

Register of enduring powers

14 The Public Guardian has the function of establishing and maintaining a register of enduring powers for the purposes of this Schedule.

PART 5
LEGAL POSITION AFTER REGISTRATION

Effect and proof of registration

15 (1) The effect of the registration of an instrument under paragraph 13 is that–

(a)   no revocation of the power by the donor is valid unless and until the court confirms the revocation under paragraph 16(3);

(b)   no disclaimer of the power is valid unless and until the attorney gives notice of it to the Public Guardian;

(c)   the donor may not extend or restrict the scope of the authority conferred by the instrument and no instruction or consent given by him after registration, in the case of a consent, confers any right and, in the case of an instruction, imposes or confers any obligation or right on or creates any liability of the attorney or other persons having notice of the instruction or consent.

(2) Sub-paragraph (1) applies for so long as the instrument is registered under paragraph 13 whether or not the donor is for the time being mentally incapable.

(3) A document purporting to be an office copy of an instrument registered under this Schedule is, in any part of the United Kingdom, evidence of–
  (a)   the contents of the instrument, and
  (b)   the fact that it has been so registered.

(4) Sub-paragraph (3) is without prejudice to section 3 of the Powers of Attorney Act 1971 (c 27) (proof by certified copies) and to any other method of proof authorised by law.

Functions of court with regard to registered power

16 (1) Where an instrument has been registered under paragraph 13, the court has the following functions with respect to the power and the donor of and the attorney appointed to act under the power.

(2) The court may–
  (a)   determine any question as to the meaning or effect of the instrument;
  (b)   give directions with respect to–
     (i)   the management or disposal by the attorney of the property and affairs of the donor;
     (ii)   the rendering of accounts by the attorney and the production of the records kept by him for the purpose;
     (iii) the remuneration or expenses of the attorney whether or not in default of or in accordance with any provision made by the instrument, including directions for the repayment of excessive or the payment of additional remuneration;
  (c)   require the attorney to supply information or produce documents or things in his possession as attorney;
  (d)   give any consent or authorisation to act which the attorney would have to obtain from a mentally capable donor;
  (e)   authorise the attorney to act so as to benefit himself or other persons than the donor otherwise than in accordance with paragraph 3(2) and (3) (but subject to any conditions or restrictions contained in the instrument);
  (f)   relieve the attorney wholly or partly from any liability which he has or may have incurred on account of a breach of his duties as attorney.

(3) On application made for the purpose by or on behalf of the donor, the court must confirm the revocation of the power if satisfied that the donor–
  (a)   has done whatever is necessary in law to effect an express revocation of the power, and
  (b)   was mentally capable of revoking a power of attorney when he did so (whether or not he is so when the court considers the application).

(4) The court must direct the Public Guardian to cancel the registration of an instrument registered under paragraph 13 in any of the following circumstances–
  (a)   on confirming the revocation of the power under sub-paragraph (3),
  (b)   on directing under paragraph 2(9)(b) that the power is to be revoked,
  (c)   on being satisfied that the donor is and is likely to remain mentally capable,
  (d)   on being satisfied that the power has expired or has been revoked by the mental incapacity of the attorney,
  (e)   on being satisfied that the power was not a valid and subsisting enduring power when registration was effected,

(f)   on being satisfied that fraud or undue pressure was used to induce the donor to create the power,

(g)   on being satisfied that, having regard to all the circumstances and in particular the attorney's relationship to or connection with the donor, the attorney is unsuitable to be the donor's attorney.

(5) If the court directs the Public Guardian to cancel the registration of an instrument on being satisfied of the matters specified in sub-paragraph (4)(f) or (g) it must by order revoke the power created by the instrument.

(6) If the court directs the cancellation of the registration of an instrument under sub-paragraph (4) except paragraph (c) the instrument must be delivered up to the Public Guardian to be cancelled, unless the court otherwise directs.

Cancellation of registration by Public Guardian

17 The Public Guardian must cancel the registration of an instrument creating an enduring power of attorney–

(a)   on receipt of a disclaimer signed by the attorney;

(b)   if satisfied that the power has been revoked by the death or bankruptcy of the donor or attorney or, if the attorney is a body corporate, by its winding up or dissolution;

(c)   on receipt of notification from the court that the court has revoked the power;

(d)   on confirmation from the court that the donor has revoked the power.

PART 6
PROTECTION OF ATTORNEY AND THIRD PARTIES

Protection of attorney and third persons where power is invalid or revoked

18 (1) Sub-paragraphs (2) and (3) apply where an instrument which did not create a valid power of attorney has been registered under paragraph 13 (whether or not the registration has been cancelled at the time of the act or transaction in question).

(2) An attorney who acts in pursuance of the power does not incur any liability (either to the donor or to any other person) because of the non-existence of the power unless at the time of acting he knows–

(a)   that the instrument did not create a valid enduring power,

(b)   that an event has occurred which, if the instrument had created a valid enduring power, would have had the effect of revoking the power, or

(c)   that, if the instrument had created a valid enduring power, the power would have expired before that time.

(3) Any transaction between the attorney and another person is, in favour of that person, as valid as if the power had then been in existence, unless at the time of the transaction that person has knowledge of any of the matters mentioned in sub-paragraph (2).

(4) If the interest of a purchaser depends on whether a transaction between the attorney and another person was valid by virtue of sub-paragraph (3), it is conclusively presumed in favour of the purchaser that the transaction was valid if–

(a)   the transaction between that person and the attorney was completed within 12 months of the date on which the instrument was registered, or

(b)   that person makes a statutory declaration, before or within 3 months after the completion of the purchase, that he had no reason at the time of the transaction to doubt that the attorney had authority to dispose of the property which was the subject of the transaction.

(5) For the purposes of section 5 of the Powers of Attorney Act 1971 (c 27) (protection where power is revoked) in its application to an enduring power the revocation of which by the donor is by virtue of paragraph 15 invalid unless and until confirmed by the court under paragraph 16–

(a)   knowledge of the confirmation of the revocation is knowledge of the revocation of the power, but

(b)   knowledge of the unconfirmed revocation is not.

Further protection of attorney and third persons

19 (1) If–

(a)   an instrument framed in a form prescribed as mentioned in paragraph 2(2) creates a power which is not a valid enduring power, and

(b)   the power is revoked by the mental incapacity of the donor,

sub-paragraphs (2) and (3) apply, whether or not the instrument has been registered.

(2) An attorney who acts in pursuance of the power does not, by reason of the revocation, incur any liability (either to the donor or to any other person) unless at the time of acting he knows–

(a)   that the instrument did not create a valid enduring power, and

(b)   that the donor has become mentally incapable.

(3) Any transaction between the attorney and another person is, in favour of that person, as valid as if the power had then been in existence, unless at the time of the transaction that person knows–

(a)   that the instrument did not create a valid enduring power, and

(b)   that the donor has become mentally incapable.

(4) Paragraph 18(4) applies for the purpose of determining whether a transaction was valid by virtue of sub-paragraph (3) as it applies for the purpose or determining whether a transaction was valid by virtue of paragraph 18(3).

PART 7
JOINT AND JOINT AND SEVERAL ATTORNEYS

Application to joint and joint and several attorneys

20 (1) An instrument which appoints more than one person to be an attorney cannot create an enduring power unless the attorneys are appointed to act–

(a)   jointly, or

(b)   jointly and severally.

(2) This Schedule, in its application to joint attorneys, applies to them collectively as it applies to a single attorney but subject to the modifications specified in paragraph 21.

(3) This Schedule, in its application to joint and several attorneys, applies with the modifications specified in sub-paragraphs (4) to (7) and in paragraph 22.

(4) A failure, as respects any one attorney, to comply with the requirements for the creation of enduring powers–

(a)   prevents the instrument from creating such a power in his case, but

(b)   does not affect its efficacy for that purpose as respects the other or others or its efficacy in his case for the purpose of creating a power of attorney which is not an enduring power.

(5) If one or more but not both or all the attorneys makes or joins in making an application for registration of the instrument–

(a)   an attorney who is not an applicant as well as one who is may act pending the registration of the instrument as provided in paragraph 1(2),

(b)   notice of the application must also be given under Part 3 of this Schedule to the other attorney or attorneys, and

(c)   objection may validly be taken to the registration on a ground relating to an attorney or to the power of an attorney who is not an applicant as well as to one or the power of one who is an applicant.

(6) The Public Guardian is not precluded by paragraph 13(5) or (8) from registering an instrument and the court must not direct him not to do so under paragraph 13(10) if an enduring power subsists as respects some attorney who is not affected by the ground or grounds of the objection in question; and where the Public Guardian registers an instrument in that case, he must make against the registration an entry in the prescribed form.

(7) Sub-paragraph (6) does not preclude the court from revoking a power in so far as it confers a power on any other attorney in respect of whom the ground in paragraph 13(9)(d) or (e) is established; and where any ground in paragraph 13(9) affecting any other attorney is established the court must direct the Public Guardian to make against the registration an entry in the prescribed form.

(8) In sub-paragraph (4), 'the requirements for the creation of enduring powers' means the provisions of–

(a)   paragraph 2 other than sub-paragraphs (8) and (9), and

(b)   the regulations mentioned in paragraph 2.

Joint attorneys

21 (1) In paragraph 2(5), the reference to the time when the attorney executes the instrument is to be read as a reference to the time when the second or last attorney executes the instrument.

(2) In paragraph 2(6) to (8), the reference to the attorney is to be read as a reference to any attorney under the power.

(3) Paragraph 13 has effect as if the ground of objection to the registration of the instrument specified in sub-paragraph (9)(e) applied to any attorney under the power.

(4) In paragraph 16(2), references to the attorney are to be read as including references to any attorney under the power.

(5) In paragraph 16(4), references to the attorney are to be read as including references to any attorney under the power.

(6) In paragraph 17, references to the attorney are to be read as including references to any attorney under the power.

Joint and several attorneys

22 (1) In paragraph 2(7), the reference to the bankruptcy of the attorney is to be read as a reference to the bankruptcy of the last remaining attorney under the power; and the bankruptcy of any other attorney under the power causes that person to cease to be an attorney under the power.

(2) In paragraph 2(8), the reference to the suspension of the power is to be read as a reference to its suspension in so far as it relates to the attorney in respect of whom the interim bankruptcy restrictions order has effect.

(3) The restriction upon disclaimer imposed by paragraph 4(6) applies only to those attorneys who have reason to believe that the donor is or is becoming mentally incapable.

PART 8
INTERPRETATION

23 (1) In this Schedule–
    'enduring power' is to be construed in accordance with paragraph 2,
    'mentally incapable' or 'mental incapacity', except where it refers to revocation at
        common law, means in relation to any person, that he is incapable by reason
        of mental disorder (within the meaning of the Mental Health Act) of
        managing and administering his property and affairs and 'mentally capable'
        and 'mental capacity' are to be construed accordingly,
    'notice' means notice in writing, and
    'prescribed', except for the purposes of paragraph 2, means prescribed by
        regulations made for the purposes of this Schedule by the Lord Chancellor.

(2) Any question arising under or for the purposes of this Schedule as to what the donor of the power might at any time be expected to do is to be determined by assuming that he had full mental capacity at the time but otherwise by reference to the circumstances existing at that time.

SCHEDULE 5
TRANSITIONAL PROVISIONS AND SAVINGS

Section 66(4)

PART 1
REPEAL OF PART 7 OF THE
MENTAL HEALTH ACT 1983

Existing receivers

1 (1) This paragraph applies where, immediately before the commencement day, there is a receiver ('R') for a person ('P') appointed under section 99 of the Mental Health Act.

(2) On and after that day–
  (a)   this Act applies as if R were a deputy appointed for P by the court, but with the functions that R had as receiver immediately before that day, and
  (b)   a reference in any other enactment to a deputy appointed by the court includes a person appointed as a deputy as a result of paragraph (a).

(3) On any application to it by R, the court may end R's appointment as P's deputy.

(4) Where, as a result of section 20(1), R may not make a decision on behalf of P in relation to a relevant matter, R must apply to the court.

(5) If, on the application, the court is satisfied that P is capable of managing his property and affairs in relation to the relevant matter–
  (a)   it must make an order ending R's appointment as P's deputy in relation to that matter, but
  (b)   it may, in relation to any other matter, exercise in relation to P any of the powers which it has under sections 15 to 19.

(6) If it is not satisfied, the court may exercise in relation to P any of the powers which it has under sections 15 to 19.

(7) R's appointment as P's deputy ceases to have effect if P dies.

(8) 'Relevant matter' means a matter in relation to which, immediately before the commencement day, R was authorised to act as P's receiver.

(9) In sub-paragraph (1), the reference to a receiver appointed under section 99 of the Mental Health Act includes a reference to a person who by virtue of Schedule 5 to that Act was deemed to be a receiver appointed under that section.

Orders, appointments etc.

2 (1) Any order or appointment made, direction or authority given or other thing done which has, or by virtue of Schedule 5 to the Mental Health Act was deemed to have, effect under Part 7 of the Act immediately before the commencement day is to continue to have effect despite the repeal of Part 7.

(2) In so far as any such order, appointment, direction, authority or thing could have been made, given or done under sections 15 to 20 if those sections had then been in force–

(a)   it is to be treated as made, given or done under those sections, and

(b)   the powers of variation and discharge conferred by section 16(7) apply accordingly.

(3) Sub-paragraph (1)–

(a)   does not apply to nominations under section 93(1) or (4) of the Mental Health Act, and

(b)   as respects receivers, has effect subject to paragraph 1.

(4) This Act does not affect the operation of section 109 of the Mental Health Act (effect and proof of orders etc.) in relation to orders made and directions given under Part 7 of that Act.

(5) This paragraph is without prejudice to section 16 of the Interpretation Act 1978 (c 30) (general savings on repeal).

Pending proceedings

3 (1) Any application for the exercise of a power under Part 7 of the Mental Health Act which is pending immediately before the commencement day is to be treated, in so far as a corresponding power is exercisable under sections 16 to 20, as an application for the exercise of that power.

(2) For the purposes of sub-paragraph (1) an application for the appointment of a receiver is to be treated as an application for the appointment of a deputy.

Appeals

4 (1) Part 7 of the Mental Health Act and the rules made under it are to continue to apply to any appeal brought by virtue of section 105 of that Act which has not been determined before the commencement day.

(2) If in the case of an appeal brought by virtue of section 105(1) (appeal to nominated judge) the judge nominated under section 93 of the Mental Health Act has begun to hear the appeal, he is to continue to do so but otherwise it is to be heard by a puisne judge of the High Court nominated under section 46.

Fees

5 All fees and other payments which, having become due, have not been paid to the former Court of Protection before the commencement day, are to be paid to the new Court of Protection.

Court records

6 (1) The records of the former Court of Protection are to be treated, on and after the commencement day, as records of the new Court of Protection and are to be dealt with accordingly under the Public Records Act 1958 (c 51).

(2) On and after the commencement day, the Public Guardian is, for the purpose of exercising any of his functions, to be given such access as he may require to such of

the records mentioned in sub-paragraph (1) as relate to the appointment of receivers under section 99 of the Mental Health Act.

Existing charges

7 This Act does not affect the operation in relation to a charge created before the commencement day of–
  (a) so much of section 101(6) of the Mental Health Act as precludes a charge created under section 101(5) from conferring a right of sale or foreclosure during the lifetime of the patient, or
  (b) section 106(6) of the Mental Health Act (charge created by virtue of section 106(5) not to cause interest to fail etc.).

Preservation of interests on disposal of property

8 Paragraph 8(1) of Schedule 2 applies in relation to any disposal of property (within the meaning of that provision) by a person living on 1st November 1960, being a disposal effected under the Lunacy Act 1890 (c 5) as it applies in relation to the disposal of property effected under sections 16 to 20.

Accounts

9 Court of Protection Rules may provide that, in a case where paragraph 1 applies, R is to have a duty to render accounts–
  (a) while he is receiver;
  (b) after he is discharged.

Interpretation

10 In this Part of this Schedule–
  (a) 'the commencement day' means the day on which section 66(1)(a) (repeal of Part 7 of the Mental Health Act) comes into force,
  (b) 'the former Court of Protection' means the office abolished by section 45, and
  (c) 'the new Court of Protection' means the court established by that section.

PART 2
REPEAL OF THE ENDURING POWERS OF ATTORNEY ACT 1985

Orders, determinations, etc.

11 (1) Any order or determination made, or other thing done, under the 1985 Act which has effect immediately before the commencement day continues to have effect despite the repeal of that Act.

(2) In so far as any such order, determination or thing could have been made or done under Schedule 4 if it had then been in force–
  (a) it is to be treated as made or done under that Schedule, and
  (b) the powers of variation and discharge exercisable by the court apply accordingly.

(3) Any instrument registered under the 1985 Act is to be treated as having been registered by the Public Guardian under Schedule 4.

(4) This paragraph is without prejudice to section 16 of the Interpretation Act 1978 (c 30) (general savings on repeal).

Pending proceedings

12 (1) An application for the exercise of a power under the 1985 Act which is pending immediately before the commencement day is to be treated, in so far as a corresponding power is exercisable under Schedule 4, as an application for the exercise of that power.

(2) For the purposes of sub-paragraph (1)–
  (a)   a pending application under section 4(2) of the 1985 Act for the registration of an instrument is to be treated as an application to the Public Guardian under paragraph 4 of Schedule 4 and any notice given in connection with that application under Schedule 1 to the 1985 Act is to be treated as given under Part 3 of Schedule 4,
  (b)   a notice of objection to the registration of an instrument is to be treated as a notice of objection under paragraph 13 of Schedule 4, and
  (c)   pending proceedings under section 5 of the 1985 Act are to be treated as proceedings on an application for the exercise by the court of a power which would become exercisable in relation to an instrument under paragraph 16(2) of Schedule 4 on its registration.

Appeals

13 (1) The 1985 Act and, so far as relevant, the provisions of Part 7 of the Mental Health Act and the rules made under it as applied by section 10 of the 1985 Act are to continue to have effect in relation to any appeal brought by virtue of section 10(1)(c) of the 1985 Act which has not been determined before the commencement day.

(2) If, in the case of an appeal brought by virtue of section 105(1) of the Mental Health Act as applied by section 10(1)(c) of the 1985 Act (appeal to nominated judge), the judge nominated under section 93 of the Mental Health Act has begun to hear the appeal, he is to continue to do so but otherwise the appeal is to be heard by a puisne judge of the High Court nominated under section 46.

Exercise of powers of donor as trustee

14 (1) Section 2(8) of the 1985 Act (which prevents a power of attorney under section 25 of the Trustee Act 1925 (c 19) as enacted from being an enduring power) is to continue to apply to any enduring power–
  (a)   created before 1st March 2000, and
  (b)   having effect immediately before the commencement day.

(2) Section 3(3) of the 1985 Act (which entitles the donee of an enduring power to exercise the donor's powers as trustee) is to continue to apply to any enduring power to which, as a result of the provision mentioned in sub-paragraph (3), it applies immediately before the commencement day.

(3) The provision is section 4(3)(a) of the Trustee Delegation Act 1999 (c 15) (which provides for section 3(3) of the 1985 Act to cease to apply to an enduring power when

its registration is cancelled, if it was registered in response to an application made before 1st March 2001).

(4) Even though section 4 of the 1999 Act is repealed by this Act, that section is to continue to apply in relation to an enduring power–

    (a)   to which section 3(3) of the 1985 Act applies as a result of sub-paragraph (2), or

    (b)   to which, immediately before the repeal of section 4 of the 1999 Act, section 1 of that Act applies as a result of section 4 of it.

(5) The reference in section 1(9) of the 1999 Act to section 4(6) of that Act is to be read with sub-paragraphs (2) to (4).

Interpretation

15 In this Part of this Schedule, 'the commencement day' means the day on which section 66(1)(b) (repeal of the 1985 Act) comes into force.

SCHEDULE 6
MINOR AND CONSEQUENTIAL AMENDMENTS

Section 67(1)

Fines and Recoveries Act 1833 (c 74)

1 (1) The Fines and Recoveries Act 1833 (c 74) is amended as follows.

(2) In section 33 (case where protector of settlement lacks capacity to act), for the words from 'shall be incapable' to 'is incapable as aforesaid' substitute 'lacks capacity (within the meaning of the Mental Capacity Act 2005) to manage his property and affairs, the Court of Protection is to take his place as protector of the settlement while he lacks capacity'.

(3) In sections 48 and 49 (mental health jurisdiction), for each reference to the judge having jurisdiction under Part 7 of the Mental Health Act substitute a reference to the Court of Protection.

Improvement of Land Act 1864 (c 114)

2 In section 68 of the Improvement of Land Act 1864 (c 114) (apportionment of rentcharges)–

    (a)   for ', curator, or receiver of' substitute 'or curator of, or a deputy with powers in relation to property and affairs appointed by the Court of Protection for,', and

    (b)   for 'or patient within the meaning of Part VII of the Mental Health Act 1983' substitute 'person who lacks capacity (within the meaning of the Mental Capacity Act 2005) to receive the notice'.

Trustee Act 1925 (c 19)

3 (1) The Trustee Act 1925 (c 19) is amended as follows.

(2) In section 36 (appointment of new trustee)–
  (a)   in subsection (6C), for the words from 'a power of attorney' to the end, substitute 'an enduring power of attorney or lasting power of attorney registered under the Mental Capacity Act 2005', and
  (b)   in subsection (9)–
    (i)   for the words from 'is incapable' to 'exercising' substitute 'lacks capacity to exercise', and
    (ii)   for the words from 'the authority' to the end substitute 'the Court of Protection'.

(3) In section 41(1) (power of court to appoint new trustee) for the words from 'is incapable' to 'exercising' substitute 'lacks capacity to exercise'.

(4) In section 54 (mental health jurisdiction)–
  (a)   for subsection (1) substitute–
  '(1)   Subject to subsection (2), the Court of Protection may not make an order, or give a direction or authority, in relation to a person who lacks capacity to exercise his functions as trustee, if the High Court may make an order to that effect under this Act.',
  (b)   in subsection (2)–
    (i)   for the words from the beginning to 'of a receiver' substitute 'Where a person lacks capacity to exercise his functions as a trustee and a deputy is appointed for him by the Court of Protection or an application for the appointment of a deputy',
    (ii)   for 'the said authority', in each place, substitute 'the Court of Protection', and
    (iii) for 'the patient', in each place, substitute 'the person concerned', and
  (c)   omit subsection (3).

(5) In section 55 (order made on particular allegation to be conclusive evidence of it)–
  (a)   for the words from 'Part VII' to 'Northern Ireland' substitute 'sections 15 to 20 of the Mental Capacity Act 2005 or any corresponding provisions having effect in Northern Ireland', and
  (b)   for paragraph (a) substitute–
    '(a)   that a trustee or mortgagee lacks capacity in relation to the matter in question;'.

(6) In section 68 (definitions), at the end add–
  '(3)   Any reference in this Act to a person who lacks capacity in relation to a matter is to a person–
    (a)   who lacks capacity within the meaning of the Mental Capacity Act 2005 in relation to that matter, or
    (b)   in respect of whom the powers conferred by section 48 of that Act are exercisable and have been exercised in relation to that matter.'.

Law of Property Act 1925 (c 20)

4 (1) The Law of Property Act 1925 (c 20) is amended as follows.

(2) In section 22 (conveyances on behalf of persons who lack capacity)–

(a)   in subsection (1)–
       (i)   for the words from 'in a person suffering' to 'is acting' substitute ',
              either solely or jointly with any other person or persons, in a person
              lacking capacity (within the meaning of the Mental Capacity Act
              2005) to convey or create a legal estate, a deputy appointed for him by
              the Court of Protection or (if no deputy is appointed', and
       (ii)   for 'the authority having jurisdiction under Part VII of the Mental
              Health Act 1983' substitute 'the Court of Protection',
(b)   in subsection (2), for 'is incapable, by reason of mental disorder, of
       exercising' substitute 'lacks capacity (within the meaning of that Act) to
       exercise', and
(c)   in subsection (3), for the words from 'an enduring power' to the end
       substitute 'an enduring power of attorney or lasting power of attorney
       (within the meaning of the 2005 Act) is entitled to act for the trustee who
       lacks capacity in relation to the dealing.'.

(3) In section 205(1) (interpretation), omit paragraph (xiii).

Administration of Estates Act 1925 (c 23)

5 (1) The Administration of Estates Act 1925 (c 23) is amended as follows.

(2) In section 41(1) (powers of personal representatives to appropriate), in the proviso–
(a)   in paragraph (ii)–
       (i)   for the words from 'is incapable' to 'the consent' substitute 'lacks
              capacity (within the meaning of the Mental Capacity Act 2005) to
              give the consent, it', and
       (ii)   for 'or receiver' substitute 'or a person appointed as deputy for him by
              the Court of Protection', and
(b)   in paragraph (iv), for 'no receiver is acting for a person suffering from
       mental disorder' substitute 'no deputy is appointed for a person who lacks
       capacity to consent'.

(3) Omit section 55(1)(viii) (definitions of 'person of unsound mind' and 'defective').

National Assistance Act 1948 (c 29)

6 In section 49 of the National Assistance Act 1948 (c 29) (expenses of council officers
acting for persons who lack capacity)–
(a)   for the words from 'applies' to 'affairs of a patient' substitute 'applies for
       appointment by the Court of Protection as a deputy', and
(b)   for 'such functions' substitute 'his functions as deputy'.

U.S.A. Veterans' Pensions (Administration) Act 1949 (c 45)

7 In section 1 of the U.S.A. Veterans' Pensions (Administration) Act 1949 (c 45)
(administration of pensions)–
(a)   in subsection (4), omit the words from 'or for whom' to '1983', and
(b)   after subsection (4), insert–
'(4A) An agreement under subsection (1) is not to be made in relation to a person
       who lacks capacity (within the meaning of the Mental Capacity Act 2005)
       for the purposes of this Act if–

    (a)   there is a donee of an enduring power of attorney or lasting power of attorney (within the meaning of the 2005 Act), or a deputy appointed for the person by the Court of Protection, and

    (b)   the donee or deputy has power in relation to the person for the purposes of this Act.

(4B) The proviso at the end of subsection (4) also applies in relation to subsection (4A).'.

Intestates' Estates Act 1952 (c 64)

8 In Schedule 2 to the Intestates' Estates Act 1952 (c 64) (rights of surviving spouse or civil partner in relation to home), for paragraph 6(1) substitute–

    '(1)   Where the surviving spouse or civil partner lacks capacity (within the meaning of the Mental Capacity Act 2005) to make a requirement or give a consent under this Schedule, the requirement or consent may be made or given by a deputy appointed by the Court of Protection with power in that respect or, if no deputy has that power, by that court.'.

Variation of Trusts Act 1958 (c 53)

9 In section 1 of the Variation of Trusts Act 1958 (c 53) (jurisdiction of courts to vary trusts)–

    (a)   in subsection (3), for the words from 'shall be determined' to the end substitute 'who lacks capacity (within the meaning of the Mental Capacity Act 2005) to give his assent is to be determined by the Court of Protection', and

    (b)   in subsection (6), for the words from 'the powers' to the end substitute 'the powers of the Court of Protection'.

Administration of Justice Act 1960 (c 65)

10 In section 12(1)(b) of the Administration of Justice Act 1960 (c 65) (contempt of court to publish information about proceedings in private relating to persons with incapacity) for the words from 'under Part VIII' to 'that Act' substitute 'under the Mental Capacity Act 2005, or under any provision of the Mental Health Act 1983'.

Industrial and Provident Societies Act 1965 (c 12)

11 In section 26 of the Industrial and Provident Societies Act 1965 (c 12) (payments for mentally incapable people), for subsection (2) substitute–

    '(2)   Subsection (1) does not apply where the member or person concerned lacks capacity (within the meaning of the Mental Capacity Act 2005) for the purposes of this Act and–

        (a)   there is a donee of an enduring power of attorney or lasting power of attorney (within the meaning of the 2005 Act), or a deputy appointed for the member or person by the Court of Protection, and

        (b)   the donee or deputy has power in relation to the member or person for the purposes of this Act.'.

Compulsory Purchase Act 1965 (c 56)

12 In Schedule 1 to the Compulsory Purchase Act 1965 (c 56) (persons without power to sell their interests), for paragraph 1(2)(b) substitute–

'(b) do not have effect in relation to a person who lacks capacity (within the meaning of the Mental Capacity Act 2005) for the purposes of this Act if–

(i) there is a donee of an enduring power of attorney or lasting power of attorney (within the meaning of the 2005 Act), or a deputy appointed for the person by the Court of Protection, and

(ii) the donee or deputy has power in relation to the person for the purposes of this Act.'.

Leasehold Reform Act 1967 (c 88)

13 (1) For section 26(2) of the Leasehold Reform Act 1967 (c 88) (landlord lacking capacity) substitute–

'(2) Where a landlord lacks capacity (within the meaning of the Mental Capacity Act 2005) to exercise his functions as a landlord, those functions are to be exercised–

(a) by a donee of an enduring power of attorney or lasting power of attorney (within the meaning of the 2005 Act), or a deputy appointed for him by the Court of Protection, with power to exercise those functions, or

(b) if no donee or deputy has that power, by a person authorised in that respect by that court.'.

(2) That amendment does not affect any proceedings pending at the commencement of this paragraph in which a receiver or a person authorised under Part 7 of the Mental Health Act is acting on behalf of the landlord.

Medicines Act 1968 (c 67)

14 In section 72 of the Medicines Act 1968 (c 67) (pharmacist lacking capacity)–

(a) in subsection (1)(c), for the words from 'a receiver' to '1959' substitute 'he becomes a person who lacks capacity (within the meaning of the Mental Capacity Act 2005) to carry on the business',

(b) after subsection (1) insert–

'(1A) In subsection (1)(c), the reference to a person who lacks capacity to carry on the business is to a person–

(a) in respect of whom there is a donee of an enduring power of attorney or lasting power of attorney (within the meaning of the Mental Capacity Act 2005), or

(b) for whom a deputy is appointed by the Court of Protection,

and in relation to whom the donee or deputy has power for the purposes of this Act.',

(c) in subsection (3)(d)–

(i) for 'receiver' substitute 'deputy', and

(ii)   after 'guardian' insert 'or from the date of registration of the
        instrument appointing the donee', and
(d)   in subsection (4)(c), for 'receiver' substitute 'donee, deputy'.

Family Law Reform Act 1969 (c 46)

15 For section 21(4) of the Family Law Reform Act 1969 (c 46) (consent required for taking of bodily sample from person lacking capacity), substitute–
'(4)   A bodily sample may be taken from a person who lacks capacity (within the meaning of the Mental Capacity Act 2005) to give his consent, if consent is given by the court giving the direction under section 20 or by–
(a)   a donee of an enduring power of attorney or lasting power of attorney (within the meaning of that Act), or
(b)   a deputy appointed, or any other person authorised, by the Court of Protection,

with power in that respect.'.

Local Authority Social Services Act 1970 (c 42)

16 (1) Schedule 1 to the Local Authority Social Services Act 1970 (c 42) (enactments conferring functions assigned to social services committee) is amended as follows.

(2) In the entry for section 49 of the National Assistance Act 1948 (expenses of local authority officer appointed for person who lacks capacity) for 'receiver' substitute 'deputy'.

(3) At the end, insert–

'Mental Capacity Act 2005	
Section 39	Instructing independent mental capacity advocate before providing accommodation for person lacking capacity.
Section 49	Reports in proceedings.'

Courts Act 1971 (c 23)

17 In Part 1A of Schedule 2 to the Courts Act 1971 (c 23) (office-holders eligible for appointment as circuit judges), omit the reference to a Master of the Court of Protection.

Local Government Act 1972 (c 70)

18 (1) Omit section 118 of the Local Government Act 1972 (c 70) (payment of pension etc. where recipient lacks capacity).

(2) Sub-paragraph (3) applies where, before the commencement of this paragraph, a local authority has, in respect of a person referred to in that section as 'the patient', made payments under that section–
(a)   to an institution or person having the care of the patient, or
(b)   in accordance with subsection (1)(a) or (b) of that section.

(3) The local authority may, in respect of the patient, continue to make payments under that section to that institution or person, or in accordance with subsection (1)(a) or (b) of that section, despite the repeal made by sub-paragraph (1).

Matrimonial Causes Act 1973 (c 18)

19 In section 40 of the Matrimonial Causes Act 1973 (c 18) (payments to person who lacks capacity) (which becomes subsection (1))–

(a) for the words from 'is incapable' to 'affairs' substitute '('P') lacks capacity (within the meaning of the Mental Capacity Act 2005) in relation to the provisions of the order',

(b) for 'that person under Part VIII of that Act' substitute 'P under that Act',

(c) for the words from 'such persons' to the end substitute 'such person ('D') as it may direct', and

(d) at the end insert–

'(2) In carrying out any functions of his in relation to an order made under subsection (1), D must act in P's best interests (within the meaning of that Act).'.

Juries Act 1974 (c 23)

20 In Schedule 1 to the Juries Act 1974 (c 23) (disqualification for jury service), for paragraph 3 substitute–

'3   A person who lacks capacity, within the meaning of the Mental Capacity Act 2005, to serve as a juror.'.

Consumer Credit Act 1974 (c 39)

21 For section 37(1)(c) of the Consumer Credit Act 1974 (c 39) (termination of consumer credit licence if holder lacks capacity) substitute–

'(c)   becomes a person who lacks capacity (within the meaning of the Mental Capacity Act 2005) to carry on the activities covered by the licence.'.

Solicitors Act 1974 (c 47)

22 (1) The Solicitors Act 1974 (c 47) is amended as follows.

(2) For section 12(1)(j) (application for practising certificate by solicitor lacking capacity) substitute–

'(j)   while he lacks capacity (within the meaning of the Mental Capacity Act 2005) to act as a solicitor and powers under sections 15 to 20 or section 48 of that Act are exercisable in relation to him;'.

(3) In section 62(4) (contentious business agreements made by clients) for paragraphs (c) and (d) substitute–

'(c)   as a deputy for him appointed by the Court of Protection with powers in relation to his property and affairs, or

(d)   as another person authorised under that Act to act on his behalf.'.

(4) In paragraph 1(1) of Schedule 1 (circumstances in which Law Society may intervene in solicitor's practice), for paragraph (f) substitute–

'(f)   a solicitor lacks capacity (within the meaning of the Mental Capacity Act 2005) to act as a solicitor and powers under sections 15 to 20 or section 48 of that Act are exercisable in relation to him;'.

Local Government (Miscellaneous Provisions) Act 1976 (c 57)

23 In section 31 of the Local Government (Miscellaneous Provisions) Act 1976 (c 57) (the title to which becomes 'Indemnities for local authority officers appointed as deputies or administrators'), for the words from 'as a receiver' to '1959' substitute 'as a deputy for a person by the Court of Protection'.

Sale of Goods Act 1979 (c 54)

24 In section 3(2) of the Sale of Goods Act 1979 (c 54) (capacity to buy and sell) the words 'mental incapacity or' cease to have effect in England and Wales.

Limitation Act 1980 (c 58)

25 In section 38 of the Limitation Act 1980 (c 58) (interpretation) substitute–
(a)   in subsection (2) for 'of unsound mind' substitute 'lacks capacity (within the meaning of the Mental Capacity Act 2005) to conduct legal proceedings', and
(b)   omit subsections (3) and (4).

Public Passenger Vehicles Act 1981 (c 14)

26 In section 57(2)(c) of the Public Passenger Vehicles Act 1981 (c 14) (termination of public service vehicle licence if holder lacks capacity) for the words from 'becomes a patient' to 'or' substitute 'becomes a person who lacks capacity (within the meaning of the Mental Capacity Act 2005) to use a vehicle under the licence, or'.

Judicial Pensions Act 1981 (c 20)

27 In Schedule 1 to the Judicial Pensions Act 1981 (c 20) (pensions of Supreme Court officers, etc.), in paragraph 1, omit the reference to a Master of the Court of Protection except in the case of a person holding that office immediately before the commencement of this paragraph or who had previously retired from that office or died.

Supreme Court Act 1981 (c 54)

28 In Schedule 2 to the Supreme Court Act 1981 (c 54) (qualifications for appointment to office in Supreme Court), omit paragraph 11 (Master of the Court of Protection).

Mental Health Act 1983 (c 20)

29 (1) The Mental Health Act is amended as follows.

(2) In section 134(3) (cases where correspondence of detained patients may not be withheld) for paragraph (b) substitute–
'(b)   any judge or officer of the Court of Protection, any of the Court of Protection Visitors or any person asked by that Court for a report under section 49 of the Mental Capacity Act 2005 concerning the patient;'.

(3) In section 139 (protection for acts done in pursuance of 1983 Act), in subsection (1), omit from 'or in, or in pursuance' to 'Part VII of this Act,'.

(4) Section 142 (payment of pension etc. where recipient lacks capacity) ceases to have effect in England and Wales.

(5) Sub-paragraph (6) applies where, before the commencement of sub-paragraph (4), an authority has, in respect of a person referred to in that section as 'the patient', made payments under that section–
- (a) to an institution or person having the care of the patient, or
- (b) in accordance with subsection (2)(a) or (b) of that section.

(6) The authority may, in respect of the patient, continue to make payments under that section to that institution or person, or in accordance with subsection (2)(a) or (b) of that section, despite the amendment made by sub-paragraph (4).

(7) In section 145(1) (interpretation), in the definition of 'patient', omit '(except in Part VII of this Act)'.

(8) In section 146 (provisions having effect in Scotland), omit from '104(4)' to 'section),'.

(9) In section 147 (provisions having effect in Northern Ireland), omit from '104(4)' to 'section),'.

Administration of Justice Act 1985 (c 61)

30 In section 18(3) of the Administration of Justice Act 1985 (c 61) (licensed conveyancer who lacks capacity), for the words from 'that person' to the end substitute 'he becomes a person who lacks capacity (within the meaning of the Mental Capacity Act 2005) to practise as a licensed conveyancer.'.

Insolvency Act 1986 (c 45)

31 (1) The Insolvency Act 1986 (c 45) is amended as follows.

(2) In section 389A (people not authorised to act as nominee or supervisor in voluntary arrangement), in subsection (3)–
- (a) omit the 'or' immediately after paragraph (b),
- (b) in paragraph (c), omit 'Part VII of the Mental Health Act 1983 or', and
- (c) after that paragraph, insert ', or
- (d) he lacks capacity (within the meaning of the Mental Capacity Act 2005) to act as nominee or supervisor'.

(3) In section 390 (people not qualified to be insolvency practitioners), in subsection (4)–
- (a) omit the 'or' immediately after paragraph (b),
- (b) in paragraph (c), omit 'Part VII of the Mental Health Act 1983 or', and
- (c) after that paragraph, insert ', or
    - (d) he lacks capacity (within the meaning of the Mental Capacity Act 2005) to act as an insolvency practitioner.'.

Building Societies Act 1986 (c 53)

32 In section 102D(9) of the Building Societies Act 1986 (c 53) (references to a person holding an account on trust for another)–

(a)   in paragraph (a), for 'Part VII of the Mental Health Act 1983' substitute 'the Mental Capacity Act 2005', and

(b)   for paragraph (b) substitute–

    '(b)   to an attorney holding an account for another person under–

        (i)   an enduring power of attorney or lasting power of attorney registered under the Mental Capacity Act 2005, or

        (ii)   an enduring power registered under the Enduring Powers of Attorney (Northern Ireland) Order 1987;'.

Public Trustee and Administration of Funds Act 1986 (c 57)

33 In section 3 of the Public Trustee and Administration of Funds Act 1986 (c 57) (functions of the Public Trustee)–

(a)   for subsections (1) to (5) substitute–

    '(1)   The Public Trustee may exercise the functions of a deputy appointed by the Court of Protection.',

(b)   in subsection (6), for 'the 1906 Act' substitute 'the Public Trustee Act 1906', and

(c)   omit subsection (7).

Patronage (Benefices) Measure 1986 (No.3)

34 (1) The Patronage (Benefices) Measure 1986 (No. 3) is amended as follows.

(2) In section 5 (rights of patronage exercisable otherwise than by registered patron), after subsection (3) insert–

    '(3A)   The reference in subsection (3) to a power of attorney does not include an enduring power of attorney or lasting power of attorney (within the meaning of the Mental Capacity Act 2005).'

(3) In section 9 (information to be sent to designated officer when benefice becomes vacant), after subsection (5) insert–

    '(5A)   Subsections (5B) and (5C) apply where the functions of a registered patron are, as a result of paragraph 10 of Schedule 2 to the Mental Capacity Act 2005 (patron's loss of capacity to discharge functions), to be discharged by an individual appointed by the Court of Protection.

    (5B)   If the individual is a clerk in Holy Orders, subsection (5) applies to him as it applies to the registered patron.

    (5C)   If the individual is not a clerk in Holy Orders, subsection (1) (other than paragraph (b)) applies to him as it applies to the registered patron.'

Courts and Legal Services Act 1990 (c 41)

35 (1) The Courts and Legal Services Act 1990 (c 41) is amended as follows.

(2) In Schedule 11 (judges etc. barred from legal practice), for the reference to a Master of the Court of Protection substitute a reference to each of the following–

(a)   Senior Judge of the Court of Protection,

(b)   President of the Court of Protection,

(c)   Vice-President of the Court of Protection.

(3) In paragraph 5(3) of Schedule 14 (exercise of powers of intervention in registered foreign lawyer's practice), for paragraph (f) substitute–

'(f)   he lacks capacity (within the meaning of the Mental Capacity Act 2005) to act as a registered foreign lawyer and powers under sections 15 to 20 or section 48 are exercisable in relation to him;'.

Child Support Act 1991 (c 48)

36 In section 50 of the Child Support Act 1991 (c 48) (unauthorised disclosure of information)–

(a)   in subsection (8)–

(i)   immediately after paragraph (a), insert 'or',

(ii)   omit paragraphs (b) and (d) and the 'or' immediately after paragraph (c), and

(iii)   for ', receiver, custodian or appointee' substitute 'or custodian', and

(b)   after that subsection, insert–

'(9)   Where the person to whom the information relates lacks capacity (within the meaning of the Mental Capacity Act 2005) to consent to its disclosure, the appropriate person is–

(a)   a donee of an enduring power of attorney or lasting power of attorney (within the meaning of that Act), or

(b)   a deputy appointed for him, or any other person authorised, by the Court of Protection,

with power in that respect.'.

Social Security Administration Act 1992 (c 5)

37 In section 123 of the Social Security Administration Act 1992 (c 5) (unauthorised disclosure of information)–

(a)   in subsection (10), omit–

(i)   in paragraph (b), 'a receiver appointed under section 99 of the Mental Health Act 1983 or',

(ii)   in paragraph (d)(i), 'sub-paragraph (a) of rule 41(1) of the Court of Protection Rules 1984 or',

(iii)   in paragraph (d)(ii), 'a receiver ad interim appointed under sub-paragraph (b) of the said rule 41(1) or', and

(iv)   'receiver,', and

(b)   after that subsection, insert–

'(11) Where the person to whom the information relates lacks capacity (within the meaning of the Mental Capacity Act 2005) to consent to its disclosure, the appropriate person is–

(a)   a donee of an enduring power of attorney or lasting power of attorney (within the meaning of that Act), or

(b)   a deputy appointed for him, or any other person authorised, by the Court of Protection,

with power in that respect.'.

Judicial Pensions and Retirement Act 1993 (c 8)

38 (1) The Judicial Pensions and Retirement Act 1993 (c 8) is amended as follows.

(2) In Schedule 1 (qualifying judicial offices), in Part 2, under the cross-heading 'Court officers', omit the reference to a Master of the Court of Protection except in the case of a person holding that office immediately before the commencement of this sub-paragraph or who had previously retired from that office or died.

(3) In Schedule 5 (retirement: the relevant offices), omit the entries relating to the Master and Deputy or temporary Master of the Court of Protection, except in the case of a person holding any of those offices immediately before the commencement of this sub-paragraph.

(4) In Schedule 7 (retirement: transitional provisions), omit paragraph 5(5)(i)(g) except in the case of a person holding office as a deputy or temporary Master of the Court of Protection immediately before the commencement of this sub-paragraph.

Leasehold Reform, Housing and Urban Development Act 1993 (c 28)

39 (1) For paragraph 4 of Schedule 2 to the Leasehold Reform, Housing and Urban Development Act 1993 (c 28) (landlord under a disability), substitute–

'**4**
(1)   This paragraph applies where a Chapter I or Chapter II landlord lacks capacity (within the meaning of the Mental Capacity Act 2005) to exercise his functions as a landlord.
(2)   For the purposes of the Chapter concerned, the landlord's place is to be taken–
    (a)   by a donee of an enduring power of attorney or lasting power of attorney (within the meaning of the 2005 Act), or a deputy appointed for him by the Court of Protection, with power to exercise those functions, or
    (b)   if no deputy or donee has that power, by a person authorised in that respect by that court.'.

(2) That amendment does not affect any proceedings pending at the commencement of this paragraph in which a receiver or a person authorised under Part 7 of the Mental Health Act 1983 (c 20) is acting on behalf of the landlord.

Goods Vehicles (Licensing of Operators) Act 1995 (c 23)

40 (1) The Goods Vehicles (Licensing of Operators) Act 1995 (c 23) is amended as follows.

(2) In section 16(5) (termination of licence), for 'he becomes a patient within the meaning of Part VII of the Mental Health Act 1983' substitute 'he becomes a person who lacks capacity (within the meaning of the Mental Capacity Act 2005) to use a vehicle under the licence'.

(3) In section 48 (licence not to be transferable, etc.)–
    (a)   in subsection (2)–
        (i)   for 'or become a patient within the meaning of Part VII of the Mental Health Act 1983' substitute ', or become a person who lacks capacity (within the meaning of the Mental Capacity Act 2005) to use a vehicle under the licence,', and
        (ii)   in paragraph (a), for 'became a patient' substitute 'became a person who lacked capacity in that respect', and

(b)   in subsection (5), for 'a patient within the meaning of Part VII of the Mental Health Act 1983' substitute 'a person lacking capacity'.

Disability Discrimination Act 1995 (c 50)

41 In section 20(7) of the Disability Discrimination Act 1995 (c 50) (regulations to disapply provisions about incapacity), in paragraph (b), for 'Part VII of the Mental Health Act 1983' substitute 'the Mental Capacity Act 2005'.

Trusts of Land and Appointment of Trustees Act 1996 (c 47)

42 (1) The Trusts of Land and Appointment of Trustees Act 1996 (c 47) is amended as follows.

(2) In section 9 (delegation by trustees), in subsection (6), for the words from 'an enduring power' to the end substitute 'an enduring power of attorney or lasting power of attorney within the meaning of the Mental Capacity Act 2005'.

(3) In section 20 (the title to which becomes 'Appointment of substitute for trustee who lacks capacity')–
    (a)   in subsection (1)(a), for 'is incapable by reason of mental disorder of exercising' substitute 'lacks capacity (within the meaning of the Mental Capacity Act 2005) to exercise', and
    (b)   in subsection (2)–
           (i)   for paragraph (a) substitute–
           '(a)   a deputy appointed for the trustee by the Court of Protection,',
           (ii)   in paragraph (b), for the words from 'a power of attorney' to the end substitute 'an enduring power of attorney or lasting power of attorney registered under the Mental Capacity Act 2005', and
           (iii)   in paragraph (c), for the words from 'the authority' to the end substitute 'the Court of Protection'.

Human Rights Act 1998 (c 42)

43 In section 4(5) of the Human Rights Act 1998 (c 42) (courts which may make declarations of incompatibility), after paragraph (e) insert–
           '(f)   the Court of Protection, in any matter being dealt with by the President of the Family Division, the Vice-Chancellor or a puisne judge of the High Court.'

Access to Justice Act 1999 (c 22)

44 In paragraph 1 of Schedule 2 to the Access to Justice Act 1999 (c 22) (services excluded from the Community Legal Service), after paragraph (e) insert–
           '(ea)   the creation of lasting powers of attorney under the Mental Capacity Act 2005,
           (eb)   the making of advance decisions under that Act,'.

Adoption and Children Act 2002 (c 38)

45 In section 52(1)(a) of the Adoption and Children Act 2002 (c 38) (parental consent to adoption), for 'is incapable of giving consent' substitute 'lacks capacity (within the meaning of the Mental Capacity Act 2005) to give consent'.

Licensing Act 2003 (c 17)

46 (1) The Licensing Act 2003 (c.17) is amended as follows.

(2) In section 27(1) (lapse of premises licence), for paragraph (b) substitute–

    '(b)   becomes a person who lacks capacity (within the meaning of the Mental Capacity Act 2005) to hold the licence,'.

(3) In section 47 (interim authority notice in relation to premises licence)–

    (a)   in subsection (5), for paragraph (b) substitute–

        '(b)   the former holder lacks capacity (within the meaning of the Mental Capacity Act 2005) to hold the licence and that person acts for him under an enduring power of attorney or lasting power of attorney registered under that Act,', and

    (b)   in subsection (10), omit the definition of 'mentally incapable'.

Courts Act 2003 (c 39)

47 (1) The Courts Act 2003 (c 39) is amended as follows.

(2) In section 1(1) (the courts in relation to which the Lord Chancellor must discharge his general duty), after paragraph (a) insert–

    '(aa)   the Court of Protection,'.

(3) In section 64(2) (judicial titles which the Lord Chancellor may by order alter)–

    (a)   omit the reference to a Master of the Court of Protection, and

    (b)   at the appropriate place insert a reference to each of the following–

        (i)   Senior Judge of the Court of Protection,

        (ii)   President of the Court of Protection,

        (iii)   Vice-president of the Court of Protection.

SCHEDULE 7
REPEALS

Section 67(2)

Short title and chapter	*Extent of repeal*
Trustee Act 1925 (c 19)	Section 54(3).
Law of Property Act 1925 (c 20)	Section 205(1)(xiii).
Administration of Estates Act 1925 (c 23)	Section 55(1)(viii)
U.S.A. Veterans' Pensions (Administration) Act 1949 (c 45)	In section 1(4), the words from 'or for whom' to '1983'.
Mental Health Act 1959 (c 72)	In Schedule 7, in Part 1, the entries relating to– section 33 of the Fines and Recoveries Act 1833, section 68 of the Improvement of Land Act 1864,

Short title and chapter	Extent of repeal
	section 55 of the Trustee Act 1925, section 205(1) of the Law of Property Act 1925, section 49 of the National Assistance Act 1948, and section 1 of the Variation of Trusts Act 1958.
Courts Act 1971 (c 23)	In Schedule 2, in Part 1A, the words 'Master of the Court of Protection'.
Local Government Act 1972 (c 70)	Section 118.
Limitation Act 1980 (c 58)	Section 38(3) and (4).
Supreme Court Act 1981 (c 54)	In Schedule 2, in Part 2, paragraph 11.
Mental Health Act 1983 (c 20)	Part 7. In section 139(1) the words from 'or in, or in pursuance' to 'Part VII of this Act,'. In section 145(1), in the definition of 'patient' the words '(except in Part VII of this Act)'. In sections 146 and 147 the words from '104(4)' to 'section),'. Schedule 3. In Schedule 4, paragraphs 1, 2, 4, 5, 7, 9, 14, 20, 22, 25, 32, 38, 55 and 56. In Schedule 5, paragraphs 26, 43, 44 and 45.
Enduring Powers of Attorney Act 1985 (c 29)	The whole Act.
Insolvency Act 1986 (c 45)	In section 389A(3)– the 'or' immediately after paragraph (b), and in paragraph (c), the words 'Part VII of the Mental Health Act 1983 or'. In section 390(4)– the 'or' immediately after paragraph (b), and in paragraph (c), the words 'Part VII of the Mental Health Act 1983 or'.
Public Trustee and Administration of Funds Act 1986 (c 57)	Section 2. Section 3(7).
Child Support Act 1991 (c 48)	In section 50(8)– paragraphs (b) and (d), and the 'or' immediately after paragraph (c).
Social Security Administration Act 1992 (c 5)	In section 123(10)– in paragraph (b), 'a receiver appointed under section 99 of the Mental Health

Short title and chapter	Extent of repeal
	Act 1983 or', in paragraph (d)(i), 'sub-paragraph (a) of rule 41(1) of the Court of Protection Rules Act 1984 or', in paragraph (d)(ii), 'a receiver ad interim appointed under sub-paragraph (b) of the said rule 41(1) or', and 'receiver,'.
Trustee Delegation Act 1999 (c 15)	Section 4. Section 6. In section 7(3), the words 'in accordance with section 4 above'.
Care Standards Act 2000 (c 14)	In Schedule 4, paragraph 8.
Licensing Act 2003 (c 17)	In section 47(10), the definition of 'mentally incapable'.
Courts Act 2003 (c 64)	In section 64(2), the words 'Master of the Court of Protection'.

Index

References are to paragraph numbers.